The Moral Economy of Elections

Do elections turn people into democratic citizens? Elections have long been seen as a way to foster democracy, development and security in Africa, with many hoping that the secret ballot would transform states. Adopting a new approach that focusses on the moral economy of elections, Nic Cheeseman, Gabrielle Lynch and Justin Willis show how elections are shaped by competing visions of what it means to be a good leader, bureaucrat or citizen. Using a mixed-methods study of elections in Ghana, Kenya and Uganda, they explore moral claims made by officials, politicians, civil society, international observers and voters themselves. This radical new lens reveals that elections are the site of intense moral contestation, which helps to explain why there is such vigourous participation in processes that often seem flawed. Demonstrating the impact of these debates on six decades of electoral practice, they explain why the behaviour of those involved so frequently transgresses national law and international norms, as well as the ways in which such transgressions are evaluated and critiqued – so that despite the purported significance of 'vote-buying', the candidates that spend the most do not always win.

Nic Cheeseman is Professor of Democracy and International Development at the University of Birmingham. He is the author or editor of ten books, including *Democracy in Africa* (2015) and *How to Rig an Election* (2018), and his research has won a number of prizes including the Frank Cass Award for the best article in *Democratization* (2015) and the Joni Lovenduski Prize for outstanding professional achievement by a midcareer scholar (2019) from the UK Political Studies Association. He is the founding editor of the *Oxford Encyclopedia of African Politics* and the founder of www.democracyinafrica.org.

Gabrielle Lynch is Professor of Comparative Politics at the University of Warwick. She is the author of over 30 articles and book chapters, and author or editor of five books, including *I Say to You: Ethnic Politics and the Kalenjin in Kenya* (2011) and *Performances of Injustice: The Politics of Truth, Justice and Reconciliation in Kenya* (2018). She is Vice President of the British Institute in Eastern Africa and Deputy Chair of the *Review of*

African Political Economy, and wrote a regular column in Kenya's *Saturday Nation* (2014–2018) and *The East African* (2015–2017).

Justin Willis is Professor in History at Durham University. He is the author of *Mombasa, the Swahili and the Making of the Mijikenda* (1993), *Potent Brews: A Social History of Alcohol in East Africa 1850–1999* (2002) and co-editor of *The Sudan Handbook* (2011) as well as numerous articles on the history and politics of Ghana, Kenya, Sudan and Uganda. He has previously served as Director of the British Institute in Eastern Africa.

The Moral Economy of Elections in Africa

Democracy, Voting and Virtue

Nic Cheeseman
University of Birmingham

Gabrielle Lynch
University of Warwick

Justin Willis
Durham University

CAMBRIDGE
UNIVERSITY PRESS

CAMBRIDGE
UNIVERSITY PRESS

University Printing House, Cambridge CB2 8BS, United Kingdom

One Liberty Plaza, 20th Floor, New York, NY 10006, USA

477 Williamstown Road, Port Melbourne, VIC 3207, Australia

314–321, 3rd Floor, Plot 3, Splendor Forum, Jasola District Centre, New Delhi – 110025, India

79 Anson Road, #06–04/06, Singapore 079906

Cambridge University Press is part of the University of Cambridge.

It furthers the University's mission by disseminating knowledge in the pursuit of education, learning, and research at the highest international levels of excellence.

www.cambridge.org
Information on this title: www.cambridge.org/9781108417235
DOI: 10.1017/9781108265126

First published 2020

A catalogue record for this publication is available from the British Library.

Library of Congress Cataloging-in-Publication Data
Names: Cheeseman, Nic, 1979– author.
Title: The moral economy of elections in Africa : democracy, voting, and virtue / Nic Cheeseman, University of Birmingham; Gabrielle Lynch, University of Warwick; Justin Willis, Durham University.
Description: Cambridge, United Kingdom ; New York, NY : Cambridge University Press, [2020] | Includes bibliographical references and index.
Identifiers: LCCN 2020047664 (print) | LCCN 2020047665 (ebook) | ISBN 9781108417235 (hardback) | ISBN 9781108404723 (paperback) | ISBN 9781108265126 (ebook)
Subjects: LCSH: Election law – Africa. | Elections – Economic aspects – Africa. | Elections – Moral and ethical aspects – Africa. | Voting – Africa. | Democracy – Africa. | Africa – Politics and government.
Classification: LCC KQC585 .C44 2020 (print) | LCC KQC585 (ebook) | DDC 342.6/07–dc23
LC record available at https://lccn.loc.gov/2020047664
LC ebook record available at https://lccn.loc.gov/2020047665

ISBN 978-1-108-41723-5 Hardback
ISBN 978-1-108-40472-3 Paperback

This book is dedicated to Sammy, a remarkable research assistant and friend who is gone too soon.

Samuel Kweku Yamoah

1982–2020

Contents

Figures

Tables

Acknowledgements

Looking back, it is quite hard to say when this project began. Devising the research, securing funding, gathering data and writing this book have taken more than ten years. The journey from research idea to book was possible only because, over that time, many people and institutions have been both generous and patient in their support. So many, indeed, that we shall certainly not manage to mention them all.

The initial seeds were sown during our observation of Kenya's 2007 election, when the possibility and significance of a research project along these lines emerged out of conversations with voters, candidates, civil society activists, analysts and academics including – but not limited to – John Githongo, George Gona, Daniel Kandagor, Karuti Kanyinga, Maina Kiai, Paul Kurgat, and Adams Oloo.

From there, the specific project evolved out of a series of conversations – and an ultimately unsuccessful first funding application – with Derek Peterson and Jim Brennan. We then benefited from working with Staffan I. Lindberg to put together a successful application to the UK's Economic and Social Research Council (ESRC, under award EL/L002345/1), whose patient support we gratefully acknowledge.

As part of the ESRC application we established an excellent advisory board of Michael Bratton, Nelson Kasfir, Clare Thomas and Lindsay Whitfield, who served for the three years of the grant. We were extremely fortunate that so many knowledgeable and insightful colleagues were willing to devote their time and energies to read research plans, assist with locating information, provide feedback on drafts and generally support our efforts. Any errors and mistakes that remain are, of course, our own.

Towards the end of the writing process we were also able to significantly sharpen our arguments as a result of three events at which we presented and received feedback on our work: one organized by Sandrine Perrot at Sciences Po, one co-organized with Mukulika Banerjee at the London School of Economics and one held at the University of Birmingham. Across these three events we benefited from in-depth comments that considerably strengthened the quality of the book both from our co-organizers and from Michaela Collord, Gordon Crawford, Chris Day, Susan Dodsworth, Jonathan Fisher, Elena Gadjanova, Peace Medie and Richard Reid – while Frederick Schaffer came from the United States to both engage with the book and give a lecture on a similar theme.

Many other colleagues have also been generous with their time and expertise. Godfrey Asiimwe, Alice Evans, Briony Jones, Dominika Koter, Cherry Leonardi, Marie-Emmanuelle Pommerolle, Mike Saward, Graeme Small and Ryan Sheely all commented on drafts and reports; so too did multiple anonymous journal reviewers. Other colleagues offered insight and advice of many kinds, from which we benefited enormously: Richard Banégas, John Barya, George Bob-Milliar, Nicole Beardsworth, Sarah Brierley, Adrian Browne, Ngala Chome, Karuti Kanyinga, Ambreena Manji, Hassan Mwakimako, George Ofosu, Gordon Omenya, Mutuma Ruteere and Hannah Waddilove.

Fieldwork would not have been possible without the help of an indefatigable and exemplary group of research assistants, transcribers and others. In Ghana, Samuel Kweku Yamoah – to whom this book is dedicated – was a whole research team in himself. In Kenya, Alex Dyzenhaus, Veronica Itimu, Mwongela Kamencu, Keffa Magenyi, Amanda Majisu, Nzau Musau, Kevin Obware, George Odhiambo, George Sayagie, Daisy Sibun and Rodrigo Vaz all helped to make the project a success; while in Uganda Sandra Auma, Adam Kakooza, Ezron Kambale Arthur Owor and Zaid Sekiito guided us through sometimes challenging fieldwork with good humour and care. The lab game in Kenya was designed and implemented in collaboration with Dominic Burbidge and those in Ghana and Uganda with Amma Panin. We also benefited from the help of several UK-based students who helped with data analysis and presentation: Sarah Gilbert, Alasdair Love and Rudabeh Shahid.

At several stages in the project we benefited from the support of the British Institute in Eastern Africa, which helped to organize a training event for principal research assistants and provided research assistants through the Graduate Attachment Scheme, and from cooperation with the Rift Valley Institute, where particular thanks must go to Mark Bradbury, Liz Mahiri and Tymon Kiepe. For the survey work, we are grateful to PSI-International (Ghana) and to IPSOS-Synovate, and especially to Tom Wolf. Throughout the research, the professional staff at our universities were excellent; particular thanks are due to Anna Hutchinson and Audrey Bowron at Durham. In Kenya and Uganda, research was undertaken with the permission of the National Council for Science and Technology of each country, and their support is gratefully acknowledged.

Beyond this, our research would not have been possible without the willingness of hundreds of people across Ghana, Kenya and Uganda to give up their time to sit down and share their experiences, ideas and insights with us – and the thousands of people who took part in surveys and lab games. We never cease to be impressed by the generosity of the very busy people we talk to, or the way in which each conversation can inspire new ideas, thoughts and directions. It is not possible to list all these people by name, but we are especially grateful for their time – this book would not have been possible without them.

Abbreviations and Glossary

AU	African Union
asantehene	customary ruler of Asante (Ghana)
CCEDU	Citizens' Coalition for Electoral Democracy in Uganda
CCG	Christian Council of Ghana
CDD-Ghana	Centre for Democratic Development – Ghana
CEON-U	Citizens Election Observers Network – Uganda
CJPC	Catholic Justice and Peace Commission (Kenya)
CODEO	Coalition of Domestic Observers (Ghana)
COG	Commonwealth Observation Group
CPP	Convention People's Party (Ghana)
CRECO	Constitution and Reform Education Consortium (Kenya)
CRO	Commonwealth Relations Office
CSO	civil society organization
DC	district commissioner
DemGroup	Democracy Monitoring Group (Uganda)
DP	Democratic Party (Kenya and Uganda)
EC	Electoral Commission
ECOWAS	Economic Community of West African States
EMB	electoral management body
ELOG	Election Observation Group (Kenya)
ESRC	Economic and Social Research Council
EU	European Union
EU EOM	European Union Election Observation Mission
FBIS	Foreign Broadcast Information Service
FBO	faith-based organization
FDC	Forum for Democratic Change (Uganda)
FORD	Forum for the Restoration of Democracy (Kenya)
ICC	International Criminal Court
IDEG	Institute for Democratic Governance (Ghana)
IEA	Institute of Economic Affairs (Ghana)

IEBC	Independent Electoral and Boundaries Commission
IEC	Interim Electoral Commission
IED	Institute for Education in Democracy (Kenya)
IMF	International Monetary Fund
kabaka	customary ruler of Buganda (Uganda)
KADU	Kenya African Democratic Union
KANU	Kenya African National Union
KCCB	Kenya Conference of Catholic Bishops
KHRC	Kenya Human Rights Commission
KEDOF	Kenya Election Domestic Observation Forum
KPU	Kenya People's Union
LRA	Lord's Resistance Army (Uganda)
MP	member of parliament
MUHURI	Muslims for Human Rights (Kenya)
NAL	National Alliance of Liberals (Ghana)
NARA	National Archives and Record Administration (United States)
NARC	National Rainbow Coalition (Kenya)
NASA	National Super Alliance (Kenya)
NCCE	National Commission for Civic Education (Ghana)
NCEP	National Civic Education Programme (Kenya)
NCCK	National Council of Churches of Kenya
NDC	National Democratic Congress (Ghana)
NEDEO	Network of Domestic Election Observers (Ghana)
NEMU	National Electoral Monitoring Unit (Kenya)
NEMGROUP-U	Election Monitoring Group (Uganda)
NDI	National Democratic Institute (United States)
NDP	National Development Party (Kenya)
NGO	non-governmental organization
NLC	National Liberation Council (Ghana)
NLM	National Liberation Movement (Ghana)
NPP	New Patriotic Party (Ghana)
NRA	National Resistance Army (Uganda)
NRM	National Resistance Movement (Uganda)
OAU	Organization of African Unity
ODM	Orange Democratic Movement (Kenya)
PC	provincial commissioner
PFP	Popular Front Party (Ghana)
PNDC	Provisional National Defence Council (Ghana)
PNP	People's National Party (Ghana)
PNU	Party of National Unity (Kenya)
PP	Progress Party (Ghana)

PRAAD	Public Record and Archive Administration Department (Ghana)
PVT	parallel vote tabulation
SUPKEM	Supreme Council of Kenya Muslims (Kenya)
SWB	Summary of World Broadcasts
TNA	The National Alliance (Kenya)
UGCC	United Gold Coast Congress (Ghana)
UHRC	Uganda Human Rights Commission
UJCC	Uganda Joint Christian Council
UKNA	United Kingdom National Archives
UN	United Nations
UNA	Uganda National Archive (Uganda)
UP	United Party (Ghana)
UPC	Uganda People's Congress (Uganda)
UPM	Uganda Patriotic Movement
USAID	United States Agency for International Development

Introduction: Writing African Elections

The constituency-level chairman and secretary of the party are busy men. We meet in a bar, where they have other appointments and business to pursue. The chairman's mobile phone rings all the time. He declines most of the calls; but still he is talking constantly, walking a little away from the table where we sit each time he decides to answer. The secretary is left to do most of the interview. Initially suspicious, he becomes more enthusiastic as he talks. He came into politics, he tells us, to 'serve my people'. Yes, he acknowledges with a smile, his party work has brought him personal benefits, though he receives no salary for it. Both Ghana's national president and the local constituency member of parliament (MP) are from his party and 'the more your party continues to stay in power, the more your aspirations will come to fruition'. But he is serious about service to his people. He proudly points to the improvements to the constituency under the current government and MP: new infrastructure projects have employed local labour and provided public amenities.[1]

Yet the constituency is not just one community, and as he talks it is apparent that he sees the population as comprised of multiple distinct groups, each with its spokespeople, all of whom must be listened to. Each little group must be rewarded for loyalty to the party. Fishermen are helped with fuel for outboard engines; small traders with loans and simple equipment; neighbourhoods with improved drains; parents with school transports for their children; and young people with an apprenticeship scheme. There are distinct scholarships for children from the Muslim community, as well as gifts of food for Eid; and there are donations to church-building projects. These men are so busy because elections are close – as the chairman complained in between phone calls 'when people see me, they ask for money'. The party office is full each day of people seeking help for their community, or personal support with school fees, or medical bills. These are not just requests, they are demands: if they are

---

[1] Fieldwork notes, Cape Coast, Ghana, 1 September 2016.

not met, the claim-makers will denounce him – and the MP – for being unwilling to help. The chair and secretary enjoy their status, but evidently feel constantly under pressure to show their virtue as patrons; as the chairman said, with a sigh, in a phrase that combined self-justification with naturalizing assertion, 'That is African politics!'

Election officials are also busy before elections. We meet one in his office in Kenya while his staff count bales of information manuals and handbooks that have arrived ready for distribution to polling station staff and party agents. This is not a public office; a police guard at the gate keeps casual visitors away. The walls are hung with organizational charts and information posters that denounce vote buying and encourage citizens to join the electoral register. The official's phone rings occasionally as we speak; the callers are junior officials reporting in on preparations. The official first trained as a teacher, and after temporary work as a polling station official applied to join the expanding staff of the electoral commission. He still thinks of himself as a teacher – educating people in their rights and duties as citizens. His work has taken him all over the country, and he is determinedly national in his outlook; the voters on his current area of work deserve the same treatment, and are under the same obligations, as those anywhere else. Like the party chairman and secretary, he sees himself as a servant of the public, but his public is more clearly national and undifferentiated. His role is to educate and guide them, not to attend to their particular problems: virtue, for him, lies in the proper performance of the processes that allow people to cast their ballot and to fulfil their duties as citizens.[2]

The election official and party organizer are both deeply committed to elections. The self-image of each is that of the moral actor: they make claims on others to behave properly, and they respond to such claims themselves. Yet they seem to have very different ideas of where virtue lies. In this, they are not unusual. The elections that we have studied are full of moral claims-making. Politicians, voters and public all make demands of one another in terms of how people should behave, of what it is to be a virtuous leader, a good citizen, or a righteous official. Such claims-making has been instrumentally employed to promote political projects: building the state, defending the community, pursuing individual or collective wealth and status. But those projects are nonetheless both represented and understood as moral ventures.

That point – that elections are a focus for multiple, discordant, appeals to morality and claims to virtue – is at the heart of this study of elections in Ghana, Kenya and Uganda. Such a starting point will seem strange to

---

[2] Fieldwork notes, Kisumu, Kenya, 7 July 2017.

many readers. Elections, after all, are notorious for duplicity and for the ruthless pursuit of power, in Africa as elsewhere in the world. Electoral violence is always a lurking possibility, and sometimes a shocking reality. Yet elections are also full of claims and demands that are explicitly moral – by which we mean not that they are good in some objective way, but rather that people cast them in terms of what is right, and what should be done. A concern with virtue – one's own, and that of others – is part of the stuff of electoral behaviour. Yet virtue is contested – people may have different ideas of what it is to be good. *That the same individuals might be torn between, or feel the need to balance, different ideas of what it is to be good is central to our argument.*

This book represents an attempt to theorize the competing conceptions of virtue that come to the fore during elections in the three countries that we study, and to understand their significance. In making this argument, we take inspiration from previous work that has foregrounded the import-ance of morality – and the limits of moral domains – in public life in Africa (such as Ekeh 1975; Lonsdale 1992a; de Sardan 1999). But we do not see what we call the moral economy of elections – a term unpacked at greater length in the first chapter – as a static form that provides a culturalist explanation of how elections function that is distinctive to Africa. Rather we use this term to describe a dynamic public process of claims-making in which more than one idea of virtue – that is, of morally proper behaviour – is in play. Our aim here is to identify the main ideas of virtue – or registers, as we call them – that are deployed around elections in Ghana, Kenya and Uganda, and to investigate the way that these shape how individuals think about elections and their relationship with the state.

We do not think that the registers that make up this moral economy are uniform across Africa; indeed there is variation even within our three cases. Nor do we think that the presence of a moral economy is unique to Africa. Representative politics everywhere involve claims-making (Saward 2006), and those claims have everywhere a moral aspect (Brunk 1980; Wolff 1994). As others have argued of Thailand (Walker 2008), the Philippines (Schaffer 2002, 2007b), the United Kingdom (Haste 2006) and the United States (Prasad et al. 2009; Skitka and Bauman 2008), electoral politics draws on ideas of virtue. What changes is therefore not the existence of a moral economy, but the way that ideas of virtue are expressed. Paying attention to this moral economy, and the registers that animate it, is important because, without it we are left with an impoverished understanding of what elections mean to candidates, officials and voters. In turn, this blind spot undermines our ability to explain some of the most interesting questions about elections in Africa and beyond. Why do many people invest so much time, effort and resources in elections, even those that are clearly not going to be free and fair? Why do the numerous and expensive voter education programmes funded by international donors do so little to discourage candidates from handing out money and other private goods? Why, when many candidates clearly believe that handouts are an effective electoral strategy, do those who spend the most sometimes lose? Does participation in elections actually turn voters into democrats? In the pages that follow we argue that attempts to answer these questions without engaging with the moral economy of elections, and with how the various claims that are made during campaigns shape popular experiences of the polls, will ultimately be unsuccessful. It is only when we recognize that elections are the sites of multiple moral projects that we can fully understand how they may contribute to – or undermine – efforts to build certain kinds of states and certain kinds of people.

Elections by secret ballot and adult suffrage, we argue, are always a way to pursue a particular kind of state-building – to persuade people that they should understand themselves as citizens, owing loyalty to a state that treats each citizen-voter equally, and able to make claims to, and about, virtue in those terms. That was the aim of the election official described earlier – and of many others like him around the world. Such demands have had a disciplinary, at times coercive, edge. Election officials insist on listing and ordering; they demand that citizen-voters see themselves as dutiful, numbered subjects. The moral claims-making pursued by elections, then, has been a way to create power. These efforts are often overlooked in the rush to highlight the multiple failures of elections and in some cases to suggest that elections are not suitable ways to select governments in the African context. Yet we argue – in contrast to Ekeh (1975) who explicitly contrasts moral and immoral publics on the continent – that the understandings of virtue asserted by the electoral official are every bit as 'African' as those of the branch chairman.

Around those state-building projects, with their emphasis on good citizenship, swirl multiple other projects of personal power or collective advancement in which very different moral claims are made. When campaigning politicians claim to be virtuous leaders, they may talk in national terms, of citizenship and the state. Yet they may also signal their virtue in other ways: as champions of local interest against outsiders, or against the state itself; as ethnic patrons willing to reward 'their' people; as big men (or more rarely women) willing and able to help out neighbours. Voters similarly press moral claims. Very often, they insist on a politics of presence and personality, demanding that leaders acknowledge them and treat them with respect.

These multiple kinds of claims-making and virtue signalling sometimes conflict, and sometimes coincide. People – voters, politicians, officials – live between and across different moral possibilities. The characters described earlier may, at first glance, be considered ideal types: the party official to embody a patrimonial politics in which personal ties and presence are central; the election official epitomizes a civic virtue that foregrounds bureaucratic process and national citizenship. As contrasting ideals, those are good to think with. Yet as people, both these characters live the messiness of human subjectivity. As we will argue, the history of the elections that we have studied suggests that any individual is susceptible – to varying degrees – to quite different kinds of moral demands, and able to make quite different moral claims. Sometimes, these may clash; sometimes they may be mutually reinforcing. As Adebayo Olukoshi (1998) and Richard Banégas (2007) have argued, the moral claims of clientship and electoral citizenship, or ethnic consciousness and civic identity, are not always incompatible. The branch chairman may on occasion speak the language of national citizenship and duty; the election official will not be immune to the affective power of ties of ethnicity and localism. There are different possibilities of virtue, and people live across them, and sometimes have to choose between them, as they justify what they do, and make demands on others. In contrast to a literature that has tended to emphasize the authorizing capacity of patrimonial ties and the lack of affective power of civic institutions and ideals (Chabal and Daloz 1999), we demonstrate that both resonate deeply with officials, citizens and leaders – and that the complex interplay of the two has profound consequences for the impact of elections.

I.1   Understanding Elections

Understanding elections in this way can help us to rethink the answers to recurring questions about elections that are relevant well beyond the three countries studied here, and beyond Africa.

The first relates to the vigour of elections. Why is it that, even where national power does not change hands, and there is widespread domestic and international scepticism about the integrity of the electoral process, incumbent regimes – and individual politicians – pour resources and time into elections, and why do voters often turn out in such large numbers? In Africa, this question seems especially pressing in the face of a persistent strand of scholarship that has suggested that the oppositional politics of multi-partyism, or the secret ballot – or both – are fundamentally unsuited to an African political culture of collectivism and consensus (see for example Lumumba-Kasongo 2005; also Anyang' Nyong'o 1988; Adedeji

1994; Owusu 1992). Yet both levels of popular engagement and survey work suggest that multiparty democracy is popular (Gyimah-Boadi 2015; Cheeseman and Sishuwa 2020). It is no doubt true that the use of coercion and financial inducements explain some electoral participation (Ninsin 2006). Yet research in our case studies suggests another reason: elections enable voters and politicians to make moral claims and present themselves as virtuous actors, and this both encourages and strengthens their participation.

The second, linked, question is about the widespread persistence – across the world – of behaviours that contravene the law, and international electoral norms. Why have practices such as what is often called 'vote buying' proved so durable in the face of repeated interventions – from a host of domestic and international actors – to promote very different norms? Our case studies suggest that, as has been argued for elections outside Africa (Schaffer 2008), behaviours that are formally illegal may be compatible with – or even demanded by – conceptions of virtue that exert a powerful hold over the popular imagination. To put this another way, deviation from official electoral rules is sustainable not simply because it is in an individual's best interest to do so, but because it is often possible for such actions to be justified, both to oneself and others, in terms of virtue. As we will set out in greater detail subsequently, popular understandings of what is justifiable – or even expected – are then shaped by socio-economic conditions, local experience, political structures and broader debates about what it means to be a good leader and a good citizen, which may vary both across space and across time.

At the same time, our work demonstrates the shortcomings of reductive frameworks that solely view African politics through the lens of ethnicity and patrimonial politics (for a critique see Aapengnuo 2010). Indeed, a third question that underpins our study is why, given the obvious importance of communal identities to voting patterns in many countries, aspiring leaders – particularly those vying for national office – spend a great deal of time during their campaigns emphasizing their commitment to the national good. Rather than being used to simply push a small sectional agenda, large rallies and television appearances are often used to extol the virtues of the rule of law and development for all (on rallies, see Paget 2019b). It is easy to be cynical, and dismiss these statements as insincere words designed either to placate international donors, or to try to curry favour with other communities whose support might be needed to win an election in multi-ethnic states (Arriola 2013). If this was the case, however, it would not make sense for candidates operating in less high-profile races in more homogenous constituencies to adopt this approach – and yet they do. We argue that the moral economy of elections provides a much more compelling explanation of why campaigns are framed in this way. Leaders go to great lengths to balance patrimonial promises to their own groups with classically civic appeals because this is how they like to think of themselves – as responsible leaders who can deliver to both nation and community – and because this is what members of *their own* community and broader constituencies demand. Failure to achieve this balance leaves candidates vulnerable to being accused of 'tribalism' – a particularly dangerous criticism – and of being seen as unfit for public office. Thus, despite the overriding focus on ethnicity around elections, political leaders ignore civic virtue at their peril.

The fourth important question that our approach opens up is the unpredictability of electoral outcomes. Although sitting presidents in Africa win 88 per cent of the elections that they contest (Cheeseman 2015a), sub-national elections are extremely competitive and incumbents often lose either at the primary or general election stage. More broadly, elections in authoritarian contexts may still involve real competition and often see heated campaigns and close outcomes (Sjöberg 2011). This raises the important question of what makes a candidate successful. If elections are – as some have argued – all about coercion and/or the transfer of money and forms of clientelistic exchange (Odukoya 2007), why does the biggest spender not always win? Our answer is that what legitimates a candidate is not simply the amount that they give out, as sometimes implied, but how effectively they present this as virtuous behaviour, and what else they are believed to have done, and are regarded as likely to do, to protect and promote the interests of their constituents broadly understood. As others have argued, election gifts offer a public demonstration that a candidate has various qualities – generosity, accessibility, resourcefulness – that are important to voters (Kramon 2017). But this only works, we argue, if a candidate's broader reputation sustains the claims that they make during elections. Someone seen to be a liar or a sell-out may find that their handouts are interpreted not as gifts but as illegitimate bribes, and so do them as much harm as good (Lockwood 2019b).

Beyond these issues, we are also interested in a fifth question: do elections contribute to what some would call democratic consolidation? Staffan Lindberg's claim (2006) that holding repeated elections, even those not of a high standard, leads to an increase in the quality of civil liberties has been repeatedly questioned. Both Lindberg and his critics have made their case through cross-national quantitative analysis (see for example Bratton 2013b; Greenberg and Mattes 2013). We approach this question from a different angle. Using a combination of qualitative and quantitative data and looking at constituency-level politics, we ask whether elections change political subjectivities – how individuals think about themselves and their relationship to the state – in a way that makes these align with international norms of liberal democracy. Our answer is that they may, but that there is nothing inevitable about this. Instead, our three cases suggest that elections often simultaneously reinforce conceptions of virtue that both support and challenge the liberal democratic project, with complex and often unpredictable implications for national politics. This moral economy has played out differently in each of our three countries. Taking a similar analytical approach elsewhere would no doubt reveal further variations, both in terms of the dominant registers of virtue and in terms of the way that they play out.

Finally, we engage with the debate about what is required for effective democratic consolidation in the African context. In part because the problems facing African political systems are often said to result from the way that patrimonial networks dominate and undermine formal state institutions (Chabal and Daloz 1999), there is a latent assumption in much of the literature that strengthening democratic bodies, and so consolidating democracy, requires the eradication of patrimonialism (see for example Lindberg 2010). Against this we suggest that at times patrimonial claims-making may be productive for democracy. While the eradication of patrimonialism might lead to greater confidence in the electoral system and a number of other positive gains such as reducing the tendency of elections to encourage corruption (Cheeseman 2015a), it might also undermine many of the affective ties that currently bind citizens to political leaders and hence the political system itself. This would risk not only engendering apathy but might also weaken the constraints on leaders by eroding their moral accountability to their communities. If this is true, then fostering more stable and rooted systems of democracy depends not on eradicating patrimonialism, but rather on channelling it in ways that harness its affective power while minimizing its corrupt and divisive potential.

As should already be clear, this is not a book about who wins elections, nor is it intended as a litany of electoral failings. Our concern is with the moral work that is done during election campaigns, and the broader impact that this has. What we are really interested in, in other words, is *the role that elections play in authorizing and constraining political action.*

I.2   Theorizing African Elections

In approaching these questions, we have followed in the footsteps of many other scholars who have written on elections, particularly in Africa. But our predecessors have not established a single path, and our work is shaped by studies that fall into three broad camps. One branch of literature has been concerned with elections as projects of state authority. A second track has concerned itself with the way that elections are shaped by existing cultural forms and ideas of identity; in this literature, ballots are always fundamentally about local projects of influence-building or advancement. A third path – now by far the most heavily trodden – understands elections as a journey to 'democratization' and has, as Dickson Eyoh (1998) dryly observed, 'a strong proclivity to combine analysis and prescription'. Where it is judged that democratization has not been reached, the central question becomes 'why elections fail?' (Norris 2015) – not what they do. The divisions between these paths have been characterized less by argument than by non-communication; they have largely proceeded separately, with little attempt to share reference points. But they are perhaps more complementary than this lack of engagement might suggest.

The idea that elections are, above all, ventures in state authority lay at the heart of the rapid expansion of the franchise in late-colonial Africa: this was part of what David Apter (1955) called 'institutional transfer'. Academic commentators, some of them doubling up as policy advisors to colonial governments, did not necessarily expect elections in Africa to replicate those in Europe or North America: as British political scientist William Mackenzie observed with unsettling prescience 'in the future we shall hear much about how elections have failed in Indonesia, or failed in Southern Sudan' (1957: 255). But he and others all shared the assumption that elections by adult suffrage were powerful mass events that could attach popular sentiments to 'symbols which comprehend the entire nation' (Shils 1960: 287; also Coleman 1960). Elections, that is, taught a citizenship that accepted and bolstered the state. The rapid abandonment of multiparty politics across much of the continent after independence led some academic observers to conclude that, in fact, Africa's politicians, or voters – or both – were unready for the responsibilities of the secret ballot (Morgenthau 1964; Huntington 1965; Zolberg 1966, 1968; Owusu 1971). But others pointed to the persistence of elections, even under single-party and "no-party" regimes, and argued that even 'elections without choice' did important political work: they produced and reproduced state power, even when they did not allocate it (Hermet, Rose and Rouquié 1978; Lavroff 1978). Elections were, in Guy Hermet's memorable phrase, 'both educational and anaesthetic' (1978: 14): they encouraged people to internalize a sense that they were subject to the authority of the state whose officials listed and registered them and made them queue (Bayart et al. 1978; Bayart 1978; Hayward 1987).

The argument that elections are primarily about the production of state power has persisted in at least some scholarship since multiparty elections returned to sub-Saharan Africa in the early 1990s (Odukoya 2007; Young 1993). Some have argued that – in Africa and elsewhere – multiparty elections have been promoted by the United States and others to ensure political continuity and so perpetuate neoliberal economics (Lumumba-Kasongo 2005; Robinson 2013). In other words, on this view multiparty polls are the device of a Gramscian 'passive revolution' (Abrahamsen 1997: 147–151) that has allowed the maintenance of national and international forms of power through what Mkandawire (1999) has called 'choiceless elections' (see also Bayart and Ellis 2000: 225–226). The implication of this literature is that multi-partyism is irrelevant, or even inimical. While some argue that only dramatic economic change can bring 'comprehensive democratisation of the state' (Nzongola-Ntalaja 2006), others follow Claude Ake's suggestion that liberal democracy is too focussed on the individual at the expense of 'collective rights' (Nasong'o and Murunga 2007: 6). Even some of the scholars who recognize that multiparty elections have the potential to produce genuine change have nonetheless argued that too often they become a tool of authoritarianism, suggesting that a 'corrupt and irresponsible African elite' (Ihonvbere 1996: 344; see also Ninsin 2006) has stripped elections of their transformative potential (Levitsky and Way 2002). In its most pessimistic version, this argument suggests that even where plural elections lead to a transfer of power, the result is no more than – as Osaghae (1999: 21) has put it – 'a drama of circulation of elites'.

The scholarship discussed so far has been only intermittently engaged with research on how people understand elections in terms of non-national identities and values, and what happens at a local level. A very different literature also began with the study of late-colonial elections, with perhaps the most high-profile strand offering a culturalist critique of elections by secret ballot and adult suffrage. In its classic form, this literature claimed that multiparty politics was unsuited to African political cultures that were concerned not with aggregating individual decisions through competitive processes, but with group consensus and the defence of what a later literature called a 'moral matrix of legitimate government' (Schatzberg 1993: 451; also Gray 1963; Ake 1991, 1993; Karlström 1996; Ayittey 2006).

This work raises important questions about political subjectivities and about the nature of emotion and affect, topics that have been explored from a range of perspectives in more recent scholarship. As Peter Pels (2007: 107) has pointed out, elections may seem to be top-down projects of discipline, but popular involvement may have quite different drivers. A series of studies have asked why people vote or involve themselves in elections in multiple other ways (Bertrand et al. 2007; Baamara, Floderer and Poirier 2016), and why both ordinary people and politicians who seek their votes might think it right to behave in ways that confound international norms (Banégas 1998; Otayek 1998; Quantin 1998; Kramon 2017). Most notably, Frederic Schaffer's work (1998, 2002, 2007b) has consistently pointed to the importance of vernacular understandings of democracy and participation. This concern with people's sense of what is right and proper – or at least what is expected and therefore to an extent legitimate – echoes both John Lonsdale's long-term effort to assert the importance of morality as a force in African history (1986, 1992b, 2004) and John Dunn's (1980) interest in understanding the rationality of voter choice in 1960s Ghana as inseparable from ideas about moral community and virtue. Elections may have been seen as state-building by those who devised and organized them, but that has not necessarily been how either voters or candidates experienced them, or sought to use them.

Perhaps the most stark argument about the importance of subjectivity and affect has emerged in a school of thought that – explicitly or not – revolves around the idea of 'expressive' voting: that voters cast their ballots to express a particular sense of who they are – that is, they vote as members of a group, rather than as individuals. At its most pessimistic, this argument is taken to imply that elections in 'divided societies' are prone to collapse into an 'ethnic census' (Horowitz 1993), which may trigger political violence (Chua 2003; Nzongola-Ntalaja 2004; Mann 2005). Yet such approaches ignore the significant proportion of voters who do not cast their vote ethnically (Bratton and Kimenyi 2008), and we have been much more influenced by a less mechanical understanding of this phenomena; expressive voting, it has been argued, is more about being than doing – electoral participation is not defined by identity, but is one of the ways in which people constitute their sense of who they are, and of the group to which they belong (Schuessler 2000).

In contrast to this focus on local meanings of competitive politics, studies that take democratization as the goal of elections have at their heart a very different ideal of virtue. That ideal is embodied by the rational citizen whose individual choice at the ballot box reflects an informed understanding of the policy differences between programmatic parties. This was the vision of the early 1990s: that elections would change the way that the state worked; that the transfer of norms would in turn transform politics and the economy (Decalo 1992; Wiseman 1995). The disappointment of that hope (Monga 1997) set the context for much subsequent literature, which recognizes that elections are often of poor quality but nonetheless tacitly assumes that they retain the potential to mould – and to be moulded by – the rational citizen-voter. At the core of this approach is the belief that elections are a means to discipline those who hold office: citizenship implies the power of the electorate to hold government accountable.

The recurring question in this research is why, given the productive potential of elections, their impact has often been thwarted (Lynch and Crawford 2011). Much of the literature shares the assumption that this is because the popular will has been denied; that this is a story of what Wale Adebanwi and Ebenezer Obadare (2011) have called 'the abrogation of the electorate'. The mechanisms for this have repeatedly been identified as institutional: the failure of elections arises from the weakness of formal and informal institutions, and/or from their subversion by incumbent elites who have 'perverted the electoral process' (Obi 2011: 379; also Diamond and Plattner 1999; Schedler 2002; Prempeh 2008; Cheeseman and Klaas 2018). Scholars have often pointed the finger at electoral management bodies (Mozaffar 2002), political parties (Elischer 2013) or first-past-the-post voting systems (Osaghae 2004: 10). At the same time, the international community is frequently presented as complicit in cheating because it prefers political stability to disruption, or because the self-appointed promoters of democracy – the United States, the European Union – are unwilling to punish regional allies (Adejumobi 2000; Brown 2001). Literature of this type often seeks explicitly to inform the search for policy interventions around institutions – such as presidential term limits (Dulani 2019), independent legislatures (Barkan 2008) and electoral commissions (Gazibo 2019) – which, if adopted, would make it harder for incumbents to rig themselves back into power. The core assumption is that electoral procedure performed correctly encourages a popular evaluative scrutiny that tames power (Lindberg 2006: 2; van Ham and Lindberg 2018: 229–234). Once this is done, it is assumed that democracy will subsequently be fostered both during elections and between them by the separation of powers between strong independent institutions (Posner and Young 2007; Signe 2019). In such literature, the possibility that there may be very different ideas of what it means to be a good representative or a virtuous citizen is at most a briefly considered afterthought (Bratton 2013a: 286–287).

In this book, we seek to engage with these different bodies of literature, informed by an awareness of the strengths and limitations of each. Understanding that elections are projects of state authority helps us to explain why even undemocratic governments seek to hold them, and why people may see participation as a national duty, in which they feel an emotional investment. Recognizing that ideas of virtue may be plural helps to explain the vigour of electoral involvement, and to understand that the electoral success of authoritarians does not rest solely on coercion and cash (Conroy-Krutz and Logan 2012). This should not, however, blind us to the ways in which elections are manipulated in the pursuit of power. Nor should we assume that the competition between different conceptions of virtue always has the same result. If the democratization literature has been too ready to assume that there is only one kind of electoral virtue, research on alternative ideas of political subjectivity has too often assumed that institutions are irrelevant-or that elections simply provide an opportunity to rehearse an unchanging idea of ethnic and clientelistic politics.

Institutions matter in the moral economy that we describe. All three of our case studies employ first-past-the-post legislative elections based on geographical constituencies. Partly as a result, they encourage a strong and direct relationship between the MP and their constituents, and local electoral contests have provided a space for a lively, personalized politics of claims-making. This stands in contrast with South Africa, for example, where it has been argued that proportional representation and a party-list system have helped to produce a 'democracy without the people' (Mattes 2002). At the same time, direct elections for the position of national president have encouraged a politics of linkage, in which presidential aspirants and constituency candidates need each other, and so must – at times – work across alternative ideas of virtue, both national and local (Waddilove 2019b).

Recognizing the potential for both institutional frameworks and local experience to generate differences both within and between countries, and in line with recent work that has emphasized the importance of addressing the interaction of formal rules and informal norms (Cheeseman 2018a), we argue that elections provide an opportunity for moral claims-making through which people's sense of self, and of what it is to be virtuous, may be shifted. Against literatures that have treated the post-independence African state as a façade, behind which a deep and enduring patrimonial-ism drives political behaviour (Chabal and Daloz 1999), or that have focussed on instrumental electoral violence and manipulation (Collier 2009), we argue for the uncertain but tenacious affective power of the idea of the state. This idea has proved to be remarkably durable, despite the weakness of the state in many African countries, and is inherently linked to a widespread notion of civic virtue: what it is to be a good national citizen, or a good public servant. The state's affective power does not go uncontested of course, and is in constant tension with the demands of multiple patrimonial forms: this book is concerned with the replaying of that tension in and through elections.

In making this case, we document the existence of two different regis-ters of virtue in Ghana, Kenya and Uganda, and explain their importance to the evolution of broader attitudes towards the state and the wider political process. Depending on the respective strength of these registers, and how they interact, the distribution of money and gifts, the falsification of results, even the use of violence in elections may appear as moral acts to voters, politicians and officials in a way that confounds some of the assumptions of the democratization literature. Yet these attitudes are not the static result of unchanging culture; political subjectivities really can change.

I.3   Research Methods

Our argument draws largely on research conducted between 2014 and 2017 in Ghana, Kenya and Uganda. One of our first intuitions was that we should expect varied electoral experience to shape subjectivity in different ways: good-quality elections that deliver uncontroversial outcomes may strengthen the hand of electoral officials because they demonstrate the possibility of 'clean' polls, while evidence of widespread manipulation and corruption may authorize further rule-breaking. Given this, our case selection deliberately selected countries that have experienced different pathways of electoral politics. Leveraging variation within a small sample is challenging, because when cases differ on a great many dimensions at the same time it can be extremely difficult to work out which factors are responsible for which outcomes. The ideal research design is therefore to compare a small number of reasonably similar cases, which makes it possible to hold some key background variables constant while assessing the significance of others. The three countries chosen all became independent from British rule with similar systems, based on parliamentary first-past-the-post constituency elections. All have remained Anglophone, as well as retaining many institutional and ritual forms of public life that reflect the colonial legacy. English is very much still the language of the state and of formal institutions, and key terms – like citizenship, democracy, nation – are routinely rendered in English, though with multiple local vernacular reflexes.

Within this similar institutional and performative context, the experience of the three countries with elections has diverged in ways that allow us to gain analytical leverage over the way in which historical processes shape political subjectivities. After independence, both Ghana and Uganda saw multiple coups, periods of military rule and at least one failed experiment with multiparty elections; Kenya has always had a civilian government and has held regular one-party or multiparty elections. Since the early 1990s, Ghana has come to be routinely touted as a success story of electoral democracy (Gyimah-Boadi 2009), while Uganda has emerged as a case study in electoral authoritarianism (Tripp 2010), and Kenya has acquired a reputation for highly ethnic politics and electoral violence (Oucho 2002). Understanding the causes and consequences of these different trajectories was central to the research.

In order to understand local politics, we also selected three areas for fieldwork in each country to vary those factors that the literature suggests impact on political subjectivities. Focussing work in three different areas of each country also ensured that we did not get captured by any one experience and allowed us to explore the 'local meanings and messiness' (Banerjee 2014: 25) of elections. More specifically, our case selection at the sub-national level was designed to vary the relationship of an area with central power: in each country we chose at least one area that had been seen as closely associated with an incumbent regime at some point in the past thirty years and another that had been widely perceived as hostile to an incumbent regime (in more than one case, a single constituency fell in both categories). We were also careful to ensure geographical variation, choosing at least one area that was urban or peri-urban, and one that was predominantly rural. Each sub-national unit was based on an area that had been a single constituency in the final colonial election: given multiple redrawings of constituency boundaries over time, and an imprecise record of this, each case therefore covered one or more constituencies as they existed in 2015–2017 (see Chapter 2 for more details).

The nine case studies also allowed us to look at another variable: the deeper history of authority. Our chosen case studies included areas that had been part of relatively centralized precolonial monarchies; and others where before colonial rule authority had been much more diffuse, through age-set systems or through lineage. That comparison was revealing, though perhaps in a negative way: while that deeper history matters in many ways, informing distinctive forms of patrimonial practice, the core tension that we identify, between civic and patrimonial virtue, is consistently apparent across constituencies and countries.

Funded by the Economic and Social Research Council of the United Kingdom, our research allowed us to bring together multiple techniques of research in a way that is unusual in this field. Our interest in political subjectivities and the ways in which elections shape norms and values meant that we needed to conduct in-depth qualitative research in addition to survey analysis, archival research and laboratory games. Each of the methods that we employed has a long history and literature complete with its own controversies, and each of the data sets that we use to build our case warrants being presented holistically so that our samples can be assessed and the precise questions we asked can be set out in full. Given the number of different methods that we draw on, doing this within these pages would have rendered the book unwieldy and added a considerable burden on the general reader; we have therefore included this material in a set of extensive online appendices that can be downloaded from the CUP website – an abbreviated version of which can be found in Appendix 1 of this volume.[3] What follows is a summary of the methods used, and how we integrate them to build our argument.

To better understand popular attitudes towards elections, quantitative analysis of existing Afrobarometer data was combined with three new public opinion surveys exploring electoral experience and political attitudes. Those surveys involved a representative national sample (1,200) and an oversample in our three sub-national units. Archival research on the history of elections in each country since the 1950s was undertaken in each country and in the United States and the United Kingdom. The aim of this work was both to recover some of the detail of electoral experience at a local level and to understand – through an examination of stated policy, and the discursive framing of behaviour – what officials and politicians (and much more rarely, voters themselves) sought to achieve through their involvement in elections. This substantial, if uneven, body of documentary material was combined with interviews in each country (over 350 in total), both in the capital city and in the three selected study areas. Interviewees were identified with the assistance of locally recruited research assistants, who often also helped with arranging interviews.

The research also involved observation of multiple aspects of the election process at national level and in each selected area – from nominations, to campaigns, to registration, balloting, counting and the declaration of results; and informal discussions and interviews with a range of individuals working with international institutions involved in what they saw as democracy promotion. All three researchers spent time in all three countries, and observed three elections: in Ghana and Uganda in 2016 and in Kenya in 2017.[4] In addition, we conducted a controlled experiment specifically focussed on attitudes to the exchange of money for votes in each country in order to generate comparative data on individual attitudes towards 'vote buying'. Under laboratory conditions, participants chosen quasi-randomly played a game in which they were either assigned the role of a voter or a candidate; candidates could gain by offering a bribe, while voters could gain by receiving one: in this way, the game tested the willingness of participants to benefit from a form of electoral manipulation.

---

[3] For full details of how surveys and lab games were carried out, as well as descriptive statistics, see the appendices available open access online at www.cambridge.org /moraleconomy.

[4] All three researchers had also observed elections in Kenya in 2007 and 2013 as part of earlier research projects.

Taken together, these diverse methods provide a range of perspectives into the question of how elections impact on citizens, and the kinds of moral conversations that this inspires. Integrating such radically different forms of data into a common explanatory framework is far from straightforward, but we have found it extremely valuable to be able to triangulate between them and to pursue those lines of thought that receive support no matter what empirical lens we adopt. The reader will find that the chapters that follow tend to draw mainly on archival and interview work to develop an argument, which is then buttressed and placed into context through the use of survey findings and, where relevant, the lab games.

I.4   The Argument

Three broad themes run through this book. The first is that elections by universal suffrage are, and have been, consistently understood by those who hold state office as necessary assertions of 'stateness'. With the singular exception of Amin's regime in Uganda (1971–1979), officials and politicians have prized the idea of mass polls as a means to produce and display legitimacy, even where – as in Uganda under Obote or Ghana under Acheampong and Rawlings – they chose to postpone these displays. The second is that elections are also popular among the public. It is true that support for multi-partyism has been less consistent, and voting is not by any means the same as choice over policy. Yet there has been repeated popular opposition to attempts to dispense with elections, or to entirely deny the ability to choose at least some of those who hold authority.

The third theme arises from these first two. If elections are necessary to produce the state, and if popular expectations demand them, what makes a proper election? There has been constant contest over how exactly people – officials, politicians and voters – should behave in elections. This is because elections provide an accessible means to articulate claims about virtue: over what it is to be a good member of society, a good leader or a good official. We express this in terms of a moral economy of elections. As we explain in Chapter 1, we do not use this term in the classic sense pioneered by E. P. Thompson (1971) and James Scott (1977) – to contrast a moral, affect-laden world of community with the chill logic of the rational market. Rather we see the moral economy as a continuing engagement between different ideas of what constitutes virtuous behaviour: an engagement that is both conflictual and productive, and that has no end point.

We use the term 'moral economy' – in preference to what might be considered a more usual political science language of norms – partly because of our strong sense, based on empirical observation, that when people need to justify or explain their own behaviour – or to criticize that of others – they look to a language of virtue. In other words, individuals are inclined to talk in terms of what is good, what is right – that is, to see themselves as moral actors, doing the right thing. There are – as we discuss in Chapter 1 – other ways of analysing this, and we have found these, notably March and Olsen's (2011) work on 'logics of appropriateness', helpful to think with. Yet in conversations, and in the documentary record, we repeatedly came across ideas of proper behaviour that were not simply expressed in terms of what is appropriate, or a shared norm, but rather as an authorizing moral force: what should I do?

We argue that, in our case studies, the moral economy has been characterized by a tension between two broad fields or registers of virtue. One is patrimonial and particularistic, stressing the importance of an engagement between patron and client that is reciprocal, if usually very hierarchical and inequitable. That engagement is rooted in a sense of commonality, based on a shared culture and or experience, which is not coterminous with the boundaries or legal definition of the state. Many different notions of moral community can be invoked in this way: people may feel moral obligations to, and make claims on, members of family, or neighbours, or people they see as sharing their ethnicity; to old school friends or worshippers at the same church.

The other register we call 'civic'. By this we mean an idea of virtue that is bureaucratic in its procedural forms; that asserts, nominally at least, the importance of a national community that is shaped by the state; and that valorizes meritocracy and the provision of public goods. This register is focussed on national community, and is most often evoked through the idea of national citizenship – a status which nominally confers rights, but also imposes expectations. Those rights and expectations are codified in law or regulation, yet are referred to in a language that foregrounds virtue rather than legal compulsion – the good citizen is celebrated as a moral being, not simply as a punctilious follower of the rules.

In contrast to some of the existing literature on morality, we do not see one of these registers as moral and the other not, as Peter Ekeh (1975) does (see also Osaghae 1995). The best-known statement of Ekeh's position comes in his seminal article on the 'two publics', in which he argued that:

The native sector has become a primordial reservoir of moral obligations, a public entity which one works to preserve and benefit. The Westernized sector has become an amoral civic public from which one seeks to gain, if possible in order to benefit the moral primordial public.

We argue that this interpretation is a mistake – at least in the three countries that we have studied. Civic virtue can lay claim to 'cultural embeddedness' (de Sardan 1999) just as patrimonial virtue may. It may not always be as powerful, and it may not always win out, but this does not mean that it is devoid of moral affect. Indeed, the pages that follow will demonstrate quite the opposite. In this sense, the interpretation offered here differs in a profound way from that offered by Ekeh, and goes against one of the key strands of the Africanist literature, which tends to contrast the affective power of primordial ties with the lack of moral purchase of civic institutions and ideals (Chabal and Daloz 1999).

Elections, we argue, provide an especially vivid moment for the making of moral claims precisely because they bring the civic and patrimonial together. Choosing representatives by ballot is very evidently linked to ideas about the nature of good leadership, and requires popular involvement. In adopting this approach, we do not suggest that elections are a distinct moral field, remote from other societal debates over virtuous behaviour. Rather, our point is that the elections, as public moments that combine the idea of a bureaucratic process with vigorous contestation and argument, reveal moral thought and disagreement that are ever present, but often lie hidden.

The evidence from our case studies suggests that the tension between patrimonial and civic ideals, and whether this plays out in a more productive or destructive way – in terms of political participation, accountability, inter-communal relations and levels of violence – is not predetermined. Of course, all patrimonial claims are exclusive in the sense that one of the core components of this register is a special preference for community members. But this requirement of leaders to first and foremost look after their own can be understood in different ways. A community may expect special treatment but also accept that the needs of other groups should be accommodated – for example, by also being given a share of land, state resources and positions. Where political parties and civil society groups regularly bridge ethnic and religious divides, the patrimonial register may encourage greater engagement in politics without generating the kind of inter-communal competition and tensions that can generate violence or withdrawal from electoral politics. By contrast, where people feel that the claims of civic virtue have little traction and institutions work to exclude rather than accommodate, the patrimonial register can pit communities against one another and encourage a more exclusive form of patrimonial claims-making that promotes inter-communal competition and violence, undermining participation.

We suggest that the type of patrimonial and civic claims-making that emerges is likely to be shaped by four key factors: socio-economic context; the structure of political institutions; historical experience; and the agency of key actors. Socio-economic context is significant because it shapes the communities within which patrimonial and civic ideals emerge and are debated. Patrimonial ideals cannot be reduced to ethnicity or 'ethnic politics' (Berman 1998), though in our three countries they are often rooted in a common ethnic – or regional, or linguistic – identity. In turn, the emergence of larger ethnic groups whose members share a sense of collective interest has both shaped, and been shaped by, electoral politics (Posner 2004). Inter-group conflict becomes more likely when different kinds of inequality overlap, so that members of the same community are disadvantaged in political, economic and social terms (Stewart 2008; Langer, Mustapha and Stewart 2009). Under these conditions, ethnic identity becomes entangled with socio-economic status, reinforcing identities and divisions. When this occurs, patrimonial claims-making may become particularly problematic, both because privileged communities come to see their status as natural, and because disadvantaged communities become more willing to support radical challenges to the status quo. This helps to explain why far-reaching political and economic exclusion has been shown to foster distrust and violent challenges to the political system (Klaas 2015).

However, the socio-economic context is not determinate. A growing number of studies have demonstrated the significance of institutions to both political identities and the effect of electoral competition. More inclusive political systems, such as consociational arrangements like executive power-sharing and minority veto, may reduce the stakes of electoral competition and lead to less intense ethnic politicking, especially if key elites have already come to an agreement over how power is to be shared. Here, our case studies show little variation: the first-past-the-post parliamentary contests that are common to all three encourage a focus on individual community leadership, exaggerating the significance of conversations about what constitutes a good leader at the local level. They also tend towards a winner-takes-all dynamic that can exacerbate tensions between rival groups, though it is apparent that a kind of power-sharing has come to the fore at certain points in Kenya, most notably between 2008 and 2013, as we note in Chapter 2.

The main institutional variation that impacts on the moral economy in our cases is, therefore, the extent to which non-state institutions do or do not cross-cut community lines and thus help to generate the possibility for greater integration of both people and ideas. Robert Putnam (1944), channelling Alexis de Tocqueville, has argued that democracy benefits when civil society features organizations that both 'bond' (strengthen an existing community) and 'bridge' (bring people from different communities into contact). While bonding institutions are important to bring people together and build social capital, bridging institutions are important to ensure that society does not become atomized and citizens understand the needs and concerns of others. In both Mali and Zambia, cross-ethnic institutions (fictional kinship in one case and trade unionism in another) have encouraged political organization beyond ethnic lines (Dunning and Harrison 2010: 21; LeBas 2013). Similarly, political parties may come to integrate and balance the desires of different groups, rather than serving as campaign groups for the interests of just one community. This may encourage a very different kind of claims-making that is less exclusive – especially if, to circle back to socio-economic factors, horizontal inequalities are relatively low.

In addition to these more structural building blocks, historical precedent is clearly important in the way that claims are made and in the emergence of new norms. There are two main ways in which this applies when it comes to the moral economy of elections; by shaping whether individuals adopt new forms of behaviour and their understandings of how institutions and leaders are likely to perform at key moments. First, there is growing evidence that individuals are more likely to change their behaviour and 'opt in' to a certain set of values if they believe that others have already done so. People look to others for cues, and seek guidance, in what they think they know of past and thus likely future behaviour. They also look to institutions for examples and guidance (Tankard and Paluck 2016: 183, 192; also Evans 2018: 362; Evans 2019). Institutions thus play an especially powerful role here, because they may structure political activity and so provide incentives for individuals to act in a certain way – yet they may lose this ability if their behaviour is inconsistent or contradictory with the register of virtue they espouse.

This is the second way in which historical precedent matters. If institutions promoting civic virtue work as they are intended to – following process, enforcing rules – opposition leaders and others will draw lessons for the future and adjust their behaviour accordingly (Moehler 2013). If they break the rules, people will be tempted to look elsewhere for their models of virtue. Transfers of power may be particularly significant in this, for, in a context of uncertainty and suspicion, candidates and voters often look to political alternation as the ultimate test of whether political institutions are credible (Huntington 1991; Schaffer 1998: 30).

Alternation may simply bring to power a new government as venal and self-serving as the last (Ismail 2018), but recent research suggests that the impact of turnovers on popular attitudes can be profound. Using Afrobarometer survey data, Michael Bratton has demonstrated that the victory of an opposition party produces a significant increase in public support for democracy – something that he calls the 'alternation effect' (2004). In a similar vein, Devra Moehler and Staffan Lindberg (2009) have argued that turnovers foster greater consensus in terms of the trust that ruling party and opposition supporters place in key democratic institutions. We therefore expect transfers of power to play an important role in facilitating, though rarely ensuring, the conditions under which patrimonial claims-making becomes less exclusive and civil ideals are more likely to resonate.

Finally, it is important to recognize the role played by individual agency, at multiple levels – from that of the individual voter to that of presidential candidates. One reason we prefer the term "moral economy of elections" to the logics of appropriateness framework is that, while many of the people we have interviewed ask 'what should an individual like me do in a situation like this?', the answers that they arrive at are sometimes different – even in very similar contexts. This suggests to us that, while it is valuable to think about norms, it is also important to leave space for different moral interpretations of the same set of choices, especially in contexts marked by considerable uncertainty in which democracy has not consolidated. When it comes to using political violence, or voting for a candidate who has paid a bribe, an individual's upbringing, background and personal principles play an important role in the decision, and this cannot be fully captured by looking at structural factors alone.

What is true for ordinary citizens is also true for political leaders. As Smith (2001) has argued, leaders may have the capacity to sway public opinion in ways that often redefine popular conceptions of rational self-interest. But this process has limits. Leaders may fail to take their supporters with them if they seek to move too far beyond what is already accepted, especially if they are not operating under extraordinary conditions that can be used as justification for radical solutions. There is nonetheless the ability to exercise agency in tight corners. Political science tends to downplay the role of leadership, not because it is unimportant but because it cannot be easily measured and hence it is difficult to analyse and compare. But in political systems with weak formal institutions, the decisions of presidents and key allies can be particularly important in shaping whether elections are manipulated and whether policies favour one group over another. Decisions made by leaders become part of the collective memory, shaping popular understandings of what is likely to happen and what is legitimate or at least justifiable. Thus, while the moral economy of elections is profoundly shaped by structural factors including formal institutions, its development is not always predictable.

The combination of these four factors can shape the evolution of the moral economy of elections in important ways. When the absence of other social cleavages such as class exaggerates the significance of ethnicity, institutions fail to integrate individuals from different communities and so reinforce existing social divisions, successive governments refuse to share power or provide public goods, and leaders respond to political challenges by exploiting what John Lonsdale (1994) has called 'political tribalism', the realization of civic ideals may look like an unrealistic pipe dream. Under these conditions, the patrimonial register is likely to resonate particularly strongly with voters.

Chapter 2 offers an analytical summary of electoral history in each of the three countries that we study. We examine the apparent difference between Ghana – often seen as a democratic success story – and Uganda and Kenya, and argue that this variation reflects the differential workings of the four factors described earlier. The mark of Ghana's perceived success is alter-nance: since 1992, power has moved back and forth regularly between the two main parties. We argue that the root of this alternance lies in very particular circumstances and the persistence of a distinctive socio-economic grouping that emerged in the colonial period, has maintained a significant degree of coherence ever since, and now forms the basis of the New Patriotic Party (NPP). That phenomenon has in turn encouraged the emergence of a competing group that has taken organizational form in the National Democratic Congress (NDC). These two groupings have become corporate bodies as much as parties, each of which has a presence across the country; they provide institutional channels for patronage and advancement at multiple levels, a network of mutual sup-port and a means for mobilization and monitoring. In turn, these corporate bodies have provided institutional support for key elements of the electoral process (notably through the work of party workers and agents). Yet their significance has been greater than that, for the existence of this support network makes political defeat bearable – so long as there is the possibility of office at some point in the future. Along with evidence that governments are willing to leave power if they lose elections, this institutional factor goes a long way to explaining the evolution of less exclusive patrimonial ideals, and a stronger civic register, in the Ghanaian case.

By contrast, neither Kenya nor Uganda has, or has had, any party with such reach or institutional robustness. In Kenya, the political salience of ethnicity – partly a consequence of colonial rule – was exacerbated by decisions made by politicians in the 1960s and 1990s. In each period, political leaders faced by a moment of change doubled down on ethnic mobilization – shaping a popular experience that influenced subsequent attitudes. In Uganda, ethnic and religious divides that emerged from colonial rule were first exacerbated by post-independence political tensions, but have more recently shifted. This change has occurred not as a result of a clear sense of shared citizenship, but by extended experience of multiple patrimonial networks that all ultimately focus (at least in the popular imagination) on the figure of the president (Vokes 2016), whose singular presence is the basis of a political stability that is rooted in both coercion and reward. Appeals to civic values have therefore often lacked credibility and, especially in Kenya, the patrimonial register has been invoked to justify political and economic exclusion.

Chapters 3 to 7, which form the empirical heart of the book, fall into two parts. The first part, 'Promoting civic virtue' explores elections as instrumental projects of citizenship. It has three chapters, each of which looks at a set of formal institutional actors whose overt commitment is to civic virtue: election management officials, election observers and voter educators. We demonstrate that in practice the behaviour of those actors may involve, and be shaped by, a patrimonial register of virtue as well as a civic one. These institutional actors have significant influence over ideas of virtue – but not enough to ensure the dominance of a civic register. The second part, 'The moral economy in action' explores the behaviour of politicians and voters, and reflects on how their response to uneven efforts to promote civic virtue has been shaped by distinctive national and local electoral histories.

Each of these empirical chapters asks a version of the same basic question: how can we understand people's behaviour in elections? This includes multiple sub-questions: why do they involve themselves in elections at all? How do they think they should behave? When they face doubt over this, how do they decide what is right? As these chapters suggest, to consider elections in terms of success or failure may misread the uncertain course – and consequences – of these multiple, diffuse, moral narratives and dilemmas. Elections, we suggest, are filled with contradictions – with tensions between different ideas of what it is to be virtuous. Those contradictions may often be productive, driving popular participation and empowering a sense of accountability; but they do not always push towards the idealized citizenship imagined by international electoral norms and can become destructive, fostering a sense of division.

Inevitably, these empirical chapters are far from exhaustive. They do not discuss in any detail a number of critical actors including security forces, judiciaries, religious leaders and so forth. They also do not discuss all of the election-related activities that the actors we focus on actually engage in and instead focus on specific areas in order to allow for a more detailed analysis of the moral economy of elections at work. Further research will be necessary to extend our analysis to other parts of the political system.

Chapter 3 examines the history of election management. It shows that since the 1990s the material culture, the rhetoric and the formal institutional framework of elections in all three countries have developed in very similar ways. The dramatic juxtaposition of the private and the public – the secret ballot, placed openly in the box – has remained at the heart of the electoral ritual, but is now increasingly surrounded by a supporting apparatus of digital identification and results transmission, in a self-consciously modern (and very expensive) display of the state's ability to know and order its citizenry. All three countries now have permanent election management bodies with professional staff, constituted in line with international electoral norms. Against Walter Oyugi's gloomy prediction (1987) that bureaucrats will always despise competitive politics, we argue that these institutions have the potential to propagate ideas of civic virtue that enable such politics. Like the Electoral Commission of India, these institutions offer a vision of fair and equal citizenship realized through electoral participation (Banerjee 2014: 14–16, 122–43).

Yet in contrast to India, these electoral management bodies have not consistently secured the confidence of the majority of the voting public. They may be directly undermined by incumbents: most notably in Uganda, where the electoral management body has been kept short of resources and directly accused of incompetence and corruption by both the opposition and by President Museveni. More importantly, their staff are always aware that there are other ideas of virtue, and that alternative moral demands may call on them to behave partially and violate procedure. The public, suspicious of such violations, are also weighing different demands on their virtue. They may decide to vote and behave as virtuous national citizens; they may decide that it is their moral duty to vote twice, or impersonate another voter, or even disrupt the election. This is not because they are unaware of, or insensible to, the possibility of virtuous citizenship; it is because on balance this may weigh less in their affective judgement of what is right in these circumstances. The challenge facing officials is therefore not simply to do the right thing, but working out what it means to do the right thing in the context in which they find themselves.

Chapter 4 discusses the international election observers who watch electoral officials go about their duties – and the entanglement of this with the workings of international 'democracy promotion'. Elections are, as many have noted, profoundly performative. They demand an audience, and since the late-colonial period that audience has always been in part an international one. Generations of political leaders, and civil servants, have sought to emphasize the disciplinary function of elections by reminding the public that 'the eyes of the world' have been upon them. Episodic and uncoordinated in early elections – when diplomats, journalists and the occasional fraternal delegation from neighbouring countries provided the audience – the international gaze has come to be increasingly formalized and expanded into an institution of its own: international election observation. This has, to some extent, turned the minatory gaze back upon the state itself: requiring and expecting behaviour in line with international norms.

From its first, unhappy, appearance in Uganda in 1980, international election observation in Africa has at times attracted more criticism than acclaim (Willis, Lynch and Cheeseman 2017). Practices have changed in response to such criticism: there have been experiments in collaboration with local civil society monitors; the deployment of long-term observers; more focus on events before and after the poll, rather than just on the day of the ballot; and, the adoption of increasingly rigorous practices for the selection of sites to be visited by observers. But observation has always faced two fundamental problems. The first has been widely noted: observers' very presence is part of the state effect of elections, conferring legitimacy, yet international observers can only report critical opinions after elections are over. Even then, there are multiple reasons to temper criticism: outright denunciation might trigger widespread violence, and/ or may close off the possibility that the next elections might be better. The logic of electoral observation is that electoral quality can and will be progressively, incrementally, improved; teleological optimism is the default mode of all reports. This links to a second problem, which is that, as observers respond to the numerous pressures they face, they risk undermining their own credibility, particularly among opposition supporters who typically demand that poor-quality polls are not just criticized but also condemned. Especially where elections have generally failed to deliver political change, as in Kenya and Uganda, this constantly undermines the capacity of international missions to encourage citizens and parties to play by the rules of the democratic game.

Chapter 5 then turns our attention to an important non-state actor: the civil society organization (CSO). Since the early 1990s, a great deal of energy has been put into persuading people of the need to act as virtuous citizens in elections. Much of this has been undertaken by organizations that have come to be routinely characterized as 'civil society'. When that term came into the literature in the 1980s, it embodied an uncertain hope that political change might come from popular action, and was rooted in the assumption that state and society were distinct: civil society was, as Bayart (1986: 111) put it (borrowing Fossaert's definition), society 'in confrontation with the state'. We share Mikael Karlström's (1999) concerns about the way that the very idea of civil society asserts a distinction between state and people that is rarely justified. As Catherine Boone (1994) has argued, the state is and always has been entangled with society.

Given this reality, our analysis is concerned with domestic organizations that promote normative international principles – such as human rights or justice – and are typically funded by Western governments. We examine one particular activity – namely, voter education – whereby these organizations seek to inform voters about their duties as citizens so as to help create 'good voters' who will elect 'good leaders' and keep 'the state' in check. We argue that the activity of these CSOs around elections is productive of the powerful illusion that state and society are distinct – it is part of the 'state effect' produced through elections, and it helps to authorize the state's demands and to legitimize power. However, despite the imaginary that it seeks to construct, civil society is not so readily distinguishable from the state: individuals move from advocacy organizations into public service or politics; a shared educational experience and sense of status binds together local officials and the literate English speakers of civil society. Indeed, each at times uses the language of virtuous national citizenship to discipline the other. However, much as the separation between state and civil society begins to blur when one takes a closer look, the individuals who work for civil society also feel the pull of different registers of virtue: they too are members of particular communities and often see the virtue of preference and reciprocation; they may also be partial, becoming involved in supporting the political campaigns of family, or other members of their ethnic group, or of friends (Monga 1995: 369). For these reasons (and others) their work may unintentionally serve to reinforce a patrimonial register of virtue; while similar approaches to voter education in very different contexts have varied consequences. As a result, while civil society's engagement in elections has had a number of positive effects, voter education has not transformed people and elections in the way that some had envisaged (Diamond 1994; Lindberg 2006).

The second part of the book looks at the moral economy of elections in action, and begins with a discussion of political aspirants and electoral campaigns. Chapter 6 poses a different version of our basic question – why do people get involved in elections? – and asks why so many people run for elected office, and how the moral economy of elections affects their campaigns. Politicians are often depicted as simply being motivated by money and the lure of power. But our research suggests that a much more complex range of considerations is usually at play, including the desire to be seen as someone with moral authority within the community. Indeed, while politicians regularly break official electoral rules, and face widespread scepticism regarding their actions and motivations, they also seek to depict themselves to voters as moral actors and construct their appeal on the basis of community expectations of appropriate leadership. Exploring these efforts, the chapter reveals how different socio-economic and institutional contexts, experiences and associated narratives, and past campaign strategies adopted, have helped to shape different ideas of proper, or at least justifiable, electoral behaviour in our three study countries. More specifically, by contrasting Ghana with Kenya and Uganda we demonstrate how, while the electoral moral economy can change over time, this does not necessarily lead to 'flawless' elections. Instead, even good-quality contests can sustain patrimonial values, while problematic processes can encourage a more exclusive form of the patrimonial register to evolve.

Chapter 7 completes our empirical investigation by exploring ideas of proper behaviour among voters. Levels of electoral participation are highest in Ghana, where power alternates between the two political corporations. They are also higher in Kenya's closely fought national elections than in Uganda, where the national outcome is never in doubt. But in all three countries, large numbers of people turn out to vote. Given the persistence of poverty and inequality, and the evident failure of national governments to deliver on the promises that they make at every election, this chapter pursues a question previously asked by Banerjee (2014): why do so many people vote for a system that leaves them poor? While recognizing the fact that many people turn out because they feel compelled to do so, we also follow Banerjee in seeing part of the answer to this question to lie in a sort of claims-making by voters, who use elections to demand that local and national politicians meet their particular needs as an ethnic community, as a local population, or even as individuals.

In addition to the numerous expectations that voters place on candidates during election campaigns, we focus on the exchange of money and gifts around elections because it is a particularly powerful lens through which to understand the complexity of moral claims-making. We find considerable popular support for patrimonial exchanges between leaders and voters in all three countries. The variations between our cases discussed earlier have also had important effects in this regard, however, because money is considerably more likely to be handed out in countries where political parties are institutionally weaker and politics has become extremely personalized, as in Kenya.

We also find that the patrimonial register only sometimes serves to legitimize the giving of money and gifts. Leaders who are seen to be authentic and who have a sustained relationship with an individual or a community can have their reputation bolstered by making handouts; in this context, gift giving is usually seen as an act of generosity and evidence of 'good' leadership. By contrast, those who lack moral authority are vulnerable to being accused of 'vote buying' – a largely illegitimate activity in all three countries, which fails to place voters under a moral obligation. In this way, a focus on gift giving reveals two important points. First, it is only by thinking in terms of the moral economy of elections that we can understand why some leaders do not benefit from handouts, and hence why the individuals who hand out the most money do not always win. Second, voters are not simply in it for themselves or their particular community. Popular condemnation of activities such as ballot-box stuffing, and the harsh criticism of those seen to be 'vote buying', demonstrate the appeal of civic virtue. The work of electoral commissions, voter educators and international observers may be partial and problematic, but it nonetheless encourages individuals – together with individuals' own gravitation to the civic register – to see themselves as citizens; voters may see themselves both as good citizens and as virtuous clients. Like election officials and politicians, voters live with the productive tensions between different possibilities of virtue.

As the Conclusion makes clear, elections are made through these contradictory processes and pressures. They do not produce the perfect citizen, obedient to the dictates of bureaucracy and deaf to particularism and clientelism. Nor do they produce narrowly parochial individuals whose only concern is for co-ethnics. Elections have not simply failed, nor are they inherently unsuitable for Africa; we share Jibrin Ibrahim's sense (1986) that, whatever the limitations of liberal democracy, it has the potential to open up space for more radical questioning. The 'politics of realism' (Eyoh 1998) demand engagement with elections; and institutional reforms can allow for a genuine popular voice through elections (Posner and Young 2007; Opalo 2019). While we share the cautious optimism articulated by others (Osaghae 1999: 22–23; 2013a), we do not locate that optimism in a belief that there is a defined electoral path to a single, universal, democratic citizenship. For those who are concerned with the quality and consequences of voting processes in Africa and elsewhere, thinking about elections as a field for moral claims-making and argument – and accepting that they are unlikely to reach any definitive conclusion – helps to explain both why the ballot does not simply transform state–society relations, and why elections may yet be worth supporting.

1   Towards a Moral Economy of Elections in Africa

Elections have never simply been about the question of who wins power. As Alain Garrigou has argued, 'Concerned with the way that voters "make" elections, we forget that the election has already "made" the voter' (1992: 18). The assemblage of technique and process that constitute an election may appear to be routine to the voter, but they are the contingent product of multiple experiments and changes. For Garrigou, their cumulative effect has been to change how voters think about themselves and their relationship to politics and the state: that is, about their political subjectivity. Garrigou was writing of France; James Vernon (1993) wrote in similar terms of England. A generation earlier, Stein Rokkan (1961: 133) had made this a general argument: elections by secret ballot and adult suffrage encourage the voter to see herself or himself as a 'unit citizen', whose relationship to the state is not mediated by other social ties.

An echo of these interpretations of the impact of elections on the established democracies of Europe can be found in the belief that the reintroduction of elections in Africa in the 1990s would give rise to two mutually reinforcing changes. In one, African political systems would become more accountable and democratic as a result of the potential to remove badly performing leaders from power via the ballot box – an *institutional* transformation. In the other, it was hoped that the process would have a disciplinary effect, teaching voters about their duties and obligations as citizens – an *individual* transformation. Staffan Lindberg's work (2006) has suggested that there is evidence for these linked transformations – a demonstration, perhaps, of James March and Jonah Olsen's point that 'rules and institutions of government' have the potential to 'turn individuals into citizens and officials by shaping their identities and mentalities' (2011: 485).

Lindberg's phrasing of his argument – that we are seeing a process of 'democratization by elections' in which repeated multiparty contests drive democratic consolidation – is relatively new. But the notion that elections could be transformative in the African context has deep roots that go back much further than the 'third wave'. Disciplinary ambitions are a very evident part of Africa's electoral history: from the civic education literature that told Kenyans in the 1960s that voting was one way to 'teach yourself citizenship', to the constant insistence on orderly electoral behaviour, to politicians' explicit demand that the public 'do their duty' by voting (Nkrumah 1961: 208; Willis 2015).[1] Elections have long been seen as the instrument of a responsibilizing citizenship by late-colonial officials, nationalist politicians and international agencies involved in democracy promotion.

In Lindberg's more recent framing of this idea, so long as elections are not of a particularly poor quality, they have the potential to train voters in democratic arts while simultaneously focussing the energies of those campaigning for stronger and more independent democratic institutions. As a result, repeatedly holding elections facilitates a process of democratization, measured in terms of an improvement in the quality of civil liberties (van Ham and Lindberg 2018). This argument, however, is consistently called into question by evidence from the ground. Between 2008 and 2018 the average quality of civil liberties in Africa fell every year according to Freedom House, and there is ample evidence of communal voting patterns and clientelist politics that challenges the vision of the 'unit citizen', guided into good behaviour by experience of the secret ballot (Nzongola-Ntalaja 2004). In Europe, moreover, the apparent disciplinary power of the secret ballot made electoral politics more sedate, less noisily public and fundamentally less participatory (Vernon 1993: 9); in Africa, elections remain vivid, vigorous, high-octane phenomena. Given this, it is all too easy to assume that neither institutional nor individual transformation has occurred.

Yet we would argue that elections in Africa have had an effect. The state as a formal political institution may be relatively weak in a number of countries, but the idea of an effective and autonomous state continues to be compelling for many actors and to play an important role in political debate. However, as is true of other parts of the world, elections have not simply been a disciplinary device that transforms a diverse populace of multiple distinct communities into a uniform citizenry; rather, they have provided a field of contestation in which voters and candidates – and a plethora of other actors besides – make claims on one another. These claims have considerable resonance because they are rooted in widely understood ideas about what constitutes proper and appropriate behaviour in different contexts. They are, that is to say, reflective of coherent sets of moral values. From electoral officials who present themselves as impartial civil servants, to voters who claim never to have accepted a

---

[1] See the leaflets 'Jifunze uraia', nos. 17 and 29, from 1963 and 1966, Kenya National Archives (KNA) DC LAMU 2/2/12.

bribe, to candidates who insist on their role as champions of a local community, elections encourage public assertions of virtue. Such performances are often clearly tailored for specific audiences; sometimes Western donors, sometimes the voters of a particular village, and so on. Yet that does not make them meaningless. Rather, they tell us something profound about popular perceptions of the kind of claims-making that will be most effective in different environments and reveal important information about political subjectivities: that is, the way in which people understand the state and their relationship to it.

Indeed, it is the very multiplicity of social settings created by elections – everything from the night meeting in a local neighbourhood, to an interview with the press, to an argument with a registration officer, to a rally with tens of thousands of cheering supporters, to a Twitter discussion over a decision by the electoral commission – that makes elections such intense foci of moral claims-making wherever they are held. Elections provide space for competing moral claims to be made, heard and resolved: over what it means to be a good leader and over the rights and responsibilities of a citizen and neighbour, relative or fellow member of an ethnic group. These processes rarely reach consensus, are often stacked in favour of those in power and frequently leave vast sections of the population dissatisfied: as the chapters to come will demonstrate, elections are also moments of greed, self-interest and violence. But ideas about good behaviour – contested, sometimes directly contradictory – run through them.

In order to ground our effort to provide a conceptual framework for how we can think about these moral narratives and the work that they do for those who use them, this chapter presents a theoretical road map for the rest of the book. In it, we draw on our experience of watching and researching elections to summarize what these moral claims and narratives typically look like in our three cases. We also engage with the literature on moral economy and state–society relations in the African context, as well as existing work on social norms within the fields of political science, psychology and anthropology, to develop a stylized theoretical framework through which to understand what we call the 'moral economy of elections'. In particular, we conceptualize our three cases as featuring a contested moral landscape in which very different interpretations of what constitutes appropriate behaviour in an electoral context coexist and, to a greater or lesser extent, compete. More specifically, we argue that it is the tension between two very different registers of virtue – one patrimonial and the other civic – that makes the moral economy of elections so vibrant and dynamic. Those calling on the patrimonial register, such as politicians and frequently voters themselves, invoke a political logic rooted in the politics of reciprocity, in which members of a given community expect preferential treatment. By contrast, those who appeal more specifically to civic ideals, classically international observers, electoral officials and civil society groups, but also often candidates and ordinary individuals, focus on the duty of voters to act as responsible citizens and on the value of a meritocratic state that is autonomous from society. We suggest that both registers carry real moral weight, arguing against an earlier literature which implied that it is only the patrimonial register that truly resonates with African publics.

It is important to note that we do not think that the moral economy of elections is unique to Africa – rather, we see it as a central feature of elections everywhere, a point to which we return in the Conclusion. What form the moral economy takes is likely to vary, however, and in-depth studies are required to reveal the nature and source of this variation. Our research process is fundamentally inductive, based on many years of conversations about elections, buttressed by months of fieldwork conducted for this project (Introduction). Our claims are therefore limited to the countries that we have studied, though it seems likely that the framework we develop can profitably be applied to other cases in which similar conditions hold. Given this, we do not argue that there is only one 'moral economy' in Africa that can be identified across all countries; that the effect of electoral participation is always the same; or that the moral values and distinctions we identify are unique to the continent. Indeed, precisely because the traction of these two registers is shaped by context – including socio-economic factors, the strength and inclusivity of political institutions, past electoral experiences, and the actions and appeals of political leaders (see the Introduction) – we recognize that both the moral economy we describe and its impact on the wider political system are likely to vary across time and space. More specifically, we find some evidence for Lindberg's (2006) proposition that good-quality elections may encourage individuals to see themselves as citizens, but also that political competition may encourage a range of patrimonial claims that may reinforce a very different set of attitudes and beliefs. Elections shape political subjectivities, then, but not always in ways that are predictable or preclude forms of malpractice such as 'vote buying' (Chapter 7).

Taken together, our interest in political subjectivities and the kinds of politics that these registers of virtue facilitate may lead readers to assume that we are effectively arguing that successful democratization in Africa requires the victory of civic narratives over their patrimonial counterparts. In fact, we reach a very different conclusion. We do recognize that when patrimonial registers gain ground it becomes harder to sustain the notion that voters and officials must follow the rules of the democratic game, increasing the risk of institutional breakdown. But we also follow Almond and Verba (1963) in seeing a vibrant democratic culture as one in which individuals are invested in the political process as a result of a range of mutually reinforcing affective ties, and we are guided by Schaffer's (2002) argument that overly sanitizing elections is likely to lead to lower levels of popular participation. Our aim is therefore not to demonstrate how patrimonial narratives can be displaced by civic ones – for this might lead to a less deeply rooted democratic process, generating as many problems as it solves. Instead, we seek to document the range of moral projects and claims-making that takes place around elections and explain why efforts to promote civic ideals so often fail to achieve their goals. In doing so, we hope to demonstrate the importance of moving election studies beyond a narrow preoccupation with the question of who wins and why, and to encourage others to look at the broader impact of political competition on how individuals relate to each other and to the state.

1.1   State–Society Relations and the Moral Economy

Our approach is concerned, at its most fundamental, with the relationship between state and society. The disciplined individual citizen-voter evoked by Garrigou is the corollary of an imagined autonomous state: distinct from society, not beholden to any interest groups and claiming legitimate authority by virtue of that separation. While a generation of scholarship on the state in Africa held that they really were separate from society (Chazan 1993) – and that this 'disjuncture' was the root cause of a continental political malaise (Osaghae 1999: 20) – it has now become common to invert this argument. Catherine Boone (1994), echoing the analyses of Philip Abrams (1988) and Timothy Mitchell (1991), has argued that the state in Africa has never been distinct from society, though the appearance of distinction has been a powerful legitimating resource for those who claim state office. State and society, that is, are not separate: they constitute one another. State actors may claim to be autonomous and separate – but they are entangled with society, and so they may behave in ways that contradict and undermine the image of autonomy – following alternative ideas of 'the right way to act' (Migdal 2001: 19–22).

This understanding of the involvement of state with society helps to explain the importance of elections and why – even in the years of single-party rule and even for authoritarian rulers who have no intention of surrendering power – the idea of elections by adult suffrage has been so attractive. As Garrigou's argument suggests, they are – at least, on one level – a bureaucratic performance. By asserting that 'the state' stands above society, they make a claim to the legitimacy of state authority that goes beyond the popularity (or unpopularity) of any individual leader: in the late twentieth and early twenty-first centuries, the election has been a quintessential demonstration of stateness for those who vote as much as for an international audience.

Yet, as Thomas Bierschenk and Jean-Pierre Olivier de Sardan (2014) have observed of bureaucracy more widely, states – in Africa and elsewhere – are always under construction. The idea of the state may be very distant from the practices of state actors. Elections may – and often do – call into question the autonomy of the state by revealing that the behaviour of both officials and publics are guided not just by ideas of civic-mindedness or bureaucratic rectitude. Other ideas of virtue may come into play, not only because people are unsure whether to behave properly, but because there are different possibilities for what constitutes proper behaviour.

It was precisely this tension between ideas of proper behaviour that inspired de Sardan (1999) to ask why people who willingly denounce corruption and who idealize the alternative possibility of an impartial civil service dealing equally with all still take bribes and flout procedure. His answer was that alternative practices and expectations, which also claim to be virtuous, create space in which behaviour condemned by international norms seems acceptable, even proper. There is, he argued, a moral economy of corruption that allows people to be aware of one model of behaviour, yet to privilege another, quite contradictory, one.

De Sardan's intervention is just one of many that has taken up the term 'moral economy' and, in doing so, has both extended and shifted its significance. The original use of the term derived traction from a teasing pun and an oxymoron: challenging the established idea of political economy and implicitly asking how economics could be moral. In E. P. Thompson's (1971) celebratory discussion of revolt as resistance, 'the moral economy' was a distinct set of pre-capitalist values, and popular action sought to defend those values; the logic of the market, by contrast, lacked morality. James Scott (1977) similarly used the idea of moral economy to evoke a distinct set of non-market values that underpinned 'everyday' resistance; the idea of a moral primordial public sphere opposed to an amoral 'civic public' was central to Ekeh's seminal work (1975; also Osaghae 1995). Some more recent usage has followed this line of thought, as with the contributions to an edited collection from Tanzania, for example (Kimambo et al. 2008). For Charles Tripp (2006), the moral economy exists as a set of values that are fundamentally in opposition to capitalism; for Tim Rogan (2017), it is the unstated organizing principle of a distinguished lineage of social and economic history that challenges the logic of capitalism.

Yet the critique of capitalism that this implies seems also to accept what Tripp (2006: 5) rightly sees as capitalism's most fundamental colonizing claim – the imaginative centrality of the rational, utility-maximizing individual, whose conscious pursuit of their self-interest through the market displaces all other ethics. If we do not accept that rationality and utility are absolute – somehow separated from human anxieties about value and virtue – then the dichotomy between the moral economy and capitalism seems analytically less useful (Genovese 1973; Booth 1994). Humans are – as John Lonsdale (1986: 127; also Sayer 2007) has put it – 'selfishly moral beings', and a concern with propriety and the opinion of others does not end with capitalism. Morality may be entangled with accumulative logics, capitalist or not: Ralph Austen's comparative study of witchcraft (1993) used the idea of moral economy as a way to understand why individual accumulation might seem proper, rather than disreputable, and Richard Banégas (1998: 87) has suggested that there might be a moral economy around elections in which money and the market played a very active part. The moral economy can thus offer a way to think about the importance of debates over virtue in multiple spheres of life in capitalist society: the way that South African mining companies seek to present themselves as virtuous actors and to make moral demands on employees, for example (Rajak 2010).

These ways of thinking with the idea of the moral economy avoid an evident danger with the term: that it becomes a 'culturalist' explanation that evades, rather than enables, analysis (Siméant 2010). Presenting behaviour as 'engrained in social habits', as de Sardan puts it, is surely accurate; but social habits are always open to challenge and can change, and it is hard to see how this can take place on the basis of a culturalist analysis alone. Lonsdale's identification of a moral economy of enduring force, which casts wealth as meritorious and poverty as delinquent, is a powerful tool for understanding Kenya's politics, from which we have drawn inspiration (Lonsdale 1992a, 1992b). But does this mean that other ideas of what Lonsdale calls 'civic virtue' – that is, the claim to moral standing within a community – are excluded from the moral economy? Are ideas about, for example, civil service impartiality not also moral claims that can be appropriated and turned to use by multiple agents? Do they not have an ability to shape behaviour and practice through that claim to virtue? We argue that Ekeh's (1975) famous distinction – summarized in the Introduction – between primordial morality and public amorality is fundamentally misleading; instead, we need to recognize the existence of different understandings of virtue, including those rooted in civic/public ideals. Moreover, citizens are not insensible to the affective power, on themselves and others, of alternative ideas of proper behaviour.

A concern with the quotidian, and with bottom-up contestations over power – the very interests that inspired Thompson and Scott – suggests a need to think about how multiple actors work between different competing ideas of virtue and to consider the contingent, shifting and apparently contradictory results of that moral work. In this way, Didier Fassin, writing of debates over migration in France, has used moral economy to mean 'the economy of the moral values and norms of a given group in a given moment' (2005: 365). Similarly, Bruce Berman and Stephen Larin, writing of the moral economies of 'ethnic and nationalist claims', define moral economy as 'those elements of culture (customs, beliefs, and practices) that normatively regulate and legitimize the distribution of resources such as wealth, power, and honour or status in a society'. This constitutes an 'economy', they note, 'because it deals with the unequal distribution of scarce resources that characterizes almost all known human communities' (2016: 4). We also use the term 'economy' because our focus on elections and leadership means that we are interested in how scarce resources are shared, but we push the idea a little further; in writing of 'moral economy' we mean the ceaseless contestation between different visions of what constitutes virtuous behaviour, whose outcomes are always contingent, that goes on in any human society. Amidst this messy process, people seek to understand themselves, and to present themselves, as moral actors; in doing so, they are enabled and constrained by their own experience and that of those around them. Moral economy, then, offers a way to think about tensions and contradictions in ideas of virtue as they apply to both leaders and citizens: why Americans who see themselves as environmentally aware may nonetheless poison their surroundings in pursuit of the perfect mono-cultured lawn; why self-consciously respectable US citizens may pursue a campaign of sabotage and violence against property (Arnold 2001; Robbins and Sharp 2003).

It is this element of contradiction and tension that leads us to think of this as 'moral'; it is the significance of this for the everyday politics of who gets what, when, how and why that leads us to think of this as an 'economy'. Alternative titles for what we wish to talk about here are social norms, dominant frames and ideologies. But while we draw on the literature that has emerged around these ideas, we argue that moral economy captures a much broader and richer way of understanding how ideas of proper behaviour may collide in ways that are both creative and destructive: not only in Africa, but in human societies more widely. To speak of a moral economy foregrounds the role of affect and arguments driven by a sense that some things are not simply routine – nor demanded by convention – but rightful and located in a wider matrix of proper behaviours. It also asserts the role of discursive exchange and co-production in the generation of morality. In other words, it allows us to see how the moral economy is a contested field in which contending notions of virtue compete, the outcome of which is best seen through its consequences for everyday life – that is, through how it makes some forms of behaviour more feasible while rendering others more costly, and so shapes political actions and outcomes. The existence of such a contest is present everywhere that elections are held, but the dynamics of the moral economy vary – notably in terms of the registers of virtue that are dominant – both within Africa and beyond it.

1.2   From Logics of Appropriateness to Registers of Virtue

Using the concept of moral economy in a way that facilitates analysis and avoids overgeneralization requires us to answer three questions: what are the different understandings of virtue that compete within a given moral economy? Where do these ideas come from, and what is their content? How do different understandings gain greater traction, and with what consequences?

This might be understood partly as a manifestation of the contested, asymmetrical process that Rogers Smith (2001) has seen as the production of 'political peoplehood' – what we would call 'political subjectivities'. Aspiring leaders, Smith argues, seek to create political communities with shared ideas of behaviour but find the possibilities of this conditioned by history and circumstance. We share Smith's sense that ideas of virtue are linked to a sense of community and that 'the forging of senses of peoplehood never takes place de novo, in a state of nature' (2001: 75); though we would emphasize that people's ideas of virtuous behaviour may straddle multiple possible communities.

The significance of people's sense of self and community in guiding behaviour is made clear by March and Olsen's (2011) work on what they call the 'logic of appropriateness' – the range of behaviours that are seen to be appropriate for certain people in a certain context. As they put it, most of the time humans take reasoned action by trying to answer three elementary questions: 'What kind of a situation is this? What kind of a person am I? What does a person such as I do in a situation such as this?' (2011: 479). Where they are widely held and deeply felt, logics of appropriateness can be called upon to authorize certain decisions or actions and 'proclaim virtue' (2011: 485). The hold that logics of appropriateness exert over individuals and groups means that understandings of political community are likely to falter if they are not viewed as suitable – that is, if they do not resonate with existing values and expectations.

While it may be obvious to someone how to behave in a situation that they regularly encounter, March and Olsen also recognize that 'in other contexts actors have problems in resolving ambiguities and conflicts among alternative concepts of the self, accounts of a situation, and prescriptions of appropriateness' (2011: 5). Sometimes, that is, people are not sure how to behave: uncertain as to what kind of person they are and/or what that kind of person should do. Such ambiguity is likely to peak during periods of political and social flux: when exogenous shocks such as war or economic collapse challenge existing ideas of behaviour, or the introduction of new institutions – such as multiparty elections – generates a new set of situations. This creates openings for the emergence of new logics of appropriate behaviour or for people to decide that existing logics should govern behaviour in a new situation. The framework of logics of appropriateness is therefore not static.

One way of expressing our interest with arguments about virtue would thus be to follow March and Olsen by conceptualizing individual uncertainty over how to behave in a certain moment as reflecting competition between particularly compelling logics of appropriateness. However, we prefer to speak about competing registers of virtue rooted in a moral economy for three main reasons. First, doing so enables us to tap into a rich seam of Africanist literature on moral economy that has sought to describe the complex evolution of different values over time in response to the realities of colonial rule, ethnicity and 'traditional' forms of government. As we noted earlier, moral economy emphasizes the way in which public morality has been co-produced through unequal relationships and discursive exchange; it recognizes the importance of language, history and the capacity of political and cultural entrepreneurs to shape popular ideas about virtue, as well as differences across time and space.

Second, we are as interested in the nature of moral claims-making and the way that moral arguments are expressed as we are in the behaviour of individuals in and around elections. In other words, our focus is not just on what people do, or how they decide to do it, but also includes the kinds of narratives that are employed to sway themselves and others, and how these are constructed. March and Olsen (2011: 485) note that logics of appropriateness are 'sometimes invoked' to proclaim virtue rather than to control behaviour directly. But claims-making around elections, when public attention is naturally focussed on questions of leadership and what constitutes a good leader, is not just *sometimes* about virtue – it is always about this.

The moral content of these claims and arguments is particularly important, because it is by referencing contending notions of virtue that individuals make sense of the situation that they face and the actions that they take.

Indeed, one of the main elements of this process that has struck us in every field site we have visited (and, indeed, in our experience of elections in the United Kingdom and elsewhere in the world) has been the consistent attempt of individuals to interpret their own actions as virtuous – to make moral meaning of their own lives. In many cases, this involves going against what most people like them are actually doing – to ask 'what should a moral person do in an immoral world'. In some cases this is done with regard to a clear reference group – to a recognized logic of appropriateness – but often it is not, in part because competing rationales have variable purchase, and in part because what is right or justifiable is dependent on how others are expected to act, and so is constantly changing. As Beek (2016) has argued in the context of Ghanaian police officers, most people live amidst and between different conceptions of virtue and so experience 'moral struggles' as they do their jobs and live their lives. Given the moral content of arguments and claims-making around elections, and the extent to which virtue is invoked, it is a much better reflection of the day-to-day reality of our cases to speak of competing registers of virtue rather than contrasting logics of appropriateness.

Third, while the logics of appropriateness framework recognizes that '[i]n other contexts actors have problems in resolving ambiguities and conflicts among alternative concepts of the self, accounts of a situation, and prescriptions of appropriateness' (March and Olsen 2011: 482), it tends to see this as being somewhat exceptional. Thus, while March and Olsen recognize that 'following appropriate rules often involves matching a changing and ambiguous set of contingent rules to a changing and ambiguous set of situations' (2011: 482–483), the absence of clarity is often said to result from a lack of familiarity, or to be driven by moments of rapid social and political change. By contrast, we understand normative ambiguity to be a pervasive and persistent feature of elections in our cases. Competing moral claims do not simply arise from unfamiliarity or institutional change, but rather should be thought of as part and parcel of a moral economy in which individuals are constantly drawn between different conceptions of virtue. In other words, we view ambiguity not to be exceptional, but rather to be woven into the fabric of everyday life.

It could be argued that we come to this conclusion because our cases are in a transition moment from one type of political system and society, with one set of associated norms and values, to another. Such an interpretation would imply that Africa is simply in between dominant logics of appropriateness, moving from a 'traditional' past characterized by communal identities and authoritarianism towards a 'modern' future in which civic values and democracy will win out. It is certainly true that an important barrier to the spread of civic ideals is the shallow roots of many formal institutions, and the way in which this undermines their capacity to prescribe and authorize certain logics of behaviour. In this sense, one might say that registers of virtue come to the fore precisely when logics of appropriateness do not offer a clear answer to the question of 'what should a person like me do in a situation like this'; that is, that the moral economy comes alive in moments of radical ambiguity begat by institutional weakness. But this would be a mistake, and would overly simplify what in reality is a much more complex picture. The arguments and narratives we describe cannot be easily categorized as either 'traditional' or 'modern', as they are both products of multiple messy interactions over the past seventy years. To abstract them out of this context would both oversimplify reality and generate misleading conclusions. As we demonstrate later, in a profound sense patrimonial and civic registers compete, but they may also be invoked by the same individuals – and sometimes at the same time – and institutions may prove to be more stable when both registers are present. Moreover, we also identify strong and effective claims-making from within the patrimonial register in situations in which democratic institutions are considerably stronger and more broadly respected, such as Ghana. We therefore do not wish to depict the patrimonial register of virtue as a residual phenomenon that only comes to the fore when existing rules are weak or break down; rather, we see patrimonialism as one aspect of a persistent preoccupation with virtue that can shift over time and space – and thus as an alternative way to think about political subjectivities in and across a wide range of societies.

It is also important to stress that we do not view African politics and society to be in any way static or exceptional. Instead, our claim is two-fold. First, in our country case studies two particular registers of virtue have emerged, and the tension between them has rendered conversations and claims-making around elections particularly complex and vibrant. Second, there is little evidence to suggest that Kenya, Ghana and Uganda are in the process of transition from a world in which different registers of virtue are in competition to one in which they are not. Teleological interpretations of political progress, in Africa and other parts of the world, are typically rooted in the assumption that, sooner or later, states will evolve strong democratic institutions, which will in turn encourage and lock in democratic norms and values. Yet the early literature on democratic transitions, which imagined smooth progress towards democratic government following the collapse of authoritarian rule, had to be revised when it became clear that many states are not on a conveyor belt towards greater levels of political liberalization (Carothers 2002). Similarly, a number of scholars have argued that the analytical category of 'hybrid' regimes that are part authoritarian and part democratic is unhelpful if this term is taken to imply that these political systems are inherently unstable and will ultimately gravitate towards one pole or the other along this spectrum (Levitsky and Way 2002). It should therefore be clear that the moral economy of elections that we describe here cannot be reduced to a 'passing phase'.

We acknowledge that, to some, foregrounding morality in the study of elections might seem counter-intuitive at best and an apologia for gross misconduct at worst. Elected office – however won – offers great prizes and contests are often associated with some of the worst excesses: violence, detention of candidates, abuse of offices and resources and so forth. In the countries studied here, political positions have, from their creation in the 1950s, been seen in part as an opportunity for rent-seeking. Whether through control over development spending, or interference in procurement, or manipulation of licensing frameworks, those chosen by voters as their representatives have always acquired new means to accumulate wealth through gatekeeping. Politics and personal accumulation are entangled, and always have been: in the early twenty-first century, as in the 1960s, running for office can seem like the only realistic route to wealth: 'once you get to parliament, [it] is like you have bid goodbye to poverty', as one aspiring candidate assured us.[2] Clearly, politicians, officials and voters all pursue what they see as their interests, and their concern to present themselves as moral actors – and be seen as such – does not preclude greed and self-interest. As one person remarked to us, in 'politics: number one is money; two, money; three, money and money, money, money. . . . Because without power you can't have the money too.'[3]

In arguing that these individuals are also engaged in morally justifying their actions, we are not exculpating behaviour that can be readily understood as self-interested, coercive, exploitative and unjust, or denying that people often do things that they know are wrong and unjustifiable. Instead, we simply recognize how the desire to see oneself and be seen by others as a moral actor is a powerful force, and shapes how people understand what their interests are and how they may properly be pursued, and how people in turn seek to justify or explain a wide range of behaviours. Frederic Schaffer's (2007a) seminal collection on 'vote buying' and Eric Kramon's (2017) recent work exemplify this point: the giving of gifts by politicians might be seen as vote buying, is certainly self-interested, and often involves a knowing breach of the law as well as of international norms. Yet, voters and politicians may all see the giving of gifts as a sign of respect and concern, and as a way of signalling virtue – not

[2] Interview KEN48a, aspiring candidate, Kisumu, 17 June 2017.
[3] Interview GHA11a, civil society activist, Ho, 9 September 2015.

as a purchase (see Chapter 7). In pursuing that point, and using the term morality, we certainly do not argue that the behaviours that we describe are moral in any absolute sense, or that they would be seen as being morally good by everyone in a particular context, or that they should be excused. Registers of virtue may be invoked to justify atrocities such as genocide as well as acts of selfless devotion. Rather, our claim is that, in order to understand what it is that people are doing when they vote, campaign and prepare for elections, we must think about how politicians, voters and officials seek to make sense of themselves, justify their actions and make demands on others by interpreting their actions through competing registers of virtue that make sense to them and to those that they interact with.

Once one starts to look for them, arguments over behaviour and responsibilities are everywhere in elections. Throughout the campaign and the preparations for the vote, elections constantly require people to justify themselves, to make demands on others – to talk of what people should do and what they should not. Politicians lecture voters about their responsibility to the nation, or their community, and make promises to them. They present themselves as moral actors: evoking shared ideas of what proper behaviour is, they point out the ways in which they have worked for their constituents. Voters applaud or heckle; they spread rumours and accusations: publicly or not, they accuse politicians of corruption, or of failing to fulfil promises, or of neglecting the needs of the voters. As they do so they affirm or question claims to virtue. Election posters and leaflets assert the virtue of candidates (and sometimes question it); voter education events and posters, training for electoral staff, workshops for agents offer visions of proper behaviour and establish their own standards of impropriety – the corrupt politician, the careless official, the voter who puts parochial interest above the nation.

Elections, then, are periods of moral contestation and claims-making over the obligations and privileges of authority and citizenship. That is why, even when voters believe that a ruling party and president cannot be ousted, campaigning and voting can still engage popular interest and enthusiasm, as long as there is some possibility of choice, some way to argue over who has behaved well and what good behaviour looks like. That many of those involved may sometimes behave in ways that defy norms – breaking their promises, breaking the rules – serves only to make this process more intense.

This invocation of virtue extends to the use and threat of violence. Violence has lurked throughout the history of elections in the countries that we study here: implied in threats and insults, casually enacted in stone-throwing, euphemized in paramilitary displays, systematically pursued in the beating of opponents by thugs or the tear-gassing of opposition rallies by uniformed security men. Again, to say that violence is a part of this moral economy of elections is not to minimize or excuse it, but how people behave, and how they justify their behaviour to themselves and others, does relate to claims to virtue – they are staking claims and making arguments. The police officers at every polling station; the ostentatious armed patrols, the direct use of tear gas, batons and firearms: these are ways for the security forces to remind everyone that they are the real guarantors of civic order. Youthful thugs may also be paid to use force, but they too will usually have a ready justification for their behaviour, for example as an assertion of the rights of the young and marginalised, or as being necessary to defend their ethnic community (Lynch 2011a).

1.3   A Tale of Two Registers

The moral economy of elections – specific as it is to time and place – is a field of contestation and claims-making, not a set of rules. Our argument that in Ghana, Kenya and Uganda this moral arena is animated by two dominant registers of virtue, the patrimonial and the civic, does not mean that we see these concepts as being rigidly defined and set in stone. Instead, we can think about the two registers of virtue that we describe here in the way that Michael Freeden (1996) analyses competing ideologies. Freeden argues that ideologies are best thought of as families of concepts, organized around a certain set of core ideas but varying in their precise formulation. We follow Freeden's example by using the terms 'civic' and 'patrimonial' to identify two 'families' of virtue that typically have certain common features but also exhibit considerable variation. When individuals invoke the civic register they touch on a wide set of ideas of virtue that revolve around impartiality, meritocracy and citizenship. In the case of the patrimonial register, the touchstones are typically reciprocity, commonality and preference. It is possible to describe the internal logics of these registers, and to identify them across different places and at different times but – as Freeden argues – these core concepts may appear in multiple combinations and permutations, so that the way virtue is understood and used to legitimize claims may vary within each register – while yet remaining in tension with rival 'families' of virtue.

In focussing on these two registers we do not suggest that there are no other forms of argument and claims-making, but we do argue that these registers, stylized though they are, provide a way to understand the place of elections in our particular case studies as an arena in which claims can be made with reference to different ideas of virtue – a site of struggle over morality with important implications or a moral economy. It is also important to note that we are not suggesting that the same registers will be dominant in all moral economies around the world. While the civic register of virtue – intimately bound up as it is with the imaginary of the autonomous state – is likely to be present wherever elections are held, what other registers hold sway, and how much purchase they enjoy, is likely to vary. It is beyond the scope of this project to specify what these alternative registers might look like, and the conditions under which they are likely to come to the fore. What is possible is to identify the factors that shape the moral economy of elections in our countries (see Introduction; Chapter 2), and to discuss the implications that this has for the kinds of registers that might emerge elsewhere, a task we take up in the Conclusion.

1.3.1 Patrimonial Virtue

Candidates and voters in our three countries regularly make demands on each other that are rooted in a common identity and a patron–client logic (Chapters 6 and 7) – and indeed spend considerable time talking about the importance of ethnicity, corruption and the role of money in politics. This preoccupation reflects the centrality of what we call the 'patrimonial register'. As Pitcher, Moran and Johnston (2009) have argued, 'patrimonialism' has been both overused and misused in writing on Africa. At its broadest, the term has been deployed to mean no more than the ability of a leader to do what they want and get away with it on the basis of their assumed dominance over a particular group or individual – that is, as a shorthand signifying compromised political institutions and 'untamed' presidents (Chabal and Daloz 1999; Prempeh 2008). Used thus, the term loses its central implication, that of moral purchase. Max Weber used patrimonialism to refer to relationships rooted in custom and trust, which implied both rights *and* obligations. The term demands that we recognize 'the reciprocities that Weber discusses along with the personal dimensions of power, governance, and compliance that feature in most contemporary accounts' (Pitcher, Moran and Johnston 2009: 127). Significantly, unless we make space for the notion of mutual responsibilities, we cannot explain how patrimonialism can give rise to powerful claims-making.

In our three cases, patrimonial moral arguments revolve around reciprocity, commonality and preference. Reciprocity refers to the practice of exchange for mutual benefit, such as the patron–client ties that often develop around elections, in which clients exchange their support for either gifts delivered in advance of the polls or the promise of access to state resources thereafter. As we explore in Chapters 6 and 7, reciprocity is often at the heart of the promises that candidates make to would-be voters, and the claims that individuals make on their leaders. In such relationships, those in power are expected to deliver to those who are not and face sanctions if they fail. Most obviously, failure to deliver on an electoral bargain may result in support being withdrawn and future defeat. Consequently, although leaders enjoy considerably more power than their followers, they do not operate without constraints. However, while the practice of leaders delivering largesse to their supporters ensures a degree of redistribution – in the geographical sense that whoever is in power directs resources away from other communities and regions and towards their own – this does not mean that it lays the foundation for an egalitarian society. Rather, patrimonial relations are inherently inequitable; leaders can only deliver if they have greater control over resources than the ordinary individual, and so the hope that patrons will take care of the community's interests is itself premised on the notion of their greater wealth and status.

Patrimonial relations differ from straightforward patron–client relationship in two important respects. First, the sense of reciprocity is not simply grounded in the exchange of money for political support but a much deeper set of socially embedded relationships in which members of a community look out for each other's interests because doing so is understood to be good for the community as a whole, and because this is what is owed by each member of the group as a result of their shared identity. In Kenya, Ghana and Uganda, this sense of commonality often takes the form of appeals to ethnic solidarity but may also be rooted in region or clan, or other communal identities that may stem, for example, from shared membership in a church or professional association. The fact that elections witness a spike in a form of patrimonial claims-making rooted in sub-national communities helps to explain why Eifert, Miguel and Posner (2010) find that they lead to individuals prioritizing their ethnic identity over their national one. Thus, in contrast to generic patron–client ties, patrimonial relationships are neither universal in their potential scope, nor are they purely contractual. Precisely for these reasons, the moral claims that they give rise to have particular power. Failing to deliver on your duties as a patron means letting down a client, but failing on your patrimonial duties means disappointing a community.

As is already clear from the discussion thus far, a third critical component of the patrimonial register is preference. When politicians seek to motivate voters through appeals to ethnic solidarity, their supporters respond by demanding preferential treatment in terms of disproportionate access to available resources. This may mean the location of development projects in the community or the promotion of community members into state employment. Tellingly, research has even suggested that voters may punish their leaders for supplying public goods that benefit everyone, rather than private or club goods targeted at community members that exclude rivals and thus implicitly recognize their preferential status (de Kadt and Lieberman 2017).

Taken together, reciprocity, commonality and preference make for a sense of moral virtue that is rooted in privileged relationships between those who share some form of collective identity. Claims for assistance and support based on this kind of reciprocity are seen not only to have power but also to be legitimate, for patrimonialism is a moral force. As Lonsdale (1992b) has argued of the Kikuyu community in Kenya, leaders are expected to give back to the community, but not because there is any notion of a deserving poor. While 'wealth ineluctably incurred obligations' (1992b: 5), the moral purchase of claims on the wealthy come not from a shared belief in the virtue of redistributing wealth per se, but from the fact that the individuals concerned were embedded within a specific ethnic and moral community and were therefore subject to an established set of reciprocal expectations.

At the same time, patrimonial virtue is internally contested. Personal ties, ethnicity and locality do not always pull in the same direction; claims or obligations may arise from shared school experience or involvement in a business organization or a club. These ties may enable electoral work: a candidate may raise campaign funds from former schoolmates (their OBs and OGs, as Ugandans call them) or fellow businessmen (Vokes 2016). But politicians, and voters, may have to weigh the relative significance of different kinds of tie: is it proper to trust, or help, other people from your ethnic group more than people who went to the same school? Your kin, rather than your neighbours? The sense that you must not let someone down – and its corollary, the belief that someone owes you something – is a powerful force, but patrimonial morality is chronically jealous: each patron therefore lives in constant fear of being replaced as a result of not having been attentive enough to their supporters' needs, and voters readily suspect their MP of favouring immediate kin over the wider ethnic group, or – worst of all – of forgetting voters and becoming part of an exclusive elite.

We use the term 'patrimonial' and *not* the more common 'neo-patrimonial' here for three main reasons. First, our aim is to describe different schools of thought and so our focus is on ideas and the conceptions of virtue that they are rooted in, rather than seeking to define or identify a certain kind of state. Appropriately used, 'neo-patrimonialism' refers to a fusion of patrimonial authority with the formal institutions of a modern state and is a way of understanding the logic of the resulting political system (Cheeseman 2018b); as a result, it is not suitable for our focus on narratives and claims-making. Second, the imprecise way in which neo-patrimonialism has been used within African studies risks reducing it to a catch-all concept that has little analytical value (Erdmann and Engel 2007; Pitcher, Moran and Johnston 2009). Finally, we see patrimonial registers as offering *one* kind of claim to moral virtue, rather than *the* claim to moral virtue. In other words, we are referring to a set of beliefs and claims that exist within a broader moral economy and which compete with other registers. We do not claim that they necessarily win out, nor that they are the dominant force. Given this, we avoid using the term 'neo-patrimonial' because it has often been deployed in the African context in a way that implies not the creative interaction of the patrimonial and the civic with unpredictable consequences, but rather the comprehensive victory of the patrimonial – and hence the notion that institutions are vacuous. Against this, we see the idea, if not always the reality, of a modern state as having become embedded in the moral economy of elections – something that is made apparent by the allure of the civic register of virtue.

1.3.2   Civic Virtue

The easiest way to think about the civic register of virtue is that it is the inverse of the patrimonial ideal type. But it is important to flesh out this register, both because it is less commonly described in the African context and because the way that this register is understood by electoral officials (Chapter 3), civil-society representatives (Chapter 5) and international observers (Chapter 4) has important implications for how it is deployed around elections. It is also necessary to demonstrate one of the central elements of our argument: that claims made through civic appeals are also a manifestation of *moral* thought and carry affective weight.

In our three cases, civic claims imply a rejection of a patrimonial logic, and instead invoke the vision of a state that is capable of delivering to everyone because it is not beholden to any particular group or faction. In line with this, those who make such claims typically invoke the value of impartiality, citizenship and meritocracy. Impartiality here means the sense that decisions are made in accordance with a principle that is intended to be applied equally to all; the kind of neutrality that emerges from ensuring that the rules of the game are followed and all parties are treated in the same way. We might think of this as a kind of technocratic logic. As Beatriz M. Reyes-Foster has argued, the focus on following the rules and on technical expertise has the potential to 'erase the voice of individual subjects' (2014: 380). But the flipside of this suppression of certain aspects of individuality is a greater degree of inclusivity, because impartiality also guards against the exclusion of minorities and those out of power.

In turn, impartiality brings with it the notion of meritocracy – the ideal that the best people and ideas rise to the top, not just those with the right breeding, or those who come from the right community. Of course, this goal is often not realized in practice – even the most effective modern states often have glass ceilings for women, those who are ethnic minorities, or are from a lower class (Reynolds 1999; Beller and Hout 2006). But this complex reality does not prevent the ideal of meritocracy from being an important part of the civic register of virtue; indeed, the notion that any voter can become president or prime minister is a critical component of the democratic project, though in reality wealth and birth always shape one's political prospects.

This strong focus on impartiality and meritocracy goes hand-in-hand with an emphasis on citizenship. Used in this context, citizenship does not simply refer to individuals allowed to live in a country, but to the notion that members of a state are born with certain duties as well as rights, and that these include acting in a civic manner, that is, to promote what is good for the whole community rather than just the individual. The combination of these three core principles generates a worldview that sees virtue as being rooted in actions that avoid particularistic or sectional considerations in order to treat all citizens equally. In this sense, the civic register often implies a commitment to some form of nationalism, and typically comes with an invocation to act in the national interest, for example, voting for candidates committed to providing public goods.

As should already be clear, the individuals in our three countries evoke notions of civic virtue in ways that are rather different to Almond and Verba's classic conceptualization of 'civic culture'. For Almond and Verba, the term 'civic' was a signifier for a specific combination of three different subcultures – the parochial, subject and participant – that were, when operating together, supportive of democratic consolidation. We eschew this formulation for three main reasons. First, we do not find these categories – which referred, respectively, to societies that were acephalous, authoritarian, and those that prized active engagement with the political sphere – analytically useful, and nor do we accept Almond and Verba's explicit argument about the Anglo-Saxon cultural prerequisites of democratic politics. Second, they envisaged each of these sets of ideas as corresponding to a prototypical 'man on the street' – that is, they conceive of certain attitudes as being held by certain types of individuals – whereas our study is motivated by the realization that the same individuals can feel moved by, and indeed make recourse to, different registers of virtue as they go about their political business. Third, our aim is less to characterize the overarching culture that prevails in a particular place and more to identify particular strands of moral claims-making and contrast them.

There are also other important differences between our approach and Almond and Verba's. Perhaps most significantly, the centrality of meritocracy to our framing of the civic register of virtue reflects the fact that such appeals are often underpinned by an attachment to a bureaucratic logic. More specifically, we find that the vision of those who invoke such ideals often rests on the assumed value of an autonomous state that is emancipated from social interests – one of the critical components in the imaginary of 'modern' nations (Bierschenk and de Sardan 2014). Thus, claims made within the civic register are typically framed as being motivated by the broader national interest rather than being driven by narrow sectional concerns, and are heavily committed to the notion of due process: they assert a kind of rational-legal authority in which the exercise of power is justified with reference to the legitimacy of the legal order. This bureaucratic ideal type rarely, if ever, exists in practice. But this has not prevented the ideal of a neutral and effective state from forming a central component of popular conceptions of civic virtue in all three countries. Indeed, evidence that the existing state has failed to uphold civic virtue often leads to impassioned pleas for individuals to behave as good citizens and to put the national interest first (Chapters 4 and 5).

1.3.3   *Alternative Registers*

It is important to recognize that there are other registers of virtue that – in our three country case studies and beyond – may compete with or reinforce one or other of the two registers outlined. This includes religious registers that interpret what is morally right as that which fits with religious teaching and serves to honour and glorify God. However, given the existence of different religions and widely divergent readings of the same religions in Kenya, Ghana and Uganda, in practice religious narratives do not represent an alternative to the patrimonial and civic registers, and instead tend to be invoked to legitimate one or the other. To take Christianity – the dominant religion in all three countries – as an example, some Christian leaders emphasize how God created different ethnic groups, sustaining patrimonial mores, while others stress how he created all men in his image, implying a form of equality that lends itself to the civic register. Similarly, while some churches teach that authority is God given and must be respected, others believe that we should struggle for social justice (Throup 1995; Sabar-Friedman 2002; Deacon and Lynch 2013). To suggest that religious beliefs may be compatible with both of the registers of virtue that we focus on here is not to suggest that they are unimportant – on the contrary, religion is central to political debate and performance across our country case studies. Rather, our point is that, in our case studies, religious beliefs do not constitute a coherent register in their own right when it comes to the moral economy of elections; they are best understood as resources that leaders seek to utilize in support of one or other of the patrimonial and civic world views.

Similarly, while ideological disagreements over socio-economic approaches – whether they be about the correct distribution of wealth or how to achieve development – are also imbued with ideas of what is moral, it is not helpful to conceptualize them as an alternative register in their own right. Debates over economic policy may feature passionate arguments over both the types of policies that governments should implement and the means that are justified to do so, but in our three cases these conversations tend to focus on whether those in authority owe an equal responsibility to all citizens or should be allowed to demonstrate favouritism in order to reward their own communities. In this way, arguments in favour of the provision of public goods on the one hand, or club and private goods on the other, tend to collapse back into the civic and patrimonial registers – which in turn explains why they are the focus of our enquiry. This particular feature of our cases should not be mistaken for a general rule, however – the situation may look very different in other countries, where more rigid religious belief systems, institutional contexts and processes of socio-economic development may give rise to alternative registers that stand in starker contrast to civic and patrimonial ideals (Conclusion).

1.4   The Moral Economy at Work

Although we argue that the patrimonial and civic registers permeate claims-making around elections in Ghana, Kenya and Uganda, our analytical separation of these concepts should not be taken to imply that there is anything neat or simplistic about how they play out in reality. While it is true that politicians and voters more frequently appear in these pages extolling patrimonial values, while electoral officials and observers more commonly advocate civic ones, there are no clean lines demarcating when and where these appeals are made. Opposition leaders regularly make use of civic arguments in order to generate greater support for electoral reforms that they hope will constrain the advantages of the ruling party (Chapter 3); they also seek to present themselves as nationally oriented to mobilize cross-ethnic support and to avoid being labelled a divisive 'tribalist' (Chapter 6). Civil society leaders who profess a deep commitment to impartiality in one forum may invoke a patrimonial register in another (Chapter 4). Similarly, voters may begin polling day extolling civic virtues and describing the kind of state they wish to live in, but end it arguing that patrimonial strategies are justified after their belief in the possibility of due process has been shaken by allegations of electoral manipulation (Chapter 7). It is therefore important to keep in mind that the registers that individuals draw on to make claims will vary both depending on their belief system and the situation in which they find themselves. Indeed, as Dominic Burbidge has shown (2014), voters thinking through the way that they should behave during an election campaign may feel the pull of both registers at one and the same time.

The real world is messy and the individuals that we describe are creative and not infrequently ingenious. Our claim is not, therefore, that people draw on these registers in isolation or that they do so in ways that are always consistent. Instead, our argument is that apparently contrasting sets of value are often in play. To illustrate the way that this contradictory pursuit of virtue manifests itself in our three cases, it may be helpful to briefly discuss three electoral moments that we witnessed in the course of our research.

(a) As we are chatting over drinks with upper-middle-class Ugandan friends in Kampala, the conversation turns to the elections to be held the following month and to the research being conducted. The men are all supporters of opposition leader Kizza Besigye and his Forum for Democratic Change (FDC); they are convinced that the opposition leader will win but are worried that his rightful victory will be denied by an uneven playing field and electoral manipulation. Much of the conversation focuses on the range of tactics that President Museveni has used to stay in power, and what the FDC and their supporters can do to protect the vote. Clearly angered by incumbent malpractice, one man jokes about how he and others voted for Besigye multiple times in previous elections. The process, as he explains it, was simple: as they exited the polling station they were careful to get the indelible ink used to guard against multiple voting only on the pad of their finger (rather than the nail); once out of the station they rushed to urinate on their finger to remove the indelible ink, and – after waiting a while and with the collusion of the local polling clerk – re-entered and voted in the name of someone who was known to be registered but out of town. After recalling the memory, the man takes on a more serious tone: such behaviour was necessary because everyone knows that Museveni engages in malpractice. It was also justifiable: Museveni had used his position for the benefit of a small elite, and it was a service to the community and country to try to bring about a more inclusive government. The implication of the story was clear: the action was illegal but deemed to have been morally sound. As a result, it was a source of pride, rather than embarrassment or regret – a story that could be told in front of both fellow FDC supporters and a foreign academic.[4]

(b) On the other side of the continent, in Ghana, morning assembly at a teacher-training college is addressed by the incumbent MP, who belongs to the ruling party. The young male and female students in white shirts and blue skirts and trousers stand in untidy rows outside the low buildings of their classrooms. Five gleaming four-wheel-drive cars have brought their guests, who are seated on plastic chairs in the shade of a large low tree. Several have already spoken, in ascending order of seniority – mostly local government officials, they are joined by one senior figure from the national party office, who is a local man. The speaker stands in the sun and, like the audience, is perspiring from the heat. He appeals for their votes – and those of their parents – in the imminent elections. He urges the importance of the national development the party will bring and the audience applauds politely. He promises that the college will be given a bus, as local schools have been, and they applaud more. They applaud most of all when the young woman who is acting as host closes proceedings by announcing that their visitors have donated equipment and cash for the development of the college's sports teams. Speakers and staff from the school go into one of the bare classrooms to sit and talk for a few minutes in private while the speakers' retinue pack the chairs and sound system away. As the party official climbs into his car a knot of excited young men gathers around the window, and something is passed out to them; the convoy then moves off in the gathering heat of the morning, raising a cloud of dust, on to the next meeting of the day.[5]

(c) In Kenya, months later, it is late afternoon in a school classroom. Since morning, the classroom has been busy with voters, for this is one of many schools across the country that is being used in the national elections. The presiding officer – wearing a high-visibility tabard that marks her status – glances at her watch repeatedly; it is almost time for voting to end. She begins to look at her manual for instructions on how to close the poll – then, suddenly, there is a small commotion. A young woman has arrived to cast her vote, but when she places her finger on the electronic device that should verify her identity, it appears that she has already voted. She denies this, so do one or two other people, who have been waiting around outside the station and claim to know her. None of the polling staff remembers

---

[4] Fieldwork notes, Kampala, 4 January 2016.
[5] Fieldwork notes, Ho, 24 November 2016.

seeing her earlier; a consensus quickly emerges that actually she has not voted, and the identification device has made an error. A dilemma – should she be allowed to vote? Since the device has marked her as having already voted, a ballot paper cannot be issued against her name. As the woman begins to argue her case, feeling grows that she should be allowed to vote. All of the agents present back the same presidential candidate, and understand that, in a close race, every vote matters. A well-known local man, who has no formal role at the polling station, talks to the agents, and they propose a solution: it is possible to override the device and issue a ballot paper in the name of another voter who has not yet voted, and is unlikely to turn up before polls close. They gather round the presiding officer, who hesitates; she is from the area, works there in her usual job as a teacher and she knows many of the agents as neighbours. Yet she has now worked three times as an election official in the last decade, and values the regulations. That sense may be heightened by the presence of a researcher, with Independent Electoral and Boundaries Commission (IEBC) accreditation. She takes a few steps away, looks at her watch, takes a few more steps – then announces that polling is closed. The young woman leaves, disappointed.[6]

Each of these moments – and many more that will be discussed in subsequent chapters – involved individuals pursuing diverse and some-times contradictory kinds of political work: building the nation, exalting civic ideals, asserting ethnic solidarity, affirming clientelism. Those instrumental political projects were rooted in performances that made arguments about virtue. Those involved presented themselves as rightful actors in society, and sought to draw others into a shared understanding of what constitutes proper conduct; however, they also behaved in ways shaped by their sense of the expectations and demands of others, and by their desire to appear virtuous. The presiding officer's behaviour reflected the importance to her of what some have called 'boundary' work whereby officials present themselves and their activities as a distinct bureaucratic sphere characterized by civic values (Lentz 2014; see also Schroven 2010). The urban professional voter was making a roundabout claim to civic virtue – only by breaking the letter of the rules could he uphold their spirit. The campaigning politicians were performing the role of national leaders committed to development, but were also compelled to respond to the expectation that they should act as patrons to a local community. All were aware of multiple gazes: the other drinkers, the politicians resting in the shade of the trees, the neighbours who were working as party agents for the day, the presence of a foreign researcher. Those audiences

[6] Fieldwork notes, Seme, 8 August 2017.

themselves made demands either explicitly or implicitly, but also felt the burden of expectation on them. In consequence, all involved were complicit in behaviours that confounded at least some notions of virtue.

1.5   Conclusion: The Productive Moral Economy

As suggested in the Introduction, looking at elections through the lens of the moral economy helps us to understand why and how the impact of elections on political subjectivities has been complicated and uneven, but may nonetheless change how individuals view their relationship with the state. It also explains why, even though many people in the countries that we study are well aware of international norms for electoral behaviour, they participate readily in elections that involve constant breaches of those norms, and why they themselves may be active in breaching them. What appear to be egregious acts on the basis of one register may be lauded as virtuous on another. More than that, the moral economy helps us to understand that elections are co-produced, albeit in very unequal ways: officials and politicians operate amidst popular demands and expectations, shaped by former elections and wider experience. For example, through demands for handouts and suggestions that they should be able to vote multiple times, citizens can undermine official rules. At the same time, through abstention, heckling and rumour, they can effectively condemn similar behaviours as improper. Moreover, when enough people see the electoral behaviour of a candidate – or a regime – as improper, the consequences are significant: the multiple malpractices of Uganda's 1980 elections left the new regime illegitimate in the eyes of many, and reliant on coercion. Virtue is contested and may take different forms – but few wish to be seen as entirely lacking it.

The moral economy can also help us to understand that change is not unidirectional, and that – while experience is cumulative – its consequences are not always predictable. Sequential elections do not always ensure the triumph of the civic register of virtue. As subsequent chapters show, elections offer ample space for the persistence of patrimonial forms, and the tension between registers of virtue has not been resolved decisively in Ghana, Kenya or Uganda. We do not think this is unusual: indeed, we see the idea that elections are shaped by persistent, unresolved, tensions around ideas of virtue as the key, generalizable intervention of this study. While the detail of the analysis offered here is specific to our case studies, the approach has much wider relevance – within Africa, and beyond it. As we have suggested earlier, the registers of virtue that we identify here – and the dynamics within, as well as between, them – take a particular form in our case studies. The moral economy of elections elsewhere may similarly involve civic and patrimonial registers, but it is likely that the productive claims-making of electoral contests may be shaped by other lines of tension.

The factors that influence how the moral economy plays out are the subject of Chapter 2, where we highlight the significance of socio-economic context, the structure of political institutions, historical experience and the agency of actors. This discussion highlights the way in which the moral economy may change over time, without one register ever becoming fully dominant. To return to Garrigou's insight, elections – everywhere in the world – do indeed make voters. But they do not simply turn them into obedient citizens or democrats, and, through the multiple claims-making of campaign and electoral process, voters, politicians and officials also make elections.

2 Elections, States and Citizens
A History of the Ballot in Ghana, Kenya and Uganda

African elections have seen remarkable variation in the way they are contested, the extent to which they have been manipulated and their potential to generate political change. If they do shape political subjectivities, we might expect these variations to lead to very different outcomes – and so we have studied countries that have similar starting points and key institutions, but which have experienced contrasting electoral pathways. Ghana, Kenya and Uganda all became independent with what one commentator drily called the 'standard set of Colonial Office democratic institutions' (Engholm 1963: 470). This meant a political system based on the 'Westminster' model, with the government elected through first-past-the-post multiparty parliamentary elections based on adult suffrage and a secret ballot. In the late 1950s and 1960s, political actors and civil servants in all three countries – and in Britain, the colonial power – had come to see elections not simply as a way of choosing a government but as an exercise in bottom-up state-building: 'training people in responsibility', as one colonial governor put it (Cohen 1957: 118). For William Mackenzie, the academic expert turned late-colonial theorist of elections, the franchise would ensure 'coherent and disciplined' African political participation.[1] Across all three case studies, then, elections have from the outset been seen not only as a necessary corollary of sovereignty but also as a way of naturalizing an exotic form of state authority, through persuading people that they are citizens.

For the political actors who, at independence, became the rulers of new nations, elections also authorized their right to lead the country to the goal of prosperity (Willis, Lynch and Cheeseman 2018). However, when it became clear that the journey to prosperity would be a long and difficult one, Africa's new rulers abandoned multi-partyism – though that abandonment took very different paths. After 1990, all three countries returned to nominally competitive multiparty politics, with direct multiparty elections for an executive president. Today, they have similar legal systems and

---

[1] Mackenzie, 'A further note on constitutional issues in Kenya', 27 October 1959, United Kingdom National Archives (UKNA) CO 822/1427.

electoral rules, such as the use of a 50 per cent plus 1 threshold for the winning candidate in a presidential election. Yet those systems apparently work very differently in practice; Ghana has seen repeated and peaceful electoral transfers of power since 1992; Uganda has not seen one; and Kenya has experienced one transfer of power and several political crises.

There are other significant differences (see Table 2.1). At the time of our research, Kenya's economy had become by far the largest of the three in absolute terms, and the government's budget is not dependent on foreign aid. Ghana, nominally the wealthiest per capita, has benefited from the export of gold and, more recently, oil but remains heavily dependent on donor support. Uganda's economy remains relatively small and donor-dependent. This might be expected to make it more vulnerable to donor pressure around democratization (Peiffer and Englebert 2012), although it is actually the state in which donors have had the least success in promoting their ideas of democratic virtue (Fisher 2013b, 2014). Crucially, what all three case studies share – along with many other postcolonial states – is the legacy of colonial state-making and developmentalism. Since the late-colonial period, state legitimacy has been explicitly tied to the promise of material improvements in the conditions of life. The nationalist politicians of the 1950s offered development in return for the support of citizens; sixty years later, that is still the explicit deal suggested by candidates at every level. This has placed a heavy burden, for popular aspirations have routinely run far ahead of state capacity; the electoral cycle moves endlessly between heady promise and bitter disappointment.

The chapters that make up the main body of the book are structured thematically, with each looking at a different type of political actor. This chapter lays the foundation for what comes next by providing a summary discussion of the electoral history of each country. Intended partly to introduce names, events, dates and institutions that will reappear in subsequent chapters, it also sets out a central element of our argument: that the history of elections has been shaped by a chronic tension between two alternative registers of virtue – a patrimonial register that revolves around reciprocity and personal relations, and which constantly locates people in terms of local moral communities; and a civic register that exalts bureaucratic order, neutrality and impartiality and emphasizes the moral claims of national citizenship. Patrimonial and civic registers of virtue are in tension, but that may be productive. One possible pattern is that people may cast ballots because personal or community ties lead them to trust and support a particular leader; yet doing so draws them into the electoral performance of citizenship. That can shift their subjectivity, encouraging them to imagine other forms of virtuous authority: voting on ethnic or

Table 2.1 *Key political features of Ghana, Kenya and Uganda (2018)*

Country	Ghana	Kenya	Uganda
Colonial power	United Kingdom	United Kingdom	United Kingdom
Year of independence	1957	1963	1962
Year that opposition parties were prohibited	1964	1982[a]	1969
2018 population	28.83 million	49.7 million	42.96 million
2018 political system	Presidential, with Westminster-style legislature	Presidential, with Westminster-style legislature	Presidential, with Westminster-style legislature
2018 presidential electoral system	Direct with 50% + 1 threshold	Direct with 50% + 1 threshold	Direct with 50% + 1 threshold
Widespread civil conflict post-independence	No	Yes	Yes
Number of national one-party/no-party polls	1	5	2
Year of 'founding' multiparty election[b]	1992	1992	2006
Total years under multi-partyism	36	30	20
Aid dependency in 2010[c]	49%	15%	45%
Formal status of electoral commission	Independent	Independent	Independent
Transfers of power via ballot box	3	1[d]	0
Gross domestic product in 2017 per capita	$1,641	$1,507	$604
Freedom House score in 2018[e]	1.5	4	5

[a] Kenya was a de facto one-party state between 1964 and 1966, and between 1969 and 1982, as no opposition parties operated. It was then turned into a de jure one-party state under the rule of President Daniel arap Moi in 1982.

[b] Founding = first election held upon return to multi-partyism. Note: Uganda held elections under a 'no-party system' from 1996 prior to opposition parties being allowed to openly campaign following a referendum in 2005. These have been included under a number of one-party/no-party polls.

[c] Aid dependency is measured by the proportion of GDP comprised of foreign aid.

[d] Kenya experienced a change of ruling party and a change of president when Uhuru Kenyatta and the Jubilee Alliance replaced Mwai Kibaki and the Party of National Unity (PNU) in 2013. However, as Kibaki and many PNU supporters moved their support to Jubilee, this is not usually considered to be a transfer of power.

[e] Average score for political rights and civil liberties. Index runs from 1 to 7, with 1 indicating most free.

localist lines may, unexpectedly, 'build the nation'. But an opposite pattern is also possible, in which the affective power of patrimonial claims may simply overwhelm those of citizenship, turning electoral politics into violent ethnic or regional competitions, or undermining belief in any kind of accountability beyond that of big men and clients.

This historical summary will suggest that our three case studies have come to lie at different points along a line between these two contrasting possibilities, their varying histories being shaped by the four interlinked factors mentioned in the Introduction: socio-economic context and the extent to which this encourages individuals to think in terms of ethnicity as opposed to class or some other form of identity; the structure of political institutions and whether this facilitates inclusion; historical precedent in terms of the extent to which formal rules are respected and power is shared; and the response of leaders and other key actors to the decisions and challenges that they face. When ethnic cleavages are undiluted by the presence of other cleavages, institutions fail to integrate citizens across ethnic lines, historical precedent suggests a winner-takes-all logic and the decisions of political leaders stoke inter-communal suspicion voters are more likely to doubt the feasibility of realizing civic ideas and instead invest in the patrimonial register.

Where our cases are concerned, the range stretches from Ghana, where more inclusive and durable institutions have led to compelling, though by no means dominant, claims of citizenship; to Kenya, where fragile and exclusive institutions have encouraged a form of electoral politics that revolves around elite dealmaking among ethno-regional brokers; and to Uganda, where the absence and apparent impossibility of electoral turn-over mean that patrimonial politics focus on the unpredictable figure of the president. Thus, while the civic register of virtue has some affective power in each country, giving the state – imagined as a nation state – a degree of resilience, the extent of that power varies considerably.

2.1   Ghana: The Country of Experiments

In the early twenty-first century, Ghana came to be regarded as a – perhaps *the* – success story of liberal democracy in Africa: 'the shining democratic star', as one account put it (Whitfield 2009: 621; also Gyimah-Boadi 2009). After multiple coups and extended periods of military rule, the re-establishment of a multiparty system in 1992 led to repeated changes of government through regular elections. We argue that multiple factors were involved in this distinctive path. Decisions by particular individuals at key moments played a part: in 2000, for example, when outgoing president Jerry Rawlings counselled the man who had sought to be his successor that he should accept the election results and acknowledge defeat; or in 2008 when the chair of the Electoral Commission (EC) faced down the threatening bluster from both sides. But perhaps more important has been the development of comparatively capable and inclusive political parties.

This institutional evolution has been made possible by particular socioeconomic circumstances. Neither state authority nor social hierarchy was a novelty brought by colonial rule; particularly in the southern half of what became Ghana, precolonial state-building and centuries of external trade nurtured a quarrelsome elite whose battles for status involved commerce and investments in European-style education as well as contest for office. Internally divided as they were, their sense of collective interest was subsequently sharpened by a process of decolonization that unexpectedly excluded this elite from power (Apter 1968). That became the basis of a remarkably enduring corporate political endeavour, the formal manifestation of which has borne various names over time and which has reasonably been called Ghana's 'establishment' (Ninsin 1998a: 59). In 2016, the current avatar of this – the New Patriotic Party (NPP) – won its third election victory since 1992. The establishment's persistence has shaped Ghana's unusually strong and enduring system of party politics, which was already being called a 'familiar tug-of-war' in the 1980s (Chazan 1987: 66). This has pitched the NPP and its predecessors against a rival political tradition that has always condemned elitism – even while itself operating as a corporate body that advances the interests of its members. That tradition, which is now manifest in the National Democratic Congress (NDC) founded by Jerry Rawlings, can be traced back to the country's first president, Kwame Nkrumah.

The rivalry between these two traditions has shaped politics in the three areas on which our research focussed – as it has politics across Ghana more widely. For convenience, we usually refer to these areas as Cape Coast, Ho and Asante Akim (also spelt Akyem), though the precise names and boundaries of constituencies have shifted a little over time. Cape Coast is a long-established commercial town and centre of learning on the Atlantic coast. A bastion of Ghana's educated establishment, and still home to some of Ghana's most famous schools and one of its leading universities, Cape Coast's disputatious elite of professionals and customary leaders pursued a long argument over representation and local government that began in the nineteenth century (Pachai 1965; Shaloff 1974; Baku 1991). Yet it also has long had many farmers engaged in cash-crop production for the market and a large population of fishermen, who have been resentfully aware that the educated elite are inclined to be disdainful of what they see as the chronic short-termism of the fishing community.

Diverse though Cape Coast's population is, many have a sense of the historical proximity of the Asante kingdom and of the pretensions to dominance that this closeness involved. Our second Ghanaian case study, southern Asante Akim, lies in that kingdom. Like other parts of the kingdom, southern Asante Akim saw a dramatic growth in cocoa farming in the twentieth century, generating multiple social tensions on gender lines and a tumultuous debate over customary authority that left the institution intact while making individual chiefs chronically insecure, and laying the basis for continuing, bitter disputes over chieftaincy (Berry 1998; Stoeltje 2010). This is a rural area, dotted with small towns and villages, and cocoa has also brought many would-be farmers to the area – which had historically been a relatively sparsely populated part of Asante (Steel 1948) – from other parts of Ghana, often to settle in distinct regional or ethnic communities; while this is very much part of Asante, many who live in Asante Akim do not consider themselves to be Asante.

Our third Ghanaian case study, Ho, is much less ethnically diverse than either Cape Coast or Asante Akim. Ho's people mostly consider themselves to be of Ewe ethnicity and historically have viewed the Asante kingdom with a wary suspicion. Lying at the boundary between a dry, sparsely populated plain that stretches towards the sea and the wooded hills to the north, the town of Ho looks and feels like an administrative centre laid out on a grid; the town and the wider area around it lie in the region east of the Volta River that was briefly under German rule before becoming a mandate (and then a trust territory) under British rule. It was in many ways isolated from the rest of colonial Ghana, though British administrative practice pushed them together (Callaway 1970). In the run-up to independence, this practice turned to a formal policy of incorporation, and independent Ghana came to include this trans-Volta area. Efforts by British officials and local cultural entrepreneurs to create more centralized chieftaincies here – remaking a precolonial model of conciliar 'village sovereignty' – had been contested (Verdon 1980; Lawrance 2005). Subsequent national policy towards chiefs in Volta – veering uncertainly between suspicion and hopeful attempts to incorporate them – left chieftaincy influential yet hard to instrumentalize for political ends (Nugent 1996). Less fertile than Asante, and without the self-confident established elite of Cape Coast, Ho is the least prosperous of our Ghanaian case studies.

The political duopoly across these different areas began with the politics of independence. Elections on a limited franchise in 1951 were seen by the British as the price of an alliance with an established elite of chiefs, professionals and merchants who would ensure a leisurely progression to 'self-government'. But Nkrumah surprised both the British and the establishment: his Convention People's Party (CPP) mobilized a more radical constituency of clerks, schoolteachers and aspiring businessmen to win a commanding election victory against the establishment party, the United Gold Coast Congress (UGCC) (Apter 1955; Austin 1976).

The CPP's victory was emphatic in all three areas studied (Garigue 1954). While Cape Coast's elite were natural supporters of the UGCC, fishermen and farmers were suspicious of the educated and enthused by the CPP's radical language of change and equality. In Asante Akim, the message of change – and dislike of chiefs – turned out voters for the CPP. Perhaps most surprising of all was the vote in Ho, where – despite a lively movement of opposition to the planned incorporation into Ghana and a partial boycott (Skinner 2007, 2015) – a CPP candidate was elected, apparently because of divisions within the Ewe nationalist movement and the coincidence of party alignment and a local chieftaincy dispute (Callaway 1970: 133–134).

After the 1951 elections, the British saw Nkrumah as the only credible political partner. The CPP won a further election in 1954, this time with full adult suffrage (Bennett 1953). Nkrumah expected this to lead to independence. But a campaign demanding that independence should involve some kind of federal government – encouraged by some former UGCC stalwarts in Asante, now organized as the National Liberation Movement (NLM), who mobilized some of the same dissatisfactions that had given the CPP such strength (Allman 1990) – threatened this plan. The British government pressed Nkrumah to hold further elections in 1956 to 'demonstrate to the world' that he had genuine popular support before independence was granted.[2] The CPP won again, though on a diminished turnout. Nkrumah and the British both argued that the election had shown the CPP still had strong support, even in Asante (where it took 97,000 votes, against 128,000 for all other parties combined): the CPP won Cape Coast, and Asante Akim very narrowly, but had by this time entirely lost support in Ho, which was won by an Ewe nationalist standing as an independent (Callaway 1970; Skinner 2007: 141).[3] Ghana became independent in 1957.

Nkrumah was much concerned with his own reputation and with Ghana's international reputation, and sought to maintain some sort of electoral legitimacy. But he also feared that, like him, others would seek to build a movement from multiple dissatisfied groups. He sought to bring all forms of associational life – trade unions, cocoa farmers groups, professional associations – under CPP control, and the opposition was subjected

[2] Lennox-Boyd to Nkrumah, 4 April 1956, CO 554/807 no. 253, cited from Rathbone (1992).

[3] Governor to Secretary of State, 23 August 1956, UKNA FCO 141/5116; results in Lamm, Consul-General Accra to Dept. of State, 21 July 1956, National Archives and Record Administration (NARA) RG59 Box 3242, Central Decimal File Ghana 1955–1959.

to an increasingly open campaign of harassment, intimidation and arbitrary detention. In 1960 a referendum was held on Nkrumah's proposal to make Ghana a republic, which was combined with a poll on whether Nkrumah should become president of that republic. The only other candidate on the ballot was J. B. Danquah, whose United Party (UP) had inherited the support of what had once been the UGCC and NLM. With the open support of the state apparatus, Nkrumah won (Austin 1970: 387). In 1964 the government organized another referendum, this time to make Ghana formally a one-party state (Austin 1970: 387–391). The campaign was even more intrusive and coercive than that of 1960: civil servants were forced to attend rallies in support of the proposal; the press and radio were filled with reports and advertisements calling for a 'yes' vote.[4] Voter education information published in the newspapers reassured voters that the ballot was secret, but also told them explicitly: 'Remember: your vote is yes'.[5] A high turnout and an overwhelming 'yes' vote were announced, but there were widespread rumours that few people had actually voted, and that many who had done so were effectively forced to support the referendum.[6]

Having disposed of open opposition, Nkrumah became convinced that the CPP itself was a source of danger, filled with local power brokers who had bought their way to election victory. Shortly before parliamentary elections scheduled for 1965, it was announced that only one candidate would be allowed to stand in each constituency on a CPP ticket, and that these candidates would all be chosen centrally – an attempt to control a chronic pattern of intra-party competition, which had seen locally popular individuals standing against centrally approved CPP candidates (Apter 1968: 292–293). There were no other parties, and no independent candidates dared stand; all CPP candidates nominated by the central party were therefore declared elected, without a ballot being cast.

A year later Nkrumah was overthrown by a military coup. The soldiers who overthrew him established a National Liberation Council (NLC) to govern, but were evidently sympathetic to the 'establishment' that had been so effectively excluded from office in the 1950s. Three years of argument over the constitution ensued, much of which effectively revolved around the question of how to prevent Nkrumah or his supporters from returning to power. The consequence was a ban on former CPP members holding public office.

---

[4] British High Commissioner to Commonwealth Relations Office (CRO), 29 January 1964, UKNA DO 195/251.

[5] 'You and the referendum', *Ghanaian Times*, 16 January 1964, p. 3.

[6] Thomas, Office of the High Commissioner, Accra to Wool-Lewis, CRO, 15 February 1964, UKNA DO 195/209.

This, and the evident support of key military officers, meant that when elections finally came, in 1969, they were won by the Progress Party (PP) – the lineal descendant of the UP, and now led by Kofi Busia (Austin and Luckham 1975). The party won in Cape Coast and in Asante Akim, where rivalry for the PP nomination was settled by the intervention of a wealthy trader who backed a compromise candidate (Twumasi 1975: 149–151). But it was defeated in Ho. This was not due to any lingering support for the CPP, which had been deeply unpopular there (Callaway 1970). Rather, a clear ethnic pattern emerged in the national vote (Card and Callaway 1970; Rathbone 1978). Komla Gbedemah, whose National Alliance of Liberals (NAL) offered the only real challenge to the PP, inherited some of the support and networks of the CPP – of which Gbedemah had been a member, before falling out with Nkrumah. But Gbedemah's support came also from his fellow Ewe, who suspected that the PP was a vehicle for Akan – and particularly Asante – dominance. The NAL won 77 per cent of the votes in the areas east of the Volta, while the PP won 77 per cent of the votes in Asante (see Table 2.2).[7]

Busia's elected government struggled to establish its authority, and was overthrown in 1972, to apparent public indifference (Le Vine 1987). The new military government benefited briefly from improving economic conditions, but then found its credibility draining away. Popular unrest – strikes and demonstrations – led first to a 'consultation' process and then to a referendum on a proposal for what General Acheampong, the leader of the military government, called 'Union Government' or 'Unigov' (Goldschmidt 1980). This would have combined military appointees with some elected representatives in a government without any role for political parties. Supported by some who denounced party politics as a failure (Owusu 1979), Unigov was denounced by multiple voices, from the self-consciously liberal establishment to radical students (Chazan and Le Vine 1979). The referendum took place amidst some confusion, and the official in charge fled the country. In the end, the government announced that the public had approved the proposals, though with a low turnout (Jeffries 1989). This claim was widely disbelieved – so widely, indeed, that decades later some interviewees were insistent that the announced result had been negative.[8]

Acheampong was quickly removed from his position by fellow officers. With the economic position increasingly calamitous, the military were anxious to hand over power. In a replay of the events of 1966–1969, a

---

[7] See the analysis in Matthews, British High Commissioner, Accra to Secretary of State, 5 September 1969, UKNA FCO 65/91.
[8] Interview GHA33a, NPP activist, Cape Coast, 31 August 2016.

Table 2.2 *Case study constituency winners: Ghana*

	Winner (party) (number of candidates) Winner's vote/turnout/registered voters			
	Cape Coast (South)	Cape Coast North	Asante Akim	Ho
1969	T Brodie Mends (PP) (3) 9,366/13,407/–	–	Nicholas Boafe Adade (NPP) (3) 9,341/12,210/–	V K Akude (NAL) (3) 11,979/15,361/–
1979	Koffi Bossah Quonsah (ACP) (6) 13,554/19,726/–	–	Samson Boafo (PFP) (4) 4,726/11,760/–	
1992	J E Ekuban (NDC) (2) 9,698/12,649/ 61,334	–	Samuel Ofosu Mensah (NDC) (1) –/–/–	Kofi Attor (NDC) (3) 20,009/25,474/ 38,720
1996	Christine Churcher (NPP) (2) 30,496/56,428/ 66,063	–	Alex Korankye (NPP) (2) 18,646/35,918/ 43,332	Kofi Attor (NDC) (5) 49,999/56,756/ 67,490
2000	Christine Churcher (NPP) (5) 31,573/56,460/ 81,265	–	Alex Korankye (NPP) (5) 19,198/33,972/ 50,036	Kofi Attor (NDC) (6) 37,131/44,562/ 74,601
2004	Christine Churcher (NPP) (4) 36,264/71,781/ 83,213	–	Gifty Konadu (NPP) (4) 24,085/40,558/ 45,061	George Nfojoh (NDC) (5) 49,463/58,675/ 67,309
2008	Ebo Barton-Odro (NDC) (5) 38,694/72,053/ 103,727	–	Gifty Konadu (NPP) (3) 23,838/39,279/ 54,041	George Nfojoh (NDC) (5) 47,036/54,734/ 82,031
2012	Kweku Ricketts-Hagan (NDC) (4) 22,150/42,603/ 50,410	Ebo Barton-Odro (NDC) (3) 21,189/43,513/ 54,655	Kwaku Asante-Boateng (NPP) (5) 31,151/51,853/ 61,084	Benjamin Kpodo (NDC) (5) 60,129/68,425/ 87,100
2016	Kweku Ricketts-Hagan (NDC) (5) 20,456/41,061/ 56,588	Barbara Asher-Ayisi (NPP) (4) 19,475/39,123/–	Kwaku Asante-Boateng (NPP) (5) 32,526/49,332/–	Benjamin Kpodo (NDC) (6) 47,330/59,852/ 95,866

Source: Compiled by authors from newspapers and other published sources. Asante Akim results are for the Asante Akim South constituency; Ho results are for either Ho Central or Ho East. Cape Coast was split into two constituencies for the 2012 elections.

constitutional commission produced a draft, which was then debated by a constituent assembly. The resulting constitution – Ghana's third republic – provided for multiparty elections and a directly elected executive president, with a very clear separation between presidency and parliament (Goldschmidt 1980: 47–48). The leader of the military government expressed the hope that multiparty elections would be economically transformative, encouraging 'healthy cooperation in the task of nation-building'.[9] Previous parties were banned, but two new parties vied for the legacy of the UP/PP. They were divided by the personal ambition of leaders, but also by disquiet over the dominance of one – the Popular Front Party (PFP) – by Asante. Against these two factions, the main rival – and self-conscious inheritor of the 'Nkrumahist' tradition – was the People's National Party (PNP), whose presidential candidate was Hilla Limann (Chazan 1992).

Limann won after the vote went to a second round, as the ethnic factor apparent in 1969 showed itself again in both presidential and parliamentary contests; the PFP was strongest in Ashanti, the PNP in eastern and northern Ghana and among Muslims (Jeffries 1980; Kobo 2010) (see Table 2.3). Asante Akim, now split into two constituencies, was won by the PFP in both presidential and parliamentary polls; Ho East by the PNP. In parliamentary and presidential votes, Cape Coast was taken by the Action Congress Party, a 'third force', which polled poorly overall but was led by a local man, Frank Bernasko (see Table 2.3).

Just before the elections, two coups – one unsuccessful, the second successful – brought a young flight lieutenant, Jerry Rawlings, to power. Rawlings' first, brief, military government was dominated by young men, low-ranking officers and other ranks. They were initially even more effusive in their endorsement of the disciplinary possibilities of elections than their predecessors: they announced that the polls would go ahead, for voting was 'more than a civic act and a moral and political obligation; it is in fact an act of faith, of gratitude and of loyalty'.[10] Rawlings handed power over to Limann's PNP government, but not before a brief and bloody period of 'house cleaning' that revealed the extent of anger at Ghana's establishment, and saw the execution of several senior military officers.[11] Limann's government also struggled in adverse economic circumstances, and at the end of 1981 it was overthrown by Rawlings, who established an avowedly revolutionary Provisional National Defence Council (PNDC) to govern the country (Agyeman-Duah 1987).

[9] 'Akuffo announces ban on political activity to be lifted', Foreign Broadcast Information Service (FBIS), Accra, 30 November 1978, SSA-78-232.
[10] 'Military Committee vice-president interviewed on election', FBIS, Bamako, 19 June 1979, SSA-79-120.
[11] J. Johnson, 'Ghana after the presidential election', 20 July 1979, UKNA FCO 65/2181.

Rawlings was to remain in power for eighteen years, during which radical economic reforms significantly reduced the state payroll and the extent of formal state control of Ghana's economy, without overturning the heavily clientelistic nature of politics (Jeffries 1989: 75). The PNDC was overtly hostile to Ghana's elite, which it accused of exploiting party and ethnic politics to entrench its position: 'there are only two tribes in this country', declared Rawlings, 'one rich and the other poor'.[12] Yet Rawlings was also driven by a sense that occasional voting had failed to instil a sense of public responsibility, and had instead encouraged an 'apathy and cynicism' that prevented 'mobilisation of our people for production and defence'. 'We are not going to put any damn paper into any box!' he told a rally. 'We are going to get involved.'[13] He and his colleagues on the PNDC argued that parliamentary government had become 'remote and distant'; instead, a 'true democracy' would be participatory, built on local defence committees chosen by consensus. Expressed in emancipatory language, the intent was disciplinary: 'the mobilization of our people towards development'.[14]

In what was presented as a process of decentralization, district assembly elections were held in the later 1980s, with a secret ballot, but on a non-party basis, intended to teach the public 'our responsibility for nation-building'.[15] At the end of the 1980s Rawlings still saw this 'new democracy' as the route to 'national productivity'.[16] A process of consultation on a new constitution was led by the National Commission for Democracy. It was framed by the insistence that a 'true democratic system' was rooted in the 'eradication of ignorance, disease, illiteracy, hunger and poverty', rather than in multi-partyism, as Rawlings continued to insist that 'democracy is not just about forming political parties'.[17] Nevertheless, the consultation showed that support for elections under a multiparty system was vocal and widespread, if hard to measure. Pushed by this consultation – and to some extent by the

---

[12] 'No turning back (a message to the nation)'; pamphlet of broadcast by Jerry Rawlings, 29 July 1982: copy in Library of Congress Africana collection.

[13] 'Chairman Rawlings questions value of elections', FBIS, Accra, 17 March 1982, MEA-82-053.

[14] 'The search for true democracy in Ghana', pamphlet, n.d., c.1986: copy in Library of Congress Africana collection.

[15] 'Rawlings speaks on 31 December revolution anniversary', FBIS, Accra, 31 December 1986, MEA-87-002.

[16] 'The evolving democratic process', pamphlet with address by Jerry Rawlings to seminar organized by National Commission for Democracy, 5 July 1990, copy in Library of Congress Africana collection.

[17] 'Annan opens 9th regional debate on democracy', FBIS, Accra, 6 November 1990, AFR-90-216; 'Jerry Rawlings addresses nation 1 January', FBIS, Accra, 1 January 1991, AFR-91-002.

government of the United States and other donors – the PNDC agreed to the introduction of Ghana's fourth republican constitution in 1992 (Boafo-Arthur 1998; Gyimah-Boadi 1994). Like the third, this featured a powerful executive president, to be elected directly on a majority vote, and a parliament elected on a first-past-the-post constituency basis (Signé 2019).

Parties reappeared rapidly; again, former parties were forbidden to reform, but simply did so under new names. Danquah-Busia clubs formed, then came together to create the NPP; PNDC supporters created the NDC, which came to claim the legacy of Nkrumahism 'if not in terms of economic policy at least in terms of its energy, its populist style and its concern for "the common man"' (Jeffries 1998: 12; also Jeffries and Thomas 1993). The NDC made full use of the advantages of incumbency in the 1992 presidential elections: 'the sluice gates of patronage were opened up', as one study of that campaign put it (Sandbrook and Oelbaum 1997: 609). The elections received financial and logistical support from donors – not a complete novelty, as this had also happened in 1969, but this time the assistance was more coordinated (Boafo-Arthur 1998). The presidential poll was won by Rawlings, standing for the NDC; the NPP alleged fraud and boycotted the parliamentary elections held a few weeks later (Oquaye 1995) (see Table 2.3). In 1996, Rawlings again won the presidential elections; the NPP had agreed to participate in presidential and parliamentary polls after intervention by donors to broker reforms in the electoral process, notably on the register and the introduction of transparent ballot boxes (Ninsin 1998b; Aubynn 2002). The NPP again alleged fraud in the presidential vote, but they won southern Asante Akim (where Rawlings had lent his support to a local chief involved in a long dispute with the paramount chief of Asante, the *asantehene* (Stoeltje 2010)) and in Cape Coast. NDC – like the NAL and PNC before it – had strong support in eastern Ghana, and won in Ho (see Table 2.2). The NDC's embrace of the Nkrumahist legacy continued to be erratic but occasionally very explicit.[18] Combined with the use of patronage resources derived from incumbency, the adoption of an anti-elitist rhetoric proved an effective corporate mobilization for elections (Nugent 1999).

In 2000, Rawlings stood down as president, having served the two terms allowed by the constitution. By not using violence to prolong his stay in power, and setting the precedent on respecting term limits, he contributed to a process of political institutionalization. In the

---

[18] For example: 'Nkrumahists urged to support NDC', *Daily Graphic,* 10 October 1996, p. 3.

Table 2.3 *Turnout and votes for main presidential candidates in case study areas: Ghana*

		Cape Coast	%	Asante Akim	%	Ho	%	National	%
1979	**Reg.**								
	Turnout	17,908		11,312		17,429		1,788,209	
	Owusu (PFP)	1,959	11	4,152	11	974	6	533,928	30
	Bernasko (ACP)	13,025	73	183	2	864	5	167,775	9
	Limann (PNP)	1,630	9	3,601	32	8,783	50	631,559	35
	Ofori Atta (UNC)	911	5	3,038	27	5,116	29	311,265	17
1992	**Reg.**	61,334				38,720		8,229,902	
	Turnout	29,299	48	20,766		35,918	93	4,127,876	50
	Boahen (NPP)	13,202	45	10,932	53	1,312	4	1,204,764	29
	Rawlings (NDC)	13,666	47	9,662	47	33,817	94	2,323,135	56
1996	**Reg.**	66,063		43,332		67,490		9,279,605	
	Turnout	56,332	85	35,547	82	56,756	84	7,266,693	78
	Kufuor (NPP)	29,959	53	18,976	53	52,970	93	2,834,878	39
	Rawlings (NDC)	25,711	46	16,056	45	3,577	6	4,099,758	56
2000	**Reg.**	81,265		50,036		74,601		10,698,652	
	Turnout	56,460	69	33,972	68	45,446	61	6,605,084	62
	Kufuor (NPP)	31,977	57	20,434	60	3,727	8	3,131,739	47
	Atta Mills (NDC)	22,834	40	12,028	35	40,165	88	2,895,575	44
2004	**Reg.**	83,213		45,061		67,309		10,354,970	
	Turnout	70,759	85	38,026	84	58,666	87	8,813,908	85
	Kufuor (NPP)	39,803	56	24,881	65	5,719	10	4,524,074	51
	Atta Mills (NDC)	29,224	41	11,687	31	52,047	89	3,850,368	44
2008	**Reg.**	103,727		54,041		82,031		12,472,758	
	Turnout	72,015	69	42,712	79	60,607	74	9,094,364	73
	NPP	31,521	44	28,455	67	4,173	7	4,159,439	46
	NDC	39,917	55	13,911	33	56,172	93	4,056,634	45
2012	**Reg.**	50,410		61,084		87,100		14,158,890	
	Turnout	42,511	84	51,833	85	68,569	79	11,246,982	79
	Akufo-Addo (NPP)	18,834	44	31,710	61	5,148	8	5,248,898	47
	Mahama (NDC)	22,683	53	18,520	36	62,363	91	5,574,761	50
2016	**Reg.**	56,588				95,866		15,712,499	
	Turnout	41,147	73	49,266		60,073	63	10,781,917	69
	Akufo-Addo (NPP)	20,977	51	33,657	68	5,998	10	5,716,026	53
	Mahama (NDC)	19,449	47	15,254	31	53,117	88	4,713,277	44

Source: Compiled by authors from newspapers and other published sources. Asante Akim results are for the Asante Akim South constituency; Ho results for the constituency variously called Ho Central or Ho East. Cape Coast was split into two constituencies before the 2012 elections; the figures given for 2012 and 2016 are for the Cape Coast South constituency.

subsequent elections, Rawlings' chosen successor, John Atta Mills – who lacked his charisma, presided over a divided NDC, enjoyed fewer resources to fund timely development projects and faced a better-organized opposition (Nugent 2001a; Briggs 2012) – lost to the NPP's candidate John Kufuor (also spelt Kufour) in the second round of the presidential election (Gyimah-Boadi 2001). Kufuor was very much a part of the Busia-Danquah tradition; he had been a minister in Busia's government and a PFP member of parliament. Some within the NDC allegedly wished to challenge the results; Rawlings advised that they should accept them. Again, the Asante Akim constituencies voted for NPP in both parliamentary and presidential elections; Cape Coast also voted – by a narrower margin – for the NPP; Ho voted overwhelmingly for the NDC, as did the east as a whole (see Tables 2.2 and 2.3).

The 2000 elections began a pattern of national alternation; the NPP won again in 2004 but lost in 2008. The NDC won in 2008 and 2012, but the NPP returned to power in 2016. Parliamentary election results broadly mirrored presidential results, and the stronghold areas of the two parties remained consistent: east and north voting for NDC, while Asante voted for NPP, with Asante Akim South becoming more of a stronghold over time (Jockert, Kohners and Nugent 2010) (see Tables 2.2 and 2.3). In this context, some emphasize the role of 'swing' voters in determining presidential elections (Morrison 2004). The role of such voters seems evident from the case study constituencies: Cape Coast has 'swung' more than once. However, it is also clear that NDC presidential defeats in 2000 and 2016 were associated with falls in turnout in their stronghold areas. It seems that, rather than vote NPP, some disillusioned NDC supporters opted not to vote at all (Nugent 2001b; Afram and Tsekpo 2017).

There are other patterns and trends. Ghana's elections have become increasingly peaceful. There was significant, sometimes lethal violence, in the elections of the 1950s, including shooting and bomb throwing. Since 1969, there has been nothing to compare with that. The elections of the 1990s saw the involvement of 'macho men', who intimidated voters and – allegedly – sought to steal or stuff ballots, as well as violent chieftaincy disputes in the north, which acquired a partisan logic and which continued to fuel significant tension around elections into the 2000s (Ayelazuno 2009; Ovadia 2011). But despite a persistent background of 'low-intensity' violence (Bob-Milliar 2014), there has been a clear change. In the 1990s, it was difficult for NPP supporters in eastern Ghana to campaign, or even show their party affiliation; by 2016, they were able to mobilize openly. Every election campaign nonetheless sees very visible and determined campaigns for peace, which urge voters to be mindful of their duty as citizens and uphold Ghana's reputation (Lynch, Cheeseman and Willis 2019).

The two-party system has remained. Other parties do exist (after a legal battle, there is even a new CPP). But these attract minimal votes in the presidential race and are only of very local significance in parliamentary elections. The parties are not really distinguished by programmes; indeed, each routinely expresses the fear that the other will steal its ideas.[19] The NPP and NDC absolutely dominate the political scene, and each party has a parallel organization among students, has friendly media outlets and radio stations, and is associated with rival football clubs (Fridy and Brobbey 2009). A successful career in politics requires long-term commitment to a party, for both NDC and NPP are careful to reward loyalty when selecting candidates.[20] While local government elections remain nominally non-party, the party affiliations of many candidates are widely known and advertised through the choice of slogans and poster design. Members of the NPP unhesitatingly place themselves in a historical tradition that stretches back to the UGCC; many prominent members belong to families for whom the Busia-Danquah tradition is a long-term commitment: one prominent member told us that the party is 'in the blood', another that he was 'born into it'.[21] There is also, however, significant factionalism within the NPP, amply evidenced by nomination contests and legal struggles, but the pursuit of collective interest continues nonetheless (Ayee 2008; Bob-Milliar 2012a; Osei 2016).

The NDC has also suffered from internal disputes, but again members are clear about their sense of belonging to a political tradition that stretches back to Nkrumah, though this is less common in Ho – where the CPP was never popular – and NDC members in general are less inclined to present this in dynastic terms and more as a matter of identification with the 'down-trodden' and of opposition to elitism.[22] Each party is – as Maxwell Owusu (1975) said of the old CPP – a corporation. The NDC, like the NPP, has its internal factions: yet each party operates as a sort of collective interest group, helping its members with employment, contracts and loans (Gyimah-Boadi and Prempeh 2012; Bob-Milliar 2012b; Osei 2012).

---

[19] 'NPP is not sincere Ahwei', *Daily Graphic*, 10 November 2000, p. 16; 'I fear Mahama will steal my new idea for NHIS – Akufo Addo', *Daily Graphic*, 26 July 2016.

[20] Interview GHA99a, parliamentary candidate, Kumasi, 10 December 2016.

[21] Interview GHA102a, NPP official, Kumasi, 14 December 2016; Interview GHA77a, NPP politician, Juaso, 1 December 2016.

[22] Interview GHA29a, politician, Juaso, 29 August 2016.

When the party is in government, jobs and money are more readily obtainable: 'when you get a government there are other – there are very many positions, that are given to the people'.[23] When out of government, members of the party benefit from a fairly sizeable private sector (Pinkston 2016) and cooperate to survive the lean times.[24] There is an ethnic element to this politics: the Volta region is still very largely NDC, while Asante is NPP. But each party has networks of supporters in the stronghold of the other; the fortunes of a region, or an ethnic group, are not wholly tied to one party or another. It is still the case that – as Kwame Ninsin (1993: 183) argued right at the beginning of the fourth republic – elections should be seen as occasions when the 'little communities' comprising Ghanaian society constitute or reconstitute their relations with the state for the purpose of realizing economic or developmental goals. Yet the intermediaries they choose to establish this linkage may come from either party. The relative political inclusion that this brings – compared to the case of Kenya, for example – has helped to reduce the stakes of electoral competition and, combined with regular transfers of power, increased public confidence in the feasibility of realizing civic ideals.

Despite this, the national reach of Ghana's parties has been quite compatible with the persistence of patrimonial politics. That patrimonialism drives party organization, and it animates the relationship between candidates and voters. As one politician told us, to campaign is to invite demands for assistance:

you pay school fees, you pay whatever. People would come to you for so many things. People will come to you for so many – for assistance – in different, different many areas. You must be able to provide some.[25]

These demands may be individual – but they are often collective, cast in the language of community and development:

the MP has become an agent of development; an agent of development and if you don't do that you are going to miss their votes ... very, very few, even decimal number will ask you the performance on the floor of parliament ... the rest want water, they want electricity, they want hospitals and clinics and their roads.[26]

Thus, while the peaceful alternance of political power has been taken as evidence of democratic consolidation, it has not necessarily meant the triumph of civic virtue or the primacy of national citizenship over other visions of community.

[23] Interview GHA33a, NPP activist, Cape Coast, 31 August 2016.
[24] Interview GHA65a, NPP official, Ho, 25 November 2016.
[25] Interview GHA1a, NDC official, Accra, 28 August 2015.
[26] Interview GHA72a, politician, Ho, 28 November 2016.

Lindberg and others have argued the emergence of a distinctive pattern of 'mature' and 'evaluative' voting in Ghana, which is not clientelistic (Lindberg and Morrison 2005, 2008; Harding 2015), and the 2016 election results have been taken as further evidence that Ghanaians vote for parties not individuals, and that they do so in an evaluative, socio-tropic way (van Gyampo et al. 2017: 33–34). Bob-Milliar and Paller (2018: 10), for example, have described that election as a 'referendum' on the economic management of the country. While we share this sense of the centrality of the party as an institution in shaping Ghana's distinctive electoral history, we would argue that individuals do matter – it is through individual ties that people are linked to parties, as activists or supporters (as we argue in Chapters 6 and 7).

Voting – or deciding not to vote – clearly has an evaluative aspect. But as a leading Ghanaian journalist (and former parliamentary candidate) recently noted with some despair, evaluation seems to have a very particularistic edge, revolving around what the party – through its local representatives – have done for the individual and their community.[27] Voters make claims, and their evaluation is one of virtue as much as economic performance: has the party's candidate lived up to local expectations of proper behaviour and generosity? We would argue that clientelism – 'big man small boy' politics, as more than one observer has described this (Price 1974; Nugent 1995) – has come to follow corporate lines defined by party affiliation. It is both rational and evaluative – but evaluation is guided by an idea of virtue in which those who hold office demand deference but are expected to show generosity. What Richard Rathbone (1973: 398–399) called the 'moral influence' of the 'man with money' has persisted. In 2016, it was still the case that – as Paul Nugent (2001b: 409) observed of Ghana's 2000 elections – 'the distribution of cash and other inducements was construed by ... politicians in overtly moral terms' (see also Ninsin 1993). It is also the case that multiparty elections have been chequered by claims of electoral malpractice (in particular, of bloated registers and multiple voting), moments of increased tension and by high levels of mistrust of key institutions including of other political parties, the judiciary and the electoral commission, complicating the picture of Ghana as one of the continent's leading democratic lights (Oquaye 1995; Abdulai and Crawford 2010; Ovadia 2011; Schmitz 2018).

---

[27] 'Maybe we want them to steal – Elizabeth Ohene writes', *Daily Graphic,* 11 September 2019.

2.2   Uganda: Military Dominance and Electoral Authoritarianism

By early 2016, Uganda had held ten more-or-less national elections since the 1950s (as well as two referenda). All have been problematic, to a greater or lesser degree. Each in turn provided a new filter of experience through which public, politicians and officials would view the next; colouring the way they understood the possibilities of behaviour and speech. Over time, they have tended to shape expectations and perceptions in a particular way, informing a widespread sense that the military will always be the final arbiter of political outcomes at a national level: 'people feel that if you have a gun, you are going to win', as one prominent politician told us.[28] As Aili Mari Tripp has argued, Uganda's 'hybrid' state is paradoxical: it offers some apparent political freedoms, yet power 'rests with the security forces' (Tripp 2010: 31). Uganda's ruling National Resistance Movement (NRM) has been described as 'at core a military autocracy' (Oloka-Onyango and Ahikire 2017: 6); violence, as Elijah Mushemeza (2001) has pointed out, has both unmade and made the Ugandan state. Electoral experience in Uganda has therefore come to encourage a popular focus on parliamentary and local government elections as a way to make claims on local representatives, who serve as emissaries to an executive presidency that is effectively beyond the power of the ballot. At the time of writing this book, there had been no transfer of power through elections in post-independence Uganda. This has been less divisive than one might have imagined, however, as a result of the nature of the NRM itself. This is far from a coherent or consistent organization (Collord 2016), and is very different to Ghana's political parties, yet it has somehow provided a structure for a politics of incorporation that has repeatedly drawn in critics who have championed local interests.[29] Partly as a result, ethnic politics has not come to the fore to the extent that it has in Kenya, though in some parts of the country many continue to question the regime's legitimacy.

As with Ghana, Uganda's deeper history and socio-economic context has shaped electoral politics, and our case studies were selected partly to capture the effects of this. Two of them come from the kingdoms of the south and west: precolonial polities that were remade through their role in the colonial system of government. Mukono (specifically for our purposes, the constituencies of Mukono Municipality and Mukono North, which lay in the pre-independence constituency of South-East Mengo) is in the east of the kingdom of Buganda, a short drive away from Uganda's

---

[28] Interview UGA14a, former DP official and candidate, Kampala, 23 September 2014.

[29] For the most recent example at time of writing, see 'Anywar's long walk to Museveni's cabinet', *Daily Monitor*, 15 December 2019.

capital, Kampala. Buganda is at the economic and political heart of Uganda. The aspirations of many Baganda – as the people of Buganda are known – to autonomy and/or primacy shaped the politics of Uganda's independence. Though Buganda (like other kingdoms) was abolished in 1966–1967, it was subsequently recreated in the 1990s as a 'cultural' phenomenon, as Museveni sought to carefully manage sub-national identities by giving them official recognition while denying them political power. Partly as a result, an affective attachment to the *kabaka*, or king, is still a powerful force. Nevertheless, the electoral power of that attachment is complicated by divergent ideas of what it means to be a good citizen of the kingdom (Brisset-Foucault 2013), and by chronic conflicts over land (Gay 2014), as well as by the presence of many people who have moved to the area from other parts of Uganda.

The pre-independence constituency of Central Tooro lay in Tooro, a smaller kingdom in the west, where precolonial central authority was more limited than in Buganda, but where the king – the *mukama* – had been more successful at using colonial rule to assert power over his chiefs (Ingham 1974: 86–118; Steinhart 1973). The constituency roughly covered the current constituency of Fort Portal Municipality and parts of Bunyangabu and Burahya constituencies. In late-colonial politics, Tooro's monarchists were caught between suspicion of the ambitions of Buganda and fear of the republican sympathies of Uganda's nationalists.[30] This kingdom too was revived as a cultural form in the 1990s, but emotional and political attachment to the monarchy is much more limited among the Batooro – those who see themselves as the people of Tooro – than in Buganda. Tooro has also seen much in-migration in recent years, and tensions over land and political office allow easy mobilization along ethnic lines. Gulu, by contrast, lies in the north of Uganda in an area predominantly inhabited by ethnic Acholi. There is no tradition of centralized authority among the Acholi, and colonial rule here struggled to engage with multiple clan chiefs, and turned to conciliar forms (Bere 1955; Reid 2017: 293). The area is much drier and more sparsely populated than Kabarole or Mukono and has seen little in-migration.

Like Tooro, Gulu is remote from Kampala, but has historically been less wealthy than either of the other study areas, and was treated as a labour reserve and/or a military recruiting ground by the colonial state. Under Idi Amin's rule in the 1970s, and since 1986 the Acholi have often experienced state authority as a hostile, alien presence. In the late 1980s and 1990s they lived through a prolonged insurgency, which pitted the Lord's Resistance Army (LRA) against the government. The LRA

---

[30] Interview UGA45a, former UPC activist, Fort Portal, 12 June 2015.

initially enjoyed some local support due to fears that the Acholi would continue to be punished for their support for Obote, and a widespread perception that '[g]overnments no longer arbitrate and provide; they periodically send soldiers to kill people' (Allen 1991: 385; Finnström 2008). However, support soon waned as people found themselves caught between the violence of the LRA, which included forced recruitment of child soldiers, and that of the government, which included forced villagization (Allen and Vlassenroot 2010). It is therefore in Gulu that the NRM has faced the greatest challenges when it comes to national integration and political mobilization.

In Uganda, as in Ghana, national elections were a late-colonial innovation, and followed a similar cycle. Elections on a restricted franchise were initially designed to recruit African allies to help prolong imperial rule; a second set of elections followed on the heels of that failed colonial project, with a much wider franchise, and were intended to establish the legitimacy of a successor elite that would take control of the state at independence. A third set of elections became necessary when particular political contingencies threatened to disrupt a smooth transfer of power (Willis, Lynch and Cheeseman 2018). In the Uganda case, it was the position of the kingdom of Buganda that provoked an extended crisis (Apter 2013). The cooperation of Buganda's chiefs had been central to the extension of British power over Uganda; consequently, Buganda had a special status, distinct from all other parts of the Protectorate, and became the economic and administrative heart of Uganda. The alliance between the British and the chiefs had set off a new phase in the long wrangle over power within Buganda. In the 1950s, that wrangling became entangled with the emerging possibility of Ugandan independence. The question of Buganda's place in such a new nation became an element in a prolonged – and successful – campaign by a new *kabaka* and some unlikely commoner allies to roll back the power of the appointed chiefs, who had established themselves as a sort of landed aristocracy during the decades of British rule (Low 1964).

This separatist urge complicated the contest between two rival parties, each of which had emerged in the 1950s claiming the role of nationalist partners to whom the British might hand power. The Democratic Party (DP) drew its mobilizing force partly from a sense that Catholics had been sidelined under British rule; the Uganda People's Congress (UPC) drew at least part of its energy from a sense of resentment – especially in northern Uganda – against Buganda's perceived dominance (Welbourn 1965; Leys 1967; Bing 1974; Gertzel 1974; Ward 1995). The UPC's leader, Milton Obote, nonetheless struck an opportunistic deal with the *kabaka*: in effect, allowing Buganda to opt out of participating in national elections, and offering a semi-federal status for the kingdom in return for an alliance against the DP. The deal propelled Uganda to independence in October 1962, with Obote as prime minster and the *kabaka* as titular president.

To the surprise of no one, the pact between Obote and the *kabaka* did not last. In a few, furious months in 1966, Obote turned first on internal critics within his own party (whom he suspected of plotting with the *kabaka* against him) and then on the kingdom of Buganda itself. Obote's chosen tool in this effective coup was the army, which stormed the royal palace, forcing the *kabaka* into exile. Parliament kept sitting, however, and Obote used it to approve a new constitution making himself president and overturning the federal arrangements of 1962, dissolving all of Uganda's kingdoms, including Tooro. The defection to the UPC of most of those who had been nominated to parliament from Buganda meant that Obote had a comfortable majority. His position was further bolstered by additional defections from the DP, whose members were worn down by intimidation and harassment – and by the systematic way in which government resources were allocated to favour UPC supporters and punish rivals (Leys 1967: 51, 101–102). Uganda thus became a unitary state, but not yet a one-party one, nor a dictatorship.

Obote's rhetoric remained that of the elected leader, but he faced a dilemma. New elections might assert his legitimacy against those rivals, and remind the population of their duties as citizens. Increasingly committed to a radical political agenda of nationalization, he wanted to mobilize the public behind this – like others, he saw the fate of Nkrumah as evidence of the dangers of losing touch with the people.[31] But what if voters were misled by wild promises, or bribed with money smuggled in from abroad? In 1969, the DP was nominally banned. But Obote's real worry was his rivals within his own party: he openly denounced them as tribalists who would pander to sectional interests at the expense of national development (Ocitti 2000: 134–146).[32] Through 1970 the president therefore devoted himself to devising an electoral system that would force all parliamentary candidates to campaign in multiple constituencies across Uganda, and would also require local party branches to ensure Obote's victory in a presidential poll (Provizer 1977; Willetts 1975).

Idi Amin's coup in January 1971 forestalled those plans, and Amin, after initial suggestions that elections would be held, showed no interest in arranging them. The years of Amin's rule were not simply a period of

---

[31] Valedictory letter, Scott, British High Commissioner Kampala to Secretary of State for Foreign Affairs, 26 January 1970, UKNA FCO 31/713.

[32] 'Obote's address to the UPC central executive committee', 1 October 1969, Summary of World Broadcasts (SWB) ME 3193 B/4.

chaos – this was a regime obsessed with order, though incapable of achieving the discipline that it idealized (Peterson and Taylor 2013). But it was also a regime impatient of resistance and disinterested in the disciplinary work that elections might do; rather, it exalted coercive force and the military. In 1979, Amin's regime collapsed in the face of a Tanzanian invasion after an ill-advised military adventure.

That elections should be held to form a new government after Amin's fall was widely accepted; but many argued for a 'no-party' parliamentary election, with candidates standing on their own merit under the 'umbrella' of the Uganda National Liberation Front. Supporters of Obote and the UPC – who were waiting in exile in Tanzania – opposed this; and they made an alliance with members of the resurgent DP (Bwengye 1985: 43–46). The subsequent election, held in December 1980, partly reprised the hopes of the independence period that elections would pull people together as citizens and reassert the legitimacy and impartiality of the state. Popular enthusiasm drove an extraordinary turnout – over 90 per cent of registered voters in many constituencies, though the reliability of the register is hard to gauge. But Obote's allies – most notably Paulo Muwanga, who took effective control of the interim government – interfered grossly to ensure a UPC victory. They did so by exploiting their offices to channel scarce goods down lines of UPC patronage and – more directly – by physically preventing the nomination of DP candidates for a number of constituencies and harassing non-UPC campaigns (Bwengye 1985: 87; Karugire 1988: 75; Willis, Lynch and Cheeseman 2017).

Muwanga also took over the announcement of results halfway through the process, encouraging the widespread suspicion that he and the UPC were simply changing the outcomes. There may indeed have been substantive tampering: in the constituency of Kabarole Southwest, in Tooro, an unusually low turnout lends credence to the DP's allegations that significant numbers of ballots simply vanished.[33] Elsewhere in Tooro, the UPC polled modestly, at best. In the central district around Fort Portal, the real race was between the DP and Patrick Kaboyo, the son of the former king, who was standing for the Uganda Patriotic Movement (UPM) of Yoweri Museveni. But in Acholi, where the UPC swept the ballot, Obote evidently had support – partly because one of his key supporters, Otema Allimadi, provided an effective channel for patronage.[34] In Buganda, where Obote's dissolution of the kingdom had been neither forgiven nor forgotten, the DP – despised by many in 1962 – had become the party of choice (see Table 2.4).

---

[33] Interview UGA47a, former DP candidate, Fort Portal, 12 June 2015.
[34] Interview UGA89a, chief and former UPC activist, Gulu, 16 January 2016.

Table 2.4 *Case study constituency winners: Uganda*

Constituency	1980	1996	2001	2006	2011	2016
				Winner (party) (number of candidates) Winner's vote/votes cast/registered votes		
Tooro: Fort Portal	[Kabarole central] Kaboha (DP) (3) 17,375/44,849/ 49,046	Apollo Karugaba (3) 5,861/10,733/ 19,131	Henry Basaliza (4) 5,912/12,632/ 29,921	Stephen Kaliba (NRM) (3) 11,719/15,150/ 26,067	Alex Ruhunda (NRM) (3) 9,732/19,051/–	Alex Ruhunda (NRM) (5) 10,322/22,524/–
Tooro: Bunyangabu	[Kabarole southwest] Henry Tungakwo (UPC) (3) 16,673/29,831/ 44,620	Adolf Mwesige (6) 11,023/31,382/ 48,042	Adolf Mwesige (3) 16,692/31,049/ 53,555	Adolf Mwesige (NRM) (3) 27,677/34,620/ 48,996	Adolf Mwesige (NRM) (4) 36,175/45,301/–	Adolf Mwesige (NRM) (6) 26,632/56,404/–
Tooro: Burahya	–	Amooti Kisembo (3) 22,703/37,682/ 63,063	Basaliza Mwesigye (3) 25,480/39,327/ 75,983	Kasaija Kagwera (3) 45,972/54,001/ 77,979	Kasaija Kagwera (NRM) (3) 37,814/62,169/–	Margaret Muhanga (NRM) (4) 36,424/83,064/–
Gulu: Gulu Mun.	[Gulu East] Otema Allimadi (UPC) 42,415/44,872/ 47,135	Norbert Mao (unopposed) –/38,172/–	Norbert Mao (3) 16,995/21,893/–	Penytoo Alex (FDC) (7) 7,756/25,718/–	Christopher Acire (FDC) (9) 10,265/30,492/–	Lyandro Komakech (DP) (8) 11,510/29,887/–

Gulu: Aswa	—	Ronald R. Okumu 6,502/20,166/ 35,666	Ronald R. Okumu (3) 17,358/20,585/–	Ronald R. Okumu (FDC) (2) 21,270/24,185/–	Ronald R. Okumu (FDC) (6) 15,542/23,906/–	Ronald R. Okumu (Ind.) (5) 16,859/30,172/–
Gulu: Omoro	—	Abednego Absalom 5,928/28,218/ 47,131	Jacob Oulanyah (6) 9,453/19,023/–	Simon Toolit (FDC) (4) 16,531/30,460/–	Jacob Oulanyah (NRM) (9) 11,044/30,322/–	Jacob Oulanyah (NRM) (5) 8,218/19,001/–
Mukono: Mukono Mun.	—	—	—	—	Betty Nambooze (DP) (5) 26,184/39,435/–	Betty Nambooze (DP) (4) 35,341/60,515/–
Mukono North	Kitaka Gawera (DP) (3) 17,894/34,704/ 37,226	Godfrey Kaitiro (5) 5,985/29,459/ 54,927	Peter Bakaluba (4) 17,324/32,712/–	Peter Bakaluba (NRM) (3) 22,680/45,539/–	Ronald Kibuule (NRM) (6) 13,343/20,532/–	Ronald Kibuule (NRM) (4) 11,261/27,906/–
Mukono South	A Ntale (DP) (4) 28,133/34,460/ 36,764	Mukwaya Janat (3) 12,764/23,701/ 40,758	Mukwaya Janat (3) 13,349/27,097/–	Mukwaya Janat (NRM) (3) 14,604/30,610/–	Peter Bakaluba (NRM) (5) 14,930/29,636/–	Johnson Muyanja (NRM) (6) 21,844/38,562/–

Source: Compiled by authors from Uganda INEC and EC reports.

Obote took office, but from the outset faced widespread scepticism over the state's legitimacy, and the reputation of elections – in particular multi-party ones – took decades to recover. The new president anyway faced a more pressing concern in the form of an active insurgency led by Museveni. By 1985, Obote found that he was unable to manage the competing demands of his political supporters and of the army, which were both internally divided. The leaders of the coup which overthrew him in July 1985 were even less able to sustain that politics; and in January 1986 Museveni's National Resistance Army (NRA) captured Kampala from a regime that had largely collapsed. As a young radical, Museveni had worked for Obote's first government, preparing for the elections that never happened. He possessed a keen awareness of the idea that elections could be managed, not only to claim legitimacy for a particular government but also to assert the authority of the state itself and to remind people of their responsibilities as citizens. Yet – not unlike Obote – he had a deep suspicion of political parties and feared that 'sectarian tendencies' would undermine the value of the vote as an exercise in citizenship, and perhaps lead voters to choose the wrong leaders (Cheeseman, Lynch and Willis 2016).[35] Having been defeated by Obote in the flawed 1980 elections, he also had a keen awareness of the way in which such processes could be undermined.

After initial experiments with a bottom-up system of electoral colleges and open 'queue-voting', with each level selecting the members of the level above, Museveni initiated a constitution-making process that involved the election in 1994 – by adult suffrage and secret ballot – of a constituent assembly (Kasfir 1991, 1998, 2000). The election campaigns for that assembly saw a vigorous patronage politics, with candidates promising particular rewards to constituents and distributing gifts (Gingyera-Pincwa 1996; Mujaju 1996: 52; Furley and Katalikawe 1999). In 1996, the Assembly – after much debate – approved a constitution that returned to the 'no-party' model some had advocated in 1980. Candidates for parliament, and for the presidency, would stand on 'individual merit'; political parties were permitted to exist but could not campaign (Reid 2017: 81–82). Museveni insisted that the return to the secret ballot was not the result of international pressure or domestic demands: 'I support free elections for my own belief, because I believe in it. That is how we are going to stabilize our country.'[36]

---

[35] 'Museveni forbids campaigning', Kampala Domestic Service, 8 February 1989, FBIS AFR-89-025.

[36] 'Uganda: President Museveni launches election manifesto', 27 March 1996, FBIS AFR-96-061.

The two subsequent presidential and parliamentary elections – in 1996 and 2001 – involved many candidates whose partisan affiliations were well known: not least Museveni himself, whose NRM nominally embraced the whole population but actually served as an uncertainly structured patronage network stretching out from the presidency downwards. Museveni won those presidential elections, and candidates aligned with the NRM won a clear majority in parliament (see Table 2.4). This success relied partly on candidates' ability to promise rewards and/or give gifts to their constituents (Muhumuza 1997; Tripp 2004). However, it also relied on immediate and threatened violence against perceived rivals to Museveni; notably in 2001, when the army and police pursued a vicious campaign of intimidation and harassment against Kizza Besigye – a rival candidate for the presidency from within the NRM – and his supporters (Tripp 2004).[37]

At the same time, Museveni and his supporters reminded people of the 'chaos' of Obote's second regime and the Amin years; the threat that this might return hung over the polls. Around Gulu, seen by some of Museveni's supporters as the stronghold of the former regime, a prolonged anti-insurgency campaign led to widespread displacement and violence in the late 1980s and 1990s (Doom and Vlassenroot 1999). But elsewhere in Uganda, levels of personal security had improved since the early 1980s, and the possibility that violence might return was a powerful incentive to vote for Museveni; in Buganda, the restoration of the kingdom in 1993 also added to Museveni's popularity. The contrast was evident in the polls. In Tooro, where the NRM had established itself early on in the insurgency against Obote, Museveni swept the presidential polls in 1996 and 2001; so too in Mukono. But in Gulu, voters overwhelmingly supported the candidate seen as most likely to beat Museveni in each election – Paul Ssemogerere in 1996, Kizza Besigye in 2001 – though neither of them was from northern Uganda (see Table 2.5). They also returned anti-NRM parliamentary candidates in almost every election from 1996 to 2006. In Tooro and Mukono, meanwhile, avowed 'Movementists' won in the 1996 and 2001 parliamentary contests (see Table 2.4).

In 2000, a referendum on returning to multi-partyism saw a majority vote against this, but also a low turnout, which was interpreted by some as a 'silent boycott' (Bratton and Lambright 2001). In 2005, a second referendum was held and this time Museveni and the NRM backed a

---

[37] 'Official denies anxiety in Mukono', *New Vision*, 29 April 1996, p. 3; 'They come like night owls', *The Monitor*, 1–3 May 1996, p. 15; 'Hit and run car kills three Besigye supporters', *New Vision*, 5 February 2001, p. 1; 'Rabwoni arrested', *New Vision*, 21 February 2001, p. 1; 'RDC attacks Besigye', *New Vision*, 22 February 2001, p. 11.

Table 2.5 *Turnout and votes for main presidential candidates in case study areas: Uganda*

		Gulu	%	Kabarole	%	Mukono	%	National	%
1996	**Reg.**							8,492,231	
	Turnout	80,422		96,266		63,178		6,193,816	73
	Museveni	5,570	7	90,901	94	45,605	72	4,458,195	72
	Ssemogerere	70,044	87	1,474	2	14,993	24	1,416,140	23
2001	**Reg.**	163,526		159,459		139,529		10,775,836	
	Turnout	89,816	55	104,943	66	94,094	67	7,511,606	70
	Museveni	8,952	10	93,414	89	57,104	61	5,088,470	68
	Besigye	72,842	81	10,586	10	34,305	36	2,029,190	27
2006	**Reg.**	133,538		153,042		120,985		10,450,788	
	Turnout	89,478	65	107,618	70	78,112	65	7,230,456	69
	Museveni	9,298	10	87,153	81	40,884	52	4,109,449	57
	Besigye	67,277	75	14,961	17	31,860	41	2,592,954	36
2011	**Reg.**	192,669		208,758		244,893		13,954,129	
	Turnout	90,030	47	124,699	60	135,863	55	8,272,769	59
	Mao	36,225	40	217	0	2,598	2	147,917	2
	Museveni	24,590	27	105,290	84	78,368	58	5,428,369	66
	Besigye	17,467	19	17,333	14	45,565	34	2,064,963	25
2016	**Reg.**	184,791		233,385		292,011		15,277,198	
	Turnout	101,588	55	168,161	72	184,919	63	10,329,131	68
	Museveni	31,391	31	122,134	73	86,328	47	5,971,872	58
	Besigye	48,594	48	35,603	21	82,858	45	3,508,687	34

Source: Compiled by authors from Uganda INEC and EC reports. Gulu column comprises the constituencies Omoro, Aswa and Gulu Municipality; Kabarole comprises Fort Portal, Burahya and Bunyangabu constituencies; Mukono comprises Mukono North, Mukono South, Mukono Municipality (from 2011) and includes Nakifuma for 2011 and 2016.

return to multi-partyism. There have been competing explanations for that change: that it was the result of pressure from international donors (whether motivated by concern with the principle of multi-partyism, or by impatience with the difficulty of pushing economic liberalization measures through parliament), or because Museveni saw this as an opportunity to secure a removal of term limits (which were packaged in the same referendum) as a *quid pro quo* (Mugisha 2004; Keating 2011). Both may well be true: term limits were removed, and there was donor pressure. But it may also have been that Museveni had identified challengers within the NRM as the major potential threat to his own position, and saw multi-partyism as part of a strategy to increase executive power: once forced out of the dominant party those rivals would be denied access to the patronage resources they needed to pursue successful campaigns, and more easily exposed to harassment (Makara, Rakner and Svåsand 2009; Keating 2011).

Museveni's confidence proved justified. In the 2006 elections, he and his supporters used the same combination of threats and outright violence, and control of state media, state officials and patronage to secure victory over the party Besigye created – the Forum for Democratic Change (FDC) – though with a reduced majority (Gloppen et al. 2006; Mwenda 2007) (see Table 2.5).[38] The 2011 elections, and those of 2016, saw less extreme violence, but brutal attacks were still conducted against the opposition, while the state's known capacity for violence and a history of instability ensured that persistent threats of violence carried real weight (Vokes and Wilkins 2016). The opposition really meant the FDC; while the DP and UPC still existed in regions where they have had historical support (Buganda and Acholi for DP; Lango for the UPC), the years of 'no-party' rule had hollowed out their local networks, as almost all patronage flowed through the NRM (Carbone 2003). These elections also apparently saw steadily growing spending by Museveni and NRM parliamentary candidates, which led some to assert that the 2011 'election was won on the basis of money'.[39] Certainly, while he denounced 'vote buying', Museveni saw no contradiction in giving out – literally – sacks full of cash during the 2011 campaign, and made absolutely explicit the connection between voting for the ruling party and the provision of government services.[40] As an opposition politician explained, the approach of NRM supporters could be very simple: 'They come to you directly and say you know what if you vote for these guys, you are not going to get anything, this area is going to be neglected, you are going to be cut off from Uganda.'[41] However, the NRM's success was also fuelled by a popular sense of satisfaction with Museveni's performance; by a widespread assumption that changing the government through elections was simply not possible; by a fear of further instability if Museveni lost; and by the weakness of the opposition (Izama and Wilkerson 2011; Conroy-Krutz and Logan 2012; Omach 2014; Perrot, Lafargue and Makara 2014).

Museveni increased his vote share in 2011, and by 2016 there was an air almost of routine to the combination of intimidation and patronage that

---

[38] 'MPs acquitted of murder, Besigye demands probe', *Daily Monitor*, 10 January 2006, p. 1; '3 killed at Besigye meet', *Daily Monitor*, 16 January 2006, p. 1; 'NRM men close Kiruhura FDC candidate office', *Daily Monitor*, 6 February 2006, p. 1; 'Govt in fresh attempt to block Besigye candidacy', *Sunday Monitor*, 12 February 2006, p. 1.

[39] Interview UGA3b, civil society activist, Kampala.

[40] 'Opposition failing me – Museveni', *Daily Monitor*, 19 January 2016.

[41] Interview UGA95a, opposition candidate, Mukono, 3 February 2016.

secured yet another victory and an increased parliamentary majority for the NRM (see Table 2.5). The regime had become adept at orchestrating electoral performances of apparent consent (Oloka-Onyango and Ahikire 2017), while inter-party competition and intra-party disputes ensured that the opposition remained fragmented (Beardsworth 2016). It was a routine that saw multiple contenders vying for the NRM nomination in many constituencies, spending liberally as they did so: the long-term effect of the return to multi-partyism has been to increase the competitiveness – and cost – of NRM primaries (Izama and Wilkerson 2011). The NRM has not funded its parliamentary candidates to any significant degree; they have funded themselves and – in the process – helped to pay for Museveni's presidential campaign (Vokes 2016; Wilkins 2016). In consequence, many have come into office with heavy debts. Their vulnerability is increased by Museveni's technique – increasingly apparent since 2005 – of not only refusing to endorse incumbent or aspiring NRM MPs, but actively encouraging voters to blame the perceived failings of government on sitting MPs, rather than on the regime as a whole (Perrot, Lafargue and Makara 2014). Debt-burdened MPs often turn to the president for help, and while this relationship may not be entirely one-sided – Museveni needs the MPs, just as they need him (Collord 2016) – their willingness to challenge his authority is evidently limited. So much was apparent when they supported the removal of the age limit on presidential candidates, preparing the ground for Museveni to stand again in 2021 – each MP having reportedly been given 29 million Uganda shillings (around US$7,500) in advance of the crucial parliamentary vote.[42]

It is not hard to find critical accounts of the abuses and malpractice of the electoral system that have emerged under Museveni (Muhumuza 2009; Makara 2010). But it is important to recognize that such politics is far from static. In 1996, patterns of ethnic and religious voting that were apparent in the early 1960s and in 1980 were still discernible, though only partly (Kassimir 1995; BakamaNume 1997). Over the next twenty years, religion seems to have become less significant in relation to political participation or voting choice. Moreover, since 2006 the vote for Museveni has become more evenly spread. Though his support is still strongest in the southwest, his home area, it is now more widely distributed across Uganda, and NRM candidates win parliamentary seats across the country (Golaz and Médard 2014; Gibb 2016). Around Gulu, for example, Museveni's vote share has steadily increased (see Table 2.5) and some of the young men who championed Acholi rights in the 1990s have become NRM stalwarts. Significantly, a number of these figures, such as

---

[42] 'MPs to get Shs 29m for age limit consultation', *Daily Monitor*, 23 October 2017.

Jacob Oulanyah in Omoro constituency, have proved adept at using access to state patronage to ensure their return to parliament on an NRM ticket. As one Gulu resident put it:

[T]he President has been visiting this side frequently. Some people think that now that he is with us, some development is being seen, road construction is going on so it has created hope in people.[43]

In this way elections, it might be argued, have provided a mechanism for a degree of popular complicity in the widening of the 'elite bargaining' that has been identified as underpinning Museveni's long rule (Lindemann 2011). They also reveal the continued strains in that bargaining. Museveni's vote share has fallen slowly in Buganda, where tension between the ambitions of the kingdom, local resentments and the claims of the central state have chipped away at his support (see Table 2.5); though it is still not entirely true to claim of Mukono – as one opposition politician did – that '[t]he most important message for our people here is that they like people who are opposing the NRM government'.[44]

National contests and party affiliations cut across local patterns of ambition and patronage, in ways that suggest that elections are by no means simply controlled by any single central hand. In Tooro, securing the NRM nomination remains a secure ticket to parliament, and incumbent MPs have an advantage. This is evident in the remarkable career of Adolf Mwesige, five-times winner in Bunyangabu constituency (see Table 2.4), whose succession of ministerial positions have enabled him to repay his constituents' support by getting the main town in the area upgraded to a municipality, and now by having the constituency itself made into a new district – both changes that unlock resources from central government. Those dynamics mean that NRM party primaries are as important – and as expensive for candidates – as the actual elections in these areas.

In Aswa, neighbouring Gulu Municipality, Ronald Reagan Okumu has a similarly remarkable record of victory, but one that is based on a record of vocal opposition to the government combined with some adept engagement with development and humanitarian agencies that has brought resources to his constituents.[45] Party matters less here; once a Movementist, Okumu has mostly stood for Besigye's FDC, but in 2016 he was unable to do so because of a quarrel over nominations. He still won comfortably as an independent. Okumu's repeated success stands in stark contrast to the turnover seen in Gulu Municipality, where parliamentary

---

[43] Interview UGA80a, civil society activist, Gulu, 25 September 2015.
[44] Interview UGA58a, DP activist, Mukono, 17 June 2015.
[45] Interview UGA77a, NRM activist, Gulu, 22 September 2015.

elections tend to be won on a plurality, with multiple repeat contenders, some of whom switch between parties (see Table 2.4).

Around Mukono, where expressed loyalty to the Buganda kingdom has become standard practice for all politicians, party discipline is also weak. Betty Nambooze, who rose to prominence by overturning a rigged election result in Mukono North in 2010 and went on to win the newly created constituency of Mukono Municipality, is nominally a member of the DP, but has openly campaigned for Besigye in presidential elections. Despite her combatively brave attitude to the NRM nationally (Médard and Golaz 2013), she is on good terms with some local NRM parliamentarians. Neither incumbency nor NRM affiliation guarantees victory here; even sitting ministers like Ronald Kibuule in Mukono North struggle to keep their seats, and win only on a plurality (see Table 2.4).

Despite the widespread assumption that elections cannot change the national government, levels of participation across the country – measured very simply in terms of voter turnout as a proportion of total population – remain significant, though they have never regained the levels of 1980 (see Table 2.8). Uganda's elections thus combine the performance of stateness with the reproduction of a clientelist politics that is both authoritarian and surprisingly lively. Yet it is an unstable combination, reliant on Museveni, for the NRM is a bundle of rivalrous factions and local networks, not a corporation.

2.3   Kenya: Negotiating Electoral Outcomes

The Kenyan experience falls somewhere between our other two cases both in terms of progress towards democratization and the competitiveness of national polls. Multiparty elections have regularly been close but have only once resulted in a genuine transfer of power. Kenya's four presidents have all been drawn from two ethnic groups – the Kalenjin and the Kikuyu. In turn, this has fuelled accusations that elections are systematically rigged in order to keep the country's more economically and politically marginal communities out of the presidency (Kanyinga and Odote 2019). Controversial elections have gone hand-in-hand with periodic reform of the electoral commission, but this has done little to sustain public confidence in the face of fresh concerns (Cheeseman, Lynch and Willis 2014). Instead, while other democratic institutions have grown stronger, most notably following the introduction of a new constitution in 2010, the electoral process is widely viewed as being compromised by the dominance of patrimonial politics (Nyabola 2018). This scepticism, along with police bruality, and the willingness of a range of political leaders to deploy ethnic violence in order to increase their chances of retaining power, has contributed to significant loss of life particularly around elections in 1992, 1997, 2007 and 2017 (Mueller 2011; Brosché et al. 2019). However, to fully understand the prevalence of ethnic politics in Kenya, and the way in which elections have come to both reflect and intensify patrimonial ties, it is important to recognize the political legacies of British rule.

Colonialism bequeathed distinctive tools, and distinctive challenges, to the rulers of independent Kenya. There were alternative ideas of nation at the moment of independence – in the northeast, among an ethnic Somali population, and at the coast (Peterson 2020) – but these lacked the wealth, geographical centrality and institutional focus that made Buganda and Asante such alarming rivals to the postcolonial state. The history of settler presence, and the extreme violence of late-colonial counter-insurgency against the Mau Mau rebellion, left Kenya with an unusually strong administration – in effect, an executive civil service, closely entwined with the security services (Gertzel 1970: 22–26). But colonial history also entrenched ethnicity as a basis for political mobiliza-tion and created a distinctive property regime (Lynch 2011a). Access to land became a means to mobilize and reward supporters, and to punish and threaten opponents. This has given local politics in some parts of the country a particular viciousness (Oucho 2002; Boone 2011). Our choice of case studies reflects that history of mobilization.

The pre-independence constituency of Kikuyu (now divided into Kikuyu and Kabete), just north of the capital Nairobi, in former Kiambaa District and now Kiambu County, has historically been largely populated by Kikuyu voters (the country's largest ethnic group), though now this is an increasingly peri-urban and ethnically diverse area. At the economic and political centre of colonial and postcolonial Kenya, Kikuyu is densely populated, agriculturally productive and has long been com-paratively well served in terms of education, communications and other services. Under Jomo Kenyatta's presidency, and again since 2002, this was very much the heartland of the incumbent government (Lockwood 2019b). Narok North, in the Rift Valley to the west of Nairobi, has by contrast been seen – by its inhabitants and others – as ill served by government and relatively remote from power, though politicians from the area were influential under President Moi. A largely pastoralist area, inhabited mostly by Maasai, Narok North has seen much settlement from other parts of Kenya – a settlement viewed by some Maasai as one part of a prolonged assault on the pastoral economy and way of life that threatens to leave them without land or cattle (Hughes 2016). Seme constituency – formerly Kisumu Rural – is in the west of Kenya, in Luo Nyanza. Lying a short drive from the provincial centre at Kisumu, the constituency is divided between a relatively well-watered ridge area and a drier, lowland that stretches to the shore of Lake Victoria. The population are almost all Luo by ethnicity. Divided by clan and locality, they – like other constituencies in Luo Nyanza – share a sense of resentment over political exclusion, in which Kenya's history can be retold as a story of repeated political betrayals of Luo interests (Wanyande 2002; Oloo 2005).

Unlike Ghana and Uganda, Kenya has never had a military government. Elections have been held regularly – more or less – since independence, though for three decades these elections permitted only contests for seats in the national assembly between members of the ruling party, with a single presidential candidate being returned unopposed at every election from 1969 to 1988. Throughout those years, Kenya's presidents liked to insist that their governments were 'freely elected'.[46] Their critics liked to point out that Kenya was a one-party state: effectively from 1969, legally from 1982 (Anyang' Nyong'o 1983: 161). Both claims need some qualification. Kenya's elections were competitive in certain limited ways, with a high turnover of MPs, but far from free (Throup 1993; Hornsby 2011). Moreover, it was not really accurate to suggest that it was the ruling *party* that held power; after a brief heyday around independence the party itself was chronically weak in organizational terms and the civil servants who controlled Kenya's administration consistently had the upper hand (Branch and Cheeseman 2006).

Kenya's administrators learned from their late-colonial mentors that elections could be a disciplinary tool, an opportunity to demonstrate and naturalize the state's claim to order its subjects. Late-colonial elections in Kenya had followed the pattern established elsewhere in Africa, but with a distinctive character shaped by a settler politics that established suffrage as the badge of adult citizenship, and made access to land a potent focus for mobilization. Late-colonial attempts to use a qualitative franchise to recruit African allies in the prolongation of imperial rule failed in the face of a widespread African demand for the franchise and self-government.

Once it was clear that the British government was more anxious to hand over power than it was to secure continued privileges for white settlers, elections became a contest between two groups of African politicians, each of which was itself internally divided. There is some truth to the jibe that the parties were 'mere federated ethnic loyalties grouped around individual personalities' (Okoth-Ogendo 1972: 13), but there was also a policy debate, which reflected the consequences of colonial educational

---

[46] 'President Kenyatta's address to parliament', Nairobi Domestic Service, 12 March 1974, FBIS, MEA 74-051.

and economic change and settlement patterns. One group, led mostly by those from Central Kenya and the western area of Luo Nyanza, who were Kikuyu and Luo by ethnicity, looked forward to the creation of a strong, centralized, independent government; they formed the Kenya African National Union (KANU). The other, led by those from the Rift Valley, western Kenya and the coast, argued for a devolved future of 'regional' government, fearing that they would lose their land, or be excluded from government employment and patronage, under a centralized government. Those who claimed to speak for them formed the Kenya African Democratic Union (KADU) (Anderson 2005).

KANU – better organized and enjoying significant financial and political support from other recently independent countries – won the 1963 elections for national assembly seats and formed the government that took Kenya to independence under a parliamentary constitution. KANU candidates won both Kikuyu constituency and Kisumu Rural, with their overwhelmingly Kikuyu and Luo electorates. But in Narok the Maasai were, as a colonial intelligence assessment put it, 'solidly pro-KADU'.[47] At the end of 1964, Kenya became a republic, and KANU's leader, Jomo Kenyatta, was chosen as president by the national assembly.

Just before that change, KADU's remaining members of the national assembly had been placed under considerable pressure to dissolve their own party, and crossed the floor to join KANU. The subsequent period of de facto one-party rule saw increasing tension within KANU, which reflected dissatisfaction over the consequences of independence. Oginga Odinga, the most prominent Luo politician, was increasingly associated with a radical group that called for more dramatic action to seize and redistribute land from settlers. Effectively driven out of KANU, Odinga and his followers formed a new party, the Kenya People's Union (KPU) in 1966. In the multiple by-elections that ensued – the 'Little General Election' – the government used a combination of patronage and coercion to ensure the defeat of most KPU candidates, with voters explicitly warned that constituencies that elected KPU candidates would be denied government resources (Gertzel 1970; Mueller 1984). Selective repression – most overt outside western Kenya – and Odinga's own campaigning style turned the KPU into a largely ethnic party. Six of the nine members who were returned to the national assembly were Luo; further by-elections whittled down their number, for as one KANU politician reportedly explained to a British diplomat:

---

[47] Southern Province Intelligence Appreciation, February 1961, UKNA CO 822/2059.

[I]t is easy enough to get the desired result without outright juggling of the figures by widespread bribery involving small sums and having your people on hand to guide the marks of the ordinary illiterate voter.[48]

The KPU was banned in 1969, in a turbulent year that saw the assassination of the only prominent remaining KANU politician from Luo Nyanza, Tom Mboya; protests against Kenyatta – ending in lethal violence – when he visited the town of Kisumu; and the widespread 'oathing' of Kikuyu as a means to consolidate community support behind the incumbent regime (Knighton 2010). That same year saw new elections to the national assembly. Since KANU was left as the only legal party, the actual polls (held by adult suffrage and secret ballot) were technically party primaries, though they were managed entirely by the administration. Kenyatta was the only candidate nominated for president, and so won unopposed, but most MPs faced challengers, and many were defeated (Throup 1993).

Local rivalries over which influential figure was best able to deliver the rewards of independence and simultaneously protect and promote local interests characterized these local contests in 1969, and in the next elections in 1974 (Hyden and Leys 1972; Hornsby 1989) Kenyatta openly encouraged voters to see elected MPs as delegates, sent to parliament to 'spell out their people's needs', rather than to engage in political debates.[49] This ensured that elections largely became referenda on the development performance of the incumbent MP, placing great pressure on politicians. Partly as a result, few politicians kept a parliamentary seat for long, and the same individuals kept running for office: in Narok, Justus ole Tipis ran in every election between 1963 and 1988, winning four times and losing twice; in Kisumu Rural, Ndolo Ayah ran in four of the five elections between 1969 and 1988, though he only once won the ballot (see Table 2.6).

This was, as more than one observer noted, an electoral system that revolved around patron–client ties and ensured a significant but not overwhelming degree of electoral participation (Bienen 1974; Barkan 1976; Barkan and Okumu 1978; Barkan 1979a, 1979b; Berg-Schlosser 1982). As Michael Chege's study of Nairobi politics showed (1981), parliamentary candidates spent heavily on campaigns, but spending alone was not enough: voters had to feel that candidates really would pursue their interests in terms of development and other public goods – from jobs to support

---

[48] Edis, British High Commission to Firman, FCO, 4 September 1968, UKNA FCO 31/209.

[49] 'Kenyatta addresses self-government day celebrations', translated, Nairobi Domestic Service, 1 June 1975, FBIS SAF-75-106.

Table 2.6 *Case study constituency winners: Kenya*

	Winner (party) (number of candidates) Winner's vote/votes cast/registered votes		
Constit-uency	Kikuyu	Narok North	Kisumu Rural/Seme
1969	Joseph Gatuguta (KANU) (3) 11,396/18,827/36,420	Moses Tenga (KANU) (2) 3,952/6,345/16,353	Wilson Ndolo Ayah (KANU) (4) 10,701/20,714/51,327
1974	Amos Ng'ang'a (KANU) (7) 15,342/26,253/32,411	Justus ole Tipis (KANU) (3) 5,575/10,758/26,375	Wycliffe Onyango-Ayoki (KANU) (4) 8,936/22,814/41,104
1979	Amos Ng'ang'a (KANU) (5) 11,235/29,598/37,146	Justus ole Tipis (KANU) (1) –/–/27,055	Robert John Ouko (KANU) (5) 23,284/38,570/51,992
1983	Peter Kabibi Kinyanjui (KANU) (4) 23,244/31,765/50,207	Justus ole Tipis (KANU) (1) –/–/38,663	Robert John Ouko (KANU) (3) 24,944/29,567/64,703
1988	Peter Kabibi Kinyanjui (KANU) (1) –/–/38,607	William ole Ntimama (KANU) (2) 14,249/26,744/36,823	Wilson Ndolo Ayah (KANU, (1) –/–/–
1992	Paul Kibugi Muite (FORD K) (5) 38,416/53,891/62,106	William ole Ntimama (KANU) (4) 24,780/39,097/49,406	Peter Anyang' Nyong'o (FORD-K) (2) 23,538/25,852/35,428
1997	Paul Kibugi Muite (Safina) (5) 48,504/54,869/68,558	William ole Ntimama (KANU) (1) –/–/46,555	Winston Achoro-Ayoki (NDP) (3) 13,508/25,283/35,436
2002	Paul Kibugi Muite (Safina) (7) 20,614/46,998/75,436	William ole Ntimama (NARC) (3) 22,025/39,500/54,211	Peter Anyang' Nyong'o (NARC) (3) 20,724/23,092/41,850
2007	Lewis Nguyai Ng'ang'a (PNU) (20) 63,421/85,879/106,688	William ole Ntimama (ODM) (8) 27,814/66,779/81,548	Peter Anyang' Nyong'o (ODM) (6) 36,481/40,860/52,937
2013	Anthony Ichung'wah (TNA) (11) 43,028/59,895/65,041	Richard ole Kenta (ODM) (3) 24,853/54,393/59,567	James Wambura Nyikal (ODM) (4) 31,025/33,638/35,735
2017	Anthony Ichung'wah (JP) (1) –/–/91,157	Richard ole Kenya (ODM) (5) 33,399/67,125/78,402	James Wambura Nyikal (ODM) (4) 32,678/44,820/53,555

Source: Compiled by the authors from IEBC reports and from the Kenya Election Database, www.facebook.com/Kenyaelectiondatabase/.

in land disputes. Citizenship did not simply impose demands on the public: it offered people a language for making claims on the state (Moskowitz 2019), and election campaigns provided an opportunity for a wider populace to make demands on those who had eaten well of the fruits of independence, as one letter to the Kenyan press made clear:

> Many company executives, businessmen, government officers, university lecturers, former MPs and the sitting MPs have flocked to the rural areas looking for votes. Our rural areas need more money to complete self-help projects, and in view of this the district commissioners should issue fund-raising meeting licences indiscriminately, so that these people can donate.[50]

The persistent inability of elected representatives to meet popular expectations meant that turnover in parliamentary seats was high. It also meant that, with national citizenship apparently an insufficient tool for making claims to development, some turned to ethnicity and kinship to provide a moral language for challenging what they saw as exclusion (Moskowitz 2019: 6–12).

When Kenyatta died in 1978, he was succeeded by his vice president, Daniel arap Moi. Moi was a Kalenjin by ethnicity, from the Rift Valley; or rather, he was one of the political entrepreneurs who had helped to craft the idea of a Kalenjin identity as a political force in the 1950s (Lynch 2011a: 51–80). Once a prominent KADU leader, he had become Kenyatta's vice president in the aftermath of Odinga's departure from KANU. His succession to the presidency had been resisted by some Kikuyu politicians close to Kenyatta; after taking office, Moi worked – discreetly at first, then more openly – to sideline those opponents, to promote Kalenjin in the civil service, and to ensure that state patronage flowed to a new set of political entrepreneurs who were not from central Kenya. KANU had remained the only registered party since 1969; in 1982, after rumours that Odinga was seeking to register a new party, the constitution was formally changed to make Kenya a de jure one-party state. Moi subsequently sought to rebuild KANU as an institution capable of wielding centralized power (Widner 1992), but Kenya never became a 'party state'. In practice, Moi continued to rely on the provincial administration, security services and local politicians (Lynch 2011a: 125). At the same time, Moi's determination to displace existing networks, as well as changing economic circumstances, led to a slow fragmentation of Kenya's post-independence elite (Widner 1992: 199–201; Cowen and Kanyinga 2002: 170; Mueller 2008; Branch and Cheeseman 2009).

---

[50] *Weekly Review*, 10 August 1979, letter from Odinga Shivachi.

Moi well understood that parliamentary elections provided an effective mechanism for allowing limited participation and disciplining aspiring political leaders. However-with a weaker political base and facing a more difficult economic context and more obvious signs of dissatisfaction (including a failed coup attempt in 1982) than Kenyatta – he also wished to use them to reward loyalty and to exclude those whom he suspected of working against him (Barkan 1987: 228; Lynch 2011a). He was consequently more willing than Kenyatta to let incumbent politicians use their positions and the civil service to protect themselves from serious electoral competition (Throup 1993). Ole Tipis sailed through the 1979 and 1983 elections in Narok North unchallenged; in 1980, Charles Njonjo – then a close Moi ally – was the only candidate in a by-election in Kikuyu, after the winner of the 1979 election stepped aside for him. Moi himself was the unopposed presidential candidate in 1979, 1983 and 1988, and so faced no poll. But by no means were all assembly elections foregone conclusions, and effective local campaigns could secure high turnouts – as in Kisumu Rural in 1979 (see Table 2.6). Constituency elections were often won on a plurality, as multiple candidates vied for support. It was ostensibly to secure more decisive public endorsement of the winning candidate that a new system of 'queue-voting' primaries, without a secret ballot, was announced in 1988 – though it was widely assumed that the real reason was to facilitate central manipulation of electoral outcomes (Throup and Hornsby 1998: 42–44).

Even this new system did not entirely prevent local competition: in Narok North, a local politician named William ole Ntimama, who had on several occasions since 1961 been persuaded not to run by allowing him a free rein in the district council, finally insisted on challenging ole Tipis (Rutten 2001).[51] Ntimama won a close race. But elsewhere the system shut out competitors – as in Kisumu Rural, where Moi loyalist Ndolo Ayah was returned unopposed (see Table 2.6). The 1988 election was widely criticized, both internationally and in Kenya itself, despite intermittently brutal repression. Given voice by an increasingly bold national press and religious leaders, and encouraged by Kenya's international donors, that criticism brought together an unlikely alliance of politicians. Veteran KANU members, including Oginga Odinga, ex-KADU and KANU members, and a number of young newcomers to politics joined forces to form the Forum for the Restoration of Democracy (FORD) in 1990. Amidst large-scale street protests, violently suppressed, donors threatened to suspend aid and Moi responded by rushing a constitutional

---

[51] Southern Province Intelligence Appreciation, January 1961, UKNA CO 822/1427.

amendment through parliament to legalize multiparty politics in 1991 (Throup and Hornsby 1998: 54–91).

The president, however, had no intention of allowing free and fair elections. Instead, his decision to end the one-party state had been part of a calculated gamble that it would be easier to hold multiparty elections and manipulate them than to entirely resist multi-partyism. This calculation proved to be correct, and Moi went on to exploit the advantages of incumbency to win disputed elections in 1992 and 1997, securing a plurality of the vote against a divided opposition (see Table 2.7). In both elections Moi and KANU spent lavishly on campaigns in which money was distributed openly: as one of his campaigners cheerfully announced: '[t]here is nothing to hide, we are going to pour an amount of money you have never seen here before to ensure that President Moi is voted in again'.[52] Opposition candidates repeatedly faced arrest or violent harassment (Throup 1993). An overtly ethnic appeal to voters alongside the organization and endorsement of violence led to 'ethnic clashes' in the Rift Valley (including Narok North) in the early 1990s and 1997, and at the coast in 1997 (Klopp 2001; Kamungi 2009; Boone 2011). In these attacks, many Kikuyu, Luo, Luhya and Kisii – who were seen as likely to vote against KANU – were cast as 'outsiders' and driven out in a savage campaign of house-burnings and murders, while local administrators actively encouraged the idea that opposition supporters should be expelled (Rutten 2001; Oucho 2002; Jenkins 2012).[53]

In advance of the 1997 elections there was international pressure on Moi's government to rein in an open campaign of violence and intimidation against the opposition, and a brave stand by politicians, clergy and the press pushed the idea that the regime's intransigence risked undermining the stability of the state itself: '[a]nyone looking at Kenya from the outside world would be excused for imagining we were in a state of war ... the country cannot sustain this state of affairs for too long'.[54] A limited deal was struck, leading to elections that were a little less violent, and where manipulation of the vote was less flagrant and direct, though still evident in multiple ways (Barkan and Ng'ethe 1998; Grignon, Mazrui and Rutten 2001; Muhula 2019).

Moi's success was facilitated by opposition disunity, itself encouraged by the government and driven by ethnic clientelism (Barkan 1993: 97; also Kanyinga 1998; Grignon, Rutten and Mazrui 2001: 15). In advance of the 1992 elections, FORD had split into FORD-Kenya, led by Odinga,

---

[52] 'We'll spend millions to win – Kanu group', *Daily Nation*, 17 November 1992.
[53] 'DO warns opposition supporters', *Daily Nation*, 23 December 1992.
[54] Editorial, 'Government must defuse this ticking time bomb', *Daily Nation*, 8 July 1997, 6.

Table 2.7 Turnout and votes for main presidential candidates in case study areas: Kenya

		Kisumu Rural/Seme	%	Narok N.	%	Kikuyu	%	National	%
1992	**Reg.**	35,428		49,406		62,106		7,956,354	
	Turnout	26,503	75	33,212	67	53,091	85	5,396,797	68
	O. Odinga (FORD-K)	24,706	93	403	1	3,392	5	944,753	18
	Moi (KANU)	1,660	6	24,055	72	869	1	1,973,337	37
	Matiba (FORD-A)	106	0	2,142	6	46,277	75	1,412,320	26
	Kibaki (DP)	15	0	6,453	19	2,488	4	1,048,932	19
1997	**Reg.**	35,436		46,555		68,558		9,063,390	
	Turnout	25,340	72	33,309	72	51,054	74	6,182,704	68
	R. Odinga (NDP)	18,986	75	450	1	704	1	667,825	11
	Moi (KANU)	4,606	18	26,775	80	2,887	6	2,500,320	40
	Ngilu (SDP)	1,116	4	247	1	5,779	11	487,538	8
	Kibaki (DP)			5,096	15	39,575	78	1,905,640	31
2002	**Reg.**	41,850		54,211		75,436		10,451,150	
	Turnout	23,123	55	39,382	73	48,102	64	5,863,472	56
	Kibaki (NARC)	22,054	95	22,515	57	23,800	49	3,647,658	62
	Kenyatta (KANU)	629	3	15,528	39	23,550	49	1,836,055	31
2007	**Reg.**	52,937		81,548		106,688		14,296,180	
	Turnout	44,735	85	66,963	82	87,257	82	9,870,201	69
	Kibaki (PNU)	406	1	21,435	26	83,182	95	4,578,034	46
	Musyoka (ODM-K)	27	0	642	1	453	1	879,899	9
	R. Odinga (ODM)	44,129	99	44,413	66	2,969	3	4,352,860	44
2013	**Reg.**	35,735		59,567		65,041		14,388,781	
	Turnout	33,153	84	54,467	91	58,701	90	12,221,053	85

Table 2.7 (cont.)

	Kisumu Rural/Seme	%	Narok N.	%	Kikuyu	%	National	%
	Kenyatta (TNA)	60	0	18,080	33	53,904	92	6,173,433	51

		Kisumu Rural/Seme	%	Narok N.	%	Kikuyu	%	National	%
	Kenyatta (TNA)	60	0	18,080	33	53,904	92	6,173,433	51
	R. Odinga (ODM)	32,754	99	34,991	64	3,350	6	5,340,546	44
	Reg.	53,555		78,402		91,157		19,611,423	
2017 (Aug.)	Turnout	44,777	84	65,320	83	77,157	85	15,593,050	80
	Kenyatta (Jubilee)	170	0	25,707	39	72,578	80	8,223,369	53
	R. Odinga (ODM)	44,440	99	39,222	60	4,046	5	6,822,812	44

Source: Compiled by the authors from IEBC reports and from the Kenya Election Database, www.facebook.com/Kenyaelectiondatabase/.

and FORD-Asili, led by Matiba, while Mwai Kibaki, a former KANU stalwart who had been turned out of office by Moi, founded the Democratic Party (DP). On Oginga Odinga's death in 1994, his son Raila sought the FORD-Kenya leadership, lost, and formed the new National Development Party (NDP) that – despite its title – became a vehicle for a distinctively Luo political mobilization (Oloo 2007: 100–101). Others too formed new parties, or split from existing ones. This frenzied formation of new political vehicles was driven, at least in part, by egotism and personal rivalry, but it drew its logic from voters' concerns with accountability: if an elected leader's task was to secure benefits for, and to promote the interests of, those represented, then ethnicity could provide the basis for moral claims on those leaders (Kanyinga 1994; Cowen and Kanyinga 2002; Lynch 2011a). In this way, successive elections reinforced a winner-takes-all political dynamic that in turn encouraged a particularly exclusive and pernicious form of patrimonial politics (Mueller 2008). As we show in Chapter 6, this dynamic has become uneasily interwoven with a more explicitly 'civic' debate, in which opposition candidates tend to present themselves as being for democracy and constitutionalism and establishment candidates as being for development and stability (Lynch 2014; Lockwood 2019a).

In local electoral contests (see Table 2.6), calculations about the ability of candidates to assist constituents and to protect and promote their interests could be linked, at least in part, to party membership or to which presidential candidate they were aligned. In 1992 and 1997, the parliamentary and presidential votes in Kisumu Rural were won by the Odinga family and the candidate of whichever party they supported. In Narok North, local big man Ntimama retained the parliamentary seat, and Moi won the presidential polls. Yet there were exceptions: in Kikuyu in the same years, the presidential vote was repeatedly won by the leading Kikuyu candidate, but the parliamentary seat by Paul Muite – who first stood for Odinga's FORD-Kenya and then for his own party, Safina. This was possible because of the courage of Muite's opposition to Moi, which was seen as standing up for his community; he combined that reputation for heroism with skill at securing donor funds for local development projects.[55]

Moi's remarkable run of electoral manipulation ended in 2002. Unable to stand again – having decided to respect presidential term limits – he anointed Jomo Kenyatta's son, Uhuru Kenyatta, as the KANU candidate for the presidency. In doing so, he succeeded in offending Raila Odinga, whom he had tempted into joining an alliance with KANU, and almost

---

[55] Interview KEN1a, former MP, Nairobi, 23 September 2016; Interview KEN3a, former activist, Kikuyu, 23 September 2016.

every other senior KANU politician. The consequence was the creation of a new opposition alliance, the National Rainbow Coalition (NARC), which brought most of Kenya's major politicians – each associated with their own, often new, political party – behind the successful presidential campaign of Mwai Kibaki (Anderson 2003). These national politics took unpredictable local form: in Narok North, Ntimama expeditiously hopped from KANU to NARC to win the seat again; Kibaki took the presidential vote. In Kikuyu, the determinedly independent Paul Muite was re-elected on the minor Safina party ticket; the presidential vote was almost evenly split between Kibaki and Uhuru Kenyatta, whose ties to the locality were much stronger than to other Kikuyu areas where Kibaki emerged predominant (Kariuki 2005). Seme voted overwhelmingly for Kibaki, and for Prof. Peter Anyang' Nyong'o – a well-known intellectual and pro-reform campaigner, and sometime supporter of Oginga Odinga and former critic of Raila Odinga, who had by then returned to Raila Odinga's camp and enjoyed a direct nomination by NARC (Oloo 2005: 186) (see Tables 2.6 and 2.7).

The NARC campaign was premised on promises of constitutional reform that would reduce the power of the presidency and widen access to government resources. The coalition held long enough to secure victory for Kibaki, but then fractured over the terms of constitutional reform (Njogu 2005; Murunga and Nasong'o 2006). Proposals for limited change, supported by Kibaki, were rejected in a referendum in 2005. Raila Odinga, a proponent of more radical change and a substantial devolution of power, led the 'no' campaign, whose symbol was an orange – and yet another new party was born, the Orange Democratic Movement (ODM) (Cottrell and Ghai 2007). This episode confirmed in the mind of many Kenyans the fundamental truth that only those who hold the presidency truly benefit from power.

The 2005 referendum established a pattern that was to endure through three subsequent electoral cycles, in each of which Odinga presented himself – with some success – as the champion of widespread resentment against the perceived economic and political dominance of central Kenya, as well as being more specifically an embodiment of Luo political aspirations. In these contests, Odinga stood against two successive candidates from central Kenya: first Kibaki himself, and then – when term limits made it impossible for Kibaki to stand again – Uhuru Kenyatta. Each of those candidates has insisted that, despite appearances to the contrary, they are national politicians. Not only has their rhetoric consciously foregrounded that claim, but their political practice has also focussed on building alliances with big men – and the occasional big woman – from around the country. The most prominent beneficiary of that politics has been William Ruto, who has sought to take on Moi's mantle as the singular leader of Kalenjin communities since the former president officially retired in 2002. Briefly allied with Odinga in 2007, Ruto was in a close but unstable partnership with Kenyatta for the 2013 and 2017 elections, which was more or less explicitly cast as a Kalenjin–Kikuyu alliance (Lynch 2014).

Parties have continued to be ephemeral in this politics of elite alliance building, despite attempts to create a legislative framework that requires party organization. Kibaki created a new party for the 2007 elections, the Party of National Unity (PNU); by 2013 this had faded, and Kenyatta ran as the candidate of The National Alliance (TNA), part of the broader Jubilee Alliance, which by 2017 had turned into the Jubilee Party. Even Odinga's ODM, which at the time of writing has endured three elections, has been organizationally insubstantial and incapable of disciplining its nominal members. Thus, while Kenya's larger parties are multi-ethnic – a necessity given the country's socio-economic make-up, and the fact that no one ethnic group is large enough to win power on its own – they have rarely provided an effective basis for the emergence of an inclusive politics.

Odinga was the declared loser in each of the hotly disputed elections held since 2005, two of which resulted in considerable political instability. The contest of 2007 dissolved into a period of prolonged violence that was triggered by accusations of last-minute rigging (Kenya 2008; Kanyinga, Long and Ndii 2010), some of which drew on powerful ethno-regional narratives of chronic injustice (Mueller 2008; Kanyinga, Okello and Akech 2010; Oucho 2010; Lynch 2011a). The crisis was ended only by an internationally brokered deal, which brought Odinga into government in the new post of prime minister. Major constitutional reform followed, intended to diminish executive power and devolve much budgetary control to elected county governments. That reform has lent new energy to local clientelist politics without decisively reducing the power of the presidency (Cornell and D'Arcy 2014; Cheeseman, Kanyinga, Lynch, Ruteere and Willis 2019). In both 2013 and 2017, Odinga went to the newly created Supreme Court to challenge the results of presidential elections where he was again declared the loser amidst significant procedural problems. In 2013, his case was dismissed (Harrington and Manji 2015), but in 2017 the court made judicial history by becoming the first judicial body in Africa to annul a presidential election (Kanyinga and Odote 2019).

Odinga withdrew from the 'fresh' poll ordered by the court in 2017, arguing that insufficient reforms had been put in place to stop it being rigged again. Kenyatta consequently won that presidential poll in a walkover, amidst opposition protests. Months of tension followed, before the crisis was abruptly resolved by a public reconciliation. Significantly, this reconciliation occurred between individuals rather than parties, further entrenching the personalization of power. 'The handshake', as it was called, offered Odinga and his closest allies an informal, negotiated access to government and called Kenyatta's alliance with Ruto into question in advance of the 2022 elections – setting off a frenzied new round of alliance building (Cheeseman, Kanyinga, Lynch, Ruteere and Willis 2019).

Weak though parties are in organizational terms, they matter. Parliamentary seats have, very largely, been won by the parties led by these national figures. Symptomatically, Muite's lengthy career as MP for Kikuyu ended in 2007, when voters chose his long-standing rival, the son of a former MP, who had secured the nomination for Kibaki's PNU. The party ticket is a claim to a connection, a demonstration of a link to national power. So those who seek election to parliament, and are influential enough to be elected, gravitate to these parties, for voters look for candidates who seem likely to be able to reward their constituents, collectively and individually. A reputation for generosity and accessibility is thus key – though voters also want candidates who will stand up for them, over land or other issues. To campaign is to donate – to church fundraisings, local schools, funeral collections or 'self-help' groups – and to draw attention to one's achievements and the shortcomings of one's main rivals. In the areas where support for Odinga or Kenyatta is at its strongest – in Kikuyu or Seme – standing on the ticket of their party has become almost a guarantee of success. In consequence, party primaries in those areas have become very vigorously contested. Since party organization is weak – with no reliable record of membership – the result has been chaotic processes, with open rigging not uncommon. Yet defeated aspirants may still stand in the elections – in 2007 and 2013 they stood for minor parties, in 2017 as independents. Where they can persuade voters that – party affiliation aside – they are more reliable patrons, they may yet win, as happened in another of the Kisumu constituencies, Kisumu East, in 2017.

This local politics of claims-making, in which virtue is displayed through generosity and courage, is entirely entangled with the national politics of alliance building. The logical conclusion of the evolution of this kind of politics over the last eighty years is that elections are characterized by complex cross-ethnic alliances and candidates promising to serve in the interests of all at the same time. More recently, the winner-takes-all logic of the first-past-the-post system has been to some extent mediated by a tendency to elite pacting, in which elections (and their disputed results) serve as negotiating tools in an apparently permanent process of pre- and post-poll dealmaking (Cheeseman, Kanyingi, Lynch, Ruteere and Willis 2019). Moreover, while more money has been spent on trying to get elections right in Kenya than in either Ghana or Uganda – and it is the only country in our sample where a problematic election result has been overturned – voters remain cynical about the feasibility of realizing civic ideals in an electoral context.

2.4   Comparative Histories

Our three case studies might readily appear to tell very different stories: Ghana as the democratic success; Uganda as cautionary tale of the limits of elections; Kenya perhaps somewhere in between. But while differences are important – and we seek to understand their significance in subsequent chapters – the similarities between, and within, the three countries are also striking. We conclude this historical survey by pointing to some of those commonalities.

Most evident is one fundamental dynamic, shared by all: the persistent assumption that government controls the resources for 'development', and that electoral politics is primarily about securing access to those resources.[56] Asked what voters want, one candidate told us simply 'they want development'.[57] Each country also sees the same chronic tension between elections as manifestations of civic order, and as sites for an intense local politics of clientelism and redistribution. That central tension has worked out in different ways in each case. As we suggest in subsequent chapters, those differences are the consequence partly of historical legacies and institutions, partly of specific circumstances or external interventions, partly of contingent decisions by key actors at particular moments; there are multiple levels of agency in play alongside that structuring tension.

Related to that tension is a second similarity: electoral contests at a constituency level in each country have largely continued to turn on the assumption that the task of elected representatives is to bring 'development' in a material sense and to defend local interests. Elections bring a local politics of ambition, claims-making and the pursuit of status together with the pursuit of national power, with consequences that are not always predictable nor readily controllable by any actor. Voters' decisions are driven by calculations about both the capacity and the trustworthiness of candidates. Candidates seek the status of recognition as virtuous leaders, but those ambitions are not readily separable from the awareness that politics offers a possible route to personal wealth in

[56] Interview UGA77a, NRM activist, Gulu, 22 September 2015.
[57] Interview GHA29a, NDC candidate, location withheld, 29 August 2016.

circumstances where entrepreneurship of all kinds is laden with risks and uncertainties. As one Kenyan businessman turned politician explained:

I am in business from 1993 and our business have been reducing because I must know somebody, I must have some political influence for me to get business. So this has made everybody to be attracted to politics.[58]

John Dunn's observation (1980: 123) that 'becoming an MP in Ghana represents dramatic upward social mobility for all except the vastly rich' is as true now as it was in 1969, and is equally applicable to Kenya and Uganda. Popular awareness of that has driven up the costs of candidacy in all three countries: 'the voters now are beginning to focus more on what is there for them . . . people say "you are going to get so much money" now, so things have changed'.[59] It has also fuelled greater scepticism about politicians and their motivations, which ensures that politicians need to invest even more time and energy in persuading people that they really will promote their interests (Chapter 6).

A third similarity is the emergence of duopolies. By 1996, all three countries had moved away from purely parliamentary systems to hybrids, with direct presidential elections; by 2016, these had all come to be two-horse races. The corollary of that is that most voters will cast their presidential vote for someone who is not from their ethnic group or their home region, but who seems most likely to promote their interests and be capable of winning. As a result, electoral politics require constant negotiation and personal dealmaking across ethnic and local lines, linking national and local politics (Chapter 6).

Perhaps the most striking lesson of these comparative histories is that electoral involvement has been so extensive, and that popular as well as state investment in elections remains so substantial. Our survey results showed that in each case study area an emphatic 80 per cent or more of respondents opposed the suggestion that elections be abolished – with the singular exception of Ho, where this figure dropped to 72 per cent. This similarity is evident not only between countries but also within them. Among Maasai, where precolonial authority diffused power among older men, adult suffrage seems as rooted as it is in monarchical Buganda, where direct elections had been seen by some in the 1950s as a dangerous challenge to the *kabaka* (Low 1962: 42), or in Cape Coast, where, from the nineteenth century, notions of authority increasingly idealized education (Arhin 1983).

---

[58] Interview KEN86a, ODM activist, Kisumu, 13 July 2017.
[59] Interview UGA38a, former MP, Kampala, 9 September 2015.

Table 2.8 shows the national electoral participation rate, measured not as nominal turnout (given the chronic unreliability of registers) but in terms of number of ballots reportedly cast as a percentage of voting age population. In countries where absolute populations have risen sharply, the figures are striking. Since 1996, Ghana's two-party system has seen very high levels of participation, with striking swings in certain years: incumbents lose when participation falls. In Uganda, the sorry record of state-sponsored violence and malpractice has reduced participation from a peak in the 1990s, but more than half of potential voters still cast ballots. In Kenya, participation dipped in 2002 but has steadily increased since.

These levels of participation may explain what could be seen as the success of elections in all three countries since 1990. It may be hard to think of multi-partyism as stable in either Kenya or Uganda, given the extent of violence and malpractice in each, and as we have shown levels of political freedom in our case studies differ substantially. But the electoral system has been remarkably robust – and so has the state itself. In 2017, angry opposition supporters in Kenya and Uganda denounced repeated electoral malpractice and talked of secession – for northern Uganda, for

Table 2.8 *Election participation: voter turnout as a percentage of estimated voting age population*

Ghana		Kenya		Uganda	
Year	Participation (%)	Year	Participation (%)	Year	Participation (%)
1969	42		34		
1979	36	1979	56	1980	72
1992	52	1992	47	1994	74
1996	85	1997	45	1996	66
2000	67	2002	37	2001	70
2004	80			2006	56
2008	73	2007	53		
2012	80	2013	55	2011	54
2016	70	2017	61	2016	56

Source: Compiled by authors from newspapers, EC reports and Nohlen, *Elections in Africa*; voting population estimated by calculation from www.populationpyramid.net. Kenya (1969, 1979), Ghana (1969) and Uganda (1980) figures are for parliamentary elections; Uganda (1994) for Constituent Assembly elections. Note that 1980 Uganda figures were depressed by uncontested seats. All others are for presidential elections; for Ghana in 2000 and 2008 these are first-round figures; for Kenya in 2017 they are for the annulled August election.

the Kenya coast.[60] But that rhetoric faded swiftly. Elections have become naturalized; and so too – for now, at least – has the state-as-nation.

Subsequent chapters ask why investment in elections has been so strong, and what the consequences of this have been. Our aim is not to explain why certain candidates won or lost. Instead, our intention is to explore what the trajectory of our cases tells us in terms of how people have understood what it means to be, and how they seek to present themselves as, a good citizen, leader or public servant. We do this by looking at some of the different groups and individuals that have sought to shape the moral economy of elections over the past sixty years.

[60] https://twitter.com/Parliament_UG/status/943102515444375553, viewed 6 May 2019; www.nation.co.ke/news/Hassan-Joho-Amason-Kingi-call-for-breakaway-of-Coast-from-Kenya/1056-4172150-2rxmh2z/index.html, viewed 6 May 2019.

Part I

Promoting Civic Virtue

3 National Exercises
Making States and Citizens through the Ballot

In the compound of the Government Training Institute, in front of a long, low block of offices and classrooms, several rows of plastic chairs have been set out on the uneven ground in the shade of some large trees. They are occupied by around seventy men and women, mostly young. They talk quietly among themselves, or look at their smartphones, occasionally drinking from plastic water bottles. Facing them sit three men, poring over a handwritten list in an exercise book, ticking off names as they go. The atmosphere is relaxed, but the oldest of the three list-checkers is evidently becoming annoyed. A week before Ghana's 2016 elections, this is one of several training sessions that he is running in his role as the constituency returning officer. Hired as temporary polling staff for the elections, the attendees need training; on the day of the polls, they will take responsibility for a polling station kit with multiple items of equipment, from mobile polling booths to indelible ink, and will be expected to follow a detailed set of written guidelines to open, close and manage the polls; to conduct the counting of ballots; and to record and transmit the results. Some will be handling the electronic devices that identify voters using biometric data, which are being used for only the second time in a national election. But not everyone has turned up – around a third of those on the list are missing. Some of those who are present are not on the list. Perhaps some, who have previous experience, see no need for training – especially as they will not be paid extra for this; perhaps some will attend other training sessions; perhaps the handwritten list and online recruitment systems differ. The returning officer – a teacher by profession, but with many years' experience as a temporary election official – vents his anger. He reminds the group of the importance of their work; of Ghana's reputation for well-managed elections; of the consequences – for them, and the nation – if they make mistakes. Then he sighs, closes his book, and the training begins.[1]

The officials who run elections are one of a number of different groups involved in promoting a distinctive kind of moral project that are

[1] Field notes, Ho, 28 November 2016.

discussed in this and the next two chapters. All share a language of neutral technology and impartial administration, all are intimately bound up with a very specific set of moral assumptions about the relationship of state and citizen. Election officials, civil society groups and election observers are all committed – officially if not always in practice – to upholding the civic register of virtue. Their role is, explicitly, to prevent partiality and particularism. However, as we shall show in this and the subsequent chapters, promoting the civic register is much more easily said than done.

Over half a century before we set foot in the Government Training Institute described earlier, the 'army' of election staff for Ghana's first national elections in 1951 was only 2,000 people strong (Lawson 1951; Russell 1951). But, even then, 'operation elections' was seen as a military exercise, combining the resources of every part of government; '[t]he opposing forces were ignorance and illiteracy, poor communications, shortage of staff, and above all lack of time' (Russell 1951: 332). The 'orderly' completion of the exercise was the object of much mutual congratulation among administrators and politicians, both British and Ghanaian (Willis, Lynch and Cheeseman 2018). There were 663,000 voters registered for those elections. By 2016, when Ghana held the seventh elections of the fourth republic, the registered electorate had reached 15,712,499, and 148,000 staff were involved. A core of full-time employees of the Electoral Commission (EC) was supplemented by a large number of women and men hired temporarily for the polls, among whom were the little group described earlier. There were almost 30,000 polling stations in Ghana in 2016; each one was issued with 97 separate items of equipment for the polls, including a biometric verification device to identify voters.

The ease with which we can provide these numbers is revealing. Ghana's 1951 statistics were assiduously publicized in accounts of this great 'experiment'; those for 2016 were broadcast by the EC just before the polls in a message intended to disprove persistent allegations of bias and to present the elections as a collective, national, endeavour: '[l]et us all do the very best for our country.'[2] The speeches and documents of those who organize elections have always been full of numbers, in Kenya and Uganda as in Ghana.[3] These figures define and proclaim adult suffrage as a triumph of

---

[2] Available at https://s3-us-west-2.amazonaws.com/ecgovgh-public/downloads/press_re lease/FINAL+PRE-ELECTION+BROADCAST.docx.pdf; for similar publicity on logistics in earlier years, see 'Voting materials to be air-freighted to the north', *People's Daily Graphic*, 29 October 1992, p. 1; 'Day of decision', *Daily Graphic*, 7 December 1996, p. 1.

[3] See, for example, Governor, Gold Coast to Secretary of State, 15 February 1951, UKNA CO 96/823/1; Editorial, 'The decision we take', *Daily Graphic*, 11 May 1979, p. 2; 'Order at the polls', *Daily Graphic*, 19 June 1979, p. 1; Editorial, 'Good faith', *People's Daily Graphic*, 4 November 1992, p. 2; 'EC despatches 40,000 ballot boxes to regions', *Daily Graphic*, 4 October 1996, p. 1.

civic virtue; but more than that they remind us that numbers are, as Theodore Porter (2006) put it, the 'quintessential form of information' – they flatten and simplify knowledge. To present staff, polling stations and equipment as numbers is to claim that all are identical, exchangeable elements that combine in a process defined by written regulation; elections are deeply involved with the ability of numbers to produce a distinctive governmentality (Rose 1991).

Kimberley Coles (2004) has presented elections as laboratories: that is, as processes that are meant to produce facts and knowledge that appear as truths. The tens of thousands of individuals become staff, impartially dedicated to the process; the population as a whole become voters, the obedient collective subject of the process; the disparate spaces pressed into service as locations for the casting of votes become polling stations. Coles's argument focusses on the idea that *techne* – the combination of artefacts, people and processes – produce democracy as a non-political phenomenon, something known and beyond question. But these processes also seek to make people's sense of self: to encourage the idea that virtue lies in following rules and regulations. Since the 1950s, those who serve – temporarily or full-time – as election officials have referred to elections as 'exercises', or even 'National exercises', emphasizing their production of an order that identifies the nation with the bureaucratic state.[4] The celebration of number and order has routinely been combined with exhortations to the public – from election officials, incumbent national politicians and newspapers – to act with 'maturity'.[5] These exhortations make multiple claims to civic virtue; officials and politicians claim authority by demanding that people understand voting as a 'sacred civic duty'[6] – as an advertisement from the Electoral Commission of Kenya (ECK) put it, 'You should vote if you love your country.'[7]

This chapter offers a summary of the development of electoral processes across Ghana, Kenya and Uganda since the 1950s. The first two sections focus on two aspects of this. The first is a steady elaboration of *techne*: things, people and processes have – in theory at least – come to be combined in increasingly complex ways in each country, with the recent move to digital and biometric technologies epitomizing this trend. The

---

[4] Governor to Ag Permanent Secretary Education, 26 June 1954, PRAAD RG 3/5/336; DC Kilifi to all heads of department, 15 July 1967, KNA CB 1/10; also PC Coast to all DCs, 4 April 1974, KNA CQ 11/2DC Taita to Director of National Parks, 10 September 1974, KNA CA 7/35.

[5] 'Minister Moi's congratulations', Nairobi Domestic Service, 15 October 1974, FBIS SSA-74–139; 'Dr Busia's address to nation about his overseas visit', Accra, English, 4 November 1969, SWB ME/3223/B/1.

[6] Editorial, 'Your day to choose', *Daily Monitor*, 23 February 2006, p. 1.

[7] Advert, *Daily Nation*, 10 December 1992.

second is the self-conscious professionalization of election management, through the establishment of what are called 'independent' or 'autonomous' institutions to manage elections (Mozaffar 2002; also Pastor 1999). This has been a global trend, but 'nowhere has the implementation of [independent] electoral commissions been so widespread' as in sub-Saharan Africa (Gazibo 2019: 175). Supposed autonomy may involve no more than inserting 'independent' in the title of electoral management bodies (EMBs). More meaningfully, it requires restricting the power of incumbent governments to appoint and fire those who run such bodies and – perhaps more important still – endowing EMBs with 'permanent bureaucracies' of their own (Jinadu 1997: 7). This in itself is a striking implicit acknowledgement that the state's wider claim to autonomy from society has been compromised (not just in Africa, it might be noted), so that electoral bodies must distinguish themselves as 'islands of integrity' (Mozaffar and Schedler 2002: 15). The convergence of *techne* and professionalization has been presented as a way to ensure impartiality, the touchstone of civic virtue.

Yet despite the recitation of number, the claims of bureaucratic success and the appeal to virtuous national citizenship, the 'voting machine' has not, in fact, entirely succeeded in instilling civic virtue: making people think of themselves solely as national citizens or turning officials into impartial bureaucrats without other links to society (Willis, Lynch and Cheeseman 2016). Instead, the third section will argue that claims to impartiality have been constantly undermined and questioned, so that elections may actually undermine the production of power through numbers. Civic virtue is never truly impartial, of course: rules and electoral procedures, even properly followed, routinely serve to authorize exclusion and inequalities of wealth and power. People who live mobile or unsettled lives, or who lack documents, are denied the right to vote; in a fundamental and persistent way, election procedures remind those with limited formal education that they are regarded as inferior to those who have been to school. Yet more than that, elections have repeatedly revealed that the state is fractured. Individuals and factions pursue personal and collective interests, seeking to gain or keep elected office – or simply to enrich themselves through the electoral process itself. As a result, politicians and officials break the nominal rules. For those involved, rule-breaking may make perfect moral sense: it may be deemed necessary or legitimate as a means to maintain order and protect group interest, or as an acknowledgement of one's obligations to friends or patrons. Putting particular interest above the creation of stateness may seem a virtuous decision, in some circumstances. As a result, elections have produced stateness, but in ways that remain contingent and contested.

That uncertainty is all the more evident because there is, as the fourth section outlines, another challenge from the public. People can and do seize elections as an opportunity to make demands. On the one hand, many accept the requirements that voting entails: being listed, named and numbered; queuing to cast their ballot. On the other hand, some also subvert the logic of the process by taking elections as an opportunity to assert other kinds of belonging or – in the face of widespread mistrust – to justify rule-breaking.

As a result, the institutionalization and expansion of EMBs since the 1990s have not in themselves ensured popular confidence in the electoral process – even in Ghana, where the EC has been held up as an exemplar of success (Debrah 2011). The claims to impartiality of Uganda's EC have been intermittently undermined – apparently intentionally – by the incumbent regime. In 2017, the reputation and morale of Kenya's EMB, the IEBC, was dealt a shattering blow when the Supreme Court nullified the presidential election, a setback followed by a grisly run of corruption scandals. In all three countries, the impartiality of 'operation elections' has constantly been questioned, even though the scale, complexity and technical armoury of the process have grown. Elections, as Mackenzie observed many years ago, are 'a sort of confidence trick'; however elaborate the processes to display impartiality may be, 'if we (or any substantial proportion of us) really doubted and began to run a whispering campaign of doubt, the electoral system could not stand the strain' (1954: 69). That confidence trick – which is, in effect, the apparent dominance of civic virtue – has never been entirely successful in the countries that we study; yet neither has it entirely failed in any of them.

3.1   Making Voters: Order and Electoral Process

In the 1950s, colonial debates about electoral organization focussed on the feasibility of adult suffrage: how would it be possible to get large numbers of voters who were illiterate and generally unfamiliar with bureaucratic process to involve themselves in a process that centred on bureaucracy (Mackenzie 1960: 466)? But a larger question overshadowed that: how could the whole voting process be kept under control? Order – as it was constantly described – was the primary concern of late-colonial election administrators and has been a persistent obsession of their successors.[8] Depictions of calmly queuing voters and helpful officials

---

[8] For example: 'We will not discriminate against any political party', *Daily Graphic*, 4 May 1979, p. 16; 'How election system works', *The Standard*, 3 February 1988, supplement.

are still staples of voter education posters (Willis, Lynch and Cheeseman 2016), and order itself is an electoral goal: as Uganda's EC put it in 2016, in a striking tautology: 'An Orderly Officer was stationed at each polling centre to ensure orderliness.'[9] Alongside the production of order, election officials have also faced the challenge of persuading voters that their choices are being accurately recorded and counted – and that they are being weighed equally with the choices of others. That is the promise of electoral citizenship, and voters have suspected – often with good reason – that it was not being kept. The consequent elaboration of processes of registration, polling, counting and tallying has been driven by the imperative to combine impartiality with what Ghana's government-owned newspaper in 1979 called 'order, stability and discipline'.[10] These two imperatives have driven the increasing elaboration of electoral *techne* across all three countries, as governments (and, sometimes, international agencies) seek to produce electoral order: this section describes that process.

In the face of concerns that illiterate voters would be able to neither read nor mark ballot papers, early experiments with the secret ballot involved a 'whispering vote' (where voters 'whispered' the name of their chosen candidate to the presiding officer, who marked the ballot paper for them). The alternative to that was the use of voting tokens and multiple boxes; each candidate was allotted a symbol, a ballot box was marked with that symbol, and voters put their ballot papers – all identical – into the box of the individual they preferred. Stories of intimidation, vote stealing and vote stuffing were rife in multi-box elections (in Ghana pre-1969, Kenya in 1969 and Uganda up to 1980).[11] If the ballot boxes were in open view, the polling officials (and others) could see the voter's choice. If they were hidden, voters and officials could – and allegedly did – take the opportunity to switch the symbols on the boxes, to insert multiple ballots, to remove ballots, or even to pour acid into the boxes (Ghana 1967: 28). As a result, over time, the single ballot box has become the norm, combined with the use of printed ballot papers that voters are expected to mark with thumbprint or pencil and with symbols to guide the illiterate.

Boasting of the move to the single ballot box in 1994, Uganda's President Museveni set out other changes, intended to make voting and counting more open to view:

---

[9] Electoral Commission, Report on the 2015/16 General Elections, p. xvi, www.ec.or.ug/docs/Report%20on%20the%202015-2016%20General%20Elections.pdf.
[10] Editorial, 'Come to the aid of the Graphic', *Daily Graphic*, 2 January 1979, p. 2.
[11] A. K. Mayanja, Buganda Minister of Education to Governor, 9 February 1962, UKNA FCO 141/18333; British High Commissioner Accra to CRO, 29 January 1964, UKNA DO 195/251.

Where, for example, there used to be a number of ballot boxes, we have provided for one. Where casting a ballot would be done in a voting booth where all types of electoral mischiefs could be committed, we have provided that voting be done in full view of the people but far enough to ensure secrecy for the voter. Where ballot papers would be ferried to be counted at one central point, we have provided that the counting of votes must be done at the polling station and on the same day.[12]

Since the 1990s, popular suspicion has combined with international electoral expertise – and finance – to push further innovations. A voter education supplement in Ghana's press listed the measures to 'prevent cheating':

Transparent ballot boxes, photo-ID cards, applying the indelible ink to the nails of voters, party agents, domestic and international observers . . . These measures, though costly, enhance the legitimacy of the ballot box as the machinery for choosing leaders.[13]

The mention of photo-ID cards highlights a second area in which practices have become increasingly elaborate. As with the casting of the ballot, innovation around voter registration has been driven by the sheer difficulty of the task – creating an ordered and accurate listing of millions of names – as well as persistent allegations of cheating that defy the linkage between individual citizenship, equality and the vote. Since the late-colonial period there have been stories of politicians and officials adding names to the register or removing them from it; of voting by those not qualified to vote (minors or non-citizens); of multiple voting; or of 'personation' (the casting of a ballot in the name of another voter).[14] The approach adopted by late-colonial regimes provided a lasting model. In all three countries registration continues to require the physical presence of the voter, this localized, labour-intensive process being explicitly linked to good citizenship: in July 2007 the chair of Kenya's ECK 'congratulate [d] Kenyans who last week expressed their patriotism by registering as voters'.[15] The process has been spasmodic: a registration period was announced, registration teams were hired and trained, and temporary registration stations established – sometimes fixed in one place for two or

[12] Similar changes had been, or were shortly, introduced elsewhere: 'Votes to be counted on the spot', *Daily Graphic*, 18 June 1979, p. 9; 'Electoral commission denies report of diversion of ballot boxes', SWB, Accra, 4 July 1996, AL/2655/A/9; 'OAU observer team "satisfied" with elections', SWB, Accra, 9 December 1996, AL/2791/A/7.
[13] 'Electoral process: what do we know?', *Daily Graphic*, 10 November 2000, p. 17; 'Electoral commission denies report of diversion of ballot boxes', SWB, Accra, 4 July 1996, AL/2655/A/9; 'OAU observer team "satisfied" with elections', SWB, Accra, 9 December 1996, AL/2791/A/7.
[14] Extract from Minutes of the 5th Cabinet meeting, 27 March 1962, UKNA FCO 141/18335; 'NPP will improve economy – Kufuor', *Daily Graphic*, 1 November 2000, p. 12.
[15] 'Poll registration nets a million new voters', *Daily Nation*, 26 July 2007.

three weeks, sometimes mobile. The imperative to gather names has been strong in such 'drives', with the clear implication that registration staff are seeking to meet targets; deadlines have been routinely extended to try to increase numbers.[16] There are now continuous registration processes in all three countries, and in Uganda voter registration has since 2016 been combined with a new national identification system.[17] But in all three countries elections have continued to be preceded by 'updates' or 'registration drives', and the urge for a massive nationwide performance remains strong: so much so that at the end of 2019 Ghana's EC announced that there would be an entirely fresh registration process for all voters before the 2020 elections.[18]

As a process, voter registration – like the census (Serra 2018) and national identification schemes – has pushed the stabilization and individualization of personal identity. These were all – as one Kenyan district commissioner (DC) proudly put it in 1979 – 'massive national exercises', into which all the resources of the state were thrown.[19] Complications over the spelling of names, cultural naming patterns and plural religious affiliations might leave an individual with variant forms of several personal names. Voter registration abhorred such flexibility and demanded that a singular name be recorded and placed alphabetically on the register.[20] The Kenyan voter who wrote plaintively of his struggle to locate the details of his own (and his wife's) registration may not have been untypical:

The name of my wife might have been spelt as 'Paulinah' and my father's name 'Mwingisi' might have been placed in front of my surname 'Madahana'. I can't remember as the registration was about two years ago.[21]

Registration has been a process: an assembling and editing of information that produces a voter who is a particular, limited form of the person – a singular citizen.

The challenge of linking individuals to the names on the register led to repeated experiments with additional paper identification that voters were required to bring to the polling station, in the face of repeated allegations of

---

[16] For example, Okech, DC Kilifi to all DOs, 2 August 1967, KNA CB 1/10; more recently 'IEBC launches mass voter registration phase 2, targets six million', *The Star*, 15 January 2017; 'EC extends voters' register display to Jan. 17', *Daily Monitor*, 9 January 2006, p. 4; 'EC extends voter register update', *Daily Monitor*, 5 May 2015.

[17] Electoral Commission, Report on the 2015/16 General Elections, pp. xiv–xv, 28, www .ec.or.ug/docs/Report%20on%20the%202015–2016%20General%20Elections.pdf.

[18] 'Election 2020: new voters' register, new BVM system coming', *Daily Graphic*, 1 January 2020.

[19] Kiambu District Annual Report, 1979, p. 1, KNA MA 12/77.

[20] Wilkinson, 'Registration of electors', 1963, KNA DC LAMU 2/2/12.

[21] J. Madahana, Kenya Shell Thika to DC Kakamega, 20 November 1969, KNA DC KMG 2/16/11.

personation. Voters' cards of various kinds – carrying a registration number, as well as a name – were used in Kenya's late-colonial and early
postcolonial elections, but later abandoned, surviving in vestigial form as
an 'acknowledgement slip' of registration, which some voters laminated to
carry with them as an assertion of their claim to electoral citizenship. The
practice produced its own problems, however. There could be mistakes or
duplications in the issuing and recording of codes, as of names, as Kenya's
colonial supervisor of elections noted in 1963.[22] More significantly, the
card could in effect become the voter. The first forged voting cards were
apparently in circulation before the first elections.[23] There have subsequently been many stories of people being bribed or bullied into giving
their voters' cards to others who use them to vote or simply destroy them to
prevent the rightful holders from voting. Indeed, stories of instrumental
malpractice around registration and voters' cards have been almost as
common as those of ballot stealing and stuffing.[24]

Voters' cards were introduced in Ghana in 1996. To tie the name on the
register more effectively to the physical voter, some carried photographs of
the bearer (an idea first touted in 1969, but abandoned because of the
cost); by 2004 this was standard.[25] More recently, digital technology has
brought election *techne* even more closely into line in all three countries.
Since around 2010, EMBs – sometimes encouraged by donors and international election experts – have turned to digital biometry to fix the link
between name and person and make the voter's body the proof of their
eligibility to vote. Digitally recorded fingerprints and facial recognition
software now supplement the photograph; the name and other data
recorded on the register have become – at least, in theory – indisputably
linked to the body of the individual voter. A press statement by Uganda's
EC in 2016 made clear the claim that this new technology represented best
practice internationally:

Through research involving benchmarking with sister election management bodies across Africa and different parts of the world, we have come to the position that
the use of biometrics for verification and authentication at the polling station
represents the best solution in strengthening the integrity of voter identification.[26]

[22] Wilkinson, Supervisor of Elections to all PCs, 21 January 1963, KNA DC Lamu 2/2/12.
[23] DC Narok to DO Olokurto, 24 October 1956, KNA OP 1/536.
[24] Lewis, British High Commission Accra to Middleton, FCO, 24 July 1969, UKNA FCO
    65/83; Editorial, 'Clean elections please!', *Daily Graphic*, 2 June 1979, p. 2; Telegram,
    British High Commission Accra to British Embassy, Luanda, 22 October 1979, UKNA
    FCO 65/2182; 'Voters cheated on KANU cards', *The Standard*, 1 February 1988, p. 1.
[25] 'IFES fact sheet: supporting the electoral process in Ghana', nd 1995, copy in Library of
    Congress Africana collection.
[26] Press statement, 19 January 2016, at www.ec.or.ug/?q=news/1912016-biometric-voter-
    verification-system-bvvs.

Voters' experience at the polling station has changed as a result. In theory, at least, they are now identified by a machine, not by the staff: between 2012 and 2016, all three countries began to use devices that scan voters' fingerprints to link them to a name on the register. The first use of the technology was problematic in both Ghana (2012) and Kenya (2013) (Barkan 2013; Cheeseman, Lynch and Willis 2014: 13–14; Piccolino 2016: 509), but in the second set of elections to use these devices (in 2016 and 2017, respectively), most – though not all – voters were biometrically identified at the polling station (EU 2017: 28–29). The links between voter, name and register have become more fixed, less open to doubt at the moment of voting. Slowly, over an extended period, and with many problems along the way, electoral organization has helped to drive a process that seeks to link each individual not only to a fixed name, but also to a unique alphanumeric code and biometric record. The process is driven by a sort of compulsion to achieve absolute identifiability: at the end of 2019, Ghana's EC announced that, since the existing biometric technology had failed to identify 0.64 per cent of those who came to vote in 2016, it was investing in a wholly new system that would combine facial scanning and fingerprint recognition.[27] This production of the identifiable citizen comes at a heavy financial cost, but it teaches all election officials and the public to think of an 'ideal' civic identity, which is individual, fixed and ultimately reliant on recognition by a state that is impartial and rule bound.

3.2   Making Officials: Impartiality, Virtue and Professionalism

The white shirts of the seated clerks stand out in photographs of late-colonial polling stations in what was then the Gold Coast.[28] They are on iron chairs, and in front of them are tables laden with the tools of work that are also symbols of their momentary authority: the voters' register, the rubber stamp and inkpad, ink for marking the fingers of those who have voted, the ballot papers themselves. The visual impression of polling stations in 2016 was very similar – though white plastic chairs had largely replaced their iron predecessors, and staff now wore high-vis tabards branded with the name and logo of the EC, rather than the pressed shirts that once marked them out as educated. In the late 1950s and early 1960s, young men were much more likely to have the formal school

---

[27] 'Election 2020: new voters' register, new BVM system coming', *Daily Graphic*, 1 January 2020.

[28] 'Polling was quiet', *Daily Graphic*, 16 June 1954, p. 12.

education that qualified them for the role; by 2016, many of the polling staff in all three countries were women, though men still tended to predominate in more senior roles, especially in Kenya and Uganda. As this section shows, the number of such polling staff has grown steadily, and they have come to be surrounded by an architecture of training and process that seeks constantly to assert the primacy of civic virtue.

Education has consistently defined the hierarchy of the polling station, but there have been changes in the background of polling staff. From the 1950s to the 1980s, presiding officers were senior teachers or local government officials; their polling clerks were the clerical staff of central or local government, teachers and senior-school pupils. In late-colonial elections, the work of these temporary election officials was supervised by those all-purpose handymen-cum-enforcers of empire, the DCs – still largely Europeans. For the European administrators, these elections became the last great organizational project of their colonial careers; they threw all their energy, and the resources of government, into the processes of registration and balloting (Willis, Lynch and Cheeseman 2018). That established a precedent: elections were a moment for a 'maximum effort drive' by government as a whole, and those who ran them expected to be able to call upon and command the staff and equipment of every department.[29]

In Kenya, where regular elections were held from the late-colonial period, and until the establishment of an independent EMB in 1992, managing elections became a routine part of the work of the DC: resented to some extent for the burden it imposed, but also valued in multiple ways. Elections offered DCs the opportunity to repair the damaged vehicles that began to accumulate at district headquarters – for both registration and polls were accompanied by an additional 'authority to incur expenditure' with some (disputed) latitude on how to spend this.[30] They allowed the DC to remind local government – and the staff of health, education, public works and every other ministry – that they were in charge and could requisition the vehicles, typewriters and staff that they needed.[31] Most of all, they provided an opportunity for DCs to publicly discipline politicians and to refine the sense of amused contempt, which characterized their view of party politics. In congratulating his staff after voter registration in 1967, one DC pointedly observed that the ruling party had been irrelevant in the

---

[29] PS, office of the Chief Secretary to all Permanent Secretaries, 3 August 1960, KNA AHC 19/8; Circular, Colonial Secretary to all Heads of Department and Chief Commissioners, 21 August 1950; DC Accra to all Heads of Department, 14 November 1950, PRAAD RG 3/5/336.

[30] DC Tana River to PC Coast, 3 April 1974, KNA CA 7/34.

[31] DC Taita to all district heads of department, all chiefs and assistant chiefs, Clerk to Council, 13 April 1974; KNA CA 7/34.

process: 'This success was Administration success.'[32] In 1969 and 1974, DCs control was made very visible through the management of joint hustings for candidates.[33] Even thereafter, the position of the DC as registration officer, nomination officer and returning officer – as well as their effective control over the licensing of public meetings – meant that politicians were subject to their statutory authority at every turn.

DCs in Nkrumah's Ghana, by contrast, were much less sure of their position vis-à-vis CPP politicians; as one allegedly told a British visitor in 1961, his main role was to ensure that the people of his district voted for the party.[34] The 1969 and 1979 elections were managed by local government administrators. In Uganda, DCs would have been the organizers of the planned 1971 elections; and in 1980, together with the chiefs who were their subordinates, they took up the task of electoral administration with an enthusiasm that revealed their desire to re-establish a bureaucratic order in the wake of the Amin era (Willis, Lynch and Cheeseman 2016).[35] Into the 1990s, Uganda's local administrators played a central role in election management.

With elections effectively in the hands of the state's administrative apparatus, the electoral commissions that had existed up to 1990 were very small or temporary, or both. But in all three countries, the 1990s saw election management pass – formally, at least – out of the hands of district administrators and into the hands of independent EMBs. This transition was encouraged by donors and demanded by opposition activists, who insisted – with good evidence – that administrators were routinely biased in favour of incumbent governments.[36] In 1991 in Ghana, 1992 in Kenya and 1995 in Uganda, a new kind of electoral commission was created: permanent bodies intended to actually run elections and manage voter education.

The claims of these commissions to autonomy were fragile. Kenya's EMB – initially the ECK, now the IEBC – was chaired from 1992 by a former bankrupt, whose partiality to the governing party was widely assumed (Foeken and Dietz 2000: 130–131, 134). Under pressure from the opposition and donors, President Moi agreed to demands for the rhetorical assertion of the ECK's independence and for an expansion of the number of commissioners in 1997 to include opposition nominees (Barkan and Ng'ethe 1998: 220–221). This produced a dysfunctional

---

[32] DC Kilifi to all DOs, 6 September 1967, KNA CB 1/10.
[33] PC Coast to DC Kilifi, 7 March 1973, KNA CA 7/34.
[34] Keeble, Office of the High Commissioner, Accra to Chadwick, Commonwealth Relations Office, 9 February 1961, UKNA DO 195/10.
[35] Gulu archive file ADM 6 ADES IV R.84, Box 529.
[36] 'Ntimama attacks DCs', *Daily Nation*, 3 October 1997, p. 16.

body that presided over a messy and procedurally flawed process (Steeves 1999: 77).[37] By 2002, however, a new chair had reorganized the commissioners and set in train a process of institution-building that went well beyond the commissioners themselves and created a full-time, permanent staff. Circa 2005, the ECK's organogram showed a headquarters staff of eighty and – crucially – a nationwide network of district offices and officials (Electoral Commission of Kenya n.d.). Similar changes were apparent elsewhere: by 2008, Ghana's EC had more than 1,000 permanent staff posted around the country (Electoral Commission of Ghana 2010); Uganda's EC had 749 permanent staff by 2016.[38]

An Interim Electoral Commission (IEC) ran Uganda's 1996 elections. The IEC chair, Stephen Akabway, had told both his staff and the public that their behaviour was being watched by the world: 'We are on a test . . . let us not be counted among the failures.'[39] The IEC warned local-level officials not to campaign for Museveni 'in their official capacity' and suspended voter educators when it was discovered that they were campaigning for him.[40] Yet the elections were condemned by the opposition and criticized by observers.[41] In their wake, a workshop for all IEC staff and a seminar – supported by donors – made recommendations for future improvement. The 'evaluation workshop' combined lament and confession – from a lack of resources to the flagrant abuse of office by incumbents and the widespread bribing of voters. The implication was both that logistical problems were somehow beyond the IEC's control – '[t]he logistics plan though always well drawn was never followed due to the unreliability of the data on especially the voters and number of polling stations' – and that politicians had led officials to 'compromise their impartiality'.[42] At the seminar, other 'stakeholders' – from political parties and what had come routinely to be called 'civil society' (discussed in Chapter 4) – echoed these complaints. All agreed on the need for a cadre of professional election officials of 'integrity and impartiality', combined with a campaign of voter education on the 'duties and freedoms of citizens' as the way to ensure free elections; clearly there was a need for 'a permanent and independent Electoral Commission'.[43]

---

[37] Interview KEN29a, former electoral commissioner, Kisumu, 13 May 2017.
[38] Electoral Commission, Report on the 2015/16 General Elections, pp. 23–4, www.ec.or
.ug/docs/Report%20on%20the%202015–2016%20General%20Elections.pdf.
[39] '8 million to vote', *New Vision*, 8 May 1996, p. 3.
[40] 'LCs advised to stop campaigns', *New Vision*, 29 April 1996, p. 1.
[41] 'Losers accuse electoral body', *New Vision*, 16 May 1996, p. 3.
[42] 'Final report for the post-election self-evaluation implementation strategies workshop for the Commission staff and field officers', pp. 13, 25, IEC 1996, Gulu ADM 6 Box 529.
[43] 'Uganda elections 1996: report of the proceedings of a post-election evaluation seminar', Gulu archive ADM 6 Box 529.

The ideal of impartiality has been foregrounded in the rhetoric of the Ugandan EC that was subsequently created: 'The vision of the Electoral Commission', according to a 2006 press advertisement, 'is to promote peaceful continuity of governance through an impeccable electoral process'.[44] Internal communication within the EC has taken a brightly bureaucratic form: 'Teamwork breeds success; concerted effort by all stakeholders, civil society and Electoral Staff remains the benchmark for all successive [sic] Electoral programmes', read one report from Gulu, signing off – as EC officials routinely do – with the national motto, 'For God and My Country'.[45] Uganda's EC has repeatedly insisted on its commitment to enforce regulations: public advertisements name voters who have registered twice; local officers reprove candidates for their conduct, and call for police investigation of alleged irregularities, and carefully file opposition complaints of harassment and malpractice.[46] As will be noted later, however, this rhetorical insistence on impartiality and procedure exists alongside multiple practical violations of that procedure and occasionally flagrant acts of partiality.

Differences between countries have persisted: in 2016, returning officers in Ghana were temporary staff (mostly teachers by profession); in Kenya they were full-time staff of the electoral commission. There are other, more significant differences – on which, more later. But in formal institutional terms and in rhetoric, the trend has been similar: EMBs in all three countries have strategic plans and 'roadmaps' for each electoral cycle; they consult with 'stakeholders'; and they maintain a traditional and social media presence.[47] Where elections were once managed by state administrators without specialist training or experience, they have come increasingly to be seen as the task of self-conscious professionals, who may see this as a career, and who are constantly engaged in processes of training and education that are intended to develop their skills. In his foreword to the lengthy manual prepared for Kenya's election officials before the 2007 elections, Samuel Kivuitu – the then ECK chair – reminded staff that '[t]he conduct of elections depends upon the integrity, competency and knowledge levels of the election officials involved' and that their task was to

---

[44] *Daily Monitor*, 6 February 2006, p. xv.

[45] Quarterly report, Election Officer/District Registrar, Gulu to Secretary, EC, 2 March 2005, Gulu Archive CR 225/6, Box 627.

[46] *Daily Monitor*, 6 January 2006, p. 23; see also 'Kalangala LC5 chairman charged with election misconduct', *Daily Monitor*, 4 January 2006, p. 5; 'Electoral Commission order Brig. Otema probe', *Daily Monitor*, 6 February 2016; Reagan Okumu to Returning Officer, Gulu, 4 March 2001, Gulu Archive CR D 225/2 Box 627.

[47] 'Launch of 2021 General Elections Strategic Plan', www.ec.or.ug/?q=election/launch-2 0202021-general-elections-strategic-plan; 'IEBC Strategic Plan, 2015–20', www.iebc.o r.ke/uploads/resources/strategicplan20152020.pdf; www.facebook.com/ECGOVGH.

'serve Kenyans' (Electoral Commission of Kenya n.d.: v). Similarly, Uganda's EC extolled the organizational 'vision' of being 'a model institution and center of excellence in election management'.[48]

At election time that core of professional staff has continued to be massively swelled by temporary staff, for no country could possibly afford to maintain the vast personnel machine of elections on a full-time basis (Pastor 1999: 10). Civil servants have been steadily removed from these roles; in Uganda, the electoral use of parish chiefs (the lowest level of administration official) was finally ended after 2006.[49] That has increased the dominance of teachers. Indeed, by 2017, temporary election staff in all three countries were almost always schoolteachers or university students. The popularity of this work – staff have not been hard to recruit – has reflected an uncomfortable reality for many; regular employment was hard to come by, and graduates struggled to find any work that they felt suitable to their training and abilities. The pay for temporary election work has been modest, but better than nothing, and the work itself a very public affirmation of status, an opportunity to work in a responsible role with a sort of brief power over voters, many of whom were neighbours and acquaintances. Students have usually worked as clerks, with presiding officers and some more senior roles being taken up by full-time teachers or graduate students (elections are usually, necessarily, in school holidays, since the process relies so heavily on school buildings and staff). For teachers, even more than for students, this was a public demonstration of status, a reminder that 'the most enlightened group that stay in the rural place are teachers ... they are role models and they are also the pace setters and they give the agenda'.[50] Those who worked as polling staff were quick to locate their motives in terms of civic virtue, stressing duty and service to the nation: 'some of us, the level of patriotism in us is so high in such a way that any national exercise, we volunteer to do it. That is why most of the exercises, [it is] teachers who normally do it.'[51]

Even among temporary staff, many have built up significant experience, working in repeated elections.[52] Recruitment processes have developed and become more overtly formalized. In the 1960s and

[48] 'Vision', on the website of Uganda's Electoral Commission, www.ec.or.ug, viewed 25 September 2018.

[49] Electoral Commission, Report on the 2015/16 General Elections, p. 24, www.ec.or.ug/docs/Report%20on%20the%202015–2016%20General%20Elections.pdf.

[50] Interview KEN48a, politician, Kisumu, 17 June 2017.

[51] Interview GHA20a, former polling staff, Juaso, 26 August 2016; see also Interview KEN8a, former polling staff, Kikuyu, 25 February 2017; Interview GHA71a, polling staff, Ho, 28 November 2016.

[52] Interview GHA39a, EC official, Cape Coast, 1 September 2016.

1970s in Kenya, civil servants were simply ordered to do this work and there was much consequent argument over whether and how they might be rewarded. Nevertheless, teachers and others would write to the DC, asking to be considered.[53] The scope for patronage and abuse was evident – whether it involved punishing refractory junior civil servants by detailing them for electoral duty in remote polling stations or using election work to reward clients. For the staff of Kenya's ECK, struggling to assert control over electoral processes from the mid-1990s, prising recruitment out of the hands of the provincial administration and local politicians was a challenging but central task.[54] In Ghana in 1992, an outraged teacher complained that returning officers – themselves hired temporarily – were choosing 'girlfriends' as polling staff, even though 'this national assignment needs qualified personnel'.[55] Such abuses have often been allegedly linked to instrumental malpractice, with polling station staff being appointed on the understanding that they would commit or tolerate rigging.[56] A process of written application – which by 2016/2017 had largely moved online – was intended to prevent such abuses, though it was evidently still combined with an offline process where personal connections and favours remained significant.

Much more than their predecessors in the 1960s, early-twenty-first-century election staff have come to be engaged in constant events that do the 'boundary work' (Lentz 2014; Beek 2016) that creates both a sense of self and 'the state'. Training encourages them to understand themselves as professionals pursuing an endless task of education and improvement that embraces themselves, their staff, politicians and the public: their work, as one put it simply, is 'teaching'.[57] Since the early 1990s, such training has been both intensified and routinized. This is partly because it is an area where donors have provided significant financial support and where multiple international agencies have sought to shape practice and to encourage the idea that elections were – as one Kenyan manual put it – 'a test time because the maturity of the democratization process of the country is under examination' (Electoral Commission of Kenya n.d.: 6). The work of election officials is presented as that of guiding the public to

---

[53] Mbela, Supervisor of Elections to all DCs, 30 March 1966, KNA DC Lamu 2/2/12; Noah Andolo, Ministry of Agriculture to DC Mombasa, 20 January 1970, KNA CQ 11/ 2; DC Taita to PC Coast, 10 December 1970, KNA CA 7/34.

[54] Interview KEN73a, IEBC staff member, Kisumu, 7 July 2017; '27,000 observers to monitor election', *Daily Nation*, 18 December 1997, p. 2.

[55] Letter, Nii Quaye, *People's Daily Graphic*, 30 October 1992, p. 5; for a similar complaint, see Alice Onek to Returning Officer Gulu, 17 June 1998, Gulu Archive CR 225/2 Box 529.

[56] Unknown to DC Kakamega, 4 December 1969, DC KMG 2/16/11.

[57] Interview KEN73a, IEBC staff member, Kisumu, 7 July 2017.

fulfil their 'essential civic responsibility', as Ghana's election staff were told in 1992.[58] Election staff also train the other actors in electoral performance. With donor funding, training for candidates and agents began in Ghana in 1992: at the initial event, the trainers were reminded of their 'collective responsibility and commitment to ensure free and fair elections'.[59] By 2008, Ghana's EC was running 'sensitization programmes and workshops . . . to educate' media and security agencies as well as candidates and agents (Electoral Commission of Ghana 2010: 14).

Trainings and workshops have been increasingly bolstered by a paper structure that sets out virtuous civic behaviour. There are polling station 'diaries' that prescribe behaviour and require completion; and since the counting of votes was moved to polling stations, the equipment provided to each presiding officer has included forms to record the count. The design of the paper forms has itself been repeatedly revised, so that by 2016 they resembled an exercise in double-entry book-keeping, requiring the presiding officer to enter multiple numbers – of ballots issued, ballots spoiled, total number of ballots, rejected ballots, number of votes for each candidate – and to reconcile these numbers on the form. Stories that these forms have been filled in wrongly, or later been altered, have abounded. That is perhaps unsurprising: mistakes are easy to make, but are also the subject of much suspicion – as in Ghana in 2012, when a change in procedure led many officials to make errors on the 'pink sheets' used to record results.[60] Paper has been buttressed with new digital technologies: in Kenya biometric registration has been combined with digital results transmission devices that were programmed to force the correlation of numbers: preventing electronic returns of over 100 per cent and requiring explanation if results declared did not tally with the number of voters identified. Paper and digital records were intended to provide a check on one another – and a guarantee of the probity and professionalism of staff.

EMBs are also engaged in educating voters: on how to register, how to vote, how to behave around polling stations.[61] 'Mass education' has been the declared goal, and the language of instruction and exhortation follows themes established in the 1950s: '[l]et's show the world that we are mature', declared the chair of Ghana's EC on the eve of the 1992

[58] 'Parties asked to probe for only the truth', *People's Daily Graphic*, 12 October 1992, p. 1.

[59] 'INEC, polling agents, share common interest', *People's Daily Graphic*, 17 October 1992, p. 3.

[60] Interview GHA39a, EC official, Cape Coast, 1 September 2016.

[61] 'INEC despatches election materials to polling stations', *People's Daily Graphic*, 27 October 1992, p. 3.

elections.[62] Initially taking the form of rather dense prose in handbooks and press advertisements – such as that issued in Kenya in 1969 (Kenya 1969) – such education, like that of the CSOs that they often work with to roll out these drives, is now often delivered through cartoons, radio broadcasts and online (see Chapter 5).[63] These campaigns are aimed at voters, but they also encourage electoral staff to see themselves as engaged in a shared educational project that defines and demands certain behaviours as virtuous: exalting impartiality, the secrecy of the ballot and the importance of individual choice. Election officials' status rests, at least in part, on their claim to superior education; their virtue lies in educating others in the ways of citizenship.

Seeing themselves as virtuous workers in the national interest entails particular views of others. In the 1970s, Kenya's district administrators reflected on the problematic 'ignorance' of those they governed: '[a] lot of effort is still required on both the part of the aspiring politicians and the administration to educate the masses politically'.[64] Decades later, election officials – both permanent and temporary – as well as other voter educators (see Chapter 5) continued to portray the public as uneducated and in need of guidance. As one Ugandan presiding officer explained:

The hardest thing about the job is people coming to vote and they do not know what to do, the majority of the people in the villages would be old women and men who are semi-illiterate, they cannot write, they cannot read.[65]

Politicians, by contrast, have been more ambiguously described. They are potential allies in the task of education, for they too usually have significantly more formal education than most voters. Educational requirements for candidacy (English language tests, then specified formal qualifications) have continued in Kenya and Uganda, reinforcing a tendency of self-selection and popular choice to foreground formal education as a necessary attribute for candidates. But if the public may sometimes be fools, politicians are knaves, chronically inclined to rule-breaking, 'irritatingly unscrupulous', and given to accusing officials unfairly of bias.[66] The guide for candidates produced in advance of

---

[62] 'Let's show the world that we are mature, says INEC boss', *People's Daily Graphic*, 3 November 1992, p. 2; 'Ballot paper to bear only names and symbols', *People's Daily Graphic*, 9 October 1992, p. 1.

[63] 'How to vote on June 18', *Daily Graphic*, 18 May 1979, p. 7; 'A guide to voters – excerpts', *People's Daily Graphic*, 30 October 1992, p. 3.

[64] Monthly report from DO Kiunga for July and August 1974, 9 September 1974, KNA CE 1/18.

[65] Interview UGA42a, former polling staff, Kabarole, 11 June 2015.

[66] 'Final report for the post-election self-evaluation implementation strategies workshop for the Commission staff and field officers', pp. 13, 25, IEC 1996, Gulu ADM 6 Box 529; Interview KEN73a, IEBC staff member, Kisumu, 7 July 2017.

Ghana's 1992 elections focussed heavily on election offences and the punishments for them (Interim National Election Commission 1992).

Over the years, EMBs have become increasingly professionalized. This has in part been driven by, but also helped to reinforce, the preferred self-image of the election official: that of the devoted nation-builder, struggling against logistical challenges, unappreciated by a public who do not understand their work and by politicians who malign them and seek to interfere with their work. As officials in Ghana bemoaned, 'the serious challenge we are having is confidence of the people';[67] political parties and their agents are also regularly cast as 'part of the problem'.[68] Yet, while election officials may readily deploy the claims-making language of civic virtue, they may respond to – and be involved in – other kinds of claims-making.

3.3 The Challenge of Impartiality

In 1957, Kenya's governor observed that '[i]t is particularly important that over the years a tradition of complete impartiality on the part of Government officers concerned with African elections should be established'.[69] Since the late-colonial period, election officials have – mostly – been enjoined to show what Ghana's NLC in 1969 called 'strict impartiality'.[70] This was the necessary corollary of the maturity expected of the public, as Kenya's President Moi declared in 1979:

I wish to tell all government employees and others involved with the supervision of the elections that they have been given strict and clear instructions that everything must be conducted without bias … I am sure that everyone will show maturity during the elections.[71]

Kenyan presiding officers have been (usually) required to swear an oath of secrecy and to sign an undertaking to observe electoral regulations.[72] Returning officers and their deputies in Ghana have been sworn in by judges from the High Court and reminded 'that their assignment is a service to the nation'.[73] After the return of multi-partyism in Kenya, Moi

---

[67] Interview GHA47a, EC official, Cape Coast, 2 September 2016.
[68] Interview GHA17a, EC official, Accra, 15 September 2015.
[69] Directive from Governor for all PCs, DCs and DOs, 24 January 1957, KNA OP 1/536.
[70] 'Afrifa's address to Regional Committee Chairmen'. Accra, English for abroad, 29 May 1969 SWB ME/3087/B/2; also 'Officials take part in mock poll', *Daily Nation*, 6 November 1979, p. 4.
[71] 'President Moi makes independence anniversary address', Nairobi Domestic Service, 1 June 1979, FBIS SSA-79–108.
[72] 'General Elections 1974. Instructions for Presiding Officers', KNA CA 7/35.
[73] '51 returning officers sworn in', *Daily Graphic*, 12 October 1996, p. 3.

called on 'the electoral commissioners to do all within their power to ensure that the election was free and fair'.[74]

These injunctions to impartiality were, as we have suggested, a technique of power; the 'impartiality' of electoral procedure has always favoured the educated and those who are adept in the use of paper (or, increasingly, digital technology). They have sometimes been mixed with praise: a Kenyan DC sent a formal letter to all presiding officers in 1974, thanking them for ensuring that elections had been conducted 'fairly and democratically'.[75] In practice, however, the claim to impartiality – and the exaltation of civic virtue and production of stateness that it entails – has always been undermined by partisan behaviour and the abuse of incumbency within the electoral process. This has created a persistent problem for election officials – from hardened DCs in 1970s Kenya to anxious young students working as polling clerks, to the self-conscious election professionals of the early twenty-first century. They cannot always know how literally to take government rhetoric, nor the demands of procedure. Senior officials in one-party Kenya might tell them that 'they were not above the law';[76] the supervisor of elections might anxiously warn that 'any "instructions" which you may receive or hear about from any source which are inconsistent with statutes, regulations, or my instructions must NOT be followed';[77] and Uganda's EC might emphasize its commitment to 'independence and impartiality' in PowerPoint presentations.[78] Yet, in practice, officials have known that they might find themselves expected, or required, to apply the rules partially or even to break them.

The partisan application of procedure has been a favourite tool of incumbent power: exemplified in the systematic barring of all Kenya People's Union (KPU) candidates in the 1968 local elections in Kenya on the basis that their nomination forms contained errors (Mueller 1984: 416) or the effectively routine denial of voter registration of certain groups.[79] The demarcation of constituency boundaries has also provided the opportunity for bureaucratized partiality. In Kenya, late-colonial constituency boundaries evidently favoured KADU (Sanger and Nottingham 1964: 35); in the

[74] 'Moi tells poll body to be fair', *Daily Nation*, 4 December 1997, p. 3.
[75] See for example DC Lamu to J Makokha, DO Central, 25 October 1974, KNA CE 1/18.
[76] 'Njonjo gives hopefuls stern warning. Police to probe poll spending', *Daily Nation*, 1 November 1979, p. 1.
[77] Circular, Norman Montgomery, Supervisor of Elections, 1 October 1974, KNA CA 7/35.
[78] 'Launching of the strategic plan', 11 December 2018, www.ec.or.ug/sites/default/files/2 020–2021-general-elections/A%20Presentation%20on%20the%20Electoral%20Com mission%20Strategic%20Plan%20and%20Roadmap%20to%20the%20%202021%20 General%20Elections.pdf.
[79] Supervisor of Elections to DC Mombasa, 26 April 1974, KNA CA 7/34.

1990s, they were engineered to favour Moi and KANU (Foeken and Dietz 2000: 131–132). In Ghana, skewed constituency allocation meant that many more votes were required to elect an NPP candidate than an NDC one in the elections of 2000 (Smith 2002: 643; Resnick 2017). In Uganda, meanwhile, the zealously uneven enforcement of campaign rules has routinely authorized coercive police action and disadvantaged the opposition (Makara 2010: 84–85).[80] The national interest may itself be evoked to demand or justify behaviour that undermines a state claim to impartiality, as when Uganda's security services responded to criticism of their evident bias in the 1996 elections by saying '[w]e are ... not just a bunch of partisans, but organs of the state with a mission to serve Uganda'.[81]

This experience of the partisan application of procedure has created doubt over whether people will adhere to the civic register and where virtue lies, making officials more willing to break the rules. This is evident, among many other examples, from reported turnouts that are either impossible or unbelievable (EU 2011: 39 on Uganda; Smith 2002: 633–636 on Ghana; Kenya 2008 on Kenya). The pattern of voter registration in Ghana strongly suggests collusion in illegal registration (Ichino and Schundeln 2012). Sometimes this rule-breaking may be pushed by intimidation; sometimes by violence; sometimes by bribery: one experienced candidate in Ghana took it as a matter of course that presiding officers might be bribed to inflate numbers at the count.[82] It may also involve demands and claims to virtue – obligation to a friend, loyalty to a patron, duty to family or country – and be encouraged, or even demanded, by voters (see 3.4).

The challenge for election officials, at every level, has not been that the language of impartiality and the independent structures are a simple sham. They are not; rules are sometimes enforced, procedures sometimes followed: those who break the rules are sometimes arrested.[83] Rather, election officials must work out for themselves which rules apply – and what they should do. By guesswork, observation or discussion with those they trust they have to decide what is the right course of action – which rules to enforce, which to enforce selectively, when to break the rules entirely. That decision reflects a sense not only of what they can get away with, but what others expect or demand from them. While this challenge has faced election officials in all three countries, it has perhaps been most acute in Uganda, where the

---

[80] 'Kayihura warns Besigye over night rallies, defends Museveni', *Daily Monitor*, 14 February 2016.

[81] 'Small group discussion report: RDCs, police and UPDF', appended with 'Uganda elections 1996: report of the proceedings of a post-election evaluation seminar', Gulu archive ADM 6 Box 529.

[82] Interview GHA29a, politician, location withheld, 29 August 2016.

[83] 'Nine EC officials arrested over bribery', *Daily Monitor*, 4 May 2015.

ostentatious transparency of the EC – which publishes a lengthy, number-laden report on each set of elections and maintains a website with an exemplary amount of information – is combined with profound and corrosive uncertainty over whether it is right to follow the rules.

The problem facing Uganda's election officials over the last two decades has partly been one of (perhaps intentional) under-funding. EMBs in all three countries complain routinely of a lack of resources, but this seems to have been especially so in Uganda. The minutes of the first meeting of the EC staff in Gulu were a sorry and revealing tale of squabbles over seniority and mutual accusations of misuse of vehicles.[84] In 2001, the registration drive in advance of elections stalled because the local administrative officials who were expected to do this had not been paid. Nationally, whether through underfunding or incompetence, registration was shambolic in 2001: voters registered, but many never received their cards; the display of registers was late and incomplete.[85] In 2006, the EC staff in Gulu were not supplied with sufficient forms or ballot papers for all their polling stations, '[s]upervisors were asked to make photocopies of the missing forms, and in the rural areas, they were asked to improvise by use of plain sheets of paper'.[86] The problem has been exacerbated by Museveni's proclivity for creating new districts (Green 2010). This is widely understood as an attempt to please local voters – on the understanding that it will bring new resources, but it also means new constituencies, and the EC has struggled to keep up.[87]

The EC's difficulties have not simply been those of insufficient resources, however. In advance of Uganda's 2001 election, a rather plaintive circular went out to local administrators who would be involved as election staff:

... you are expected to stop engaging in illegal practices such as:

  i. Being an agent of a candidate
 ii. Confiscating or withholding of voters' cards
iii. Directly or indirectly influencing another person to vote or refrain from voting for a candidate.[88]

---

[84] Minutes of the first meeting of the Election Commission staff, Gulu, n.d. 2000, Gulu Archive, CR 225/3, Box 627.

[85] 'EC fails to issue cards', *Daily Monitor*, 1 March 2001, p. 3; Editorial, 'It is an election, not a war', *Daily Monitor*, 1 March 2001, p. 8; 'Election postponed', *New Vision*, 2 March 2001, p. 1.

[86] Quarterly report, Election Officer/Assistant District Registrar Gulu to Secretary, EC, 28 April 2006, Gulu Archive, CR 225/6, Box 627.

[87] 'EC hit by lack of funds: activities on a standstill', *Daily Monitor*, 7 April 2019.

[88] CAO to all sub-county and parish chiefs, 16 January 2001, Gulu Archive, CR 225/3, Box 596.

Stephen Akabway, the chair of the EC at the time, presented himself as the embattled champion of proper procedure, telling the press that '[t]here are many people against us but we shall continue'.[89] The dilemma facing EC staff was highlighted by the extraordinary verdicts of the Supreme Court on petitions challenging the results of elections in 2006 and 2016 – which had been marked by the widespread abuse of incumbency and high levels of violence or intimidation against Besigye and his supporters. The judgments comprehensively denounced the EC itself for its conduct of the elections, but avoided criticism of the president and ruling party, and refused to cancel the results (Murison 2013; Sekindi 2017). Unable to act impartially, the EC were nonetheless denounced for failing to do so. After the 2006 elections, events became more bizarre: one of the commissioners of the EC was arrested, accused of ordering extra voters' cards to enable vote-rigging. Charges against her were dropped, and she later claimed that she had been wrongly accused by other members of the commission to cover up a scandal over the inflated cost of procuring the photographic voters' cards.[90]

After the 2001 elections, the new chair of the EC, Badru Kiggundu, repeatedly presented himself as being committed to 'transparency', but somehow powerless in the face of the 'power, hunger and idleness' of politicians and voters.[91] More remarkably, he went on to effectively accuse his staff of failing in their duty to ensure a reliable register for the 2006 elections: 'you ask yourself whatever happened to the ethical values of the officers who were trusted with this work? ... What do I do? My hands are tied'; and admitted that '[w]e cannot say that the system is 100 per cent clean'.[92] Yet he was silent in the face of some apparent abuses and presided over the creation of new polling stations whose location remained unannounced until shortly before the election, encouraging suspicion that this was to facilitate rigging.[93] Meanwhile, Museveni has responded to by-election defeats for the NRM by accusing the EC of corruption.[94] While the handbooks issued to Ugandan polling staff in 2016 insisted that 'you are called upon to carry out your responsibilities with integrity, impartiality, transparency and fairness throughout the day', polling staff must have doubted whether anyone else would. It seems unsurprising that, despite the elaborate architecture of handbooks

---

[89] 'Register display begins next week', *New Vision*, 17 February 2001, p. 3.
[90] 'Commissioner Miiro gets bail', *Daily Monitor*, 6 April 2001, p. 3; 'EC official exposes 2001 election racket', *Daily Monitor*, 19 February 2006, p. 1.
[91] 'Kiggundu blames insecurity on poor laws', *Daily Monitor*, 12 January 2006, p. 17.
[92] 'EC boss speaks out on election preparedness', *Sunday Monitor*, 5 February 2006.
[93] '2,400 new polling stations trigger fear of rigging', *Daily Monitor*, 16 January 2006, p. 1.
[94] 'Opposition rigged Luweero elections – Museveni', *Daily Monitor*, 28 May 2014.

and forms, there was widespread failure to follow regulations at polling stations in those elections (EU 2016: 30–31).[95]

The problems of Uganda's EC have been extreme, but not unique. In Kenya, two successive EMBs have slowly been built up as professional bodies; each has then failed disastrously, prompting a sudden decline in public trust (Khadiagala 2008; Barkan 2013; Erlich and Kerr 2016; Cheeseman, Kanyinga, Lynch, Ruteere and Willis 2019). Election staff who had the patience to read through the 60 pages of guidance issued by the ECK in advance of the 2007 elections would have found – alongside the schematic diagrams of how to lay out the polling station and how to rearrange it for the count, and the template forms for oaths of secrecy – the very explicit demand that they should be 'impartial' and 'transparent' (Electoral Commission of Kenya n.d.). But as the formal inquiry into those elections later found, the tallying of votes was deeply problematic (Independent Review Commission 2008: 126–127). A man who served as a polling station presiding officer in Kikuyu, in the heartland of Kibaki's PNU, offered an explanation for that disparity: he insisted to us that he and his staff had followed those rules, counting the votes and submitting results. But he claimed that, once reports started to come in of suspiciously large votes for Kibaki's presidential opponent, Odinga, in the latter's home area, the attitude at the tallying centres in central Kenya changed, and polling officials – convinced that their colleagues elsewhere were doing the same – decided that collective ethno-regional interest required them to abandon bureaucratic virtue: '[t]hey were just changing the form. Just like that, it's not that people voted'.[96]

The IEBC, created in the wake of that fiasco, was larger, better resourced and apparently more professional than the ECK. In 2017, it deployed the latest digital equipment for voter identification and results transmission. Yet the election results were annulled because of evidence of widespread malpractice in the tallying process (EU 2017a: 5–6, 28–30). Some forms were missing; others seemed to be inconsistent in design or appeared to have been altered to change results; biometric technology did not, in the end, effectively discipline staff into following the rules. As one voter had said to us before those elections, '[w]e put our thumbs – but we go back home, then they go with the machines, we can't know what they are going to do with the machines'.[97]

---

[95] 'Polling officers pocket facts', EC, 2016, www.ec.or.ug/pub/Pocket_facts.pdf.
[96] Interview KEN8a, former polling official, Kikuyu, 25 February 2017.
[97] Interview KEN55a, former chief, Seme, 21 June 2017.

3.4   Popular Malpractice

This deviation from bureaucratic virtue may sometimes be demanded by a voting public, rather than simply being pushed by politicians. Electoral processes may be devised as performances of citizenship, but people constantly use them in ways that complicate that performance. Some of those ways may be legal, notably the widespread practice (especially common in Kenya) of registering to vote at 'home' – understood not as the place of residence (or even of birth), but in ethno-regional terms. As one voter living in Nairobi explained in 1969, 'I am a person from Kakamega [in the west of Kenya] district, and I wanted to have my election there.'[98] 'I always vote at home', one interviewee told us, though he has not lived in that home for many years.[99] Registering and voting may make the individual a national citizen, but they also assert membership of ethnic and regional community. Constituency boundaries are shaped by popular demand as well as elite scheming; the revision of boundaries has long been the cue for a rush of ethnic claims-making on behalf of particular groups demanding separate constituencies.[100] Such claims-making can evoke very localized forms of moral collectivity – as with the prolonged and ultimately successful campaign by people in the former Kisumu Rural constituency to redefine this for the 'Seme community'.[101]

The very local making of claims and demands spills readily into registration and into the polling station: as one man pointed out to us, local-level election 'officials are not strangers, these are people from the village, and they recruit at the village level'.[102] There are multiple consequences to that, for such officials face real moral dilemmas. In Ghana, the NPP has long alleged that the NDC brings Togolese from across the border to boost their vote in Volta – a technique that may involve a degree of complicity by registration staff, as well as by local chiefs and a wider public (Robert-Nicoud 2019: 3). The registration of voters who are, formally, underage has been relatively common, in Ghana at least.[103] In 2012, international observers of Ghana's elections noted with a mixture of puzzlement and outrage that registering staff must have been aware of

---

[98] Morris Ong'ang'o, East African Airways to DC Kakamega, n.d. 1969, KNA DC KMG 2/15/1.
[99] Interview KEN54a, voter, Kisumu, 21 June 2017.
[100] For example: John Kikuyu, Special Committee KANU to National Assembly Boundaries Commission, 9 November 1966, KNA 12/11; 'The wananchi of Bunyore location to Secretary Electoral Commission', 11 August 1973, KNA 12/11.
[101] Interview KEN55a, former chief, Seme, 21 June 2017.
[102] Interview KEN14a, civil society activist, Kisumu, 15 March 2017.
[103] 'Electoral fraud in K'si', *Daily Graphic*, 29 November 2000, p. 1.

this (Commonwealth Secretariat 2012: 18–19; see also Ichino and Schündeln 2012). No doubt they were; but those staff, locally hired, connected by kinship and multiple other ties to those with whom they were dealing, may often have found it difficult to resist. Voters' cards, once introduced, became useful identification tools in Ghana; banking, registering your phone line, all kinds of other bureaucratic processes required one. To refuse one to a friend or relative would be an affront, a refusal to help that might have other social consequences. Where partisan sympathies were strong, it might also seem an affront to the political interests of a wider community – reducing the collective voting potential of the group. That sense of shared interest may also readily provide a virtuous explanation for suspiciously high turnouts in parts of Ghana, which are presumably the consequence of either multiple voting or personation with the complicity of polling staff (Smith 2002: 635–636). The very common practice of 'assisted voting' in Kenya – where voters declare themselves in need of help, because of illiteracy or other cause – may turn the ballot into a more-or-less public act, allowing or requiring the voter to signal their virtuous membership of the local community (Carter Center 2017: 12; also Chapter 6). Multiple voting, as the example of FDC supporters discussed in Chapter 1 reveals (see 1.4), also requires the involvement of voters in collaboration with local officials. This practice was also revealed by other interviewees, including one activist in Seme who explained how, in Kenya's 2007 election, he had helped boost Odinga's presidential vote with the help of locally hired ECK officials:

> [W]e said we do not want to see the turn-out of less than 90 percent. Because a turnout of less than 90 percent would be disastrous for everybody. We had areas in the other parts, in central where the turnout was more than 100 percent ... so after people have finished voting, let's say 4pm, we look at how many ballot papers have not been cast, we look at the percentages, if we are at 40 or 50 percent, or 50 or 60 percent then we have to push it, so we have to mark them and stuff them, that has to be done.[104]

There are then the even more specific and very local challenges to bureaucratic virtue. One Kenyan man told us how he and his relatives – and, presumably, polling staff – conspired to allow him to vote using his sister-in-law's voting card in one of Kenya's one-party elections, because they shared the feeling that the incumbent MP was a drunkard and should be voted out. Another explained how he voted in 2013, without any form of identification and even though the biometric device was not working,

---

[104] Interview KEN14a, civil society activist, Kisumu, 24 March 2017.

simply because the presiding officer was a friend of his parents.[105] The vignette in the introduction to this book suggests the very immediate nature of the challenge to polling staff: what if someone appears at the polling station who is locally known, but missing from the register for reasons that no one can understand. Should they be allowed to vote? Are they not an adult, a member of the community – and perhaps politically supportive of a locally very popular candidate? Civic virtue might demand that they be denied a vote, but a local sense of community would demand that they should be allowed to cast a ballot.

3.5   Conclusions: The Electoral Confidence Trick

Elections, as we have suggested earlier, have become ever more logistic-ally challenging and expensive exercises. Uganda's EC reported that it employed a total of 643,162 people in the course of the 2016 elections cycle, a remarkable figure in a country with an adult population of around 21 million. In surveys, between 4.8 per cent (Ghana) and 7 per cent (Kenya) of respondents reported that they had themselves worked as paid election staff at some point in their life.[106] That reach has been selective, however, privileging those with formal education. It has also come at a cost: the overall price of an election is hard to gauge (as the use of government resources may provide something of a subsidy, and donor funds are not easy to track), but some broad trends are evident. The budget for Ghana's 1979 elections was 5 million cedis (around USD 1.8 m at the official rate or USD 1 for every vote cast); that for the 2008 elections 58 million cedis (USD 60.5 m), around USD 6.60 for every vote cast. For 2016, it was 826 million cedis (USD 200 m); that is USD 18.5 per vote cast (Electoral Commission of Ghana 2010: 21).[107] The budget for organizing Kenya's 1963 elections was GBP 81,715 or a little less than USD 0.14 for each vote cast; Kenya's 2017 elections cost more than USD 25 per vote cast.[108] Donors do provide electoral support and have at times covered the cost of new digital equipment, but the great majority of this cost comes from national funds: the report by Uganda's EMB on the

---

[105] Interview KEN58a, former politician, Narok, 25 June 2017; Interview KEN54a, voter, Kisumu, 21 June 2017.
[106] Electoral Commission, Report on the 2015/16 General Elections, p. 23, www.ec.or.ug/docs/Report%20on%20the%202015–2016%20General%20Elections.pdf.
[107] www.pulse.com.gh/news/politics/election-2016-this-is-the-cost-of-elections-in-ghana-id5772116.html.
[108] Webb, for Chief Accountant to all DCs, 16 April 1963, KNA DC KMG 2/1/77; 'Chebukati wants poll materials reused in 200 to cut expenses', Daily Nation, 12 September 2018.

2016 elections suggests that less than 1 per cent of the cost was covered by donor funds.[109]

Elections, then, appear as expensive, embracing national events, marked by ever-greater elaboration of process. Transparent ballot boxes, printed ballot papers to be marked by the voter, counting at the polling station, digital identification: elections are buttressed by an increasingly complex *techne* in these three countries. Professionalization of institutions and the elaboration of practice have encouraged a fixing and bureaucratization of personal identity and have made familiar the linkage between citizenship, responsibility and civic order; elections really do produce 'state effects'.

Interpreted another way, this might also be a story of divergence, contrasting the success of Ghana's EC with the persistent weakness of electoral management in Kenya and Uganda. Ghana's EC has established an international reputation for impartiality and professionalism, acknowledged even by commentators who are generally sceptical of stories of Ghanaian exceptionalism (Abdulai and Crawford 2010: 31; see also Omotola 2013). In Kenya and Uganda by contrast, despite the investment of money and energy in staff, training and equipment, the EMBs have struggled to demonstrate efficiency or build a reputation for impartiality (Erlich and Kerr 2016), and have instead been waylaid by allegations of malpractice and corruption. This might appear as evidence of a cycle of civic virtue – successful electoral management creates confidence in the electoral process, encouraging all involved to follow the logic of civic virtue, while problematic elections foster mistrust. As researchers, we found the staff of Ghana's EC consistently open and helpful, confident that we would be sympathetic to them as professionals; their colleagues in Uganda were guarded and anxious by comparison.

Yet public opinion complicates that story. The Afrobarometer data set out in Table 3.1 demonstrates that, as we might expect from recent experience, public trust in the electoral management body has regularly been higher in Ghana than in Uganda, and especially Kenya. This is particularly the case after transfers of power. Around Ghana's 2000 election, public trust increased to 63 per cent and rose to 67 per cent around the 2008 elections. This pattern demonstrates the significance of changes of government to public confidence in the electoral process (see Introduction and Chapter 2). Our own survey data also finds that Ghanaians recognize that their electoral commission has, over time, 'helped to improve the quality of elections' (Figure 3.1). Not only do

---

[109] Electoral Commission, Report on the 2015/16 General Elections, pp. 26–8, www.ec.or.ug/docs/Report%20on%20the%202015–2016%20General%20Elections.pdf.

Table 3.1 *Trust in national EMBs as reported by Afrobarometer*

	Trust in Electoral Commission	Round 1 (1999–2001) (%)	Round 2 (2002–3) (%)	Round 3 (2005) (%)	Round 4 (2008) (%)	Round 5 (2011–12) (%)	Round 6 (2014–15) (%)	Round 7 (2016–17) (%)
Ghana	Don't trust[a]	31.5	40.6	20.6	28.9	40.1	59.4	41.3
	Trust[b]	62.6	49.1	74.7	66.6	58.8	37.4	54.0
Kenya	Don't trust	-	42.4	34.8	72.7	30.6	48.9	59.2
	Trust	-	50.9	52.9	24.8	53.0	45.7	33.9
Uganda	Don't trust	8.3	73.9	29.6	55.5	53.9	40.4	54.1
	Trust	76.4	20.3	64.4	39.8	42.7	53.3	41.8

[a] Don't trust = 'Don't trust' + 'trust just a little'
[b] Trust = 'Trust somewhat' + 'a lot'
- = No data available
Source: Data from www.afrobarometer.org, compiled by the authors

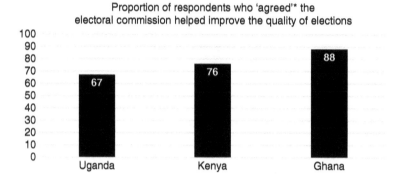

Figure 3.1 The impact of the electoral commission on the quality of elections (%)
* Agree = those who stated that they 'agreed' or 'strongly agreed' with the statement. The other options were 'disagree', 'strongly disagree' and 'neither agree nor disagree'.
Source: Authors' own survey data

the vast majority of Ghanaians (88 per cent) agree with this statement, the sentiment is felt by both opposition (83 per cent) and ruling party (93 per cent) supporters. This stands in stark contrast to Uganda, where almost a third of citizens do not agree that the EC has helped to improve elections, and this figure rises to 45 per cent among those who back the opposition FDC.

However, while these findings conform to our expectations, they are not the whole story. Ghana's politicians have constantly and publicly questioned the impartiality of the EC (Ayee 2017; Robert-Nicoud 2019),[110] and recent elections have witnessed a number of controversies. The Afrobarometer data reflects growing concern over the independence of the EC and documents a fall in trust between 2008 and 2015. Moreover, in the latter year, and in 2000, public confidence was actually higher in Uganda than in Ghana, despite the disparity between the two countries when it comes to the quality of democracy. Indeed, levels of public mistrust of EMBs have been quite high in all three countries, peaking after polls that were especially strongly disputed by the opposition, falling back where results were more broadly accepted. This effect is particularly profound in Kenya, where the transfer of power in 2002 and the defeat of the government in a national referendum in 2005 led to a

---

[110] For two examples: 'Allegations are incredible', *Daily Graphic*, 21 November 2000, p. 1; 'Demo against EC in Kumasi tomorrow', *Daily Graphic*, 5 April 2016.

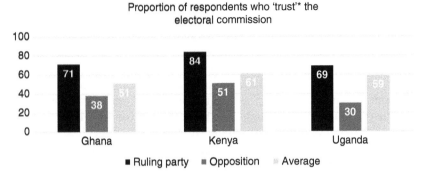

Figure 3.2 Public trust in the electoral commission (%)
* Trust = those who responded that they 'trust' or 'trust a lot' the electoral
commission. The other options were 'don't trust at all' and 'trust a little'.
Source: Authors' own survey data

significant increase in public trust to a high of 53 per cent, which was then
lost following the flawed polls of 2007 (Erlich and Kerr 2016).

Our own surveys conducted in 2016/2017 confirm the fragility of
public opinion and the extent to which it is shaped by recent events
(Figure 3.2). Trust was higher in Kenya (61%) than in Ghana (51%).
Interviews conducted at the same time suggest that these results are an
accurate reflection of the political mood. Many of those we talked to in
Ghana were quick to express the belief that the EC was not, in fact,
impartial (though they sometimes praised local staff).[111] Much has been
made of the independence of Ghana's EC, but in the run-up to the 2016
general elections the retirement of the much respected Chair Kwadwo
Afari-Gyan led to a crisis of confidence in the commission when the
NDC government appointed Charlotte Osei as his replacement (Ayee
2017; Cheeseman, Lynch and Willis 2017b). NPP leaders alleged that
Osei was a life-long NDC supporter and that her appointment was
designed to enable an unpopular government to manipulate the polls.
Despite the relatively high quality of Ghanaian elections, or perhaps
because of it, this concern resonated with many citizens. Even though
she subsequently presided over an NPP victory and there was no evidence of any wrong doing, Osei was later sacked by the new government,
in part because senior figures remained convinced that she would have
manipulated the polls if the opposition had not been able to compile a

[111] Interview GHA77a, parliamentary candidate, Juaso, 1 December 2016, p. 9.

complete list of results to prove that it had won (Cheeseman and Klaas 2018).[112] In the run-up to the 2020 elections, the announcement that there would be an entirely new voter registration process was denounced by the NDC (and minor opposition parties), who once again openly questioned the impartiality of the EC.[113]

As this story suggests, trust in the electoral commission is heavily partisan: in areas generally associated with the opposition, absolute mistrust[114] was especially high – 31 per cent in Kisumu, 31 per cent in Gulu and 54 per cent in Asante Akim. More broadly, while those who felt close to the ruling party expressed high levels of trust in Ghana (71 per cent), Kenya (84 per cent) and Uganda (69 per cent), opposition supporters were much more sceptical. These results demonstrate that, even in more consolidated democracies such as Ghana, citizens do not expect electoral commissions to be fully neutral. Instead, the partisan divide in trust in the electoral commission is evidence of the widespread suspicion that civic ideals will be undermined, either by incompetence, patrimonial politics or self-interest (Moehler and Lindberg 2009).

There may, then, be a third way of reading the history of electoral commissions in our case studies. The apparent success of Ghana's recent electoral history – manifest in a relative absence of violence and in a political stability that does not rely on authoritarianism – does not reflect the wholesale triumph of an idea of civic virtue, spread through professional election management. Ghana's EC staff do prize professionalism and impartiality, and they are more able to follow the demands of impartial duty than colleagues in Kenya and Uganda. Yet procedure is not always followed, and politicians and the public openly question the impartiality of the EC. In other words, the reputation of Ghana's EC is in part a consequence of a party system that has allowed the repeated alternation of power; results are accepted because two competing corporate parties each know that their turn will come again. In turn, this has reduced the pressure on the electoral commission, facilitating its professionalization.

This suggests two, slightly contradictory, lessons. Significant numbers of people – even in Uganda – are apparently willing to accept the possibility that electoral officials might follow the rules, and, therefore, that they might be the citizens of an impartial state. But that acceptance is not universal and seems contingent; many people, much of the time, doubt

[112] 'Why Charlotte Osei and two EC deputies were sacked – CJs report', *Daily Graphic*, 29 June 2018.
[113] 'Opposition parties initiate "yenpene" demo against new register', *Daily Graphic*, 6 January 2019.
[114] I.e. the number of citizens saying that they 'don't trust at all'.

that possibility. It is not the perceived integrity of the EC that has made the 'national exercise' of election organization less disputed, and less violent, in Ghana. Instead, it is a particular combination of the four factors we have identified: the emergence of two corporate parties, each with some claim to a national reach; key decisions by major politicians; and a consequent, spreading, experience of accepting the result of polls even where they are controversial. Across all three countries, it seems clear that the vigour and extent of popular electoral involvement is not based simply on a belief in institutional impartiality, despite constant innovations in electoral management. The electoral production of citizen and state is powerful, but it is not unquestioned.

4   The Eyes of the World Are upon Us
The Aspirations and Limitations of International
Election Observation

The election observers driving towards Olympic Primary School polling station were nervous. Over Christmas lunch two days previously they had been discussing the prospects for the Kenyan general elections of 2007 and the fact that the country stood at an important crossroads. Having experienced a first democratic transfer of power in 2002, Kenya appeared to be on the verge of a second, with opposition leader Raila Odinga forging a narrow lead in some opinion polls ahead of the vote. A second transfer of power would signal growing political maturity and mean that for the first time in Kenyan history the president would not be Kikuyu or Kalenjin. But the potential for further political liberalization was not the only possibility: a flawed election could see democratic gains rapidly disappear.

Now, driving slowly past a snaking queue of voters that lasted for at least two kilometres, the observers came face to face with people who had been waiting in line from as early as 3 a.m. to cast their ballots. It was an inspiring sight, but it also brought home just how high the stakes of the election had become. As if to emphasize the point, the car transporting them was stopped by a gang of young men wielding sticks, who demanded to 'inspect' the contents to make sure that no pre-filled ballot papers were being smuggled in. That incident quickened pulses, but as the observers entered the polling station a cheer went up from the crowd, instantly relieving the tension. Olympic Primary School is located in the Kibera "slum" in Odinga's Langata constituency. The voters in the queue overwhelmingly planned to cast their ballots for the opposition and, believing that Odinga could only lose the election if it was rigged, saw election observers as allies. 'You will protect the election for us', said one, 'you will make sure that Raila wins.'

This positive mood did not last for long. By the time that the polling station was due to open, parts of the electoral register had still not turned up. Worse still, the sections that were missing included names starting with the letter 'O', which forms the beginning of most Luo surnames, meaning that many in the queue could not cast their ballots. The longer the delay went on, the tenser the situation became. The observers had decided to monitor events at Olympic Primary School because a rumour had circulated ahead of the polls that the ruling party might try to rig Odinga out of his own legislative constituency. Due to a quirk of the Kenyan political system at the time, which fused elements of the British and American electoral models, prior to the 2010 constitution successful presidential candidates had to both win a plurality of the popular vote in a direct presidential election and be returned as a member of parliament (MP) in a first-past-the-post constituency election. Given this, the logic of the rumour went, it would be much easier to manipulate the vote in one constituency than in the whole country. As fears of rigging escalated, some voters began to point accusingly at the election officials, complaining that observers were not doing enough to rectify the situation and alleging that – as in the past (Brown 2001) – they were siding with the ruling party at the expense of Kenyan democracy.[1]

First hailed as guarantors of impartiality, then accused of complicity in malpractice, the experience of the observers at the Olympic Primary is illustrative of the hopes and suspicions that surround election observation. As observers, they knew that they could not intervene in the process; their only role was to watch and comment in retrospect. The logic of this process is that it is the very act of observation that matters: by being there, observers deter malpractice. But to the crowd, their silent presence affirmed international approval of the process – evoking anxieties about external interference and manipulation that have deep roots in historical experience.

Like many of the other actors discussed in Part I of this book, election observers are part of a broader set of structures that have emerged through the entanglement of political projects that seek to build states and manage political change through elections. Since the 1990s, in particular, those aims have routinely been presented as democracy promotion, rooted in the assumption that Africans want a liberal democracy based on electoral citizenship, but need assistance to achieve this. Such an approach constructs democracy as a fundamental human right – what Michael McFaul has referred to as a 'world value' (2004: 147) – and is rooted in the belief that elections, if properly held, will facilitate more representative, accountable and effective – and hence more legitimate and prosperous – government. This is why so many international peacekeeping operations view the holding of elections as the ultimate marker of success, after which the mission can be drawn down (Cheeseman 2015a).

---

[1] The researcher was registered as an observer by the ECK as part of his research on the elections and, while not attached to a formal observer mission, was clearly recognizable as an observer as he wore the green individual ID issued by the ECK.

This understanding of the value of democracy promotion, and of elections in particular, has been communicated in speeches, codified in the policies of international bodies such as the European Union (EU) and supported through the investment of considerable funds: it is estimated that in total more than USD 1 billion a year is spent on democracy promotion activities around the world (Dodsworth and Cheeseman 2018: 302). The adoption of democratic models of government and 'good governance' has also been pushed through more coercive mechanisms, most notably the attachment of political conditionality to the economic assistance provided by the likes of the International Monetary Fund (IMF) and the World Bank.

Yet, while democracy promotion is almost always sold on the basis that it is driven by altruism, from the very start it has served a variety of different motivations. During the Cold War, US assistance to European democracies was intended not only to aid recovery after the destruction of the Second World War but also to expand the market for American exports and insulate allied states from the expansion of communism. Programmes such as the Marshall Plan reflected the belief of successive American leaders that the country would be safer if it could mould the world into an idealised image of itself (Agnew and Entrikin 2004). Similarly, recent efforts to promote good governance by the IMF and the World Bank approved the creation of 'very superficial democratic institutional forms' precisely because their ultimate goal was not to advance civil liberties but to facilitate the structural adjustment of African economies (Abrahamsen 2000: 195). These realities – and the fact that Western powers have frequently formed alliances with authoritarian regimes to promote their own security and geo-strategic interests – have led to accusations of hypocrisy and worse, especially in the parts of the world with a recent memory of repressive European colonialism (Brown 2001).

Against this backdrop, international democracy promotion efforts have tended to adopt a strong focus on promoting a certain technocratic view of civic virtue. In this formulation, democracy promoters focus on the way in which impartiality and equal respect for all citizens are enhanced by ensuring due process – that is, that the stipulated rules are followed – for both theoretical and strategic reasons. Theoretical, because much of the classic literature emphasizes the significance of the rule of law to the consolidation of democracy (Mansfield and Snyder 2007). Strategic, because holding a country to its own standards and adopting a technocratic focus on easily observable outcomes help to minimize accusations that foreign governments are infringing on states' sovereignty. Emphasizing due process thus makes intuitive sense, while also operating as a self-defence mechanism for Western donors. Viewed in this context, election observation is not simply one element of a broader moral project of democracy promotion but is rather an essential component of an international regime that tends to pay more attention to the question of whether the rules are followed than who they are designed to benefit. In this sense, they epitomize the kind of civic ideal of virtue described in Chapter 2, with its focus on impartiality, meritocracy and due process.

This chapter provides an overview of the work of election observers across our three countries in order to answer two questions. The first is how election observers have understood their role and the kind of civic ideas that they have promoted. The second is the extent to which these groups have been able to persuade voters and political leaders that they are credible purveyors of civic values in order to strengthen confidence in democratic institutions. This is significant for our purposes, because such confidence is often expected to reduce the lure of claims made in the patrimonial register, which may encourage individuals to ignore the national good – or to subvert political processes – in order to protect, or to maximize the benefits accruing to, a sub-national community. Through a historical and comparative analysis of our cases that pays particular attention to the way in which observers present their work in official reports and statements, we document the way that organizations such as the Carter Center and multilateral bodies such as the EU set themselves up as impartial and professional institutions. A critical component of this stated goal is that observers have become deeply invested in developing their work as a science whose credibility is rooted in strong methodological foundations. Attempts to strengthen observation have therefore led to the adoption of increasingly elaborate procedures over the last three decades. As part of this process, researchers have devised checklists and quantitative measures to try and make observation more effective (Elklit and Svensson 1997; Elklit 1999; Elklit and Reynolds 2005), with academic writing feeding into a relentless quest for greater rigour.

There is some evidence that despite the well-known limitations of observation – such as an excessive focus on polling day itself and an inability to observe all the processes that make up an election (Geisler 1993) – operating on this basis has enabled monitors to reduce electoral fraud (Hyde 2007; Merloe 2015; Hyde and Marinov 2014). We demonstrate, however, that despite this, the capacity of international observers to promote a civic register of virtue is frequently undermined by a range of challenges – some contingent, some inherent. Contingent challenges include the inconsistent foreign policy of Western states, the fact that different observation groups will sometimes provide contradictory evaluations and evidence that observers do not always condemn more subtle forms of electoral manipulation

(Cheeseman and Klaas 2018). Recent criticisms have demonstrated, for example, that observation can simply move electoral fraud around – from more visible to less visible forms (Simpser and Donno 2012) and from observed to unobserved polling stations (Asunka et al. 2019) – rather than actually eradicating it. As a result, some have suggested that authoritarian incumbents exploit the presence of observers to validate flawed elections (Odukoya 2007: 153), implying that observation is very much a political art rather than a science (Kelley 2012).

These challenges are very real because they eat away at the core of observers' credibility, especially when they appear on the front pages of national newspapers and are circulated on social media. As we will see, the media plays an important role in shaping how the 'international gaze' is experienced – and observers have limited control over press reportage. Even careful statements can be reported as condemning an election or giving it a clean bill of health depending on the disposition of journalists and editors. As weighty as they are, these problems could, in principle, be overcome – for example by adopting new observation techniques and achieving greater consistency in international practice. What is more problematic is the set of inherent issues that only become fully apparent when observation is viewed in the longue durée. The first is that, even as the repertoire of observation techniques has expanded, observers are easily depicted as ignorant outsiders who are easily duped – or even worse, as willing accomplices in malpractice. As Kelley points out, 'Western actors led the advocacy, practice and funding of election monitoring' (2008: 244), rendering observation profoundly vulnerable to the accusation that it is a colonial enterprise – an inherently conservative project intended to ensure stability. Given this, it is ultimately not the self-confidence and professionalism of observers that really matters, but whether politicians, officials and voters can be persuaded to believe that they are impartial.

This is far from straightforward given the inherently cautious nature of the observation industry, which is exacerbated by what we have elsewhere called the observers' dilemma: what should observers do when elections seem unfair or openly fraudulent (Willis, Lynch and Cheeseman 2017)? On the one hand, overlooking electoral manipulation generates controversy and undermines the idea that observers are independent arbiters of electoral quality. On the other hand, to denounce elections entirely may lead to violent disorder and advertises the fact that the presence of observers, on its own, is insufficient to secure compliance with international norms. In turn, this runs the risk of both encouraging scepticism about the efficacy of observation and locking Western donors out of the process, undermining their ability to contribute to efforts to strengthen democracy in the future.

In light of the potential downsides of both options, it is unsurprising that the mere presence of observers is insufficient to persuade political leaders or citizens that they should strictly adhere to the rules of the democratic game, safe in the knowledge that everyone else is doing likewise. While Kelley (2008) is surely right that the presence of international observers has become an international norm – with their absence often taken to imply that a country is not a democracy – this does not mean that observation missions have the capacity to drive norm change, that is to promote civic values over patrimonial ones, within the countries in which they operate. To use the language developed by scholars of international relations, the presence of an international norm does not necessarily mean that it will be domestically internalized (Björkdahl 2002). Instead, the salience of a norm depends on the extent to which it is reflected in everyday legislative, judicial – and we would add electoral – practice. In turn, this is shaped by a variety of different factors. For Cortell and Davis, Jr (2000), some of the most significant are whether there is a 'cultural match' between international and national understandings, and the extent to which national rhetoric, the material interests of domestic actors and key political institutions encourage adherence.

International observers might be thought to have a distinct advantage when it comes to shaping domestic agendas in this way. In contrast to some international organizations, they have a high-profile presence for a significant amount of time. They also have a domestic equivalent in the form of local observer groups that are formed by civil society and religious organizations and which are usually funded by the international community, and so can push the civic register from 'above' and 'below'. In this sense they bridge the domestic/international divide in a way that promises to give them greater authority. But as Tankard and Palluck (2016) have argued, when the legitimacy of organizations is called into question, the capacity of otherwise powerful institutions to authorize norm change is undermined (see Chapter 1). This is also a problem for domestic observer groups, which make the same claims to neutrality as their international counterparts and are generally seen to be more legitimate on the ground, but are manned by nationals – and often by people from civil society – who also have partisan preferences and ethnic allegiances, and so are vulnerable to accusations of patrimonial bias (see Chapter 5). Fostering a civic register against this background can be particularly difficult.

To return briefly to Olympic Primary School, the growing tension was relieved when the full electoral register turned up and Odinga won the seat by a landslide. But the chaos of the national vote drew multiple observation groups into the political crisis (Cheeseman 2008). Most notably, the EU challenged the credibility of the vote and was accused by the government of bias and of triggering post-election violence (Kagwanja and Southall 2009). Ten years later, during the 2017 general elections, EU observers were again critical, but this time chose not to condemn the polls. As a result, they faced a fierce backlash from the opposition and negative press coverage including satirical cartoons and headlines that implied they had ulterior political motives. In both cases, the idea that observation can be separated from the particular interests of foreign powers was called into question.

While these tensions are present in all three of our cases, it is important to keep in mind that the effect of observation is not uniform. In addition to documenting the disciplinary potential of the international gaze and the efforts of both domestic and international observers to assert their autonomy from domestic forces, we leverage the variation within our sample to demonstrate considerable differences. Although observers have been drawn into domestic disputes in each country, this has not occurred to the same extent due to variation in both historical precedent and the credibility of key institutions (Introduction). In line with the argument of the previous chapter, it is in Ghana – where elections have been less problematic, the electoral commission and key observation groups have developed greater independence and capacity, and transfers of power attest to the willingness of the international community to work with a variety of political parties – that leaders and voters have been more willing to suspend their scepticism. However, in Kenya and Uganda, where flawed polls have kept the same party in power for long periods, the perceived conservativism of observation has encouraged greater cynicism. As a result, there is considerable evidence that it is only in Ghana that the presence of observers has significantly strengthened the purchase of civic registers of virtue.

We begin with a short history of observation to set the scene, before moving on to a discussion of how observers seek to assert their credibility, and the challenges that they face in doing so.

4.1   A Brief History of Observation

Late-colonial elections combined multiple, sometimes incoherent projects. They were supposed to encourage an emergent cohort of African political leaders into constitutional processes that would preserve key aspects of the colonial state, while also disciplining the aspirations of an increasingly frustrated populace. Following a number of elections in which colonial powers typically failed to manipulate the process in favour of more moderate leaders, they were also intended to transfer power into African hands and cast a positive light on the colonial project. By holding orderly polls, colonial officials hoped to prove to a watching world that colonial rule had ultimately been a successful nation-building project, while nationalist politicians hoped to establish their legitimate right to rule (Willis, Lynch and Cheeseman 2018). As the *Daily Graphic* editorialized in 1954 'we are being tested before the world and it is up to us to prove that we have not only the ability to carry out the functions of government in a democracy but that we can also comport ourselves with dignity and restraint'.[2]

Elections were also supposed to educate, to instil a set of norms of political behaviour. All these projects had a performative element; they required an audience to give them meaning. Both colonial officials and African politicians encouraged a kind of observation. Officials from Belgian-governed Rwanda and independent Sudan were invited to Uganda's 1958 elections, while Ghana's 1956 elections were watched by six British MPs and a delegation of seven Nigerian nationalists, as well as an election official from Sierra Leone and multiple journalists.[3] As documented in Chapters 2 and 3, nationalist politicians constantly impressed on voters that they were under scrutiny: as Ghana's voters were reminded in 1951, proper behaviour 'would demonstrate to the outside world that they were capable of taking their place with other free nations'.[4]

This preoccupation with stability and discipline continued into the postcolonial era, in part inspired by early evidence from Congo (now the DRC) and Nigeria of the potential for elections to exacerbate ethnic tensions (Cheeseman 2015a). In the decades after independence, incumbent politicians and civil servants – and the press, on their behalf – evoked the international gaze repeatedly in pursuit of order and stability. As Kenyatta announced in advance of the 1969 polls 'the whole world was watching to see how the people of Kenya were conducting their second General Election since independence'.[5] Order, as Atieno Odhiambo (1987) has pointed out, really meant the acceptance of the authority of the state. In that context, elections were intended to teach people to observe the rule of law – and the world was waiting to see whether they had mastered their lessons. As Kenya's press pointed out before the 1974 elections, 'the rest of Africa and the wider world are watching'.[6] The implication was that

---

[2] Editorial, *Daily Graphic*, 11 June 1954, p. 5.
[3] Ag. PC Northern province to Supervisor of Elections, 27 August 1958 and Vice-Governor general, Ruanda-Urundi to Governor Uganda, 2 September 1958, Uganda National Archive (UNA) Elections 1 L/117; Lamm, Consul-general Accra to State, 16 July 1956, NARA RG 59 Box 3242.
[4] Commissioner Special Branch to Kingston, Ministry of Defence and External Affairs, 9 February 1951, UKNA FCO 141/4926.
[5] 'Eastern Province out in force for President', *East African Standard*, 1 December 1969, front page.
[6] Editorial, *Daily Nation*, 23 September 1974.

it was voters who were being observed, as postcolonial leaders seeking to ensure discipline instrumentalized the power of the global audience to exhort voters not to embarrass their new nations. Electoral violence was particularly dangerous, for example, because disorder might be taken to imply that the country had not been ready for self-rule.

In evoking this gaze, African politicians perhaps exaggerated its intensity. In such international scrutiny as there was, larger narratives of Cold War politics weighed more heavily than questions of due process (Attwood 1967; Westad 2005). The British High Commission reported an entirely negative verdict on Ghana's 1964 referendum in a confidential despatch to London; similarly, confidential accounts of Kenya's 1969 elections were more forgiving but condescending.[7] In neither case, however, was there a formal, public, verdict on the management or fairness of the vote. Nor did the wider world demonstrate anything like a consistent commitment to elections – as the undisguised British and US satisfaction at the overthrow of Nkrumah in 1966, and of Obote in 1971, made abundantly clear. The legacy of these years, when numerous participants published memoirs that evidenced Western complicity in the fall of more independent and critical African leaders (Attwood 1967; Stockwell 1978), further undermined the international community's claim to be committed to electoral integrity. Moreover, the only example of formal electoral observation in this period – the Commonwealth mission that endorsed Uganda's flawed polls in 1980 – offered a ready reference point for subsequent scepticism about the impartiality of the international gaze (Willis, Lynch and Cheeseman 2017).

The political landscape shifted significantly following the reintroduction of multiparty politics in the early 1990s. After this point, the public commitment of Western donors to support democratic consolidation in Africa meant that the international gaze could now be turned against incumbent governments by opposition parties and civil society groups seeking to expose abuse. Ruling parties sought to resist this trend: ahead of Uganda's competitive (but no-party) elections in 2001, a government-controlled newspaper still demanded good behaviour of the public:

The whole world is looking on with abated [sic] breath, to see if Ugandans are really mature enough to sort out their own political affairs ... We must not embarrass ourselves. Voting in a new leader is supposed to be a very peaceful exercise.[8]

---

[7] High Commissioner, Accra to Secretary of State, 29 February 1964, UKNA DO 195/251; Edis, British High Commission Nairobi to Purcell, FCO, 10 December 1969, UKNA FCO 31/355.

[8] Editorial, 'Give democracy a chance', *Sunday Vision*, 11 March 2001, p. 10.

However, in the context of a liberalized media and growing civil society (Chapter 5), governments could no longer channel the international gaze as they once had. When the front page of a self-consciously business-focussed regional newspaper bore the message 'The eyes of the world are upon you' ahead of the Kenyan elections of 2013, the words were printed over photographs of the major party leaders.[9] Discipline now was demanded not only of the public – it was politicians, too, who must behave.

Turning that gaze around – away from voters, and onto politicians and election officials – was the aim of the rapid development of election observation as a formal endeavour of specialists, rather than of journalists and diplomats. The context for this was the wider investment of bilateral donors and multilateral organizations in funding civil society groups, training journalists and advising electoral commissions in order to 'promote' or 'deepen' democracy. The United States Agency for International Development (USAID) created the Centre for Democracy and Governance in 1994, and expenditure in this area increased from USD 103 million in 1990 to more than USD 1 billion in 2005. For its part, the EU was collectively spending around Euro 2,500 million on democracy assistance by 2010 (Cheeseman 2015a: 114).

Election observation grew alongside this multiplying suite of external interventions in response to the increasing number of countries holding multiparty polls. According to data collected by Kelley (2012: 4), the total number of national-level election observation missions increased from around 30 a year in the 1980s and early 1990s, just 10 per cent of all elections held, to 80 in 2004 – some 82 per cent of all elections. In many ways the period 1989–1992 was a 'tipping point' (Kelley 2008: 227–228), as it was during this period that influential regional organizations such as the Commission on Security and Cooperation in Europe and the Organization of American States officially endorsed the principle of international observation. In turn, this created the conditions necessary for the emergence of the observation industry.

The Carter Center, the not-for-profit US-based non-governmental organization (NGO) established by former President Jimmy Carter to 'advance democratic elections and governance consistent with universal human rights',[10] deployed its first mission to Panama in 1989 (Carter Center 2016). Since then, the Carter Center has increasingly focussed its activities on election observation, monitoring 'more than 100 elections'

[9] *The East African*, 2–8 March 2013, p. 1.
[10] Carter Center, 'Democracy programme', n.d., www.cartercenter.org/peace/democracy/index.html.

across 38 countries by early 2019.[11] The year 1989 was also particularly significant for our three cases because it saw the first observation effort of the Organization of African Unity (OAU), which joined a mission to Nicaragua (Odeh 2016: 3). In the decade that followed, the growing requests of member states for the OAU to play a constructive role in the democratization process eroded a prior emphasis on the importance of non-interference. In turn, this contributed to a growing sense that elections that were not observed were not legitimate. In the twenty-five years that followed, the OAU and its successor the African Union (AU) observed more than 250 elections (Karume and Mura 2012). A number of regional organizations subsequently followed suit, such as the Economic Community of West African States (ECOWAS), which has observed elections in Ghana.

A similar process also led the Commonwealth Secretariat to recommend – again in 1989 – that henceforth it should begin formally monitoring the elections of member states and thus our three countries.[12] The EU was a little slower to join the party but observed the first democratic and multiracial elections in South Africa in 1994. Initially, EU observation efforts were rather ad hoc and at times disorganized, despite the creation of the EU Election Unit in 1995. In 2000, however, the European Council's Communication on EU Election Assistance and Observation adopted a new approach to provide a central focal point for election activities. This led to the development of a more integrated approach, known as European Union Election Observation Missions (EU EOMs). The EU's commitment to election observation was further entrenched in 2010, with the creation of the European External Action Service – effectively its Foreign Ministry – and over the next 19 years, it deployed 10,000 observers to 65 countries in 130 missions.[13]

The language of observation groups is typically one that emphasizes not only the rule of law but also the value of inclusive and transparent politics. In this sense it places particular weight on the significance of citizenship and due process within the civic register of virtue. Ahead of the re-run of Kenya's 2017 presidential election, for example, fears that the judiciary was being intimidated by supporters of the ruling party, and that this had resulted in a number of judges failing to turn up for work, led the EU EOM to talk openly of the risk of 'political interference' and to call on Kenyans to 'respect the rule of law, the separation of powers, and to grant

[11] Ibid.
[12] The Commonwealth, 'Observing elections', n.d., http://thecommonwealth.org/agv/obs erving-elections.
[13] Trastec, 'EU election observation missions', n.d., www.transtec.be/website20/fields_o f_activity/EOMs.

each other security, rights and freedoms'.[14] Similarly, in a press release ahead of the Ugandan elections of 2016, the Chief Observer of the EU EOM noted that he had held numerous meetings to discuss 'the importance of the transparency and inclusiveness of the electoral process'.[15]

The notion that citizens have certain rights (to be able to vote, to free speech) along with responsibilities (to be orderly, to follow the rules) is rarely far from the surface of such statements. The EU statement on the 2017 Kenyan elections cited above references 'security, rights and freedoms', while the Carter Center, in lauding Ghana's 2008 polls, commended an 'honest election ... as well as the rights of all Ghanaian citizens to participate freely in the political process'.[16] Moreover, the joint statements that observer groups sometimes release, especially around elections that are controversial or expected to be conflictual, usually include a strong emphasis on rights and freedoms in addition to rule following. The day before the Kenyan elections of 2013, for example, a group that included the AU, Carter Center, East Africa Community and the EU called on Kenyans to 'respect the right of fellow voters to choose their elected representatives free from fear of intimidation or violence'.[17]

This component of international engagement has at times proved controversial, in part because the idea that there are universal human rights is not accepted by all African governments, but also because international institutions have often been accused of promoting them inconsistently[18] and of ultimately prioritising stability over democracy (Lynch, Cheeseman and Willis 2019). Thus, while regional observation groups such as the AU use a similar language to their Western counterparts, they tend to focus less heavily on human rights and to instead reference general progress towards democracy and development. In line with this, the invocation of citizenship typically goes hand in hand with an

---

[14] European Union EOM Kenya, 'EU EOM Statement, 25 October 2017', 25 October 2017, https://eeas.europa.eu/sites/eeas/files/eu_eom_kenya_2017_state ment_wednesday_25_october_0.pdf.

[15] European Union External Action Service, 'Chief Observer Eduard Kukan presents final EU Election Observation Report on 2016 Uganda Elections', 18 February 2016, https://eeas.europa.eu/headquarters/headquarters-homepage/13092/chief-observer-eduard-ku kan-presents-final-eu-election-observation-report-2016-uganda_en.

[16] Carter Center, 'Ghana's voters renew commitment to open and competitive elections', 8 December 2008, www.cartercenter.org/news/pr/ghana_elections_prelim_state ment_2008.html.

[17] International Observation Groups, 'Observer groups call for peaceful polls, urge Kenyans to await results', European Union External Action Service, 3 March 2013, http://eeas.europa .eu/archives/eueom/missions/2013/kenya/pdf/joint-missions-statement-03-03_en.pdf.

[18] European Union External Action Service, 'Uganda debates European Union contribution to human rights, 5 December 2018, https://eeas.europa.eu/election-observation-missions/eom-kosovo-2017-%E2%80%93-municipal-mayoral-elections/54880/ugand a-debates-european-union-contribution-human-rights_sq.

emphasis on solidarity and the importance of national identity. These features reflect a more cautious approach to intervening against the wishes of domestic governments and the historic focus of the OAU on promoting pan-Africanism and defeating colonial rule.

In the framing of ECOWAS electoral statements, for example, inclusive citizenship is often assumed to be intimately connected to the unifying force of nationalism. For example, following Ghana's 2012 elections, when there was considerable controversy regarding the quality of the election and the functioning of new digital technology, the ECOWAS Election Observation Mission called on the media and party leaders 'to exercise restraint and *demonstrate a high sense of patriotism* as the Electoral Commission endeavours to rectify the situation' [our emphasis].[19] Similarly, after a much smoother process in the country's 2016 general elections, the ECOWAS Commission congratulated the Ghanaian electorate 'for the high sense of patriotism and civic responsibility they displayed'.[20]

This variation serves as an important reminder that registers of virtue are neither uniform nor set in stone. Instead, while claims made in the civic register share a family resemblance and tend to feature a number of core elements – due process, citizenship – this emphasis may be combined with other values and expressed in different ways depending on the context and the actor.

4.2   International Election Observation and the Quest for Credibility

Although they issue high-profile press releases and appear on national media, observers have not found the promotion of adherence to democratic rules straightforward. In part, this is due to the presence of other actors who promote patrimonial forms of claims-making and often go against official rules and regulations (Chapters 6 and 7). But it is also rooted in the fact that observers' rhetoric has not always matched reality. The plethora of organizations that emerged in the 1990s contributed to the challenge of establishing credibility. While the explosion of observation groups increased the manpower and resources invested in watching elections, and the range of groups on the ground from different

---

[19] ECOWAS, 'Ghana's electoral process peaceful, transparent – ECOWAS poll observer mission', Relief Web, 9 December 2012, emphasis added, https://reliefweb.int/report/ghana/ghana%E2%80%99s-electoral-process-peaceful-transparent-ecowas-poll-observer-mission.

[20] ECOWAS, 'Communique on the Outcome of the Ghanaian Elections 2016', 9 December 2016, emphasis added, www.ecowas.int/communique-on-the-outcome-of-the-ghanaian-elections-2016.

backgrounds facilitated 'action that might otherwise have been blocked for political reasons' (Kelley 2009: 59), the failure of observers to coordinate on a common strategy led to what Carothers (1997: 27) has described as 'unnecessary observer clutter'. At the same time, the 'different biases, capabilities, and standards of organizations' sometimes led different missions to 'contradict each other or work at cross-purposes' (Kelley 2009: 59). This is particularly significant because it threatens two of observers' strongest claims to credibility: that they are neutral and apply a rigorous scientific methodology. After all, how can neutral observers applying the same methods come to different conclusions?

A growing recognition of the dangers of disagreements gave rise to two broad and related trends. In the first, bodies such as the Carter Center and EU set about developing 'an increasingly standardized approach' to their methodology (Carter Center 2016: 5). Consequently, there are now professional observers, analysts and country experts who go from one election to another. Long-term observers arrive in country months before an election is held and are advised by country experts who better understand local contexts. Not all groups have developed their practice in this way, however. Most notably, the Commonwealth Observation Group (COG) have maintained smaller and less technocratic missions and tend to produce shorter reports heavily shaped by the disposition of the head of the delegation – though at times this can lead to critical reports, as in Uganda in 2011 when Dame Billie Miller, the former Deputy President of Barbados, was evidently outraged at the range of electoral malpractice on show (Commonwealth Secretariat 2011). More recently, however, the COG has also taken steps to make its approach more rigorous, publishing a Compendium of Commonwealth Good Practice in 2016.

In the second trend, leading observation groups sought to build agreement around minimum standards and principles that should be applied by all observers. In particular, Western-based groups such as the National Democratic Institute (NDI)[21] and Carter Center, afraid that their efforts will be undercut by less critical regional organizations, worked with the United Nations to establish a common approach (Kelley 2009). In 2005, this movement achieved a notable success with the agreement of the Declaration of Principles for International Observation and Code of Conduct for International Election Observers. The Declaration stresses above all the need for observers to act impartially – a word that appears seven times in the first three pages alone – and outlines key 'dos' and 'don'ts'. It was initially endorsed by 22 organizations including the AU,

---

[21] NDI is a non-profit organization aligned to, but not formally part of, the Democratic Party of the United States.

with a further 28 signing up over the next 14 years, though there continues to be considerable variation in the practical application of these principles.

These challenges notwithstanding, the justificatory language of observers has increasingly cast their tutelary presence in terms of analysis and technical expertise: as the EU puts it, observer missions adhere to 'fundamental principles of independence, impartiality, consistency, a long-term approach and professionalism'. In doing so, they explicitly cast themselves as unbiased because they employ 'a robust and comprehensive methodology' and only rely on 'facts that are witnessed or verified by the observers'.[22]

The EU's official *Handbook for Election Observation* further emphasizes this point. The 14-point code of conduct includes the following provisions:

> 6. Observers will maintain strict impartiality in the conduct of their duties, and shall at no time express any bias or preference in relation to national authorities, parties, candidates ...
> 10. Observers will base all conclusions on well documented, factual, and verifiable evidence ....
> 14. At all times during the mission, including during private time ... each election observer should behave blamelessly, exercise sound judgement, and observe the highest level of personal discretion. (EU External Action Service 2016: 21)

In addition to this concern to broadcast independence and methodological rigour, the practice of election observation reflects a growing investment in self-consciously scientific methodologies. The positioning of observers in polling stations on election day is sometimes done on the basis of a random sampling of constituencies stratified by key demographic data from the latest census to ensure a representative distribution. When observers are in place, they are given standardized forms to complete which do not encourage individuals to voice their own opinions, but rather to record exactly what happens on the basis of a 'tick box' checklist (EU 2016: 167). The growing length and breadth of such forms is a useful indicator of the industry's quest for more robust and defensible methods: the Carter Center's form for polling station observation increased from 37 items to 45 between 2002 and 2013. This checklist approach is particularly attractive because it promises to generate standardized data that can be aggregated to generate a thorough and reliable set of reports – usually an interim report released shortly after polling day, and a final report released some

---

[22] EU External Action Service, 'Election Observation Missions (EUEOMs)', 10 August 2016, https://eeas.europa.eu/topics/election-observation-missions-eueoms/4 21/election-observation-missions-eueoms_en.

months later. In this way, observers aim to demonstrate that they embody their principles.

Unsurprisingly for an industry in search of greater consistency, the language of election reports has converged around a common electoral bureaucratese. Reports usually begin by praising the electorate, for example noting that '[v]oters showed exceptional commitment and determination to cast their ballots' (EU 2017: 1). They then list a series of strengths and weaknesses before implying – usually, but not all of the time – that even in cases where there is considerable evidence of electoral malpractice, this is insufficient to warrant rejecting the results outright. This conclusion, however, is rarely stated explicitly. Having long ago moved away from talking about whether elections are 'free and fair', it is now much more common to hear heads of observation missions talk of the importance of 'credible and peaceful' polls. But when it comes to written reports, even this is rarely stated explicitly. Rather, recognizing that the contested nature of electoral processes often generates deep suspicions among losing parties and their supporters, observers typically refrain from actively endorsing the process. Instead, in controversial elections the verdicts of European and North American monitors are typically revealed through an act of omission. Rather than grading the election along a clear scale, or providing a one-line statement that the election was acceptable, the reader is left to infer from the absence of statements to the contrary whether or not the election was flawed.

While observers often recognize the limitations of sitting on the electoral fence, they struggle to find a viable alternative. There are two main reasons for this. Most fundamentally, international observers have failed to resolve a key dilemma: how to expose and reduce fraud without undermining the very industry and political system that they are seeking to strengthen. While observers genuinely aim to combat malpractice, they often fail to condemn it because to do so would risk the long-term viability of the observation model (Willis, Lynch and Cheeseman 2017). This is not just because more confrontational verdicts might lead to them not being invited back. It also relates to the tight parameters within which missions operate. Observers are supposed to be a moral presence: they can only really have an effect if they change behaviour by simply being there, for they cannot intervene in real time – they can only watch and report.[23] Broadcasting evidence of manipulation advertises the limitations of this model, especially when it happens in successive elections.

---

[23] EU External Action Service, 'Election Observation Missions (EUEOMs)', 10 August 2016, https://eeas.europa.eu/topics/election-observation-missions-eueoms/4 21/election-observation-missions-eueoms_en.

It is therefore unsurprising that, although the Commonwealth mission in Uganda in 1980 came to be seen as an embarrassment characterized by 'inadequate preparation and political naiveté' (Sives 2001), its conservative positioning is often repeated, especially in countries where the maintenance of peace is a primary consideration for the international community. The Final Report of the EU on Kenya's 2017 elections, for example, contains both a list of 'Key Conclusions' and a lengthy 'Executive Summary'. However, despite the intense controversy around the polls neither section includes a single clause that provides a clear and explicit statement about whether the 8 August elections were acceptable. For example, the Executive Summary argues that errors in the tallying process 'did not appear to consistently advantage one candidate', implying a legitimate outcome. But this conclusion is not explicitly drawn. Instead, the summary moves on to note that 'in a closer race, such problems could have a decisive impact on the outcome' and that the 'lack of IEBC explanation or acknowledgement of errors and omissions' undermined public confidence (EU 2017: 6).

A similar approach was adopted by the EU with regard to the Ugandan presidential election of 2016. The controversy surrounding the contest ensured a charged atmosphere at a press conference held just after the election at which the EU EOM presented its preliminary report. The report catalogued multiple dubious practices while commending the public for their 'remarkable determination on election day', explicitly suggesting 'voter enthusiasm for the democratic process'.[24] While this non-committal position was feasible on the page, it was harder to maintain in public. When faced with pointed questions from journalists about whether the EU mission believed that the results were credible, given that there was a discrepancy between the official results and the figures recorded by its observers in 20 per cent of polling stations that were observed, mission representatives refused to give a straight answer. Instead, they directed the audience to read the report 'and draw their own conclusions'.[25] This inherent conservatism helps to explain why between 15 and 35 per cent of elections with a 'major flaw' are nonetheless endorsed by international monitors (depending on the type of irregularity, see Kelley 2012: 164).

Such linguistic obscuration is rooted in the urge to show impartiality, as well as the desire to avoid controversy. While the criticism meted out to observers of Uganda's elections in 1980 and 2016 suggests that this

[24] Nic Cheeseman, Gabrielle Lynch and Justin Willis, 'How election monitors are failing', Foreign Policy, 29 April 2016, https://foreignpolicy.com/2016/04/29/how-election-monitors-are-failing-uganda.
[25] Ibid.

approach may not work, observers are even more exposed when they do make explicit statements. In the Kenyan elections of 2017, for example, John Kerry, the former US Secretary of State and the head of the Carter Center observation team, issued an incautious initial endorsement of the process as 'free, fair and credible'.[26] The response of opposition leaders and civil society groups was swift and fierce, with one caustically accusing the observers of simple incompetence:

You don't just visit one primary school where voting takes place and make a conclusion that everything is right ... The observers did not do their work properly.[27]

Taken together, the experience of observers in Kenya and Uganda demonstrates that both publicizing and downplaying evidence of malpractice in close elections are likely to expose observers to accusations of partisan bias as a result of pre-existing suspicions about their motivations. Historical experience and continuing examples of inconsistent behaviour and willingness to trade democracy off against other priorities have generated a set of suspicions regarding international actors that is evidenced by the nationally representative surveys that we conducted in each country (Figure 4.1). We asked individuals a range of questions including whether they think that election observers should be present during an election and whether they have improved the quality of elections over time (Figure 4.2). In all three cases, international observers are less trusted than their domestic counterparts and, within the category of international observers, those from the African Union are seen to be more legitimate than teams from the EU or the United States.[28] The magnitude of this gap is striking. While a majority of respondents favoured the presence of observers, in each country around 25 per cent more people felt this way about domestic observers than about their American counterparts.

The consistency of these patterns across our three cases, despite their very different experiences of international engagement, is strongly suggestive of the extent to which popular attitudes are shaped by perceptions

---

[26] Lily Kuo and Abdi Latif Dahir, 'Foreign election observers endorsed a deeply flawed election in Kenya', Quartz, 6 September 2017, https://qz.com/africa/1068521/kenya-elections-deeply-flawed-questions-foreign-observers.

[27] Leela Jacinto, 'Kenyan court ruling puts "election observer industry" in a tight spot', France 24, 1 September 2017, www.france24.com/en/20170901-kenya-court-ruling-election-observer-industry-missions.

[28] The question about the United States did not specify whether the observers came from the Carter Center or other groups such as the NDI and International Republican Institute (IRI). It is possible that some respondents did not have any of these organizations in mind and instead imagined observers coming directly from the US government.

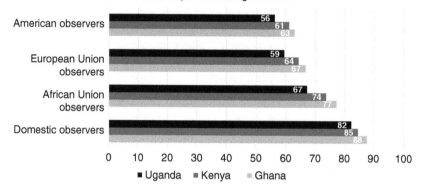

Figure 4.1 Public support for the presence of election observers (%)
* Agree = those who stated that they 'agreed' or 'strongly agreed' with the statement. The other options were 'disagree', 'strongly disagree' and 'neither agree nor disagree'.
Source: Authors' own survey data

of the motivations of observation groups, which in turn cannot be separated from their perceptions of the states from which they originate. In particular, the higher support for AU observers as compared to groups from the EU or the United States appears – given the regular criticism of the limited effectiveness of the AU – to reflect a prior belief that African leaders and officials are more likely to act out of a spirit of genuine solidarity. As a result, Western observation groups face an uphill struggle to change the attitudes and behaviours of political leaders and voters.

4.2.1   Cross-National Variation in the Credibility of International Election Observation

While all observers face a challenge to establish their credibility, their capacity to overcome these challenges is heavily shaped by the past experience of voters and politicians. As we have seen, in both Kenya and Uganda, the combination of successive election controversies, the absence of political change via the ballot box, business deals and geostrategic alliances between Western powers and incumbent governments has heightened suspicion regarding observers' capacity and willingness to ensure due process is followed. In Ghana, by contrast, the situation has been very different; while observation began much as it did in Kenya and Uganda, it was later acclaimed as a force for democratic progress.

The significance of recent experience is clear from the fallout from the Supreme Court's decision to invalidate the results of the Kenyan election that John Kerry had praised. According to Odinga, the Supreme Court's verdict 'put on trial the international observers who moved fast to sanitize fraud'.[29] In the furore that followed, opposition supporters began to link Kerry's position, and the lack of support that they felt they were receiving from the US Ambassador, into a single narrative that emphasized American (and Western) willingness to sacrifice Kenyan democracy in order to sustain a privileged relationship with the incumbent government.[30] That narrative drew on a long history of perceived US support for incumbent regimes (Brown 2001; Gibson and Long 2009), as well as from pre-election reports of corrupt military deals.[31] In this context, the fact that most observation groups are headed by political leaders – in order to give their statements greater weight – became a liability, because it facilitated the politicization of their activities.

Observers have been able to play a much more constructive role in Ghana not because there have never been controversies, but because over time transfers of power have reduced suspicions of partiality. In the 'founding' multiparty election, President Rawlings' decision to invite international observers and effectively veto domestic ones created the impression that he believed that he could fool foreigners but not Ghanaians themselves (Anglin 1998: 492). This created the perception that international observers were accomplices to authoritarianism, especially after Rawlings secured a controversial victory and 'opposition parties criticized the COG and the Carter Center for failing to spot many instances of electoral malpractice' (Aubyn 2012: 240). Yet by 2016, the presence of international monitors had come to be frequently identified as having strengthened democratic norms and values.

One of the main reasons for this is that, although the 1992, 2008 and 2012 elections were controversial, the regular transfer of power has generated greater confidence, among both the electorate and the political elite, that the electoral commission and the wider international community are willing to see political change (Chapter 3). In particular, the

---

[29] Lily Kuo and Abdi Latif Dahir, 'Foreign election observers endorsed a deeply flawed election in Kenya', Quartz, 6 September 2017, https://qz.com/africa/1068521/kenya-elections-deeply-flawed-questions-foreign-observers.

[30] Ibid.

[31] Njeri Kimani and Simon Allison, 'Kenya's very own "arms deal" scandal", Daily Maverick, 10 March 2017, www.dailymaverick.co.za/article/2017-03-10-kenyas-very-own-arms-deal-scandal.

willingness of donors to recognize governments of both political stripes has made possible the performance of impartiality: where two established parties compete and exchange power, observers can point out that they have endorsed victories by both sides.

In turn, popular perceptions of observers and the wider international community as supportive partners have enabled observers to present themselves as upholders of civic virtue and bureaucratic process. Thus, one of the most respected authorities on Ghanaian elections, E. Gyimah-Boadi, argues that in Ghana's 2008 election 'the visible presence of a large number of international election-observer groups ... as well as foreign media increased transparency and public confidence in the process' (2009: 146). Similarly, Aubyn concludes that 'the mere presence of election observers ... has in itself also helped to deter overt acts of electoral fraud, violence, chicanery and corruption' (2012: 262). The word 'overt' is a significant qualifier there, but it is clear that in Ghana transfers of power have fostered confidence in both the political system and those sent to oversee it. This is not simply because the observers have behaved differently in Ghana; as we have explained, their perceived efficacy is in large part the product of favourable circumstances.

Further evidence of the variation in attitudes towards observers between our three cases, and its relationship to transfers of power, is provided by our surveys (Figure 4.2). While a majority of respondents in each country agreed that international observers have helped to improve the quality of

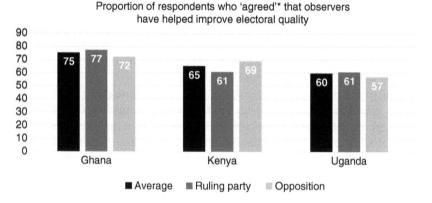

Figure 4.2 The impact of international observers on the quality of elections (%)
* Agree = those who stated that they 'agreed' or 'strongly agreed' with the statement. The other options were 'disagree', 'strongly disagree' and 'neither agree nor disagree'.
Source: Authors' own survey data

elections, the figure was highest in Ghana (75 per cent) and lowest in Uganda (60 per cent) – a difference of some 15 per cent. Moreover, in both Ghana and Uganda, ruling party supporters are more positive about the impact of international observers than their opposition counterparts, in part because they are far more likely to be satisfied with the quality of elections and democracy overall. The reverse is true in Kenya where – in a survey conducted in the run-up to the 2017 elections – opposition supporters were 8 per cent more likely to think that international observers have played a constructive role. It is difficult to disentangle exactly why Kenya bucks the trend from the survey data alone, but the most plausible explanation is that the 2007 Kenyan election is the only one in our sample in which observers rejected the result – and in so doing were seen to side with the opposition, at least prior to the 2017 polls. This interpretation is supported by the fact that when it came to EU observers – the group that was most critical in 2007 – 71 per cent of those who felt close to an opposition party believed that they should be present during an election campaign, compared to just 54 per cent of those who felt close to the ruling party.

The high levels of popular support for international observation in Ghana and much lower levels in Kenya and Uganda suggest that observation works best when it is needed least. Significantly, there is no easy way for observers to improve this situation. While condemning poor-quality processes might appease democracy activists and opposition parties – and sustain the notion that observers are neutral – it also risks damaging the legitimacy of key electoral institutions and challenges the fundamental authorizing fiction of stateness; namely, that the state is autonomous from society. In turn, this has the potential to undermine the resonance of bureaucratic ideals and thus the civic register by demonstrating the extent to which the rules of the game are undermined by patrimonial considerations and self-interest. Indeed, because accusations of malpractice may both undermine the credibility of domestic institutions, while simultaneously dragging observers into controversial political disputes – as in Kenya in 2007 – they may paradoxically represent a worst-case scenario regarding the spread of the civic register, at least in the short term. Promoting democratic norms through election observation is therefore much more challenging than it first appears.

4.3   Domestic Monitors and the Challenge of Autonomy

During the 1990s, certain aspects of the international gaze became increasingly domesticated through the exponential increase in the number of foreign-funded NGOs (see Chapter 5). One particularly significant dimension of this process occurred through the work of the domestic election observation groups, which are typically funded by foreign donors and adopt much of their approach. In the early literature on Africa's re-engagement with multiparty politics, domestic observation was often seen as something of a silver bullet (Nevitte and Canton 1997): the greater size of domestic missions meant that they could provide more thorough coverage; their local knowledge meant that they would be harder to dupe (Geisler 1993; Carothers 1997).

The rapid growth of domestic observation efforts in the early 1990s brought a large number of people into direct engagement with the electoral process, in stark contrast to the small nature of international missions, and initially suggested that domestic observation would be able to live up to this billing. In Kenya, for example, local civil society groups came together ahead of the 1992 general elections to form the National Electoral Monitoring Unit (NEMU) and deployed an impressive 8,000 observers (Rutten 2000: 296). By the time of the 2007 elections, NEMU had been replaced by Kenya Election Domestic Observation Forum (KEDOF), which mobilized 17,000 people based on a broad coalition of both religious and secular groups (Kanyinga, Long and Ndii 2010). In Uganda, the later return to multiparty politics meant that it was not until 2001 that a large-scale domestic observation effort was launched. In that election, the NGO Election Monitoring Group–Uganda (NEMGROUP-U) fielded some 18,000 monitors. By the time of the 2016 election, monitoring was being coordinated by the Citizens Election Observers Network–Uganda (CEON-U) – itself managed by a Steering Committee that represented 18 different CSOs (CCEDU 2015). In Ghana, the pattern was somewhat different. As noted earlier, the 1992 elections saw more international observers than domestic ones (Gyimah-Boadi, Oquaye and Drah 2000: 21). However, by 1996 this situation had changed, and a combination of greater funding and the controversy over the 1992 results led to a significant scaling up of activities under an umbrella group called the Network of Domestic Election Observers (NEDEO), which deployed 4,100 monitors (Gyekye-Jandoh 2016: 42). By 2016, NEDEO had been superseded by the Coalition of Domestic Observers (CODEO), which deployed 8,000 individuals, drawing on a coalition of 42 civil society, faith-based and professional associations. As in international observation, this evolution went hand-in-hand with efforts to develop new scientific methodologies, including the adoption of parallel vote tabulation (PVT) – discussed in greater detail later in this chapter.

We have already seen (Figure 4.1) that there is greater popular support for domestic as opposed to international election observation. However, the challenges that international observers face are also present – and in

some cases are even more acute – when it comes to their domestic counterparts. On the one hand, domestic observers – just like the CSOs from
which they are usually formed – are embedded in the societies in which they
operate and so can easily be perceived as biased as a result of their ethnicity,
location or past political affiliation (Chapter 5). As a result, despite promising to take a non-partisan approach to observation, they often struggle to
convince voters that they operate on the basis of a civic rather than
a patrimonial logic (Mapuva 2013). On the other hand, the 'domestic'
status of such groups does not necessarily generate greater credibility,
because they tend to be largely funded by international donors and so are
vulnerable to the accusation that they serve foreign political agendas
(Mesfin 2008: 6). This concern is not without foundation, as domestic
groups often face their own version of the observers' dilemma, in which
more critical groups may have to consider whether to moderate critical
statements in line with the position of the international community in order
to safeguard the financial support that they depend on.

Recent electoral history evidences these tensions in all three countries
but also reveals the same variation identified above. The ability of domestic
groups to promote the civic register is shaped by the greater cohesiveness
and credibility of the broader civil society that they are drawn from.
Operating in a more conducive environment, Ghanaian domestic observers have gradually built up capacity and credibility, and some organizations are now recognized as leaders in the field.[32] By contrast, their
equivalents in Kenya and to a lesser extent in Uganda have often faced
difficult questions over their approach and have been criticized for reflecting, rather than overcoming, social divisions. Thus, while the quest for ever
more scientific methods of election observation has seen the introduction
of new methods, their capacity to strengthen the authority of domestic
observers has been more limited in Kenya and Uganda.

4.3.1   Ideas of Virtue and Variations in Credibility
among Domestic Observers

In all three countries, observation groups see their work as central to the
fight for democracy and explain their commitment to it in terms of civic
virtue – as the names of organizations imply through their claims to be
'national' or 'citizen' bodies. Although the core staff of most domestic
observation teams are professional, they rely on individuals to monitor
polling stations either on a voluntary basis or in return for very small
remuneration. Given that the risks of monitoring an election are not

---

[32] In particular, Ghana Centre for Democratic Development (CDD-Ghana) has been
lauded by organizations such as NDI.

negligible, this suggests a genuine interest in, and commitment to, the electoral project. Reflecting on the motivation of individuals to join domestic observation groups in Ghana, a prominent domestic observer noted that

one thing I have realized is that when you engage people to work as observers ... they feel so elated, so happy, so enthusiastic that even wearing the T-shirt ... I think it's something that they also feel proud of.[33]

Those involved in Uganda came to a similar conclusion. For example, a member of CCEDU, which monitored the 2011 elections, argued that most of the people who helped to identify and report malpractice did not 'do it because they are going to get money out of it, but it was a duty. They wanted to serve their country'.[34] This may be a touch generous – and many are no doubt also motivated, at least in part, by the compensation involved and connections potentially created (Bodewes 2014: 80) – but this is a near ubiquitous interpretation and is certainly how observers frame their own activities when speaking to others.

Domestic monitoring missions routinely use this kind of language in formal descriptions of their own activities. In Ghana, CODEO's principles communicate a deep commitment to civic virtue. Not only does the organization promise to '[m]aintain independence from partisan associations and promote an image of impartiality', it also commits to ensuring 'the integrity of its undertaking' and pledges that 'plans once laid out must be executed'.[35] These three statements embody the holy trinity of civic virtue: autonomy, engaged citizenship and due process. The same is true of Uganda's CCEDU, which aims to 'promote integrity, transparency and active citizen participation in Uganda's electoral process'.[36] As we describe in greater detail in Chapter 5, many of the programmes undertaken by groups such as CCEDU focus on themes such as 'Honor Your Vote', which explicitly constructs the good citizen as one who is politically engaged and who gives their support to the candidate with the greatest merit. Within this moral frame, patrimonial behaviours such as selling one's vote or choosing a candidate on the basis of ethnicity are explicitly looked down upon.

But as with international observers, the efforts of domestic groups to stand above politics have frequently been undermined by the processes within which they are embedded. In the run-up to the 2007 Kenyan

---

[33] Interview GHA5a, Kumasi, 3 September 2015.
[34] Interview UGA7a, Kampala, 17 July 2014.
[35] CODEO Ghana, 'Our objectives and principles', n.d., http://www.codeoghana.org/about-us.php?p=T3VyIE9iamVjdGl2ZXMgJiBQcmluY2lwbGVz.
[36] CCEDU, 'Home page', n.d., www.ccedu.org.ug.

elections, the success of the 2002 election – when the country experienced its first democratic transfer of power – encouraged the formation of a large and self-confident domestic observation group, KEDOF. The urge to reach an ambitious target of 35,000 monitors allowed some individuals to register despite lacking a direct institutional affiliation with any of KEDOF's affiliate organizations. Although a day of training was provided for observers, there was relatively little vetting.[37] Taken together, these problems, combined with the limited capacity of the secretariat, meant that 3,000 monitors 'failed to submit their observation checklists after the exercise' (IREC 2008: 68).

KEDOF also experienced tensions between its secular and religious leaders, especially as evidence emerged of electoral manipulation. Disagreement over whether to reject the declared results exacerbated a 'deep-seated antagonism' within the organization (IREC 2008: 68). Much of this reflected mismanagement (Long 2008: 8), personality clashes and competition over control of resources between different groups 'each of which felt that it was uniquely placed to manage the coordination and funding' (IREC 2008: 68). It also, however, reflected partisan and ethnic considerations and so undermined KEDOF's claim to neutrality (Kanyinga, Long and Ndii 2010: 379). According to the report written by the donor programme that helped to found KEDOF and provided it with technical support, the domestic observers 'reflected in microcosm the ethnic, political, personality and other divisions that exploded so dramatically after the election' (as quoted in IREC 2008: 68).

This combination of internal disagreement and external criticism undermined the credibility of KEDOF, and its claim to bureaucratic legitimacy and civic virtue. As a result, the model was abandoned and international donors and CSOs agreed to build a smaller body that would be better trained and more integrated – and hence less likely to generate accusations of political or ethnic bias. Thus, Election Observation Group (ELOG) was born and monitored the 2013 elections with a much smaller group of observers. However, deploying just 7,000 people (Bland 2015: 16) in a country with more than 40,000 polling stations meant that it was not possible to achieve comprehensive coverage. As a result, this change went hand in hand with another, the introduction of a PVT, a sample-based election observation methodology that had been gaining ground for the previous 20 years.

The core idea of a PVT is that, by observing the electoral process and recording the results at a representative sample of polling stations, domestic observation groups can generate a projection of the presidential

---

[37] Cheeseman witnessed this first hand and was able to register despite not being a Kenyan national.

election result – with a margin of error that falls as the sample size grows. A typical sample of around 1,200 would give a margin of error of plus or minus 3 per cent. Precisely because designing the sample of polling stations requires the application of rigorous social scientific principles, and the process generates a binary outcome in terms of whether the official results are credible or not, the use of a PVT promises to bring mathematical precision to a discipline that has often been criticized for its reliance on individual observation and personal judgements – though at the cost of obscuring some issues behind a wall of numbers.

Most notably, while a PVT allows domestic observers to give a clear 'yes' or 'no' when asked whether the official result reflects the votes cast, it also risks deflecting attention away from important questions such as whether background conditions were conducive to voters freely expressing their political beliefs. Indeed, the very language and methodology of PVTs confers a greater sense of certainty on the whole process, granting domestic observers access to their own distinctive language of neutrality and scientific certainty; for, unlike international missions, domestic missions can marshal the numbers of people needed to run PVTs. Thus, Ghana's CODEO confidently describes PVTs as 'employing time-tested statistical principles' that ensure that '[n]o biases are shown'. Echoing the way that the method is promoted more generally, CODEO emphasizes its scientific foundations, noting that specially trained clerks are required to process the data, which is communicated via mobile phone networks to a tailor-made central database. According to CODEO, the ability of these processes to generate representative and accurate findings means that the PVT is 'a unique observation tool'.[38]

Given the great potential of PVTs, it is easy to see why they became extremely popular after the method was first pioneered in the Philippines in 1986 – becoming the tool of choice for international assistance to domestic observation (Garber and Cowan 1993). Over the last 30 years the NDI has 'assisted civic groups in 52 countries perform over 200 parallel vote tabulations (PVT) and continues to help citizen groups evolve in the methodology that they use to oversee their election processes'.[39] It also hosts PVT academies to foster and spread best practice.[40] In line with the trends in international observation described earlier, the language used by the NDI to describe the academies and the work done within them explicitly constructs election observation as a scientific endeavour,

---

[38] CODEO Ghana, 'PVT overview', n.d., www.codeoghana.org/pvt-overview.php.
[39] NDI, 'Parallel Vote Tabulations', 15 December 2019, www.ndi.org/pvt.
[40] NDI, 'NDI organizes Parallel Vote Tabulation academy', 20 November 2019, www.ndi.org/NDI_Organizes_Parallel_Vote_Tabulation_Academy.

'which demand[s] precision in training, communications, analysis and reporting', and which involves methods that can be honed over time to generate an increasingly robust and reliable process to ensure 'electoral integrity'.[41] This optimistic message has resonated across the continent and beyond (Cheeseman and Klaas 2018: 178). In addition to promising to encourage a broad range of democratic processes, PVTs are also popular with donors because their focussed nature means that they can be conducted with a relatively small team, and so are compatible with declining aid budgets in this area. This combination of domestic demand and external supply means that '[i]n countries as varied as Indonesia, Mexico, Croatia and Ghana, PVTs are now part of the electoral culture'.[42]

Framed in this way, the PVT approach appears to be something of a panacea – a way to promote and protect electoral integrity with such precision that accusations of partisan or ethnic bias are simply taken out of the equation. It is therefore no accident that Kenya's first experience of a PVT was in 2013, after the controversy surrounding the elections of 2007, while the first PVT in Uganda was conducted in 2006, following the flawed polls of 2001. In some cases, the evidence sustains the claims made for this new approach to observation. However, the emergence of new methods has not worked to insulate domestic observers from controversy – and hence to sustain their ability to persuade citizens to place their faith in the official rules of the game – in precisely those cases in which their independence has been most challenged. This is because – despite the language of science and numbers – the power of a PVT is rooted in popular belief and confidence in the organization deploying it. Much like opinion polls (Wolf 2020), critics may allege that the sample selected is not representative and question how a small number of observations can accurately predict the overall outcome – an argument that infuriates statistics experts but resonates with many voters, who have little exposure to sampling methodology and the mathematics that lie behind it.[43] A related problem is that, in the context of a close election and small sample size, a PVT may 'confirm' that the leading candidate plausibly secured more than 50%+1 of the vote, but would also have confirmed the opposite – as both results fell within the margin of error – which is what happened in Kenya in 2013 (Ferree, Gibson and Long 2014: 157).

Second, PVTs are limited in what they can tell us about an election. In particular, they are not designed to provide a comprehensive overview of

---

[41] Ibid.
[42] Ibid.
[43] As with opinion polls, it seems likely that those making these allegations understand that the methodology is reliable and deliberately play on the suspicions of their supporters.

the campaign and whether the broader environment was conducive to a credible election. Partly as a result, PVTs often 'confirm' the result of an election that has a number of serious flaws. For example, the findings of the PVT conducted by domestic observers in Uganda in 2011 confirmed the official results, yet this jarred with the many limitations that opposition leaders – and many observers themselves – identified with the process. In addition to the illegitimate use of state infrastructure and funds to support the campaign of the ruling party, EU observers reported that logistical failings led to 'an unacceptable number of Ugandan citizens being disenfranchised', while 'the power of incumbency was exercised to such an extent as to compromise severely the level playing field between the competing candidates' (EU 2011: 5). A litany of other abuses was also noted, including the refusal of the police to operate impartially, while 'poor application of basic procedures revealed inadequate training of polling station staff and implied insufficient safeguards against fraud' (EU 2011: 7). Despite their reluctance to condemn the process outright, these observers' comments arguably gave a more accurate account of the polls than did the numerical wizardry of the PVT.

The failure of the PVT to persuade opposition leaders in Kenya and Uganda that recent elections were acceptable ultimately undermined the ability of domestic monitors to confer legitimacy on the process and bolster support for civic virtue.[44] The contrast between the experience of these two countries and that of Ghana is instructive. Although the Ghanaian presidential elections of 2008 and 2012 featured significant controversy, with the losing party alleging electoral manipulation, there was relatively little debate over the PVTs that confirmed the results or of the organizations that carried them out. While Nicolas Cook suggests that 'US-supported CODEO PVTs in 2008 and 2012 appeared to contribute to public trust in those close elections' (2018: 3), we would argue that the experience of Kenya and Uganda makes it clear that the greater confidence witnessed in Ghana did not come from anything inherent within the PVT, but rather from the context in which the PVT was implemented, as described in Chapter 3. Repeated transfers of power, public confidence in the electoral commission and the emergence of one of the most respected observation bodies on the continent, the Ghana Centre for Democratic Development (CDD-Ghana) – which established CODEO in 2000 – conferred credibility on the PVT process. Precisely because credible organizations are required to hold

---

[44] Xan Rice, 'Ugandan leader wins presidential election rejected as fraudulent by opposition', *The Guardian*, 20 February 2011, www.theguardian.com/world/2011/feb/20/ugandan-leader-wins-presidential-election.

a credible PVT, this methodology alone has little independent capacity to promote civic virtue.

Public opinion across our three cases reflects both the extent to which observers are operating under favourable conditions – that is in a political system in which transfers of power are possible – in addition to the reputation of domestic groups (Figure 4.3). Fully 91 per cent of Ghanaian respondents agreed that domestic observers have improved the quality of elections, reflecting the particularly high esteem in which Ghanaian domestic observers are held. By contrast, the controversy over the politicized nature of domestic observers and civil society in general (Chapter 5) explains why only 71 per cent of Kenyans gave the same answer – a difference of some 20 per cent. Thus, despite the adoption of PVT technology in all three cases, it is only really in Ghana that there is evidence that it has conferred greater credibility on electoral processes and those who observe them.

Our point in making this argument is not to critique the use of PVTs themselves, but rather to demonstrate that the success of efforts to strengthen electoral integrity is itself conditioned by the context within which they are introduced, and whether voters and political leaders have reasons to trust claims made in the civic register. Especially where citizens have come to expect patrimonial bias or criminality and have been given little reason to believe in the efficacy of democratic rules and institutions, domestic observers will struggle to win hearts and minds in the absence of

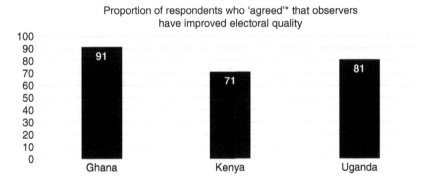

Figure 4.3 The impact of domestic observers on the quality of elections (%)

* Agree = those who stated that they 'agreed' or 'strongly agreed' with the statement. The other options were 'disagree', 'strongly disagree' and 'neither agree nor disagree'.

Source: Authors' own survey data

a transfer of power. Voters and candidates alike know only too well that the proof of the pudding is in the eating.

4.4   Conclusion: The Challenge of Promoting Civic Virtue from the Outside-In

This chapter has shown how election observation missions – both domestic and international – have consistently sought to promote civic virtue. In doing so, they have taken part in an important kind of claims-making, demanding that participants follow norms that are understood in terms of due process. The moral authority of such claims, however, is weakened by internal contradiction: while observers work hard to embody and broadcast impartiality, their audience suspects that in fact they are motivated by a range of other considerations. History and inconsistent behaviour encourages scepticism when European or North American governments assert their neutrality, and past experience suggests that international observation has an inherent conservative bias. Domestic observers suffer less from the historical baggage of colonial rule, the Cold War, problematic economic policies, the 'war on terror' and questionable business deals, but may nonetheless struggle to assert their autonomy from the political processes in which they – to an even greater extent than their international counterparts – are enmeshed.

In stressing this point we do not mean to imply that election observation does not provide incentives to those in power to moderate their behaviour around elections, or that making demands in terms of civic virtue is never worthwhile. Recent research has demonstrated that observation has the capacity to modify strategies of electoral manipulation, if not always to curtail them (Asunka et al. 2019). Rather, our argument is that observation on its own cannot ensure the greater acceptance of civic registers of virtue. Ultimately, the claims of observers to neutrality, like the claims of election officials (Chapter 3), are only really accepted where power changes hands – and that is beyond the control of domestic and international missions.

This point suggests that we need to carefully rethink the way that we conceptualize international democracy promotion strategies. Many recent analyses of the ability of Western governments to effect reform in sub-Saharan Africa have followed Levitsky and Way (2006), who view this as a function of the degree of Western leverage (how vulnerable a government is to external pressure) and linkage (the density of a country's ties to the United States, EU and multilateral institutions). This approach has considerable traction when it comes to explaining the ability of Western states to use economic or military coercion to force through formal policy change – though even in this context it risks understating the capacity of African leaders to exercise agency in tight corners (Fisher 2014). It has far less to say, however, about the ability of donors to use what Nye (1990) famously called 'soft power' to persuade political leaders and populations to adopt new norms and practices.

While Uganda has often been the most aid-dependent case in our sample, for example, it is arguably the country in which the international community has been least effective at fostering civic registers of virtue. This is partly because Museveni has proved to be a world leader at manipulating international engagements for his own ends (Hauser 1999; Fisher 2013a, 2014). But it is also because, while economic and coercive powers are important components of the authority of international institutions, they are not sufficient to ensure their credibility and efficacy. Accounts of international democracy promotion therefore need to place greater emphasis on the significance of popular and elite perceptions of international actors and their proxies.

This conclusion suggests another: that it is important not to exaggerate the significance of the international gaze. As we have argued elsewhere (Willis, Lynch and Cheeseman 2018), elections in Africa have become so dynamic precisely because they were rapidly embraced and domesticated. Many countries on the continent now have a 70-year history of holding elections of one form or another, and they have become part and parcel of the political system, a ritual that has become a critical component of state identity and legitimacy. Thus, the reason that African leaders do not stop holding elections is not simply to avoid international condemnation. An equally if not more compelling motivation is that to do so would in effect be an admission that they are not running a respectable 'modern state', which in turn would generate intense resistance from a range of domestic constituencies including opposition parties, civil society groups, ordinary citizens and significant components of the ruling party itself. The significance of the international gaze is therefore not that it sustains democracy and elections in Africa but that it has been one of the important – if problematic – sources of civic ideas of virtue.

Looking forward, it is important to recognize that the effect of the international gaze is profoundly shaped by proximate events and the composition and balance of power within the international community itself, which is constantly shifting. In recent years, efforts at electoral manipulation have been exposed in Gambia and Venezuela but condoned – or at the very least tolerated – in Bangladesh and the DRC by exactly the same Western actors (Cheeseman and Klaas 2018), reinforcing popular suspicions that observation efforts are characterized by inconsistency and double standards. At the same time, the illusion of Western hegemony following the collapse of the Soviet Union in 1991 has now given way to recognition that the world is becoming increasingly 'multi-polar'. In addition to the growing role that China is playing in sub-Saharan Africa (Large 2008), a range of other countries have become increasingly economically significant, including Saudi Arabia, Iran, Turkey and Russia (Chege 2020). These authoritarian states may valorize aspects of the civic register, such as the significance of the rule of law, but they have less interest in promoting other elements such as active citizenship. Moreover, although it is true that some of the new 'non-traditional' countries engaging in Africa do not explicitly promote authoritarianism, the success of countries such as China, with its very different political system and underpinning ideological foundations, has encouraged African leaders to emulate a very different set of role models (Fourie 2014). Promoting civic virtue is therefore going to be even more complicated in the future than it has been in the past.

5   Creating Democrats
Civil Society and Voter Education

Loud music blared from the truck cruising slowly down the street; on its flat back, a group of young people danced; one called out over the amplified music to urge citizens to vote in Uganda's upcoming election. One could easily have mistaken the colourful and noisy roadshow for a party campaign vehicle. Yet instead of being festooned in the usual party colours – yellow for the National Resistance Movement (NRM), blue for the Forum for Democratic Change (FDC) or orange for Go Forward – the vehicle and its passengers were all dressed in purple. The performance was part of a national voter education drive conducted by a collection of civil society organizations (CSOs) under the banner of the Citizens' Coalition for Electoral Democracy in Uganda (CCEDU), which called on Ugandans 'to *topowa*' (or 'not give up') and to 'honour their vote' and 'focus on issues'.[1] As a CCEDU TV advert of the time declared:

[M]ost of us complain about our bad roads, poor health services ... and so many other things. But do you know that you have the power to change everything? Yes, with your vote. Your vote has the power to improve our roads ... [it] can end poverty, corruption and improve the lives of all Ugandans ... so *topowa*. Honour your vote. Your choice can make the difference.

Similar motivational performances have been seen across all three countries since the return to multiparty politics. They blame national woes on corrupt leaders who work for themselves or a narrow support base rather than for the country as a whole and extol the virtues of following the rule of law and of nationally minded citizenship. In so doing, a particular type of civil society has sought to educate and empower people to 'take their civic duty seriously and make demands for accountable leadership from their leaders' (KNCHR 2007: 5).

These efforts to cultivate civic virtue among citizens who then elect civic-minded leaders are not a new phenomenon. In the run-up to pre-independence elections, newspaper editorials tutored people on what to consider when marking their ballot[2] and clergymen urged people to

---

[1] Fieldwork notes, Fort Portal, 8 February 2016.
[2] 'Choosing the new assembly', *Uganda Argus*, 25 April 1962, p. 4.

'weigh the issues' and to vote as a 'matter of conscience'.[3] At the same time, multiple forms of associational life played an active role in electoral politics; most notably, trade unions (particularly in Kenya, see Kyle 1999) and churches (particularly in Uganda, see Ibingira 1973). After independence, governments in all three countries moved to curtail and/or incorporate those organizations and movements that had proved so useful in anti-colonial mobilization (Cooper 2012: 58–59). But associational life did not end. Civil society in Uganda enjoyed a resurgence during the no-party democracy years, with a powerful women's movement capable of winning significant concessions (Tripp 2001). The reintroduction of multiparty politics in 2005 hardened partisan divides, while government repression of overt criticism made it more difficult for civil society groups to operate. But even after this, associational life – from religious groups to professional associations and NGOs – has played an important role in calling for governance reforms and in supporting democratization (Oloka-Onyango and Barya 1997; Tripp 2010). In Ghana, it was middle-class organizations – students, lawyers, doctors – that both empowered and divided the resistance to Acheampong's Unigov plans in the late 1970s (Chazan and LeVine 1979) and which continued to back 'good governance' reforms in the 1990s and early 2000s (Arthur 2010). In Kenya, ethnic associations continued to play an important part in post-independence politics until they were banned in the early 1980s, when professional, student and religious organizations became increasingly prominent (Atieno Odhiambo 2004: 169). In turn, it was Kenya's main-line churches – Presbyterian, Anglican, Catholic – that provided an organizational basis and a moral language for a critique of queue-voting and single-party rule in the late 1980s and early 1990s (Sabar-Friedman 1997). Through such activities, bodies such as the National Council of Churches of Kenya (NCCK) seemed to realize the idea – or even, perhaps the 'Idea' (Comaroff and Comaroff 1999: 1) – of civil society as it came to be imagined during the 1980s, namely as a body that could both educate and represent the citizenry vis-à-vis a bloated yet rootless state that was blamed for everything from underdevelopment to conflict (Bayart 1986; Diamond 1994).

The involvement in electoral politics of multiple associational forms that seek to fit, but which also clearly fall beyond, this Idea is still apparent. As Chapters 6 and 7 show, various local associations – from transport cooperatives to market associations – provide arenas for multiple claims-making that help to constitute election campaigns, as do groups based on ethnicity or locality. As Karlström has argued, such organizations may not

---

[3] 'The Christian voter in a general election', *Daily Graphic*, 8 June 1956, p. 7.

fit into a common conception of civil society, but they do provide ways to 'conceive and enact' an engagement with the state (1999: 117). However, in this chapter we focus on the civil society that gained prominence with political and economic liberalization and the 'good governance' agenda, namely those formal organizations that have a recognized structure, staff and vision, and seek to bring about and support 'an informed, active and responsible citizenry; and a responsive, accountable and effective government' (CRECO 2019; also VonDoepp 2019).

The 'third wave' of democratization has seen an efflorescence of such organizations. In Kenya, the number of registered non-governmental organizations (NGOs) – comprised mainly of development and governance-oriented organizations – increased from several hundred in 1990 to more than 8,000 by 2012 (Brass et al. 2018: 136), with those registered to provide civic education increasing from fewer than 20 in 1991 to more than 130 in 1996.[4] In Uganda, the growth has been less explosive, but nevertheless impressive: the number of registered NGOs grew from approximately 1,000 in 1996 to more than 4,000 by 1999 (Dicklitch 2001: 31), with more than 800 involved in CCEDU by 2018.[5] The lack of specific laws to regulate CSOs in Ghana renders it more difficult to give national-level figures, though it is clear that the 1990s saw a similarly rapid proliferation (Tsikata, Gyejye-Jandoh and Hushie 2013: 23 and 8).

Many of these organizations focus largely (or exclusively) on development and social service provision (Hearn 1998; Katusiimeh 2004; Tsikata, Gyejye-Jandoh and Hushie 2013; Brass 2016). However, many also focus on good governance and democratization and undertake a mix of inter-linked work packages on areas such as voter and civic education, documentation (including domestic election observation), advocacy and litigation (most notably for electoral reform) and peace-messaging/building (Lugano 2020). These governance programmes vary in scope and scale from small stand-alone projects to large collaborative projects conducted in conjunction with government agencies, international NGOs and other CSOs. Activities tend to be funded by the international community – be it by large multilateral and bilateral agencies, such as the United Nations (UN), United States Agency for International Development (USAID) or European Union (EU), or international organizations or foundations, such as the National Democratic Institute (NDI) or the Ford Foundation (Mercer 2002; Hearn 2007; Brass et al. 2018).

As the scale and scope of civil society have grown, the divisions and tensions within it have become increasingly apparent. So too has the extent to which activists and organizations are actually entangled with

---

[4] 'Civic education and donors', *The Standard*, 28 January 2002.   [5] www.ccedu.org.ug.

the state, embedded within particular communities and externally oriented. In this vein, critics have pointed to how organizations can be urban, elitist, ethnically biased, divorced from the societies that they purport to represent, and characterized by their own form of personalized rule; how their reliance on external funding can ensure that their activities reflect donor, rather than local, concerns; how 'activists' often 'straddle' state and civil society; and how civil society groups may be co-opted by, share interests with, or unintentionally help to sustain existing political cultures and forms of power (e.g. see Fatton 1995; Ndegwa 1996; Allen 1997; Oloka-Onyango and Barya 1997; Hearn 1998 and 2007; Dicklitch 2001; Mercer 2002). As we will discuss in this chapter, such entanglement with state structures, embeddedness in societies and external orientation or extraversion (Bayart and Ellis 2000) can reveal and reinforce a perception of a biased patrimonial state and/or undermine civil society's assumed capacity to promote civic virtue. This undermines civil society's capacity to organize and represent various societal interests in a way that, as Larry Diamond has put it, is 'concerned with *public* rather than private ends ... *relates to the state* in some way but does not aim to win formal power or office ... [and] encompasses *pluralism* and diversity ... [with] different groups represent[ing] different interests' (1994: 6–7; emphasis in original). Instead, examples of entanglement, embeddedness and extraversion suggest that CSOs may often not differ from the state that they are meant to help keep in check and are therefore unable to ensure the 'accountability, responsiveness, inclusiveness, effectiveness, and hence legitimacy of the political system' (Diamond 1994: 11).

Informed by such critiques and insights, this chapter focusses on voter education efforts and the ideas of moral citizenship and leadership that these seek to cultivate. We define voter education not in the narrow sense of 'information on how to vote' (UHRC 2016: 28–29), but more broadly as all avowedly educational efforts aimed at voters. This focus is in part pragmatic – it is impossible to look in any detail at all the different types of democracy support work that CSOs do in a single chapter. It is also a product of our approach – voter education is all about what people *should do* and *why* and thus provides an excellent example of how different registers of virtue may play out in the moral economy of elections. By drawing on our interviews and participant observations we differentiate between five types of voter education: information, mobilization, decision-making or 'issue-fication', comportment, and vigilance (see 5.1). However, while our research points to important variations in approach, the similarities that we witnessed outweighed the differences. Voter education in all three countries seeks to change individual behaviour by making people into 'good citizens' who participate in elections as considered, issue-oriented, orderly and peaceful individuals. In so doing, voters are framed, as with civic education efforts elsewhere, as 'not-yet-good-enough citizens ... [who need] to learn what being a good citizen means and how they should act' (Pykett, Saward and Schaefer 2010: 529). At the same time, voter education efforts seek – through the collective action and power of the vote – to facilitate the emergence of 'good leaders' who are honest, fair and committed to the general good. Both voters and politicians are thus encouraged to internalize a civic, rather than patrimonial, register of virtue: the 'good' voters and leaders that voter education explicitly seeks to cultivate follow the rules, rise above societal pressures and prioritize national interests.

In the process, voter education campaigns help to imagine the Idea of civil society outlined above, namely as a form of associational life that is of, and for, society and separate from, and capable of checking, the state. Within this framework, educational campaigns are cast as an activity that is conducted by 'expert citizens' (Bang 2005) who adhere to, and who simultaneously help to promote, a civic register of virtue that values impartiality, meritocracy and the national common good. CCEDU's self-definition is typical: 'The overriding agenda of this coalition is to advocate and promote integrity, transparency and active citizen participation in Uganda's electoral process.'[6] Similarly, Uraia – which was formed in 2000 and by the 2010s was 'the premier national civic education organisation in Kenya' – lists its organizational values as 'integrity, equity, transparency, professionalism, nonpartisan, equality'.[7] Voter education not only helps to imagine a particular kind of civil society, it also serves – or so we argue – to help 'produce the apparent separateness of the state' from society (cf. Mitchell 1991: 91) that is so vital to the Idea of an impartial bureaucratic state that adheres to civic virtue.

However, the messy reality of political life ensures that these visions are constantly called into question. First, while voter education efforts seek to strengthen a civic register of virtue, they sometimes inadvertently strengthen a patrimonial register whereby voters primarily see themselves as members of sub-national groups and support those who have assisted them. This can happen in various ways. Voter education efforts can reinforce a sense that others will act according to the patrimonial register; fail to provide clear moral direction about what people should do when others do not adhere to official rules; and applaud, and even enact, the reciprocity and preference of the patrimonial register.

This is not to say that voter education by civil society does not have important effects – they are just not always the impacts that were

[6] www.ccedu.org.ug.   [7] http://uraia.or.ke.

intended. The language and behaviour that it propagates can promote civic virtue and produce the appearance that the state is separate from society. However, while civil society efforts are very similar across our three country case studies, the nature of their effect – or the productiveness of this electoral work – varies. Local context – and most notably, the perceived salience of sub-national identities and historically informed expectations regarding the likely behaviour of key actors and institutions – influences how similar voter education efforts are received and interpreted. The chapter starts by introducing a schema of voter education efforts, before moving on to a comparison of voter education and popular evaluations of civil society in our country case studies and to the implications for efforts to cultivate 'good' civic-minded voters and leaders and for the type of civil society and state that is enacted.

5.1   The Educational Imperative

In all three countries the institution with the primary mandate to conduct voter education since the return to multiparty politics has been the electoral management body (EMB). In Ghana and Uganda other state agencies are mandated to conduct broader civic education; namely the National Commission for Civic Education (NCCE) and the Uganda Human Rights Commission (UHRC), respectively. These efforts are then supported by various CSOs and a range of other actors including the media, political parties, individual candidates, state officials and multiple other public employees and local figures, from teachers to chiefs. Voter education efforts are thus multi-sectoral and pervasive. They are also increasingly diverse in approach with efforts ranging from posters, newspaper adverts and infomercials to workshops, public debates, roadshows, roaming public service vehicles, plays, cartoons, games, sermons, social media campaigns and much more.[8] The majority of citizens will have seen, read or heard a voter education message ahead of an election day. To use figures that only capture a single type of voter education during a single electoral cycle: 58 per cent of respondents in a study in Kawempe, Kampala, said that they had been encouraged to vote by religious leaders during sermons in the run-up to the 2011 elections (Feree, Jung, Dowd and Gibson 2018: 12), while it is estimated that Kenya's 'YVote Campaign' – conducted by the Independent Electoral and Boundaries Commission (IEBC) in conjunction with

---

[8] For an example of how some of these different approaches may be combined in one voter education drive see the Yvote Youth Outreach in Kenya video at www.ifes.org/news/wor king-kenyan-youth-get-out-vote-during-2017-electoral-period.

CSOs ahead of the country's 2017 elections – reached almost 170,000 people through face-to-face interactions and 17 million through social media.[9] Radio jingles, television infomercials, newspaper adverts and posters with information on how and why to vote were ubiquitous during our research in Ghana, Kenya and Uganda ahead of their 2016 and 2017 elections.

Despite such a diversity of actors and approaches, voter education efforts share common aims, namely to create 'a climate of knowledgeable participation by all potential voters' (KCCB 2017: 41) and to foster a 'mature political culture' (NCEP cited in Finkel and Smith 2011: 418). Voter education is predicated on the assumption that elections 'cannot be easily comprehended' by voters (Wanyande 2002: 55). The implication – as Frederick Schaffer has argued of largely middle-class civic educators in the Philippines – is that many educators 'not only have contempt for "dirty" or incompetent politicians, but also have misgivings about the poor who keep re-electing them' (2007b: 167). Fearing that voters are prone to violence, they insist that peace is a 'prime civic duty' (Lynch, Cheeseman and Willis 2019).[10] This focus on potential chaos is often reinforced by a Fanon-esque internalization of colonial tropes. As one member of Ghana's peace infrastructure remarked in 2016:

[C]onsidering, I mean, our attitude and character as blacks and Africans, you know, when you don't engage [people], I mean the likelihood of them I mean, doing a whole lot of things to mar the whole [electoral] process is, is, is there. So we engage them.[11]

Against such shared concerns, voter education in all three countries, we argue, is aimed at addressing five perceived informational gaps, namely that citizens might not know how to register and cast a valid ballot; fail to understand the importance of voting; fail to understand the basis on which they should support candidates; fail to grasp how they should behave as voters; and fail to understand the ways in which they can help to ensure that others follow the relevant rules and procedures. This leads us to differentiate between five types of facilitated learning: voter information, voter mobilization, voter decision-making or 'issue-fication', voter comportment and voter vigilance.

The first type of education, voter information, is the most obvious and consists of relaying key things that citizens need to know if they are to

---

[9] See the Yvote Youth Outreach in Kenya video at www.ifes.org/news/working-kenyan-youth-get-out-vote-during-2017-electoral-period. Statistics are listed 4 minutes and 30 seconds into the video.

[10] 'Let's have a peaceful end to campaigns', *Daily Nation*, 27 December 1997, p. 6.

[11] Interview GHA48a, Ho, 23 November 2016.

become effective voters: how to register, how to find one's polling station, how to mark and cast one's ballot paper. Unsurprisingly, the nature of voter information is heavily influenced by where a country is in the electoral cycle, by whether an election will adopt new technology and by recent experience. For example, CDD-Ghana increased its voter information efforts in the lead-up to the 2016 election after an evaluation underscored the high number of rejected ballots in 2012.[12] Similarly, information on the colours of different ballot papers was foregrounded in Kenya's 2013 elections following the inauguration of a new constitution in 2010 amidst widespread acknowledgement that the task of voting for six different levels of elected posts on a single day would render the country's elections one of the most complex in the world.

The second strand – voter mobilization – assumes that many people do not understand the importance of voting and need to be encouraged to become active citizens. A common theme is that people are either apathetic or sceptical and do not appreciate the power of their vote. CCEDU's educational drive ahead of Uganda's 2016 elections began with a 'votability' campaign that sought 'to motivate Ugandans to engage' with the update of the country's voter register (CCEDU 2015: 1) and then moved to call upon citizens to 'not give up' in their efforts to have their voices heard. Some organizations also call on people to mobilize their families, friends and neighbours to vote. In this vein, Kenya's 2017 'YVote' campaign 'enlisted youth ambassadors and experiential marketers' through 'a combination of online messaging and door to door activation . . . to encourage youth to "make an election day plan" to go out and vote with family and friends' (Technical Working Group 2018: 67).[13]

Mobilization is often closely intertwined with education on appropriate logics for selecting a favoured candidate. At the heart of this is the aim of ensuring that voting decisions are informed by individual judgements on issues – hence the term 'issue-fication', favoured by some CSOs (Jesuit Hakimani Centre 2017). Voters, it is assumed, must be dissuaded from voting along patrimonial lines and from being unduly influenced by money, personal ties or co-ethnicity, which reinforces a cycle of corruption and poor leadership. Given such assumptions, voter education aims to instil a sense of 'responsibility to vote for ethical men and women' (KCCB 2017: 11). As one civic educator in Kenya bemoaned, many people tend to vote 'with their stomach, rather than with their head', which has 'entirely eaten the moral fabric of our society' such that the

---

[12] Unrecorded interview, civil society activist, Accra, 26 September 2018.
[13] For an example of a YVote 'motivation video' see www.ifes.org/news/youth-vote-activation-and-digital-media-campaign-gearing-2017-kenyan-election.

country continues to get bad and corrupt leaders.[14] In a similar vein, CCEDU's 2016 'Topowa – Honour your vote' campaign included a 'People's Pledge':

We the people of Uganda, commit to participate peacefully, actively and responsibly in the forthcoming elections. We undertake to focus on issues, reject inducements, financial or otherwise. We honour our vote. For God and my country. (CCEDU 2015: 19)

This call for active citizens that follow rules and focus on peace, the national interest and God's will is common to 'issue-fication' drives across all three countries; with relevant 'issues' thus clearly defined in line with the civic register.

As campaigns for 'issue-fication' have become increasingly central to civil society voter education efforts, they have also become more sophisticated and multi-layered. Calls to denounce vote buying and to 'vote with our conscience and not our stomachs' (CJPC 2017: 6) are increasingly intertwined with efforts to help voters know an aspirant's position on particular issues and to hold them to account. This has included the organization of public debates, such as those for presidential candidates held in Ghana since 2000, Kenya since 2013 and Uganda in 2016. These events are staged (at least in part) to encourage aspirants to focus on issues (IEA 2014: 12), but they are also meant to be educational for voters by providing them 'with the kind of information that they need for them to make [informed] choices' (Crabbe 2013: 7).

These debates are also meant to help cultivate a sense of candidates as respectful peers, who share an understanding of what the main issues are and how politics should be conducted. As one religious leader who helped to organize the 2016 presidential debate in Uganda explained, 'the idea behind holding this debate is all about promoting peace ... because if now the top leaders can sit together ... why do you [as an ordinary Ugandan] hate each other to the extent of seeing one another as enemies?'[15] The Kenya Presidential Debate Coalition made similar claims days before the country's 2013 election when they insisted that 'the debates have contributed to the emergence of an issue-based political culture' and that by bringing opposition candidates and positions together they had also 'lowered political temperatures'.[16]

Such ideas point to a fourth strand of voter education – voter comportment – which focusses on how voters should behave so as

---

[14] Unrecorded interview, clergyman, Nairobi, 3 October 2018.
[15] Interview UGA108a, religious leader, Gulu, 25 February 2016.
[16] Advertisement: 'Kenya presidential debate coalition: "Supporting presidential debates in Kenya"', *Sunday Nation*, 3 March 2013, p. 55.

to help ensure that an election is credible, orderly and peaceful. As one civil society activist in Ghana suggested, voter education would teach 'when you go to the polling station this is how you'll have to conduct yourself and then comport yourself in such a way that you don't infringe on the right of other people'.[17] Comportment efforts often combine details on electoral rules – for example, against wearing party paraphernalia inside a polling station – with an emphasis on order and peace. In the words of one voter education message in Uganda, '[i]t is your duty and responsibility to peacefully accept the legitimate outcome of an election' (CCEDU 2015: 13). In so doing, such efforts help to promote an election that is not only orderly and peaceful, but one in which voters purposively adhere to a civic register (by following the rules and prioritizing the national good) and, in so doing, suggest an image of an unbiased and bureaucratic state that adheres to the same.

It is important to stress that education for electoral peace is not a small focus or new phenomenon. On the contrary, while such efforts have grown with the expansion of civil society from the early 1990s, and were particularly intense following Kenya's post-election crisis of 2007/2008 (Cheeseman, Lynch and Willis 2014; Elder, Stigant and Claes 2014), they have long been part of voter education efforts across all three countries. This includes Ghana, where – unlike Kenya and Uganda – multiparty elections have been relatively – though not wholly – peaceful since the 1990s (Lynch, Cheeseman and Willis 2019).

Voter vigilance, finally, encourages the public to see themselves as citizens involved in a task of mutual discipline, collectively ensuring that others also adhere to electoral rules and thus the civic register. In this vein, the Kenya Conference of Catholic Bishops' (KCCB) *Civic, Voter and Peace Education Handbook* described the right to vote as including a responsibility to

ensure that every other citizen exercises his or her right to vote without being intimidated or ensuring there is no bribery of voters, that every institution and public officer performs their role in ensuring free and fair elections, that there is no violence or intimidation, [and] that those who violate the law and commit electoral offences by being involved in corruption, hate speech, incitement, promoting war like activities and such like offences are barred from contesting or are punished for crimes they are suspected to have committed. (2017: 19)

As the country's Catholic Justice and Peace Commission (CJPC) made clear in their annual civic education drive in 2016, '[a] truly responsible citizen sometimes must go an extra mile to do things which help the society' (2016: 10). To this end, CSOs (often in collaboration with

---

[17] Interview GHA4a, civil society activist, Kumasi, 3 September 2015.

relevant government agencies, and/or with donor funds) have established hotlines and crowdsourcing mechanisms to involve citizens in reporting and preventing malpractice.[18]

These various educational strands can come into tension with each other, but they are fundamentally similar: often cast as purely technical, they are in fact all concerned with the promotion of moral behaviour and with the civic register of virtue. They do this by casting certain activities – such as rule adherence, individual choice and the prioritization of national interests – as virtuous. Others – such as rule-breaking, vote buying and the prioritization of individual or ethnic interests – are presented as immoral and dangerous. The cross-cutting theme: if good citizens choose good leaders, credible elections will deliver stability and development, and the civic register will come to trump the patrimonial.

This intertwined bundle of normative goals is most obvious when it comes to 'issue-fication', which presents issue-based politics as being largely absent, yet achievable through collective action. CCEDU's 2016 campaign insisted that '[i]f we all vote, our roads, hospitals and education can improve. Let's all go and vote for leaders who can end poverty, create jobs and ensure security ... Your vote makes a difference' (CCEDU 2015: 18). Or, as the preface to a Kenyan CJPC civic education campaign argued in 2017, 'responsible' citizens who hold officials accountable can expect 'quality services' (Korir 2017: 7). However, these normative goals are also central to the other four strands of voter education including (perhaps least obviously) voter information, which involves both the dissemination of facts regarding electoral rules and regulations *and* a plea (sometimes implicit, often explicit) for popular adherence to the same. In this vein, efforts to inform people on how to vote also imply that people *should* vote. In turn, efforts to inform voters of the legal implications of 'vote buying' – for example, that 'it's very dangerous, you'll be arrested'[19] – relay official laws (Kramon 2017: 22) but also seek to persuade people to not be swayed by the same.

Civil society efforts around elections therefore seek to bring about a political transformation through popular attitudinal and behavioural change. Before turning to some of the tensions between the civic and patrimonial registers involved in such efforts, we provide a brief sketch of variations between our three cases. In so doing, we highlight how, in terms of the approaches adopted, there are a number of common features but also how different contexts – most notably in popular experiences and

---

[18] Advertisement from IED, CJPC and NCCK: 'Together for peaceful elections', *Daily Nation*, 26 December 1997, p. 9; Interview UGA5a, civil society activist, Kampala, 16 July 2014.
[19] Interview conducted by research assistant, voter educator, Nairobi, 11 December 2018.

perceptions of CSOs and key political institutions – lead to significant variation in terms of public evaluations of civil society's involvement in elections. These differences have important implications for the impact of civil society voter education efforts on voter behaviour and on the Idea of civil society and the state that is produced.

5.2   A Common Agenda, Different Contexts

A common goal of creating civic-minded citizens does not mean that civil society voter education efforts have been the same across time and space. The approaches have varied as a result of the regimes in place, institutional learning and donor funding.

In terms of strategies adopted, Ghanaian CSOs have often been innovators, for example, through the introduction of presidential debates in 2000 and non-denominational prayers for all parties in 2008 (Arthur 2010: 212). Voter educators in Kenya, meanwhile, have been able to use a relatively dense network of CSOs and faith-based organizations (FBOs) to periodically conduct particularly intensive education drives, such as the Kenyan National Civic Education Programme (NCEP) of late 2001 to December 2002, which consisted of 'some 50,000 discrete workshops, plays and puppet shows, and community meetings conducted by nearly 80 Kenyan NGOs' (Finkel and Smith 2011: 418). By contrast, the efforts of Ugandan CSOs have appeared – at least in relative terms – to be fairly limited in scale and imploring, rather than exhortatory, in tone.

These differences largely stem from varying levels of state control. While governments in all three countries were highly suspicious of, and sought to curtail, voter education efforts by CSOs during the elections of the 1990s (Dicklitch 2001; Orvis 2003; Botchway 2018), the three countries have since diverged. Ghana has become increasingly open; Uganda has remained highly controlled; and Kenya became more open, until the government and prominent CSOs locked horns following the International Criminal Court's (ICC's) intervention in 2010 (Lugano 2020). The consequences are clear: Ghanaian CSOs operate in an increasingly conducive space, while, in contrast, CCEDU's Topowa campaign was briefly suspended by the Ugandan EC ahead of the country's 2016 election (UHRC 2016), and President Kenyatta warned donors against interfering in the country's sovereignty through civic education ahead of the country's 2017 elections. In response, donors invested fewer resources and the intensity of voter education declined.[20]

---

[20] Interview conducted by research assistant, voter educator, Nairobi, 11 December 2018.

Levels of partisanship also play a role in shaping how voter education efforts are rolled out and received. In Ghana, high levels of partisanship for the two main political parties amidst regular transfers of power ensure that there are prominent CSOs and activists associated with both parties: the Institute of Economic Affairs (IEA), for example, with the NPP, and the Institute for Democratic Governance (IDEG) with the NDC. That undermines claims to civil society impartiality but has given both the NDC and NPP reason to allow space for CSOs to work. In Kenya, by contrast, partisan links have reduced the space for CSOs to work, rather than expanding it. In the 1990s, prominent CSOs were generally seen to be dominated by certain ethnic groups (Mercer 2002: 14) and as 'bastions of opposition politics' (Orvis 2003: 256). In the early 2000s, organizations became increasingly divided over their attitudes to the NARC government (2003–2007), which they had helped bring to power and then differed sharply in their responses to the country's post-election crisis of 2007/2008 (Lugano 2020). By the 2017 elections, the leadership of some organizations, such as the NCCK and Supreme Council of Kenya Muslims (SUPKEM), had become publicly associated with the ruling Jubilee Alliance, while other organizations, such as the Kenya Human Rights Commission (KHRC), InformAction and Muslims for Human Rights (MUHURI), were clearly antagonistic to the government. This was reflected in the approaches adopted. In 2017, the NCCK ran a fairly classic voter mobilization and 'issue-fication' campaign, while 12 more critical CSOs formed a new coalition – *Kura Yangu, Sauti Yangu* ('My Vote, My Voice')[21] – which called for electoral reform and voter vigilance. Uganda represents a third trend: CSOs working on governance are largely anti-regime/NRM and periodically join forces with opposition politicians to campaign for electoral reform. Consequent government hostility has meant that such groups have been forced to pull their punches, lest their voter education work be banned entirely (Dicklitch 1998, 2001).

There are also important intra-country differences, which relate, in large part, to whether or not an area is predominantly pro-government, opposition or swing, and local experiences – most notably of violence. Fieldwork in Ghana confirmed that civil society activists are more likely to be pro-NDC in Ho and pro-NPP in Kumasi. In Uganda, the most vibrant civil society space was found in Gulu due to the legacy of the Lord's Resistance Army (LRA) and influx of international NGOs. In Mukono, CSOs are relatively active due, in large part, to the area's proximity to Kampala, while Fort Portal – as both a more rural constituency and an NRM stronghold – had the least active civil society. In Kenya, the recent

---

[21] https://web.archive.org/web/20170813033047/http://kurayangusautiyangu.org/about-us/.

history of election-related violence prompted a multitude of externally funded interventions and has ensured high levels of civil society activity around recent elections in Kisumu County – an oft-cited potential 'hotspot' – and, to a lesser extent, Narok. In Kiambu, by contrast, there has been less CSO-led election-related activity.

Overall, however, the similarities in voter education efforts across the three countries outweigh the differences. Peace and order have been consistent themes across all three countries (Lynch, Cheeseman and Willis 2019). 'Issue-fication' has become increasingly prominent during the second and third decades of multiparty politics, as organizations became increasingly concerned with the widely perceived 'commercialization' of politics. CSOs have also developed more sophisticated campaigns that take advantage of the proliferation of community radio stations and rapid uptake of social media (Tettey 2019), and voter vigilance has come to the fore during recent elections, driven by repeated allegations of malpractice in all three countries.

Another key similarity is dependence on donor funds. The fact that voter education is generally cast as non-partisan, as empowering of ordinary citizens, and as helping to promote both electoral credibility and peace, has ensured that it has remained one of the favoured democracy support initiatives of major donors across all three countries alongside support for key electoral institutions and observation (Chapters 3 and 4). The resurgence of debates around the need for civic education within donor countries may have encouraged this – studies around the same time in the United States, for example, proposed civic education as a means to address low levels of political participation (Galston 2001; see also Crick 2002 for the United Kingdom).

This reliance encourages certain patterns of behaviour – from increased attention to issues of particular concern to donors (such as devolution in Kenya following the inauguration of the 2010 constitution) to a fairly conservative approach to political engagement (see 5.3). But approaches to voter education efforts are not simply determined by donors. Instead, the focus and approach of voter education efforts are primarily shaped by a particular image that CSOs have of themselves as civic-minded actors that seek to encourage adherence to a civic register of virtue among citizenry and state alike, by the approaches adopted by other voter educators (such as EMBs and the media) and by popular concerns. The prominence of peace-messaging, for example, stems from a widespread concern in all three countries that elections might turn violent, from the nation-building role that CSOs have envisaged for themselves, and from the attention given to peace by other national and international actors (Lynch, Cheeseman and Willis 2019).

The fact that EMBs have enjoyed the primary mandate for voter education since the return to multiparty politics accounts for another similarity: while civil society voter education efforts across all three countries look to mobilize citizens to hold leaders accountable and the state in check, they also have to work closely with state institutions to conduct their work. As Karisa Cloward notes of civil society work in Kenya, '[b]y controlling the purse strings or access to the communities NGOs serve, government agents are unavoidable middlemen whom NGOs must satisfy if they hope to succeed or even survive' (2019: 24). In the field of voter education more specifically, CSOs in all three countries need to be recognized by the EMB to conduct activities and often rely on the assistance of local administrators to reach largely rural populations. Moreover, with more donor funding channelled through state institutions in the 2000s (Evans and van de Walle 2019), many CSOs find that they increasingly need to work in close collaboration with EMBs and other state bodies, such as the Ghanaian NCCE or Kenyan NCIC, to conduct voter education campaigns.

Finally, donor dependency and the need to work with the state have ensured that high-profile voter education drives in all three countries have largely been conducted by a small number of 'usual suspects'. These national organizations are usually urban-based and manned by educated and committed individuals; they tend to enjoy good relations with the international donors who fund them and to have troubled relations with incumbent regimes and to be heavily involved in other democracy support work packages such as domestic election observation. Examples in Ghana include CDD-Ghana, the Christian Council of Ghana (CCG), IEA and IDEG. In Kenya, they include the CJPC, the Constitution and Reform Education Consortium (CRECO), the Institute for Education in Democracy (IED), KHRC, NCCK, SUPKEM and Uraia. And in Uganda they include the Democracy Monitoring Group (DemGroup), CCEDU, the Uganda Joint Christian Council (UJCC) and Uganda National NGO Forum. This brief – and far from exhaustive – list points to another important aspect of voter education in all three countries: the blurring of secular and religious organizations and messages. Religious and secular organizations will often coexist within the same network. In turn, while secular organizations regularly include references to God in their materials and activities (e.g. see CCEDU 2015), 'the bulk of the language used by [FBOs] ... echoes [the] rather standard discourse of "secular" donor-funded civil society actors' (Alava and Ssentongo 2016: 681).

The five key strands of voter education – which collectively seek to create 'good' citizens and leaders – thus cut across the civil society space in, and the territory of, all three countries. Yet these similar approaches then play out in very different contexts. Ghanaians are much more confident than Ugandans of their ability to elect a new government (Chapter 7), and the salience of ethnic identities in Kenya encourages more people to interpret the likely behaviour of others (including CSOs) through an ethnic lens (Chapter 6).

Popular attitudes to CSOs both reflect such realities and have important implications for the varied impact of voter education programmes. In the national surveys that we conducted, an absolute majority of citizens in all three countries believed that civil society groups have overall had a positive effect on the quality of elections. However, in each case a significant minority disagreed (Figure 5.1). Citizens were most positive about the role of civil society groups in Ghana, where a number of technically capable CSOs have emerged, and domestic observation – along with its international counterpart – is widely believed to have contributed to an improvement in the conduct and management of elections following divisive polls in the early 1990s (Chapter 4). By contrast, the public was most critical of the role of civil society in Kenya, where domestic observation has frequently been the source of controversy (Chapter 4), and political leaders have been relatively outspoken in their criticism of CSOs (CRECO 2019).

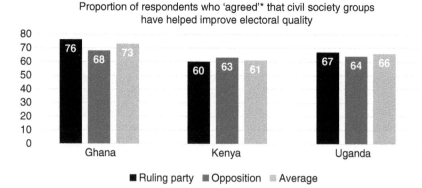

Figure 5.1 The impact of civil society groups on the quality of elections (%)
* Agree = those who stated that they 'agreed' or 'strongly agreed' with the statement. The other options were 'disagree', 'strongly disagree' and 'neither agree nor disagree'.
Source: Authors' own survey data

Interestingly, while there was a partisan gap in attitudes to civil society groups in each country, it was not that substantial. In Ghana and Uganda, ruling party supporters appeared to have a more positive attitude towards civil society groups, most likely because they believed that the country had made greater strides towards democratic consolidation, whereas opposition supporters were more likely to say that their country is not a democracy at all. This pattern is reversed in Kenya where we found the lowest approval ratings of any sub-group among ruling party supporters – this reversal is probably best explained by the controversies surrounding civil society-led domestic observation efforts (Chapter 4) and the government's sustained attack on prominent governance CSOs following the 2007 elections (Lugano 2020).

Unsurprisingly, we found the same pattern was repeated when it comes to popular support for the active participation of civil society groups in elections (Figure 5.2). While fully three-quarters of Ghanaians agreed that civil society groups should be present during election campaigns, and almost as many Ugandans agreed, Kenyans were considerably more sceptical. The partisan divide was also the same: ruling party supporters were more likely to support the involvement of CSOs in elections in Ghana and Uganda. By contrast, opposition supporters (70 per cent) were more likely to give civil society groups their backing in Kenya than those who felt close to the government (64 per cent). Our survey data therefore reveals considerable

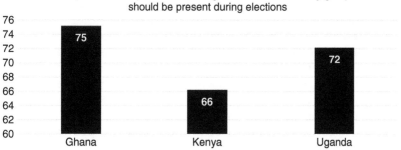

Figure 5.2 Popular support for the presence of civil society groups during elections (%)
* Agree = those who stated that they 'agreed' or 'strongly agreed' with the statement. The other options were 'disagree', 'strongly disagree' and 'neither agree nor disagree'.
Source: Authors' own survey data

public support for the 'third sector', but also some of the tensions that lie at the heart of its work.

These variations in public evaluations are important as they ensure that the way in which similar voter education campaigns are interpreted and the impact that they have differ between and within our country case studies. Most notably, where citizens have less trust in CSOs, and more people disapprove of their engagement in the electoral arena, it is much harder to persuade voters that they are impartial and credible institutions, and hence to encourage citizens to promote the civic, over patrimonial, register. Such distrust also undermines the Ideas of a civic civil society and bureaucratic state that elections can potentially help to produce. It is to such effects that the final sections of this chapter turn.

5.3   Making 'Good Citizens'

Through voter education, CSOs have worked hard to promote civic virtue. Yet three common problems have afflicted these educational efforts to shape citizenship. The first is a failure to fully understand voter behaviour and associated motivations and pressures; the second is a tendency to unintentionally strengthen the patrimonial register; the third is a lack of clarity on what virtuous citizenship entails when other actors break the rules. These shortcomings are important as – together with the issues discussed in 5.4 and 5.5 – they help to shape the ways in which voter education actually influences the moral economy of elections.

Voter education programmes have consistently oversimplified the causes of commonly cited 'problems', such as invalid votes, low turnout and vote buying. Voter educators tend to assume that no one would want to 'make a vote intentionally invalid' and that invalid votes are simply due to a 'lack of information, lack of knowledge of what he is doing'.[22] This may often be true: the number of invalid votes tends to be higher in rural areas with low levels of formal education,[23] while the number of invalid votes fell from 2.57 per cent of the total vote to 1.52 per cent in Ghana between the 2012 and 2016 elections following a concerted voter education drive to combat the problem. Yet not all invalid votes are the result of voter error. Partisan polling clerks may intentionally spoil ballots with dirty thumbs during the sorting process; opportunistic party agents may demand the invalidation of some votes for their opponent even where the voter's intention is clear.[24] Frustrated voters may also intentionally spoil

---

[22] Interview UGA42a, clergyman, Fort Portal, 11 June 2015.
[23] Interview GHA5a, civil society activist, Kumasi, 3 September 2015.
[24] Fieldwork notes, Gulu, 18 February 2016.

their vote as a political act: like the voter in northern Uganda who – likely knowing that all votes are counted in public – wrote 'Fuck M7' across their 2016 presidential ballot.[25]

The idea that the problem lies with ignorance or misinformation is even more questionable when it comes to non-voting. While voter education drives insist that each vote counts, potential voters – particularly in Kenya and Uganda where historical experience has informed strong narratives of electoral injustice (see Chapter 2) and deep scepticism of election administrators and observers (Chapters 3 and 4) – are acutely aware that their vote might not count. They may stay home, not because they do not understand how politics works, but because they understand how it works only too well. As one well-educated Ugandan woman put it:

[T]he first presidential elections that were held [in 1996], there were of course the usual complaints of rigging ... and yet, the reports of the official monitors of the elections were [that the] elections were free and fair. So from that point on I somehow got this feeling that there was no need, my vote didn't count. Yes. I never registered to participate in any other elections.[26]

Or, as one civil society activist in Kampala put it, 'The importance of voting does not correlate with the results.'[27]

A decision to not vote may also be informed by the strength of partisan identity and thus constitute a moral position. For example, while voter education efforts in Ghana have intensified over time, voter turnout rates fell in 2000 and 2016. This was due, in large part, to the strength of party identification and the fact that, especially in the NDC heartlands of Volta, many voters – who found it difficult to shift their loyalty from one party to another – simply stayed at home as a way to 'punish' the NDC government (Nugent 2001b: 421–422; Afram and Tsekpo 2017). On the other side of the continent a year later, and in a very different context in which opposition supporters did not want to legitimize a process they deemed to be flawed, the Kisumu Governor Anyang' Nyong'o justified the opposition's boycott of Kenya's repeat presidential election by noting that 'if the government subverts the sovereign will of the people ... then people are entitled to rebel against this government' (cited in Waddilove 2019b: 346).

Moreover, while voter education tends to see poor illiterate voters as 'the problem', there is evidence that upper upper-middle citizens may turn out in relatively low numbers (Nathan 2016 on Ghana). Athough it is true that

---

[25] M7 is a nickname for President Museveni; Interview UGA80b, civil society activist, Gulu, 25 February 2016.
[26] Interview UGA10a, researcher, Kampala, 19 July 2014.
[27] Interview UGA4a, civil society activist, Kampala, 16 July 2014.

the destitute are the least likely social group to vote, rural dwellers turn out more regularly than urbanites (Bratton, Mattes and Gyimah-Boadi 2005: 298). This may stem from party mobilization strategies, which often target those in lower income brackets (Nathan 2016), and from the fact that elections may matter more to the less privileged. As Mukulika Banerjee (2014) has argued of elections in India, those who feel socio-economically marginalized may be more appreciative of the performance of recognized citizenship that voting provides, while upper-middle-class citizens may be put off by the long, hot and dusty queues and fear of insecurity. This point was echoed in remarkably similar language by a businessman from Kisumu, who noted that 'the enlightened ... we never used to go and register as voter because you don't want to queue'.[28] Abstention is thus not necessarily a consequence of ignorance.

That voter education might misunderstand the average voter is most glaring when it comes to 'issue-fication' and calls for people to not be 'blinded' or 'silenced' by money.[29] As we will show in Chapter 7, handouts that are perceived as bribes usually fail to sway voters. In turn, candidates hand out money and other gifts – not because they believe that everyone who takes this cash will vote for them – but to appear as credible and generous leaders (Kramon 2017). Handouts are also encouraged – and even demanded – by voters who see such payments as a right or as a display of virtue and electoral viability. Calls for people to not 'sell their votes' thus over simplify decision-making and are likely to have little impact. Indeed, they may, as Schaffer (2007b) has shown in the Philippines, have a perverse impact of reinforcing a sense that CSOs are elitist and divorced from local realities.

Similar problems extend to a common educational assumption that ethnic support is entirely separate from issue-based voting. As one voter educator warned, 'In multi-ethnic societies like Ghana, there is the danger that if you do not give voter education to the people, they will focus on ethnicity, personality and neglect issues' (cited in Botchway 2018: 12). However, in practice, ethnic support is often intimately intertwined with issues such as development and security. If the 'issue' is 'will this candidate build a school in my area?', shared ethnicity may be a very relevant consideration, for it may increase trust and offer a moral basis for subsequent accountability. Collective narratives of injustice may also help to shape positions on certain key policies – such as land reform – which can be seen to be in or against the interests

---

[28] Interview KEN86a, political campaigner, Kisumu, 13 July 2017.

[29] As summarized by a Uraia voter education advertising campaign in 2013. For example, see full-page adverts published in the *Daily Nation* on 27 February 2013 (p. 25) and 1 March 2013 (p. 40).

of a particular area or community (Lynch 2011a; Long 2019). This is especially true in Kenya where there is a relatively strong perception that politics has been, and is, 'ethnic' and that it therefore makes sense to vote for one of your 'own' and against particular 'others' even if one is focussed on such important issues as land, development or security (Lynch 2011a, 2014).

Voter education also fails to fully appreciate individual behaviour in another sense, namely to consider the ways in which people's decision to cast a ballot and to vote for a particular candidate may not be a matter of individual choice. For example, as the history of Kenya and Uganda reveals, insecurity and displacement can disenfranchise (Kamungi 2009); fears of violence tend to discourage turnout; people may feel an obligation to vote in line with family heads or key opinion leaders (whether as a result of moral expectation or a more straightforward fear of physical consequences), while those known – or likely to be assumed – to be supporters of the 'wrong party' at the local level may fear the repercussions of casting their vote. All of these possibilities are complicated by the fact that voting is not always secret. The involvement of party agents to 'assist' voters was evident in all three countries, including in Uganda where it is officially illegal. In Ghana and Kenya, party agents are allowed to oversee the process when a voter is assisted by an EMB official to ensure fairness, and it is common for multiple agents to become involved. These pressures are also all gendered: women are more likely to stay at home in the face of insecurity, wives are more likely to feel swayed by husbands and more women than men require assistance to cast their vote (Carter Center 2018: 9). They are also context-specific: for example, residents of areas where ethnic and/or religious divides overlap partisan divides and which have suffered a history of violence and displacement may feel a particularly strong obligation and/or direct pressure to vote for particular candidates (Ferree, Jung, Dowd and Gibson 2018). As Christine Bodewes (2010) has argued with respect to civic education in Kibera, Nairobi, information is not necessarily empowering when those who receive it still fear intimidation, violence or a loss of access to key patrons and resources.

Not only does voter education often fail to fully appreciate the ways in which a range of other factors can help to determine voter turnout and preferences, but it can also unintentionally help to strengthen the patrimonial register it seeks to undermine. As will be discussed in 5.4, education efforts sometimes provide new arenas for an aspirant to flaunt their personal wealth and political connections. Voter education – particularly in contexts such as Kenya where ethnicity is particularly salient or Uganda where many are highly sceptical about the possibility of presidential turnover – can also encourage scepticism over the feasibility of realizing the civic virtue that it seeks to promote. In short, constant references to the widespread problems of voter bribery and apathy, or to the unreliability of key institutions, may render people even less likely to take on the suggested behaviour of a 'good citizen', because they suggest that others are unlikely to follow suit (cf. Tankard and Paluck 2016).

Indeed, research shows that civic education conducted by CSOs 'antagonistic toward governments' can have 'a direct, negative effect on participants' levels of institutional trust' (Finkel, Sabatini and Bevis 2000: 1868 and 1851 on the Dominican Republic; also Bratton and Alderfer 1999 on Zambia). Kenyans who participated in a 1997 civic education programme were more aware of democratic shortcomings – such as the ways in which local authorities might demand bribes, engage in partisan harassment, or physically abuse people – than non-participants (Orvis 2003: 262). Even the injunction to 'have faith in the Electoral Commission' – as displayed on a roundabout in Accra in 2016 – may trigger doubt rather than confidence, while stories of malpractice may encourage 'a reinforcing cycle of expectation and action' (Lynch 2011a: 218). As one opposition supporter with ample experience of voter education efforts explained in September 2017 (before National Super Alliance (NASA) had announced their boycott of the 'fresh' elections), he would look for people on election day and pressure them into voting. Recognizing that this might conflict with the vision of civic virtue that he himself had promoted, he nonetheless saw this as the right thing to do: when government and electoral institutions were (in his eyes) breaking the rules, intimidation of voters became justifiable, even virtuous, as a means to protect local interests.[30]

This distinctive understanding of voter vigilance suggests a further problem with civil society efforts to promote civic virtue: there is often a lack of clarity about what people should do when different strands of voter education come into conflict or when others do not adhere to the rules. If people believe that the playing field is uneven, should they turn out and potentially help to legitimize a flawed process, stay home or stage a protest? Can it be legitimate to take money from a candidate in a context where personal experience and rumour both suggest the ubiquity of bribery in public service? Voter education generally avoids such questions; at times it is contradictory. Placards placed by the Scout and Guide Fellowship-Ghana around the Danquah Circle roundabout in Accra in 2016 advised citizens that '[t]here must be justice for all' and '[e]rrors do not cease to be errors simply because they're ratified into law'. Yet similar

[30] Unrecorded interview, ODM activist, Seme, 14 September 2017.

placards around the same roundabout, as well as other voter education efforts ahead of that election, encouraged citizens to prioritize peace (in the sense of short-term order) and to leave oversight and struggles for justice to other institutions. As one Kenyan clergyman put it, people 'should look for legal and peaceful means to settle grievances' (Korir 2017: 8). Yet this presupposes 'a level of social [and institutional] justice that may not exist' (cf. Chambers and Kopstein 2001: 860). Voter education efforts tend to be silent on this key conundrum: voters are required to be both orderly and vigilant – but what should they do when there is no orderly way to exercise vigilance? Teaching citizens to be 'governable' (Pykett 2007) in the face of electoral problems may erase the possibility of civic virtue embodied by an 'insurgent citizen' who has a right, 'and perhaps [the] responsibility – to make claims on the state and their representatives' (Dorman 2019: 469).

As a result, voter mobilization campaigns may unintentionally undermine broader civil society efforts to cultivate the civic register. For example, in 2011, and having unsuccessfully pressed for electoral reforms to an evidently unfair system, Ugandan CSOs abruptly switched their focus 'to voter mobilization/education'. As one CCEDU activist explained:

[W]e were inspiring people to participate actively in the electoral process, calling people to remain vigilant to secure their vote but also asking people to participate very, very peacefully. That was amidst calls for a boycott that had been mounted by the opposition at that time and we said look, because there is challenges, you don't walk away from the challenges but we seek to correct them. And so that was our guiding sort of thinking that let's mobilize everyone. If everyone is keen on the vote, then there wouldn't be spaces to steal a vote.[31]

A larger opposition vote may indeed make it more difficult for incumbents to steal an election, but the CCEDU strategy – while perhaps unavoidable – implied either a confidence in the process that it had previously denied, or a willingness to accept that the ballot, however flawed, was the limit of political action. Voter education, it seems, is always at risk of implying that legitimate political participation is restricted to the act of voting.

The potential contradictions of voter education are particularly apparent in more authoritarian contexts where experience leads many to doubt the credibility of election results – as in Kenya and Uganda – than in relatively open contexts that experience regular turnovers of power – such as in Ghana (Lynch, Cheeseman and Willis 2019). In turn, the extent to which voter education efforts are likely to unintentionally strengthen patrimonial registers by questioning the behaviour of others appears to

---

[31] Interview UGA97a, civil society activist, Kampala, 4 February 2016.

be highest in Uganda – where many do not feel that their vote counts – and Kenya – where messaging and civil society behaviour may also inadvertently reinforce a belief in the political salience of ethnicity. To fully understand how this plays out, it is important to consider what kind of 'good leaders' such campaigns envisage, and the type of civil society and state that voter education helps to produce.

5.4   Making 'Good Leaders'

An avowed aim of voter education efforts is to ensure the election of leaders who are both legitimate (as a result of having been elected through credible polls) and 'good' – that is, law-abiding and interested in the common good. Less clear, or even actively contradictory, is how people should identify good leaders and what the common good actually is. This lack of clarity complicates educational efforts to promote a civic register of virtue.

On the issue of voter choice, educators tend – in line with the civic register and common theories of democratic citizenship – to encourage people to use their ballot in ways that maximize the common or national good. However, democratic theory is unclear as to whether the common good is best promoted through a collation of individual preferences or whether citizens should put their personal or parochial preferences aside and consider what is in the nation's interests (Wolff 1994). This tension is echoed in the practice of voter education drives across our three cases: while some suggest that voters should examine the candidates and select 'the one who undertakes to advance national values and principles of [the] common good' (KCCB 2017: 11), others emphasize how voting 'gives you the power to elect leaders who promote your interests and to remove those who have failed to promote your interests and retain those who have performed well' (Gathaka 2012: 3).

This issue is exacerbated by a tendency for voter education materials to imply that the 'common good' is obvious and lies in accountability, development and stability (e.g. CCEDU 2015). Most notably, this approach presents a technocratic and inherently apolitical view of political decision-making, which fails to recognize that interests may clash and that there may be differing opinions on what the public good is, what the priorities are and how goals might best be achieved. This is evident at the national level, for example, in terms of whether one favours state intervention or 'trickle-down' economics, but also at the local level, for example, when neighbouring communities differ over development priorities or the just resolution of a land dispute (as in Narok), or even over where a new administrative headquarters should be situated (as in Adaklu, next to Ho).

Voter educators are generally agreed that 'good leaders' should promote peace and shun violence, but they are less clear on what this
involves. For example, does peace require one to avoid issues that might
provoke conflict? Or does peace require a strong state that can ensure
order? Or does it involve struggling (and perhaps even fighting) for
justice, a more inclusive political system and sustainable peace?
Generating answers to these questions is complicated by the fact that,
while incumbent candidates – particularly in Kenya and Uganda – tend to
support an 'ideology of order' (Atieno Odhiambo 1987), opposition
candidates are often associated with struggles for justice, and voter educators may be divided between the two along partisan lines.

Similar questions arise with respect to other aspects of voter education.
While civil society groups are generally agreed that good leaders should be
national in outlook, it is not always clear what this means in practice given
that every elected politician bar the president represents a sub-national
constituency. Should these leaders just be 'committed to [the] welfare of
all and to the attainment of the common good',[32] or should they also
'understand our problems and [be able to] mobilize the community to
seek solutions for their problems' (Gathaka 2012: 10)? If the latter, then
who constitutes the relevant community? Vague answers to such critical
questions can play to the advantage of a patrimonial register of virtue,
which views the good leader as someone who is a strong defender and
promoter of particular sub-national interests (Chapters 6 and 7).

The lack of clarity in voter education programmes is most glaring when
it comes to evaluations of the distribution of cash and other gifts by
candidates, which in turn reflects the reality of the patrimonial register
as an arena of moral debate that can – just like the civic register – appear as
right and legitimate. At one extreme, a handful of educators reject all
handouts and particularistic modes of assistance as immoral and encourage voters to only focus on a politician's formal duties. In this vein, one
educational pamphlet in Kenya insisted that '[a]n MP should not: give
gifts and bribes to potential voters and supporters … supervise
harambees[33] and fund-raising meetings in the constituency; create, fund,
deliver or guarantee "development projects" such as schools, hospitals,
roads and factories; be a tribal chieftain or leader' (Centre for Governance
and Development 2005: 17). However, this line of argument clashes with
the notion that political representatives should also be responsive to local

---

[32] Church newsletter published in July 2017 by the Catholic Bishop of the Diocese of
Lodwar.
[33] 'Harambee' is a widely used term in Kenya for local fundraisers.

needs and runs counter to a long experience of development rhetoric that emphasizes the value of grass-roots initiatives directed by local politicians.

Further confusion arises from the way in which voter education efforts oscillate between condemning immoral 'vote buying' and lauding virtuous 'development-mindedness' without considering how acts that may be regarded as 'vote buying' by some might be regarded as a display of generosity and 'development-mindedness' by others (Chapter 7). In this vein, CCEDU's 2016 Topowa campaign called on Ugandans not to 'sell your vote ... [but to] use your vote wisely to vote for leaders who will improve our education, roads, health services, create jobs and end poverty' (2015: 15). This, like the NCCE's emphasis on 'matters of concern to the Ghanaian voter' in Ghana's 2012 and 2016 elections, may encourage praise for leaders who focus on national development, but it can also encourage praise for those who say – as one Kenyan voter educator enthusiastically explained of a candidate in his constituency – 'I cannot bribe you to go and sell your vote ... But I am ready to assist where there is big need.'[34] Or, to put it another way, a focus on 'development projects' and 'assistance' opens a 'grey zone' in which most handouts – including those that most voter educators are clearly trying to critique – can be interpreted as signs of development-mindedness and thus virtue. This includes sizeable contributions to fundraising events, as well as money given to rally participants to 'buy refreshments' – both of which can (and often are) read as signs that an aspirant is generous and cares about people's well-being and may be likely to invest in local development projects, rather than as a simple attempt to buy support.

Given these tensions, it is unsurprising that civil society messaging has failed to erode a popular politics that sees the role of MPs as largely being about the provision of personal and club goods (Lindberg 2010; Chapter 6). The uncertain zone between vote buying and development-mindedness is a particular problem for 'issue-fication' efforts, which may actually reinforce patrimonial politics. This was evident, for example, during a civil society-organized parliamentary debate in Nakuru, Kenya, in 2013 where the questions posed to local aspirants, and the answers they gave, focussed not on how they would meet their official duties in parliament or on the policy manifestos of their parties, but on what they had done for their communities and what they would likely do in the future. While voter educators approved of this discussion as focussing on issues rather than identities, the debate's focus on service to local communities actually played to the patrimonial register. As an

---

[34] Interview conducted by research assistant, voter educator/clergyman, Nairobi, 7 December 2018.

NCCE official noted of parliamentary debates organized in conjunction with CSOs ahead of Ghana's 2016 elections in Ho:

[W]hat we are saying is that the campaigning should be issue-based . . . we've also created a platform for all the political aspirants . . . we want them to have that platform, they meet the constituents, the constituents meet them, they interact, you see. If we give you our mandate, *what are you going to do for us?*[35]

The challenges that these tensions present for the erosion of patrimonial logics are further exacerbated by the ambiguous status of voter educators themselves. CSO activists and workers may straddle partisan and civil society roles (Orvis 2003). Tasked with disseminating messages extolling the virtue of neutrality and due process, they may also be known to have strong political opinions and affiliations – or reveal those affiliations during the campaign, as when a radio talk-show host discusses voter education with a civil society guest, who later displays ethnic chauvinism or bias when the conversation turns to the merits of particular candidates.

Another example of such contradictory messaging is provided by religious organizations and clergy who – in all three countries – engage in voter education but also conduct fundraisers for specific parties, praise those who give generous donations to faith-based projects, and may even give their public support to leaders in ways that demonstrate how they are enmeshed in patronage networks and/or ethnic logics. For example, in Kenya, the CJPC's annual Lenten campaign booklets, which often focus on voter education, regularly call upon people to dismiss those who give out handouts. At the same time, about half of the pages in these pamphlets consist of a list of the funds raised by each parish. This is included as a form of accountability, but it may reinforce the sense that individual contributions to local community projects are virtuous acts that should be reciprocated with support.

In some cases, the dividing line between civil society and active politics is further undermined by the decision of a number of religious leaders to vie for elected positions (Deacon 2015). Even those who spurn such direct engagement in politics may host politicians at their churches, mosques and temples and attend political rallies. Through these interactions, many religious leaders publicly engage in and/or acclaim behaviour that plays to a patrimonial register of virtue. This may include helping to campaign for particular candidates. Indeed, while candidates have long sought to use religion to mobilize voters, religion has become increasingly prominent in election campaigns, especially in Kenya, where religious 'blessings' of aspirants have become a particularly

[35] Interview GHA60a, civic educator, Ho, 25 November 2016; emphasis added.

common feature of rallies since 2013 (Deacon 2015; Nyairo 2015). At a more general level, while religious leaders may ask politicians to adhere to the official rules of the game, their own behaviour often exposes their 'questionable neutrality' (Gyimah-Boadi and Markovits 2008: 219; also Chacha 2010) and suggests that co-ethnicity and/or patronage (Alava and Ssentongo 2016) – or what one Ghanaian clergyman wryly called 'stomach direction religious leadership' – has determined their loyalties.[36]

Together with the tendency for religious leaders to emphasize the need for peace, such support often plays to the advantage of the incumbent – particularly in Kenya and Uganda where there is a more entrenched political establishment and mainstream churches are typically enmeshed in 'networks of patronage' in part due to their 'vulnerability to state intimidation' (Alava and Ssentongo 2016: 678 on Uganda). In 1997, for example, Kenya's Archbishop David Gitari declared that 'it was better to accept rigged elections than to risk chaos'. These comments were widely believed to have been motivated by the fact that Gitari – an ethnic Kikuyu – had 'been bought' by the Moi government (Peters 2001: 65). However, it is also clear that patrimonial logics can lead clergy to voice support for the political opposition. Thus, while religious leaders in Central Kenya and the Rift Valley tended to support Jubilee's re-election campaign in 2017, many in Western and Nyanza openly expressed their support for Odinga. To give just one example, at NASA's Mashujaa Day (or 'Heroes Day') rally in Kisumu on 20 October 2017,[37] several religious leaders blessed Odinga and his team in ways that reinforced ethnic logics. As one charismatic neo-pentecostalist bishop told the largely Luo crowd – amidst anger that the police were targeting Luo in their suppression of demonstrations – while 'some are celebrating, [we are] mourning … pray for our leader Joshua Raila Odinga … [they] want to kill us, want to destroy us… [But it is] for Raila to take us to Canaan'.[38] The response of proximate people in the crowd suggested that the relevant 'us' was ethnic Luo as exemplified by a man who – in a #LuoLivesMatter T-shirt – talked about the Luo community's problems and how they would be resolved by Odinga's success.

Finally, patrimonial expectations of what politicians *should do* are also fostered by the way that voter education is rolled out, which often mirrors the strategies used by candidates themselves. This includes the way that

---

[36] Interview GHA53a, clergyman, Ho, 24 November 2016.
[37] Across Kenya Mashujaa Day celebrations are usually a 'national' event presided over by the National Administration. However, due to the fallout over the presidential election, a 'national' celebration was not held in Kisumu in 2017 due to security concerns and instead NASA organized a political rally.
[38] Fieldwork notes, Kisumu, 20 October 2017.

civil society groups seek to attract and engage participants – from the T-shirts and posters distributed to the sitting allowances paid. As one voter educator noted of civic education efforts in Kibera, Nairobi, ahead of Kenya's 2002 elections:

[W]e enticed the community to attend [the workshops] by putting them in nice hotels, paid their transportation and gave them posh meals. For most of the participants, it was nothing more than a money-making venture. (cited in Bodewes 2014: 75)

Many also participated, it later became clear, in the hope that it would lead to further paid work as domestic election monitors (Bodewes 2014: 80).

This conflux of contradictory practices and multiple identities can undermine individual and institutional reputations, particularly in contexts in which people have reason – for example, due to historical experience or the perceived salience of ethnicity – to be suspicious. This was evident in Kenya in September 2017, for example, when an event in Kisumu organized by the NCCK – an organization that was widely deemed to be pro-Jubilee – was disrupted amidst claims that it was a cover to buy constituents' voter cards and so prevent opposition supporters from expressing their democratic rights in the 'fresh' presidential election.[39] Such perceptions of bias and feelings of mistrust – which are higher in Kenya and Uganda due to popular scepticism about the neutrality of political institutions and the salience of ethnicity in the Kenyan case – undermine the ability of CSOs to promote the civic register of virtue. They also highlight the numerous ways in which the idea of a 'professional' civil society that stands separate from the state and which acts to keep it honest and accountable can be called into question – an issue to which this chapter now turns.

5.5   Productions of Civil Society and the State

The idea of civil society as comprised of 'expert citizens' who can understand and relay information that is poorly understood by the average citizen is intimately intertwined with the idea of a particular type of associational life that sits between 'the people' and 'the state'. This imagined divide, which is central to the Idea of an impartial and unbiased bureaucratic state (Comaroff and Comaroff 1999), is both reproduced and simutanouesly undermined by the electoral work of CSOs.

---

[39] Unrecorded interview, civil society activist, Kisumu, 14 September 2017.

At one level, voter education efforts – from the newspaper adverts and radio talk shows to the hotel workshops and public theatre – help to perform and (re)produce an ideal vision of civil society. Voter education is conducted by registered organizations with work plans and staff and by organizations that usually also have websites, offices and publicly listed objectives. This construction of civil society as a professionalized sphere of democracy promoters is an important electoral effect, which – together with other organizational activities from election observation to public litigation cases – has far-reaching implications. Among these is the consequent capacity of CSOs to raise funds to sustain their wider operations, and the way that their visibility enables them to take up prominent positions as both opinion leaders and important 'stakeholders' who should be consulted in government decision-making (Mercer 2003).

Yet, at another level, voter education efforts call this vision of associational life into question. First, and as we have already seen, the civil society sector often manifests the same divisions that characterize the societies that they seek to educate and reform. Second, as largely urban-based and externally oriented organizations, many CSOs are entwined with society, yet hardly representative of it. The professional staff of CSOs – distinguished by their education and their familiarity with government – are often much closer to the people who comprise the state. They may have studied with politicians and state officials, at school or university, and contracts for civil society work will often require coordination with state institutions or be directly funded by them. Involvement in an NGO can also act as a springboard into politics (Alava and Ssentongo 2016; Orvis 2003). This is perhaps most common in Kenya, which has a particularly extensive civil society space. Indeed, of 549 national and county-level aspirants interviewed by Karisa Cloward and Keith Weghorst ahead of Kenya's 2017 elections, 30 per cent had some CSO background and 15 per cent had held a paid position in the NGO sector (2019: 2–3), while almost a quarter of Kenya's 2013–2017 parliament who revealed their previous employment record had worked with a CSO (Cloward 2019: 17).

The willingness of activists and organizations to operate in ways that fuel perceptions that they are partisan or ethnically biased – or at least, simply interested in making a living – also has important implications for voter education. Generic messages may be interpreted as partisan and dismissed. For example, when CJPC ran an education programme in Kenya in 2002, some assumed that this must be a sign of partisan support for Mwai Kibaki, the only prominent Catholic presidential candidate (Bodewes 2014: 77). As one Kenyan civil society activist noted in 2018, 'if you have a programme and you talk about bad leadership ... some people ... [will say] "well this one is really hitting my person"'.[40]

The perception of CSO bias creates space for authoritarian-minded incumbent regimes – and sometimes opposition candidates, too – to question or suppress voter education messages that might endanger their position. Given differences between our three countries – in terms of the perceived biases of CSOs and levels of authoritarianism (5.2) – it is unsurprising that politicians in Uganda and Kenya have denounced CSOs' elitist character and dependency on donor funding more frequently than their peers in Ghana, by dismissing them as puppets of foreign influence out of touch with the public (Bodewes 2014: 68–69; CRECO 2019). This kind of critique is significant at three levels. First, it leads ordinary people to question the motivations and content of voter education campaigns. One civil society activist noted that, when Kenyatta denounced civil society-driven civic education in December 2016 as a tool for external interference, 'even the general citizenry started to ask, who are these civil society guys? What is their agenda? ... I mean they just started having doubts ... [and to ask] "should I even listen to what these guys are talking about?"'.[41] Second, such narratives can be used to justify the imposition of state restrictions on CSOs (Dodsworth and Cheeseman 2019). They also encourage self-censorship – as in Uganda where religious leaders silenced the 'most outspoken of the moderators' in the country's first presidential debate in 2016 to ensure that President Museveni did not feel 'uncomfortable' (Alava and Ssentongo 2016: 684). This, as Alava and Ssentongo note, 'is the "give and take" of Uganda's hybrid regime: to enable continued engagement with the state, public figures must refrain from saying things the state does not wish to hear' (2016: 684).

The overall impact of voter education programmes on the Idea of the state is also mixed. On the one hand, elections help to enact 'the apparent separateness of the state' from society (Mitchell 1991: 91). It is the state that implements electoral rules and regulations, registers voters, organizes for balloting and counting, announces and inaugurates the victor, deals with petitions, and provides security. In turn, by guiding the public into the role of voting citizens, by seeking to encourage a sense of optimism about what the state can achieve and provide, and by ultimately encouraging public acceptance of the legitimacy of the electoral process, voter education contributes to a powerful state effect of elections by reinforcing an image of the bureaucratic state that sits above, and acts separately

---

[40] Interview conducted by research assistant, voter educator, Nairobi, 11 December 2018.
[41] Interview conducted by research assistant, voter educator, Nairobi, 11 December 2018.

from, society. In so doing, voter education helps to cast the Idea of the state as impartial and autonomous, and as helping to promote the national common good and thus as a loyal adherent of the civic register of virtue.

These are powerful effects. Yet voter education, like electoral administration, may also reveal the reality that state institutions, and those who work for them, are actually entangled in society (Chapter 3). Those delivering the education may be seen as too close to the ruling party or, conversely, as agents of the opposition. Moreover the education that they provide may alert citizens – either implicitly or explicitly – to the fact that politicians or officials may often break the rules and do not always exemplify civic virtue. The reception and interpretation of such voter education messages will depend, in large part, on the local contexts and, in particular, on people's historical experiences and expectations as regards the likely behaviour of others. Voter education efforts thus help to produce the appearance of an autonomous state – powerful through its separation from society – but can also suggest that state institutions may act at the behest of vested interests and powerful individuals. There is a perverse effect here: voter education is apparently dedicated to the promotion of civic virtue, yet may strengthen a patrimonial register, particularly where there is already uncertainty over how others will likely act and ongoing debate over what constitutes virtuous behaviour.

5.6   Conclusion: The Impact of Voter Education

Governance CSOs in all three countries have shown a commitment to the ideals of adult suffrage, the secret ballot and electoral choice. Many members have braved arrest, intimidation and even death, and their activism and lobbying have made significant contributions to democratization (Arthur 2010; Muhula 2020). Voter education efforts, however, have had a mixed impact and have fallen short of the transformative effect that some had envisaged.

On the one hand, voter education has helped to relay key information and there is evidence that voter education has helped to reduce the number of invalid ballots (5.3). Voter education has likely also contributed to increasing levels of electoral participation (Chapter 2) – although it is difficult to separate out the impact of voter education from the ground-intensive campaigns conducted by aspirants at all levels (Chapter 6). Voter education has also likely encouraged people to think more carefully about who they should vote for and why and fuelled popular concern with accountability. As Finkel and Smith concluded in their study of the 2001 to 2002 NCEP civic education campaign in

Kenya, '[c]ivic education, especially when it is conducted with active, participatory teaching methodologies, *can* work, and it can have direct and immediate effects on strengthening democratic attitudes and heightening political awareness among adults in new democracies' (2011: 432; emphasis in the original). Finally, by raising potential and real problems with the state, voter education can feed into lobbying and other forms of activism in constructive ways (Arthur 2010; Muhula 2020).

On the other hand, and despite several decades of concerted voter education efforts that explicitly seek to promote the civic register of virtue, that register is yet to trump the patrimonial register. This is evident from the electoral success of politicians who rely largely on patronage to mobilize support; from the fact that increased electoral competition has gone hand in hand with increasingly expensive campaigns; and from the pressures that politicians face to be generous and to assist their constituents in accordance with the patrimonial register (Chapters 6 and 7).

A moral economy approach can help to explain this disjuncture between aims and outcomes. More specifically, it helps to highlight how voter education campaigns that seek to promote the civic register are often undermined by a misunderstanding of the 'problems' that need to be solved, by a failure to provide clear moral direction when other actors do not adhere to official rules, and by the complex and often contradictory roles played by civil society actors themselves. CSOs and their representatives may become enmeshed with state institutions, parties and local communities, which can undermine their perceived neutrality and hence their ability to credibly advocate for a civic register of virtue. Voter education – like much civil society activism – also tends to be inherently conservative (Fatton 1995; Gyimah-Boadi 1996; Oloka-Onyango and Barya 1997; VonDoepp 2019), which can encourage a perception that the organizations that undertake it support the incumbent. At the same time, the way that voter education is conducted explicitly constructs civil society as a particular type of associational life and the state as emancipated from society, while simultaneously providing participants with information that calls both images into question.

Finally, a focus on the civic and patrimonial registers of virtue can help to explain differences in both how civil society efforts are received and their impact. Thus, while the majority of citizens in all three countries see value in civil society's support for democracy, the fact that – ahead of recent elections – ruling party supporters in Kenya were the most sceptical of any group in all three countries is understandable when we consider the extent to which civil society's adherence to, and contribution to, the civic register had been challenged by the Kenyan government itself

(5.2). In turn, while voter education seeks to promote the civic register of virtue, popular acceptance of that message is contingent. In Kenya, the suspicion that civil society institutions embody ethnic divides, rather than bridging them, vitiates the effects of their work. In Uganda, historical experience of sectarian politics and the apparently elite nature of CSOs have combined with the reflex authoritarianism of Museveni's regime to render voter education work seem both suspect and ineffectual. In Ghana, the experience of alternance makes the imagined goal of voter education – the informed, rational citizen enabled to make a political choice by an impartial state apparatus – seem more achievable, if still distant.

Part II

The Moral Economy in Action

6 Performing Virtue
Politicians, Leadership and Election Campaigns

On 27 June 2017, over a thousand people gathered in a marquee in Nairobi to launch the National Super Alliance (NASA) manifesto in advance of Kenya's general elections. An initial skit cast Raila Odinga as Joshua, leading the Israelites back to Canaan, and throughout the prayers, speeches and songs that followed, the message was clear: NASA was going to win. Besides optimism, the performance was carefully choreographed to suggest NASA's inclusivity: a video, which punctuated the entertainment and speeches, outlined NASA's agenda of people-oriented development and security and relayed messages from citizens across the country – including the government strongholds of the former Central and Rift Valley provinces. The audience was similarly stage-managed to ensure that it comprised of politicians and activists from each of the country's former eight provinces, while prominent politicians from across the country were recognized and a selection were given a chance to speak. As one of NASA's leaders, Moses Wetang'ula, put it, the alliance sought to 'create one big happy family called Kenya'; the incumbent Governor of Nairobi welcomed 'faces from across the country'.[1]

The event made a claim to virtue that appeared firmly located in the civic register: NASA – in contrast to successive regimes that had betrayed the 'Kenyan dream' – was composed of leaders who had struggled for progress and would ensure that everyone benefited from social justice, development and national cohesion. However, this overt emphasis on impartiality, meritocracy and national citizenship sat uneasily alongside multiple implicit appeals to the patrimonial register and associated ideas of particular preference. The manifesto was launched by Odinga and his four 'principals'[2] – four male former cabinet ministers whose political capital lay largely in their assumed ability to mobilize co-ethnics – which raised hopes (and fears) that they might favour certain communities.[3] Just as NASA was presented as an inclusive, nationally oriented and

---

[1] Fieldwork notes, Nairobi, 27 June 2017.
[2] Kalonzo Musyoka, Musalia Mudavadi, Moses Wetang'ula and Isaac Ruto.
[3] Unrecorded interview, civil society activist, Nairobi, 25 July 2017.

civic-minded alliance, it was simultaneously depicted as a multi-ethnic coalition, which – like other explicitly multi-ethnic political platforms before it – 'could assist, protect, and defend diverse interests'. This would be achieved by ensuring that various groups had a regional or community patron to represent and assist them, and through NASA's inclusion alliance, which was implicitly pitched against a rival more exclusive ethnic coalition (Lynch 2011a: 104).

In this chapter, we argue that appealing to both the civic and patrimonial registers of virtue is a common feature of political campaigns across our three country case studies. Although parliamentary candidates are more likely than their presidential counterparts to emphasise the patrimonial, and certain candidates will sometimes focus (albeit for often fairly limited periods of time) on a single register, politicians routinely present themselves as the embodiment of civic virtue, committed to impartial national stability and progress. These public utterances are often undercut, however, by the efforts of the same politicians to present themselves as leaders attending to the moral demands of 'their' people, and hence as practitioners of patrimonial virtue. This is true of official campaign periods, but also of politicians' interactions more broadly – for actual and aspiring politicians know that their behaviour is always under scrutiny.

This felt need to speak to both registers stems, first and foremost, from the fact that both hold moral weight among the publics that politicians seek to mobilize (6.1; Chapter 7). It is reinforced by 'decampaigns' whereby an aspirant's rivals seek to attack their viability, capacity and virtue (6.3.3). Those who adhere too closely to the civic register may thus be denounced – by their opponents, as well as by broader publics – for forgetting their constituents or for being too mean or too poor to assist them. By contrast, candidates who mainly speak to the patrimonial register risk being accused of tribalism and corruption and of caring only for their 'own'. The fact that a sense of relevant 'we-ness' can collapse into ever smaller categories – of clan, kin or immediate families – ensures that this can be a dangerous charge even in a largely ethnically homogenous constituency (Lynch 2011b).

Efforts to balance the two registers – with 'balance' here understood as a precarious and often extremely uneven combination, rather than as a state of equilibrium – are complicated by the fact that people want their elected representatives to be and do different and potentially contradictory things: to be present and generous, to help with jobs and social services, to protect and promote particular interests, to be upstanding and honourable, and to advance development, security and justice more broadly speaking (Barkan 1979a; Wanyande 2002; Bratton and Kimenyi 2008; Lindberg 2010). To navigate these demands, and to cultivate their reputations among different audiences, politicians must attend a range of public and private events and be visibly present in their constituencies. Many also adopt a mix of styles or brands: a capable technocrat might inspire trust that they can bring specific rewards and/or foster national development; a strong fighter that they will struggle for justice and progress for their community and/or country.

In building their reputations, politicians are aided by a productive ambiguity in the interpretation of their statements and activities. Presence, generosity, the provision of development projects, the defence of interests and promotion of public goods (such as prosperity or peace) can all be valued as evidence that a politician has brought (or will likely bring) particular benefits to a sub-national community; but they can also all be understood as a sign that a politician will be impartial, meritocratic, and work in the national interest. However, while effective communications and productive ambiguity can help aspirants to speak to both registers in a single campaign, their efforts are constantly challenged by the obvious tensions between the two registers – of impartiality versus preference, of meritocracy versus reciprocity and of commonality versus national citizenship – and by the decampaigning efforts of their opponents.

Understanding electoral campaigns in this way – namely as a struggle by politicians to speak to both the civic and patrimonial registers of virtue – can help to explain why campaigns are so ground-intensive, vibrant and varied and often so unpredictable. It also allows us to nuance a common argument that African politicians are Big Men who simply combine coercion with the distribution of goods to gain and sustain their position through neo-patrimonial politics (LeVine 1962; Ekeh 1975; Chabal and Daloz 1999). Whether the patronage involved is interpreted in simple rational choice terms – as handouts and goods distributed close to elections (Hyden 2006: 75) – or as part of longer-term efforts to develop a track record that one is of a 'redistributive type' (Kramon 2017: 11), these analyses present electoral politics as driven by voters' assessment of a leader's ability to deliver them material benefits (Barkan and Okumu 1978; Barkan 1979b; Lindberg 2010; de Torrenté 2013).

Our analysis goes beyond such accounts by recognizing the importance and limitations of patron–client relationships. As we will argue in Chapter 7, politicians need to ensure that handouts are interpreted as a sign of virtue in order to benefit from them electorally (Nugent 2007). At the same time, the ubiquity of handouts ensures that a reputation for patrimonial virtue is best cultivated through the promotion and defence of group interest more broadly speaking (Gadjanova 2017a), while politicians have to simultaneously respond to the popular appeal of the civic register. This reality helps to explain why candidates combine handouts with development projects, advocacy, policy pledges and decampaigns (6.3), and why patronage is often distributed more fairly than a purely clientelistic logic would suggest (Harris and Posner 2019).

Understanding campaigns through the lens of the moral economy can also help to explain why ethnic identities can become so politically salient, but why elections are not a mere 'ethnic census' as is sometimes suggested (Horowitz 1985; Ishiyama 2012). Colonial and postcolonial histories have ensured that – due to collective narratives of injustice and desert, popular perceptions of accountability and likely assistance, and constituency boundaries – the relevant 'commonality' of the patrimonial register is often a shared ethnic identity (Berman 1998). However, no politician can either assume or rely on ethnic support. Many need to mobilize cross-ethnic alliances and/or compete against fellow co-ethnics (Long 2019). They also face constituents who view both the civic and patrimonial registers as virtuous. As a result, even those who emphasize their claims to patrimonial virtue must make some claim to civic virtue and/or justify their deviation from that virtue as a necessary expedient forced on them by the nepotism or tribalism of their rivals.

The availability of these two, quite different, positions helps to explain how patrimonial appeals can be more or less ethnically divisive. When what is good for an ethnic group is understood as compatible with the national public good, the tension between the patrimonial and civic registers is minimized and it becomes easier for a politician to appear as both a 'good' member of their community and a 'good' national leader to co-ethnics and non-co-ethnics alike. Under these circumstances, politicians face strong incentives to locate themselves in the 'middle-ground' and campaign for the votes of a range of different communities. By contrast, when the interests of different ethnic groups routinely come into conflict – for example, when a 'winner-takes-all' logic ensures that the victory of some results (or is widely perceived to result) in the exclusion of others (Berman, Cottrell and Ghai 2009; Kanyinga 2009) – such cross-over appeals are likely to fall on deaf ears. In such contexts, politics can escape from the constraints of 'moral ethnicity' to become the 'political tribalism' of inter-group competition (Lonsdale 2004: 76 and 1994: 131), and, in extreme cases, leaders can rally co-ethnics by depicting 'others' as 'an existential threat' to group survival who 'should' be expelled or even killed (Nyabola 2018: 178).

The political landscape that politicians face – the socio-economic context, structure of key political organizations, past experiences and actions of others – helps to shape campaign strategies, with certain messages likely to resonate in some contexts but not in others. However, it is important to recognize how aspirants also help to shape the political landscape – through the divisions that they foster or salve, the institutions that they build or undermine, and the experiences that they imprint. It is this interaction of political landscape and aspirant agency over time that explains intra- and inter-country variations in electoral campaigns. For example, presidential candidates face greater pressure to play to a civic register than their parliamentary counterparts who are meant to represent a particular constituency. At the same time, local narratives of injustice generate variations in the pull of the patrimonial register between certain areas and countries (Lynch 2011a).

In Kenya, where public confidence that others will adhere to a civic register has long been undermined by perceptions of ethnic bias, the abuse of power (Oucho 2002) and a sense that 'others' do not value the same national goods – whether democracy and constitutionalism or peace and stability (Lockwood 2019a) – more explicit and exclusive forms of patrimonial politics have gained ascendancy. In Uganda, Museveni's concerted efforts to mobilize support across the country – through patronage, the promise of peace and repression of the opposition (Vokes and Wilkins 2016) – have encouraged aspirants to adopt less explicitly ethnic campaigns and to argue that either their proximity to, or distance from, the president will help them to promote particular interests and the national public good. In Ghana, peaceful transfers of power, more inclusive development policies and political institutions that integrate people across different communities (Gyimah-Boadi 2009) have reduced the tension between the civic and patrimonial registers and enabled a balance that is skewed more heavily towards the civic register.

To begin to tease out such complexities this chapter focusses on the moral economy of parliamentary election campaigns. The first section provides an overview of public expectations that help to shape the landscape in which aspirants campaign. The second section focusses on politicians' motivations to stand and argues that both popular expectations and electoral promises entangle ideas of civic and patrimonial virtue in ways that fuel public scepticism towards the 'political class'. The chapter then turns to politicians' efforts to mobilize support as they struggle to present themselves as electorally viable and as the most appropriate kind of 'good leader' – and the different behaviours that this leads them to adopt. The final section then seeks to explain some key commonalities and variations between our cases, which reveals the extent and limits of politicians' agency.

6.1   Pressures from Below

Through their campaigns politicians seek to shape public opinion, but they also need to respond to popular expectations. Candidates gain insight into these realities through opinion polls and voting patterns. More striking, however, are the claims and emotions that constituents express in various public forums, from radio phone-in programmes and online debates to conversations in local markets and interactions at political rallies. As John Lonsdale notes, power 'may control the public address system, but crowds also have a voice, generally a murmur, at times a roar' (2004: 76).

However, it is not always easy to tell what people want. When we asked survey participants whether politicians 'have a responsibility to take care of the people who vote for them before they assist others' or should rather 'rule in the interests of all', 86 per cent of Ghanaians, 88 per cent of Kenyans and 77 per cent of Ugandans strongly agreed with the latter option.[4] This prioritization of the civic register may reflect the particular context of a survey conducted by international researchers, yet the fact that this was readily produced as the 'right' answer is suggestive. Indeed, there is considerable evidence that support for politicians (and particularly for presidential candidates) stems, at least in part, from evaluations of their actual or likely performance in delivering key national public goods, such as economic growth, public services and security (Bratton and Kimenyi 2008; Lindberg 2010; Conroy-Krutz and Logan 2012).

The power of the civic register is also evident in the speed with which people castigate those perceived to be 'nepotistic' or 'tribal'. For example, when commentators on a popular blog tried 'to bring in ethnicity' during Kenya's post-election crisis of 2007/2008, they:

> were immediately reined in by fellow commenters. Thus, when Gaisha94 wrote: 'i WONDER IF YOU ARE ALL IUOS', other commenters reacted with: 'keep our discussions civil and productive, with an eye toward the "we" we want to become' and 'hakuna ukabila hapa' [There is no tribalism here]. (Brinkman 2019: 79)

Voters and candidates also feel the relentless promotion of civic virtue by other actors – from election officials and international actors to CSOs and religious leaders (Chapters 3 to 5; Elder, Stigant and Claes 2014).

However, while there may be strong support for civic neutrality in the abstract, in the cut and thrust of everyday politics, the patrimonial register often comes to the fore. Indeed, politicians in all three countries often lament how the popular voice that they hear is profoundly patrimonial in its claims. As one aspirant put it: 'When you go out to the village, people

---

[4] Authors' own survey. The full question was 'I am going to read you two statements. Please tell me whether you Agree with A, Agree with B, or Agree with Neither. Statement A: Political leaders should rule in the interests of all Ghanaians/Kenyans/Ugandans and should not privilege their own community. Statement B: Political leaders have a responsibility to take care of the people who vote for them before they assist others.'

will say "What are you giving us?"[5] That lament is itself a claim, of course: an assertion that, as one Kenyan politician assured us, while he understands the importance of civic virtue, he is forced away from it by popular pressure: 'should we give handouts? I have been against it, but again I think they [those who demand these] are winning, because I am beginning sometimes to give.'[6]

There are good reasons to be sceptical of the claim that politicians would operate in a 'civic' way if only they could. A long-standing critique of Africa's politicians is that they encourage patrimonial politics as a way of preventing the emergence of a class politics that would threaten their position (Mafeje 1971; Nyangira 1987). As Cheeseman, Kanyinga and Lynch have written of Kenya, 'the willingness of elite actors to work across ethnic lines to maintain their access to political power and economic opportunities' helps to explain 'the highly unequal nature of the country's political settlement' and the country's relative stability (2020: 22).

However, the apparent tension between these two accounts can be resolved if we recognize how they may both be true for different individuals and/or at different times. It is certainly the case that politicians have come to constitute a sort of class, a rivalrous elite distinguished by their greater wealth whose position is sustained by the existing order (Cheeseman, Kanyinga and Lynch 2020). Yet some politicians recognize the limitations of this model and would prefer to reform it. Moreover, as individuals, politicians experience demands for patrimonial politics as a pressure from below that they cannot ignore:

[Y]ou go to attend a burial they expect you to give money. You go on a wedding meeting, they expect you to give them money. You go on a fund-raising drive for the erection of a school, they expect you to give them money.[7]

In short, it is clear that – despite the strong majorities in favour of the civic register in our survey – many feel that politicians should be acting as patrons and giving direct assistance (Chapter 7), while '[s]ome people have become so pessimistic about what politicians will do for them to the extent that they would want to charge them for their votes'.[8] As a result, politicians face constant demands for handouts and assistance (Chapter 7), and sceptical voters often support those known to be corrupt or

[5] Interview UGA55a, politician, Mukono, 16 June 2015; Interview GHA1a, NDC official, Accra, 28 August 2015; Interview KEN10a, activist, Seme, 14 March 2017. See also Elizabeth Ohene, 'Maybe we want them to steal?', www.myjoyonline.com/opinion/2019/September-11th/maybe-we-want-them-to-steal-elizabeth-ohene-writes.php.
[6] Interview KEN51a, politician, Seme, 19 June 2017.
[7] Interview UGA27a, politician, Mukono, 23 March 2015.
[8] Interview KEN14a, youth leader, Seme, 24 March 2017.

ethnically biased (Bratton and Kimenyi 2008; Faller 2015). Similarly, while people are quick to denounce 'tribalism', they also tend to reject those who do not help out their kith and kin as 'mean',[9] and many engage in activities – such as the reposting or sharing of online material – that encourage ethnic chauvinism and division (Nyabola 2018).

Popular expectations of assistance were evident from our surveys when we asked participants what the most important thing that people thought their current MP did to win the last election. We coded open-ended responses under six headings that incorporate different aspects of leadership: being loyal to the political party, making legislation and defending democracy, representing the constituency at the national level in parliament and the media, personally assisting citizens and making donations to those in need, leading and supporting development activities, and showing interest by attending local events such as weddings and funerals. In all three countries development activity was identified as the single most important activity, followed by assisting people and making donations (see Figure 6.1). It is therefore clear that, despite their stated preference for civic-minded leaders, most people believe that political success revolves around delivering material benefits – whether club or private – to their constituents.

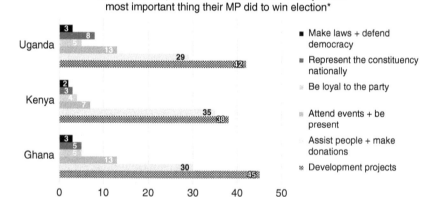

Figure 6.1 The effectiveness of campaign strategies (%)
* Respondents were asked to mention only one activity. Other answers that do not fit into any of these categories have been omitted.
Source: Authors' own survey data

---

[9] Interview KEN81a, parliamentary aspirant, Seme, 10 July 2017.

Material patronage was not the only criterion, however. The third most common response in each country was that the most valuable thing the MP did was to attend events and be present – 13 per cent in Ghana and Uganda, and 7 per cent in Kenya. Eric Kramon (2017) has argued that such activities may be valued, at least in part, as an informational cue about future patronage, but presence is also significant in and of itself as a symbol of solidarity and belonging. There was also recognition that representing the constituency could generate support, especially in Uganda (8 per cent), while a small number of people mentioned the importance of being loyal to the party (4 to 5 per cent), and making national legislation and defending democracy (2 to 3 per cent).

One might expect there to be differences in the responses of rural and urban respondents (Harding 2015). However, while we do find differences, the pattern is far from straightforward (cf. LeBas 2010; Nathan 2016). Thus, while urban residents were slightly more likely to say that candidates need to be loyal to the party and to represent the constituency nationally, there was no shortage of focus on patrimonial issues. Indeed, although we might expect less of an emphasis on development in urban areas, given the greater availability of public services, the opposite was the case. As demonstrated by Figure 6.2, which shows the difference in how often an activity was mentioned in rural as compared to urban

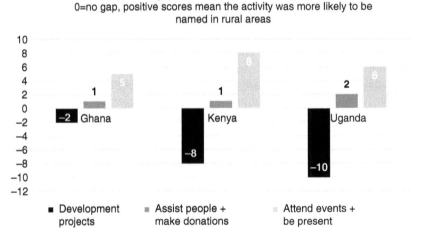

Figure 6.2 Urban/rural variations in the importance of campaign activities (%)
Source: Authors' own survey data

constituencies, urbanites were *more* likely to identify the promise of development projects as the most important thing done by their MPs than their rural counterparts. While the difference was negligble in Ghana (2 per cent higher in urban areas), it was considerable in Kenya (8 per cent higher) and Uganda (10 per cent higher).

Interviews, along with previous studies (Nugent 2007; Conroy-Krutz and Logan 2012; Kramon 2017), further nuance these survey responses by revealing how evaluations of 'development activity' are influenced by an assessment of a politician's motivations and thus by other factors – from the salience of ethnicity and levels of partisan identification, to levels of public mistrust in key institutions and the candidate's track record. As one journalist in Kisumu noted, an evaluation of development-mindedness 'depends on who gives ... If Jubilee comes [here] and dishes out money or projects, the idea is that they're trying to buy [votes]; while if Raila [does the same], then he's not trying to buy, but he cares'.[10] In short, whether politicians' efforts are regarded as virtuous is a matter of interpretation rather than scale (Chapter 7). Moreover, while the importance placed on 'development' and 'assistance' may be taken as evidence that the patrimonial register clearly trumps the civic on the ground, the ambiguous status of assistance – which may be seen to contribute to either particular interests or to national development (6.3.2) – means that individual acts need to be understood in their local context. In addition to the potential for the distribution of patronage to be called into question for being too narrowly focussed on friends, family or clansmen, this means that, while aspirants often feel compelled to emphasize the patrimonial register, they ignore the civic register at their peril.

These findings, which are elaborated upon in Chapter 7, suggest three broad points. First, MPs are encouraged to engage in a variety of behaviour across the patrimonial and civic registers. Second, the patrimonial expectations of constituents are not solely focussed on the exchange of patronage and assistance but also include showing solidarity with the community. Third, it is important not to exaggerate the difference between urban and rural election campaigns, as candidates in both contexts face strong pressures to provide personal assistance and focus on local development projects. However, before we turn to politicians' efforts to navigate these complex, and often contradictory, demands, it is important to look at why politicians vie for office and how people interpret their motivations.

---

[10] Unrecorded interview, journalist, Kisumu, 11 July 2017.

6.2   Why Stand?

Popular expectations that candidates will invest in development projects, provide direct assistance and be accessible ensure that election campaigns are expensive. Aspirants routinely complain not only of the cost of campaigning, but more generally of the cost of being constantly expected to play the role of patron.[11] Many aspirants risk becoming heavily indebted or declared bankrupt (Wilkins 2018: 219). They also run the risk of harassment, intimidation, direct violence and, if they are opposition leaders in countries such as Uganda, imprisonment (Abrahamsen and Bareebe 2016). Despite such costs and dangers, electoral races, particularly at the sub-presidential level, remain crowded, and it is clear that many people who have not run harbour ambitions of vying for political office at some point in the future. So why does elected office have such an allure, despite its evident costs? And how do popular perceptions of politicians' motivations help to shape the moral economy of elections?

Candidates often claim that they are motivated by the shortcomings of incumbents and the opportunity to serve and assist people that elected office provides. In such explanations, personal ambition is readily glossed as public service: 'I want to be the person to link local people with the leaders' or, even more frankly, 'I decided to engage the community by becoming their leader'.[12] However, it is often unclear whether this stated desire is informed by a commitment to impartiality and meritocracy, and thus the civic register, or a desire to protect and promote the interests of a particular community, and thus the patrimonial register, or whether it is a façade that masks self-interest. As one MCA aspirant in Kiambu County explained ahead of Kenya's 2017 elections:

I looked at the [incumbent] ... and I tried to analyse him and then I noted he has completely done nothing for this community ... [so I decided] let me get into politics ... there are resources, a lot of money that is set aside to assist the people.[13]

This vague evocation of a 'community' or 'people', for whom 'maybe I could make a difference'[14] – which could refer to either reciprocity or impartiality – was not uncommon.

However, some suggested that they were motivated by a more explicitly civic commitment to national development and democratization.

---

[11] For example, see Interview KEN7a, politician, Kikuyu, 18 February 2017; Interview KEN14a, political campaigner, Seme, 15 March 2017; Interview GHA15a, politician, Accra, 10 September 2015; Interview UGA56a, politician, Mukono, 16 June 2015.

[12] Interview UGA98a, politician, Gulu, 9 February 2015; Interview UGA73a, politician, Kampala, 12 October 2015; Interview KEN51a, politician, Seme, 19 June 2017.

[13] Interview KEN24a, Kikuyu, 11 May 2017.

[14] Unrecorded interview, former councillor, Njoro, 25 July 2017.

This was the claim of a former Kenyan MP and well-known member of the pro-democracy movement of the early 1990s, who explained to us how:

[Q]uite honestly I was not interested in going into politics at all . . . [but after the repeal of the constitutional clause banning multi-party politics in 1991] the penny dropped, and I realised these people don't have the same commitment that we have on principle. Their only beef that [they have] with government is that they're out of power; if they get in there, I am not persuaded they'll be any different.[15]

Many candidates are encouraged to stand by those around them (Carter Center 2018). A cliché of politics across our three countries is the politician's insistence that – as someone who had acquired a little more wealth, education or influence than those around them – they were persuaded 'to go and get [a] political post'[16] by neighbours and kin. As one former MP for Kikuyu put it, once he began to support projects in his home area, 'people started nudging me'.[17] Such explanations may be self-serving, but encouragement is clearly commonplace. The logic may be crudely instrumental: as soon as someone declares themselves to be a candidate, their kin and neighbours have greater leverage to request handouts or assistance. But at the same time, many are actively looking for someone who will be more effective at dealing with government, at bringing development, fighting for rights and justice, and ensuring security (Barkan 1979b; Waddilove 2019b).

These different commitments – to local, group and/or national interests – may overlap. A female candidate might wish to improve the status of women collectively (Carter Center 2018), but also think that her victory may help her to accumulate wealth and/or help to promote sectional interests. It is possible to view the development and promotion of one's constituency as a sectional and/or national good: local-level changes can advance specific group interests, but they can also be impartially applied within a constituency and be regarded as an MP's civic (albeit incremental) contribution to national development and stability. Similarly, while talk of national development may be informed by the civic virtues of impartiality and inclusive citizenship, it can constitute a cover for the promotion of community-level interests (Lynch 2016a).

While civic and patrimonial considerations are no doubt often important, many are motivated, in part or primarily, by the opportunities and perks of office: 'People think that their solution to poverty is in politics and they go there . . . they will go to amass wealth for themselves.'[18] This is

[15] Interview KEN1a, former parliamentarian, Nairobi, 23 September 2016.
[16] Interview KEN76a, politician, Seme, 13 July 2017.
[17] Unrecorded interview, former MP for Kikuyu, Nairobi, 10 May 2017.
[18] Interview UGA79a, NGO activist, Gulu, 24 September 2015.

also, of course, a motivation for close supporters of candidates: as one businessman explained of his involvement in the Kisumu County gubernatorial campaign in 2017, while he believed his preferred candidate would do a better job than the incumbent, he also wanted 'to be part and parcel of a political group so that I can also influence business and get business. It's unfortunate but that's another motivation factor'.[19] The oft-cited possibility of financial gain is intertwined with the more general appeal of status and power of being an 'honourable' member (Daddieh and Bob-Milliar 2012). In all three countries, politicians are famous and – apparently, at least – rich. Their rallies can be intoxicating displays of enthusiastic applause and support. They enjoy the power and influence that stems from official duties as well as from a place in more informal networks. There is then the comradery of collective struggle and the appeal, which for some appears almost addictive, of the political game – in out-smarting others, of being in the thick of intrigue and plots.

Finally, while many aspirants expect or at least hope to win, others stand even though they know that they have no real chance. One reason to do this is to establish themselves as possible contenders for future elections and/or to build a reputation as someone who can (or has) mobilize(d) support for higher-level candidates in the hope of being co-opted in to powerful political networks. This strategy has encouraged many lower-level candidates to campaign for Museveni in Uganda (Wilkins 2018). In Kenya, the devolution of significant power to 47 county governors in 2010 has led to a complex pattern of sub-national candidacies that have benefited both the incumbent president and the opposition (Waddilove 2019a). In Ghana – where it is difficult for aspirants to win without being known by the NDC or NPP – and where being an active member of either party can offer some support to everyone from the humblest member to the most senior politician (Bob-Milliar 2012b) – standing for one party in the stronghold of the other will not lead to electoral success, but it may well bring other rewards, such as an appointment to an administrative post if one's party secures the presidency.[20]

Politicians therefore have various motivations to run, but being seen to run for the right reasons is critical to their success. Popular perceptions tend to foreground the self-seeking motivations of socio-economic gain (Ayee 2011: 378) and, while communities encourage those who have some wealth or local influence to run for office, they are quick to denounce those who stand as self-seekers. This is true of incumbents, but also of opposition

---

[19] Interview KEN86a, political campaigner, Kisumu, 13 July 2017.
[20] Unrecorded interview, former parliamentary aspirant and party strategist, Accra, 11 July 2019; Interview GHA99a, parliamentary candidate, Kumasi, 10 December 2016.

candidates who are widely mistrusted across the sub-continent (Bratton and Logan 2015). Such popular scepticism is important as it helps to explain why politicians have to work so hard to display their virtue and why they are always so vulnerable to 'decampaigning'.

6.3   On the Campaign Trail

Just as political aspirants often draw from a diverse 'menu of manipulation' (Schedler 2002), they also adopt a mixed 'menu of mobilization'. This is unsurprising. Not only do voters demand multiple things, they comprise members of multiple, overlapping groups – young and old, men and women, urban and rural, rich and poor, professionals and informal workers, co-ethnics and non-co-ethnics, Christians and Muslims. The challenge of running an effective campaign is then further complicated by popular scepticism and rivals' efforts to undermine each other's reputation. This section provides an overview of four intertwined pillars of electoral campaigns in Ghana, Kenya and Uganda – namely viability, virtue, decampaigns and communications – before we turn to the use of more problematic strategies and inter-country variations in campaign trajectories.

6.3.1   Electoral Viability

A politician's ability to promote particular or national interests is closely tied to their perceived capacity to secure power. Voters – whether they prioritize the patrimonial or civic register – are often reluctant to support a candidate who has no chance of winning, particularly if they dislike, or even fear, one of the other candidates or parties in the race. Campaigns are therefore in part a confidence trick (Schaffer and Schedler 2007: 27), as candidates compete to exude confidence in terms of their electoral viability (Kramon 2017).

At one level, this is about demonstrating popularity. During extended campaign periods, everything from buildings to trees and vehicles are plastered with posters; crowds at rallies become 'moving billboards';[21] motorcades to submit nomination papers are noisy and large; public defections by supporters or officials of rival parties are engineered (Perrot 2016); and candidates jostle to be endorsed by influential figures. But viability is also intimately interlinked with virtue signalling. This requires a careful negotiation of the patrimonial and civic registers (6.3.2), and displays of 'ordinary virtues', such as trust and honesty

---

[21] Interview GHA89a, civic educator, Juaso, 6 December 2016.

(Ignatieff 2017: 52). In the face of an increasingly pervasive 'Pentecostalist cultural style' (Meyer 2008), the adoption of religious discourse and imagery has become increasingly important to the latter: those who enjoy God's favour can present themselves as spiritually virtuous and as destined to succeed (Deacon 2015). As the NPP campaign slogan in 2012 and 2016 succinctly put it, 'The battle is the Lord's.'[22]

Viability is also linked to party affiliation. In Ghana, a candidate's prospect of victory in a party stronghold largely depends on their ability to secure the locally popular party ticket, and even in 'swing' areas electoral success is all but impossible unless one is nominated by the NDC or NPP (Chapter 2). This ensures that the campaigns for those party nominations are often fought more closely than the subsequent general election and may be more closely associated with various abuses – from claims of outright vote buying to intimidation.[23] In Kenya, party primaries, particularly in 'stronghold' areas, are also often fiercely fought and associated with widespread malpractice (Oloo 2007; Wanyama 2010). In Uganda, the centrality of Museveni's patronage and his ability to provide (and deny) security ensure that electoral viability is closely linked to how a candidate relates to the president – with NRM candidates (and some independents) seeking to display their proximity to Museveni, and opposition candidates looking to demonstrate their capacity to stand up to him (Lynch 2016b; Wilkins 2018). Yet as much as the image of viability is important, successful electoral campaigns also require more direct performances that a candidate is, and will be, a good leader.

6.3.2   Cultivating Virtue and Productive Ambiguity

To be regarded as virtuous according to the patrimonial register, aspirants need to cultivate a reputation for being accessible to constituents, as well as for assisting them, and to 'develop personal repertoires and styles of giving tailored to the political messages of their candidature' (Vokes and Wilkins 2016: 591; also Roelofs 2019). While all are expected to give some money and material items to voters, expectations vary according to an aspirant's position and wealth (Chapter 7). Moreover, while some rely on handouts to show that they are of a 'redistributive type' (Kramon 2017: 11), others adopt a strategy that places greater emphasis on their track record in facilitating development more broadly speaking and/or

---

[22] 'NPP holds final "Battle is the Lord's" rally today', *Ghana Star*, 4 December 2016, www .ghanastar.com/news/npp-holds-final-battle-is-the-lords-rally-today.

[23] Unrecorded interview, civil society activist, 28 September 2018.

their strength in struggling for particular rights and interests. The most successful appeals to the patrimonial register combine multiple forms of patronage – from handouts and the provision of club goods to community advocacy. The long-term MP for Narok North, William ole Ntimama, for example, was generous with individual patronage, an ostentatious sponsor of community development projects and a belligerent advocate of Maasai land interests (Throup and Hornsby 1998: 542–543; Rutten 2001; Hughes 2016). Similarly, the long-term MP for Aswa, Ronald Reagan Okumu, has used his connections with development and humanitarian agencies to bring resources to his constituents,[24] but has also developed a reputation for vocal opposition to the government (including over the highly emotive issue of elite land grabs in the region).

A carefully cultivated track record as a philanthropist, service provider and/or advocate can be reinforced, or undermined, by other informational cues. A sense of community matters: the vast majority of elected MPs self-identify as a member of a locally prominent religious group (Takyi, Opoku-Agyeman and Kutin-Mensah 2010). The vast majority also hail from the constituencies that they represent and share an identity with the most numerous local ethnic group or clan (Byrd 1963; Hornsby 1989; Morrison 2004). The idea that one is autochthonous – or a local 'son of the soil' – is often particularly important as a sign that one is 'from', and thus more likely to be 'for', a local community (Lynch 2011b). But identity alone is insufficient to secure victory. Aspirants also need to cultivate a reputation for being a 'good' son of the soil through substantive displays of their accessibility and commitment to a community (Roelofs 2019). In this vein, politicians across all three countries speak of the need to have a house in their constituency: 'they know that any time they need me I will be at my house'[25] (also Nugent 2007; Kavulla 2008; Gadjanova 2017: 612). They must also regularly travel to (and around) their constituencies (Mattes and Mozaffar 2016), while careers can be boosted through displays of cultural embeddedness – from the relaying of local myths to a skill for singing songs in the vernacular.[26]

It is also important that aspirants show respect for, and be endorsed by, locally popular or influential figures, though the identity of such local power brokers varies. In Kenya, self-declared local 'elders' have become prominent in endorsing candidates or even appointing them as fellow elders – seeking, perhaps, to demonstrate their own status as much as to benefit those they support (Willis

---

[24] Interview UGA77a, NRM activist, Gulu, 22 September 2015.
[25] Interview UGA57a, politician, Mukono, 16 June 2015.
[26] Interview KEN10a, woman activist, Kisumu, 14 March 2017.

2009).[27] In Ghana, customary chiefs enjoy widespread respect and, despite a legal prohibition, are routinely drawn into electoral politics – though their influence has proven hard for any candidate to consistently instrumentalize (Nugent 1996).[28] In other words, while chiefs in Ghana 'can't tell [their] adult children who to vote for',[29] they can often call a candidate's character into question in a way that is less common in Kenya. As one chief explained:

[A]s a chief you have to ... remain neutral ... [but, as a politician] when you are about to come to my community, you have to inform me earlier on. Now you don't come with the empty hand. At least two bottles of schnapps in addition to the envelop ... [If you don't, then] when you are off I will call my people back to the palace again, I will tell them that because of the behaviour of this candidate, please don't vote for him or her. ... I think 2004 elections ... somebody do this ... I called my people not to vote for him, he lost ... Coming to my town, no two bottles of schnapps or small envelop ... this is disrespect to [me/the chief]![30]

In Uganda, too, customary authorities can be locally influential in electoral politics – though this varies significantly between different areas. Legally barred from active politics, the *kabaka* and his ministers play a complex game of allusion and indirect signalling to offer support to some candidates, and few candidates in Buganda would stand in open defiance of the kingdom.[31] As one candidate explained, 'when [I] introduce myself [I] tell them, I'm so and so, [I was] born here, I support the *kabaka*'.[32] When Andrew Senyonga first vied for the Mukono LC5 chairmanship in 2011 he was unsuccessful – even though he spent generously – because of doubts about his commitment to Buganda. Ahead of the 2016 elections, he contributed generously to *kabaka* projects and was invited to kingdom events. Seen now as a loyal subject of the kingdom, he ran again and won the seat. In contrast, the historical weakness of traditional leaders in Acholiland and government involvement in the reinvention of customary authority made chiefly endorsement of little importance in Gulu – and endorsement by the recognized paramount chief potentially toxic.[33]

Yet, as strong as the pull of local authenticity is, candidates understand that there is a risk that if they focus exclusively on one community they will

[27] 'Monkey's tale: DP Ruto crowning as elder "revoked"', *The Star*, 29 May 2018.
[28] 'Three traditional councils endorse Prez Mahama', *Daily Graphic*, 31 October 2016; 'Sefwi Anhwiaso chief endorses NPP's "1-Factory-1-District" policy', *Daily Graphic*, 11 August 2016.
[29] Unrecorded interview, IDEG observer, Kumasi, 10 December 2016.
[30] Interview GHA101a, chief, Asante Akim, 12 December 2016.
[31] Unrecorded interview, LC5 candidate, Mukono, 16 January 2016.
[32] Unrecorded interview, LC5 candidate, Mukono, 16 January 2016.
[33] Interview UGA92a, politician, Gulu, 17 January 2016; Interview UGA109a, politician, Gulu, 26 February 2016.

come to be seen as a zealot and hence be branded a 'tribalist'. Even the late Ntimama – who might be regarded as one of Kenya's most patrimonial leaders – did not wholly neglect the idea of civic virtue. Instead, while his defence of Maasai land rights was rooted in ethnic land claims, which presented non-Maasai as 'guests' who had failed to behave properly (Jenkins 2012), he also evoked national citizenship through the argument that the protection of Mau Forest, which feeds various rivers and lakes in southern Kenya, was ultimately to the benefit of the entire nation.[34] Moreover, while the exclusive logic inherent to Ntimama's fiery rhetoric made such appeals to civic virtue appear disingenuous to many, others balance civic and patrimonial claims more credibly. For example, Betty Nambooze, the MP for Mukono Municipality from 2010 to date, is known to be loyal to the Buganda kingdom and to give money to constituents facing medical or other crises,[35] but she has also effectively presented herself as a strong advocate for justice and as a patriotic Ugandan who stands up to corruption and poor governance (Médard and Golaz 2013: 549).

Across our three country case studies, aspirants are assisted in such precarious balancing acts by ground-intensive campaigns and targeted messaging (see 6.3.4) and by a level of ambiguity as to whether their actions speak to the patrimonial or civic registers. Cultivating a reputation for development mindedness often involves behaviour that – at first glance – appears to fall squarely within the patrimonial register. Certainly, giving money, bags of cement or other private goods to individuals or particular groups may simply be an attempt to build community-specific or reciprocal support. But it can also be an attempt to display civic virtue, for example, if the aspirant argues that they are helping those most in need or contributing – albeit incrementally – to national development. In this way, a school or road can be situated to benefit a particular ethnic group or support base, but it can also be presented as evidence of one's commitment to the public good (Harding 2015). Support for a land dispute can be cast as supporting local 'sons of the soil' or as protecting a national resource, such as an important water catchment area (Meinert and Kjær 2016). Such productive ambiguity is deepened by the use of different languages, metaphors and cultural inferences. For example, when talking about land, aspirants do not need to talk in explicitly patrimonial language for audiences to understand that – according to autochthonous logics – the beneficiaries of their policies or advocacy will be their own community (Manji 2020).

---

[34] Unrecorded interview, clergyman, Narok, 1 June 2017.
[35] Interview UGA35a, politician, Mukono, 27 March 2015.

In this way, ambiguity can be productive for aspirants, enabling them to favour their supporters, while suggesting that their efforts will actually be to the benefit of all and so minimizing accusations of 'vote buying', 'nepotism' and/or 'tribalism'.[36] Ambiguity can also, however, be dangerous: the lines between development and vote buying or ethnic chauvinism are by no means clear, and interpretation is not controlled by the candidate: supplying poles for a local electrification project might be presented by a leader as an act of patrimonial or civic virtue, but it can also be denounced by rivals as vote buying.[37]

To negotiate such complex terrains, aspirants often seek to cultivate a particular style or persona. Options include a 'populist' style, whereby politicians play on the idea that people are (ab)used by establishment elites; a 'progressive' style that relies on expertise, foresight and technocratic capacity (Roelofs 2019); a 'conciliatory' approach that emphasizes an ability to work with others; and a 'combative' approach that underscores a candidate's strength and courage in standing up to power (Wanyande 2002; Médard and Golaz 2013; Lockwood 2019a). The utility of these styles rests, at least in part, in their capacity to cut across both registers of virtue and in how they can be mixed and matched. For example, in Kenya's 2013 election, Kenyatta and Ruto used a 'combative' response to the ICC's intervention to argue that they would defend the reputation and position of both 'their' communities and the nation against a neo-colonial West (Burbidge 2014; Lynch 2014). At the same time, they presented themselves as young 'progressives' who – unlike their 'analogue' opponents – would help to foster digital innovation and growth. In contrast, Odinga benefited from a reputation, at least among his supporters, as a combative populist: 'a principled person'[38] who 'embodies the struggles that people have had' at both local and national levels.[39] In neighbouring Uganda, an NRM activist explained how he persuaded constituents of how, 'by getting closer to government', they would benefit from national public goods (most notably peace and development) and be able to tackle those things (such as boreholes and community roads) that had literally 'broken down' at the village level. This conciliatory style was then interwoven with references to his education and background in finance and to how – as an implied 'progressive' – he could understand and explain the workings of the national economy to citizens.[40] These styles play a central role in the moral economy of elections because – together with a productive ambiguity as to whether an action or promise is civic or patrimonial and

---

[36] Unrecorded interview, RPP monitor, Kisumu, 10 July 2017.
[37] Interview GHA74a, local NDC official, Juaso, 1 December 2016.
[38] Interview KEN55b, retired chief, Seme, 12 July 2017.
[39] Interview KEN81a, parliamentary aspirant, 10 July 2017.
[40] Interview UGA 77a, Gulu, 22 September 2015.

ground-intensive campaigns (6.3.4) – they help to explain how politicians are often able to simultaneously present themselves as both 'good' civic *and* patrimonial leaders despite the potential contradictions between the two registers of virtue.

6.3.3   Decampaigning

Campaigns involve efforts to mobilize support for particular candidates, and against others, as aspirants try to encourage citizens to accept their 'friend–enemy dichotomy' (Ost 2004: 242). The need to constantly negotiate, and to find an uneasy balance, between the civic and patrimonial registers offers much scope for such decampaigning. Emotive performances and messages are often divisive. For example, while wealth can be regarded as evidence of success and capacity, it can be dismissed as a product of corruption or witchcraft (Geschiere 1997). Investment in a local development project can be lauded as evidence of generosity and development-mindedness, but it can be criticized as biased towards co-ethnics and funded by corruption. Similarly, a track record of combative politics in defence of people's interests can be taken as a sign of bravery and commitment to a cause, but can also be used to dismiss a leader as a 'noise maker' who is unable to help their supporters in more practical ways.[41] For example, while Nambooze mobilized support in 2016 on the basis of her reputation as being 'part of the struggle' against poor governance, local NRM activists used this – albeit unsuccessfully – to suggest that she 'only knows how to abuse the president' and thus question her capacity to bring development.[42] In other contexts, the same approach was more successful and helped to build Museveni's presidential vote around Gulu from 2006 and to win the Omoro constituency for the NRM in 2011 (Omach 2014: 364; Lynch 2016b).

Decampaigning efforts are often highly personalized. While the support of well-known figures can be a major boost to a candidate, their reputation can also be besmirched by their association with more influential figures, since the support of prominent individuals can open the door to claims that one is a mere 'puppet'. Similarly, the narratives that are woven around national figures can trickle down to local contests. In Ghana, the idea that Rawlings is 'a jumped-up dictator with blood on his hands', or that NPP leaders are 'self-interested elites' (Jeffries 1998: 206), continues to pervade local campaigns. There are then more specific

---

[41] Unrecorded interview, NDC activist, Cape Coast, 27 November 2016.
[42] Unrecorded interview, civil society activist, Mukono, 19 January 2016; unrecorded interview, journalist, Mukono, 15 January 2016.

slurs. For example, during the 2008 campaigns, '[t]he NDC presented the NPP's candidate ... as a drug dealer and cocaine addict ... [while the] NPP fought back by stigmatising the NDC's candidate ... as a walking corpse, weak and politically powerless' (Schmitz 2018: 237). Similarly, while the FDC has cast Museveni as old, authoritarian and corrupt, the NRM has responded with equally personalized attacks – from allegations that Besigye was HIV+ and an agent of the dictatorships of the 1970s and early 1980s (Dagne and Harding 2001: 2) to laying charges against him for treason and rape (Mwenda 2007: 26). In Kenya, efforts to depict Odinga as divisive and dangerous in the 2007, 2013 and 2017 elections drew on various rumours – from his alleged involvement in the 1982 coup to his support for radical Islam, responsibility for the post-election violence of 2007/2008, and support for the ICC (Willis 2008; Lynch 2014; Nyabola 2018). In these cases and many others, the types of decampaigning narratives that emerge tend to target the kind of virtue claimed by the leader, whether patrimonial or civic.

However, while politicians are often tainted by such associations and scandals – from the demonization of party leaders to stories of corruption, sexual exploits, involvement in crime and violence, and examples of electoral malpractice – these associations do not necessarily herald the end of a politician's career. This is evident from the number of politicians who have their victory nullified in an electoral petition but nevertheless go on to win a by-election (Murison 2013; Sekindi 2017). But negative associations and scandals are not irrelevant: stories abound of prominent candidates whose chances were dashed by negative propaganda (Lockwood 2019b), while others turn 'problems' into part of a winning campaign strategy (Lynch 2014). In short, what is critical is not the factual accuracy of the allegations, but whether it appears plausible to the target audience and, if so, whether it undermines an aspirant's claims to be viable and virtuous. Do people dislike the influential figures with whom a politician is associated, or does this alliance render them more popular? Do rumours of wrongdoing undermine an aspirant's perceived ability to work for their constituents, or might it actually speak to their capacity to be a good strong leader? The answer to all these questions is partly shaped by the effectiveness of an aspirant's communications strategy.

6.3.4   Communications

In all three countries campaigning has been facilitated by the opening up of the airwaves and spread of social media (Osborn 2008: 316; Gadjanova, Lynch, Reifler and Saibu 2019). The role of social media in particular has prompted significant debate in recent years as academics discuss the changes wrought (e.g. Nyabola 2018; Brinkman 2019; Omanga 2019 on Kenya), and aspirants complain that social media has facilitated the spread of falsehoods against them – from allegations of their involvement in corruption to their use of 'charms' or 'voodoo'.[43] The power of social media is also not lost on those who look to take advantage of this new technology. One campaigner in Kisumu explained how:

> I have five Facebook accounts, only one has my name and the rest have other names and a lot of people do that. So you can do a post and five people react and those five people are you, to get people's attention. Because people will always comment on what others have commented on and you can also post whatever you want.[44]

The role of such strategies and propaganda – together with the import-ance of ensuring that people know about one's efforts to 'bring develop-ment', 'security' and/or 'struggle for justice' and to simultaneously guard against the decampaigning efforts of others – encourages candidates to invest heavily in both traditional and social media coverage.[45] Yet while different media are important their impact is mixed. Social media, for example, can be used to circulate rumours and falsehood and can reinforce patrimonial logics as politicians use their online presence to advertise donations and development projects. It can also be used, how-ever, for voter education, to promote peace and other national goods and to hold leaders accountable (Nyabola 2018; Gadjanova, Lynch, Reifler and Saibu 2019). Significantly, because leaders typically do not want to be associated with the worst personal attacks on their rivals and 'other' communities – which would undermine their cross-over appeal and claims to civic virtue – these are often conducted by lower-level activists and 'foot soldiers'.

Moreover, while important, the opening up of the airwaves and rise of social media have not changed the fundamental logics of electoral cam-paigns, which in all three countries remain ground-intensive (Paget 2019b) and heavily reliant on physical presence (Nyabola 2018; Gadjanova, Lynch, Reifler and Saibu 2019; Cheeseman, Fisher, Hassan and Hitchin 2020). Political rallies remain a popular campaign tool across the board, in large part because of the multi-layered performances they feature. This includes the mode of an aspirant's arrival, the campaign songs adopted and commissioned, the entertainment provided, the line-up on the dais, the language, tone and content of the speeches given, and the audience's response. This complexity ensures that – when carefully stage-managed – rallies, like the NASA manifesto launch discussed

---

[43] Unrecorded interview with NDC MP, Accra, 12 July 2019.
[44] Interview KEN14a, political campaigner, Seme, 24 March 2017.
[45] Interview KEN86a, political campaigner, Kisumu, 13 July 2017.

earlier, can perform both viability and virtue. In a single event, a candidate can bring together supporters who are rewarded (with food, drink, T-shirts and money) for their presence; pay a local journalist to focus in on the crowds gathered and so exaggerate their popularity; and speak to national issues in English to establish their civic credentials, while leaving less prominent figures to speak of more ethnically relevant and potentially divisive issues in local vernaculars.

Holding rallies is not straightforward, however. A dismal showing can undermine claims to viability (Paget 2019b), a rival can mobilize youths to heckle or disrupt an event, and media accounts can narrow in on moments of ethnic chauvinism or popular rejection. The careful management of media coverage is particularly important given that messages that are popular in one area are often unpopular in others. For example, while the NPP's 'displays of "big mannism"' were effective in Asante in Ghana's 1996 election, in the north and Volta region 'the triumphalist tone of the NPP campaign merely confirmed a well-entrenched stereotype of Ashanti arrogance' (Nugent 1999: 308). In Kenya's 2017 election, reports that Odinga had urged Maasai at a rally in Kajiado not to sell their land to outsiders 'who have come to invade' proved popular among Maasai as a patrimonial pledge,[46] but were gleefully exploited by Jubilee in other areas since they played into a long-standing accusation that – in contravention of the civic register – Odinga was a 'tribalist'. As Ruto asked pointedly at one rally in Nairobi: '[A]re we not Kenyans?'[47]

Even more important than the big rallies are the myriad small-scale meetings. In the weeks before an election, every candidate faces a dizzying series of diary commitments, most of which will involve a donation of some kind as well as a speech. This includes stop-off meetings in small trading centres, 'town hall' meetings with various local groups (hairdressers, motorcycle taxi drivers, parent-teachers associations, etc.), and attendance at different places of worship, weddings and funerals. The perception of the latter as 'a communal thing'[48] ensures that funerals have become a particularly popular venue for political aspirants to display their commitment to a particular area and/or community and thus their patrimonial virtue – a commitment made manifest by their presence, the gifts of food for the funeral meal, pledges of future assistance to the bereaved and other promises made. Especially intense during official campaigns, these engagements are

---

[46] Conversation with a NASA rally attendee, Narok, 28 June 2017.
[47] Fieldwork notes, Jubilee rally, Nairobi, 24 July 2017.
[48] MCA aspirant, East Seme, 15 March 2016.

sustained and pervasive; in between elections, any aspiring candidate must be mindful of the need to be seen, whether in person or through intermediaries.

These smaller meetings are valued, just like rallies, for the audiences that can be reached and for the different images that can be performed through a carefully stage-managed appearance. For example, while many like to speak in churches, mosques and temples because they provide 'a ready audience [that] won't cost a lot',[49] attendance also provides an opportunity to display generosity by donating to building funds and the like, to speak of struggles and the importance of justice, to gain the endorsement of influential figures, and to appear as God-fearing and morally upright (Bompani 2016).

A range of activities are also valued because they help candidates to navigate a locally appropriate balance between the patrimonial and civic registers. More specifically, a candidate can combine an espousal of civic virtue at public rallies and religious meetings when journalists and 'bloggers' are around with more explicitly patrimonial messaging through door-to-door canvassing, 'night meetings' with key 'stakeholders', closed-door meetings with community groups and the use of 'foot soldiers'. This combination of public and private messaging is important as it allows for a cultivated image of civic virtue to be accompanied by explicit commitments to more particular needs and claims that might be regarded as irresponsible or offensive if given more oxygen.

Finally, this array of activities helps to build and sustain a network of local intermediaries. All politicians require point men across their constituency on whom they can rely to inform them of local issues, organize people to come out to register and vote, and serve as party agents during the polling, counting and tallying processes. These local activists are crucial to electoral politics, and their involvement tends to be profoundly patrimonial. As one woman activist told us 'when you start doing politics, you see people coming to you, with their problems', and 'politics gives you that power, so that people know that I come to [her name] I can eat'.[50] While one such man in Uganda complained of the financial as well as physical burden of the role – 'the moment you enter politics, that is complete loss' – he went on to explain how he derived both wealth and status from his role as gatekeeper: the man who could get a form authorized quickly or get the MP to provide transport for a funeral: 'Don't I benefit from that? Therefore people say, "This is our man!"'[51] Or, as

---

[49] MCA aspirant, East Seme, 15 March 2016.
[50] Interview GHA32b, NPP activist, Cape Coast, 6 December 2016; Interview GHA32a, NPP activist, Cape Coast, 31 August 2016.
[51] Interview UGA74a, NRM activist, Kampala, 12 October 2015.

one activist in Ghana told us, 'The reason why I went to work for the party is future. Because, in particular, I have something to chop.'[52] The more elevated of these local intermediaries may themselves be appointed to some parastatal or local government role. For those who are business-people, contracts and licences become easier to get, while others may find their local community favoured with piped water, mains electricity or school uniforms for local children,[53] and some look to use their position to build their own political careers.[54] Across all three countries, then, ground-intensive campaigns create opportunities for local mobilizers to become mini patrons who help politicians to adhere to the patrimonial register in ways that minimize the inherent tensions between being a 'good' civic and patrimonial leader.

6.4   Doing the Wrong Thing

Candidates lay claim to virtue, but pursuit of electoral victory will often lead them into behaviour – such as bribery, intimidation and rigging – that is morally dubious in both civic and patrimonial terms. They manage that tension partly by strategies of deniability, publicly distancing themselves from problematic behaviour, but often also by an explicit argument of moral exigency: insisting that problematic behaviour is actually required in pursuit of virtue. In order to demonstrate how candidates seek to justify such behaviour, this section addresses the role of intimidation and election rigging – the issue of vote buying is taken up in Chapter 7.

6.4.1   Intimidation and Violence

Intimidation and violence are a common part of electoral campaigns – from the low-intensity and decreasing levels of violence witnessed in Ghana over the years (Gyimah-Boadi 2001; Bob-Milliar 2014; Schmitz 2018) through to the extensive use of harassment and intimidation of opposition leaders by the Ugandan state (Abrahamsen and Bareebe 2016; Nkuubi 2017; Sjögren 2018) and the combination of state violence, gang and ethnic violence in Kenya (Mueller 2008; Mutahi and Ruteere 2019). Political violence is sometimes deadly, but more often it is not, in part because it does not have to be in order to be effective. Small-scale violence may achieve 'an intense psychological effect' (Schmitz 2018: 237) with

---

[52] Interview GHA82a, NPP activist, Cape Coast, 2 December 2016.
[53] Interview GHA29a, parliamentary aspirant, location withheld, 29 August 2016; Interview GHA32a, NPP activist, Cape Coast, 31 August 2016; Interview GHA44a, NDC local official, Cape Coast, 2 September 2016.
[54] Interview GHA93a, NDC local official, Cape Coast, 8 December 2016.

previous experiences of violence making euphemistic evocation extremely powerful – 'shaking the matchbox' as it is called in Zimbabwe (Beardsworth, Cheeseman and Tinhu 2019: 8).

Aspirants can use violence to undermine their main opponents. This includes the physical disabling of candidates (from arrests to murder), the intimidation and displacement of supporters, and disruption of rallies or balloting (in the party primaries and/or general election) (Mutahi 2005). Incumbents enjoy a clear advantage when it comes to such political violence given their control of state security forces, but opposition leaders can also deploy a degree of repression in their own strongholds. Violence can often be a particularly useful strategy because it enables candidates to simultaneously intimidate rivals while demonstrating the costs of defection to allies (Cheeseman 2015a: Chapter 5). It can also build an emotive sense of unity against ethnic 'others'. For example, in the Rift Valley region of Kenya in the early 1990s, the government instigated 'ethnic clashes' to unite the president's co-ethnics as much as to intimidate opposition supporters (Holmquist and Ford 1995: 178). Violence can also be used to reward supporters: during the aforementioned clashes, some government supporters took advantage of forced displacement to acquire land (Galaty 2005: 177).

However, while intimidation and violence have often been used to great effect, they come with significant costs. This arises partly from domestic and international scrutiny (Chapter 4), but also from popular feeling; violence is likely to attract opprobrium as the overwhelming majority of voters believe that it is wrong and should be punished (LeBas 2010: 10; Chapter 7). Individuals seen to be excessively thuggish are likely to be criticized in newspapers and may be abandoned by supporters who do not wish to be associated with or who abhor such tactics. Candidates may therefore seek to deny culpability, using proxies to try to distance themselves from any bloodshed. As one interviewee in Kenya explained, most people 'will not like someone who uses violence to win an election, so that violence would occur but it would be difficult to understand who are behind these young men who are causing violence'.[55] Such deliberate obscuration may also involve deliberate efforts to sow confusion and lay the blame at the feet of rival leaders. As one Kenyan activist explained of his involvement in a 2013 parliamentary campaign:

[O]ne incident is when we went to a place and sponsored certain people to put on an opponent's t-shirt and beat up some of the people. You beat them up with an

---

[55] Interview KEN22a, civil society activist, Kisumu, 19 March 2017.

opponent's t-shirt ... and so, it is that candidate's people ... beating others, so the message would spread around the constituencies.[56]

The ever-present possibility that such dirty tactics have been used is also politically useful as – together with the difficulty of ascertaining the true culprits – it helps any politician who was involved to deny culpability.

In other cases, the use of violence is excused as an unfortunate, but necessary, part of the political game. As Adrienne LeBas notes:

> In conversations prior to the 2007 elections, local and national politicians alike suggested that candidates had become trapped in a violent 'race to the bottom': as soon as one candidate in a given field hired youths or organized militia, other candidates felt compelled to 'organize security' for themselves as well. (2010: 8)

Violence can also, however, be presented as morally necessary according to both the patrimonial and the civic register. In both Kenya and Uganda, incumbent governments have presented themselves as the guarantors of national peace and have used this to present the systematic use of security forces against opposition supporters and candidates as a way to ensure order (Abrahamsen and Bareebe 2016; Vokes and Wilkins 2016; Nkuubi 2017; Mutahi and Ruteere 2019; Lynch, Cheeseman and Willis 2019). In the face of this, some opposition supporters offer their own moral narrative, casting violence as the necessary and virtuous response to oppression. This was evident in the repeat election in Kenya in October 2017, when ODM supporters prevented polling stations from opening across four counties in former Nyanza Province (Waddilove 2019a). The disruption of a national election might intuitively seem like the ultimate contravention of the civic register. Indeed, some local activists saw it as the necessary pursuit of Luo interests and thus justified according to the patrimonial register.[57] As one Seme resident explained, in a context in which 'the government is hell bent on making sure we don't raise our heads ... we just need to be tough', what mattered was not the law, but 'what the community thought was wrong'.[58] Others however, took a very different route – Odinga, for example, justified his actions as a display of national civic virtue and a defence of democracy: 'if we [in Kenya] fall to dictatorship all of Africa is in danger'.[59]

As a result of such different interpretations, the threat or use of violence can be used to perform and do multiple things at once – from weakening one's opponents to the cultivation of narratives of civic virtue and patrimonial reward. In this way, Rebecca Tapscott explains how the NRM's

---

[56] Interview KEN14a, political campaigner, Kisumu, 24 March 2017.
[57] Unrecorded interview, ODM activist, Kisumu, 20 October 2017.
[58] Unrecorded interview, youth leader, Seme, 19 October 2017.
[59] Fieldwork diary, TV News.

expansion of its Crime Preventer programme ahead of the country's 2016 election – 'nominally a community policing initiative intended to curb crime in local communities and supplement security during the election' (2016: 693) – exacerbated a sense of intimidation and possible violence. Similarly, at one and the same time the programme provided patronage to youth and presented 'crime preventers as active and engaged citizens invested in the country's future' who – under Museveni's leadership – would help 'manage Uganda's unruly population' to promote the rule of law (2016: 704). Such examples are a reminder that violence, while widely denounced, may be sold as a virtuous electoral act according to the civic and/or patrimonial register if a politician can develop a narrative which resonates with enough people.

6.4.2   Rigging

Alongside the use of intimidation and violence are a host of other methods that can be used to try to tilt an election in a candidate's favour – from the gerrymandering of constituency boundaries to ballot-box stuffing and imaginative tallying (Cheeseman and Klaas 2018). As with violence, electoral rigging tends to be undertaken in ways that allow a candidate to plausibly deny involvement, since they are both illegal and broadly unpopular (Chapter 7). Given this illegality and public opprobrium in the abstract, some interviewees were surprisingly candid about their personal involvement. This was true of one activist in Seme who told us how he had helped to rig a party primary for a local councillor in 2007 and boost Odinga's presidential vote in 2007 and 2013:

We helped him [the local councillor] rig ... it was a mockery of an election ... There were no ballot papers, so we got exercise books and we would cut them into pieces ... in one polling station where I was ... we were able to cut very many of them and we were able to stuff them into the ballot box...

... what people would concentrate on at the general level would be ... how do we ensure that Raila Odinga gets more votes here, if the turnout is 50% then you have to force the turn out to be 90% ... You see the ECK officials are not strangers, these are people from the village ... so they are people who are party supporters ... so after people have finished voting, let's say 4pm, we look at how many ballot papers have not been cast, we look at the percentages, if we are at 40 or 50%, or 50 or 60% then we have to push it, so we have to mark them and stuff them, that has to be done.[60]

For this individual – and for others with whom we spoke – the main justification for such malpractice was an assumption that other candidates were doing the same rendering it necessary to bend 'some rules ...

---

[60] Interview KEN14a, youth leader, Kisumu, 24 March 2017.

just to be able to make their end'.[61] As the man explained of the councillor-level primaries in 2007:

Yes, of course [our opponent also tried to stuff], only that we stole more than they could. I mean that is, is not the best thing to see but politics is about winning. It is not about being second.[62]

This felt need to counter the rigging that one's opponent would likely engage in was then often intertwined – either implicitly or explicitly – with the idea that one had to prevent the 'other' from winning because their election would, for one reason or another, 'be disastrous for everybody'.[63] In this vein, an activist who admitted that his preferred candidate for a county seat in Kisumu had rigged the ODM party nomination in 2017 proffered a two-fold justification. On the one hand, his candidate had 'tried to do the right thing, but then the others wanted to do the wrong thing. So it's hard, [you] end up having to do the wrong thing'. While, on the other hand, his fears that a more corrupt and less developmentally oriented candidate would win led him to believe that 'at times this democracy is not a very good thing. At times we have to guide it.'[64] Or, as a Ugandan lawyer who admitted to casting multiple votes for Besigye in previous elections explained, his actions were necessary – as Museveni was known to engage in widespread malpractice – and justifiable given the desirability of political change.[65]

Critically, this perceived need to manipulate the process can be presented as necessary according to either the civic or patrimonial register of virtue: with an opponent potentially presented as disastrous for the prospects for a meritocratic, impartial and law-abiding future for the nation but also for the capacity of leaders to exchange support for preferential treatment. In our interviews this question of who the relevant 'everybody' was – for whom a candidate would be 'disastrous' – was often unclear. However, from looking at the broader conversations with these individuals it is evident that, while some were seeking to protect and advance sub-national interests, many saw these interests as compatible with the national good and thus saw electoral malpractice – in a morally imperfect world – as justifiable according to the civic and/or patrimonial registers of virtue.

---

[61] Interview, KEN81a, parliamentary aspirant, Seme, 10 July 2017.
[62] Interview KEN14a, youth leader, Kisumu, 24 March 2017.
[63] Interview KEN14a, youth leader, Kisumu, 24 March 2017.
[64] Interview KEN86a, political campaigner, Kisumu, 13 July 2017.
[65] Fieldwork notes, Kampala, 4 January 2016. This example is discussed in more detail in 1.4.

6.5   Different Political Trajectories

There is much that is similar between our country case studies. As discussed, campaigns are expensive and, while the majority of MPs belong to a political party, parties – including the NDC and NPP in Ghana – provide little support for non-presidential candidates. In turn, while many are motivated to go into politics by the possibility of wealth, and some politicians do become rich while in office, elected politicians tend to have a track record of local generosity and to belong to a national and/or local elite *before* they vie for office (Byrd 1963; Hornsby 1989; Pinkston 2016). The importance of being relatively wealthy – but also educated and well connected – has ensured some common backgrounds: late-colonial politicians tended to be teachers and civil servants, and sometimes the sons of chiefs. As the relative wealth and status of teachers have declined over the last few decades, the proportion of former administrators, businessmen, lawyers and CSO workers elected to national assemblies has increased (Hornsby 1989; Morrison 2004; Cloward 2019; Cloward and Weghorst 2019).

The importance of the patrimonial register also ensures that successful candidates tend to be male. Women tend to have less control over family finances and thus less capacity to fund expensive campaigns than their male counterparts. They also face 'a socio-cultural discourse of women's place in society', a '"masculine model" of political organization' and the gendered nature of electoral violence (Bawa and Sanyare 2013: 288; also Madanda 2017; Bauer 2019; Bouka, Berry and Kamuru 2019; Mitullah 2020), which collectively ensure that it is more difficult for them to appear as viable, to assist according to the patrimonial register, to engage in malpractice and to guard against it. Certainly, at independence every single party leader and successful parliamentary aspirant across all three countries was male (Byrd 1963: 9; Hornsby 1989: 282; Nketiah 2005: 87), and the number of women elected to open seats remains small (Bawa and Sanyare 2013; Gibb 2016; Bouka, Berry and Kamuru 2019).

Yet being male is insufficient. Elected politicians have overwhelmingly been 'men', not 'youths' – the latter term referring less to a specific age and more signifying those who, critically for the patrimonial register, have limited status and are not able to provide for their family and kin (Gyampo 2019; van Stapele 2020). Africa's first parliamentarians were youngish men, many in their thirties – the products of relatively recently introduced systems of colonial education and employment. Over time, however, the average age has crept up and many MPs are now well past retirement age. Relative wealth, job profile, a visible track record of assistance, the extent to which leaders are known within a community and enjoy the support of local opinion leaders: all these tend to favour older men. Older candidates do not inevitably win, however. While the idea of eldership suggests that more mature figures 'may have the capacity to help others in difficult situations' (Omobowale 2008: 215 on Nigeria), younger candidates can claim virtue by casting older politicians as having tried and failed, by playing on the idea of generational renewal (Ocobock 2017) and by focussing on their ability to struggle for a community and/or nation.

In addition to these similarities, political campaigns also play out differently across the three countries. Once again, these variations reflect the influence of different socio-economic contexts, realities of social organization, historical experience and leadership. In Ghana, the electoral strength of the NDC and NPP has had a significant impact on politicians and their campaigns. The dominance is striking. No other party has ever even come close to winning a presidential election or a parliamentary majority during Ghana's Fourth Republic; every elected government in Ghana's history has come from one or other of these political traditions. In 2012, the NDC and NPP won 270 of 275 directly elected seats in parliament[66] and 98 per cent of the presidential vote. Similarly, in 2016 the two parties secured 98 per cent of the presidential vote and all 275 seats. Party switching is also less common than in our other countries: most MPs are long-standing party members, and acute suspicion surrounds those who swap sides.[67] It is not only candidates who must belong to a party to make their way in politics: so too must activists. The everyday evidence of the strength of Ghana's political parties is the ramified structure that, in both the NDC and NPP, ties the basic level of party organization to every individual polling station in the country. Service at this level is the essential first step for anyone who aspires to prosper through party activism. Together with a relatively strong private sector (Pinkston 2016) and a history of presidential alternance, this underpins Ghana's distinctive politics.

The close association of the NDC and NPP with two political traditions (Chapter 2) is mirrored in a wider bifurcation of associational life, from FM radio stations to student unions and football clubs (Fridy and Brobbey 2009). In turn, this division has helped to reproduce slightly different socio-economic profiles in the two parties. Many of the CPP candidates in Ghana's 1957 elections shared Nkrumah's background in teaching or had worked as government clerks; the UGCC by contrast tended to recruit 'among old-line merchants, intellectuals, and

---

[66] There were four independent candidates, and one from a minor party.
[67] Unrecorded interview, civil society activist, Accra, 19 September 2015.

professionals' (Morrison 2004: 424). More recently, the NPP's presidential candidates have either been lawyers (Kufour in 1996, 2000 and 2004; and Akuffo-Addo in 2008, 2012 and 2016) or university professors (Boahen in 1992) and have come from established political (and sometimes royal) lineages. In contrast, Jerry Rawlings – the NDC candidate in the country's 1992 and 1996 elections – rose up through the military and was 'neither university educated nor lineal heir of privileged classes' (Morrison 2004: 425). John Atta Mills – the NDC candidate in 2000, 2004 and 2008 – was a legal scholar but did not hail from such an established family as Kufour or Akuffo-Addo, while John Mahama – the NDC's candidate in 2012 and 2016 – was a former teacher. These profiles help to maintain a sense of difference between the parties despite their very similar manifestos (Ayee 2011).

These established political traditions have allowed for the persistence of strong regional/ethnic voting patterns with very little overtly ethnic campaigning, which guards against the more exclusive, and thus potentially violent, tendencies of patrimonial politics. In many ways, the pattern that emerged in 1969 has been maintained: Volta votes for the self-avowed Nkrumahist tradition (now NDC) and Asante for the Busia-Danquah tradition (now NPP). But in contrast to 1969, local and national politicians carefully avoid reference to these ethno-regional relationships. Indeed, while the 'majority of Ghanaian voters, view the dominant parties as representative of Asante and Ewe interests' they 'base their evaluations of the "Asante" and "Ewe" parties ultimately on things other than ethnicity' (Fridy 2007). This includes which party is most likely to foster development and security in their local area and/or nationally, and the distribution of club goods (Lindberg 2010). In turn, while government spending patterns do reflect a regional bias (Abdulai and Hickey 2016), aspirants and activists are quick to denounce any aspect of their rival's presidential campaign that suggests a party will favour a particular area – such as Mahama's comments in 2012 that voters in northern Ghana should support him as a fellow northerner (Kelly and Bening 2013: 476).[68]

In addition to a strong sense of party identity, the regular transfer of power, capacity of parties to organize across the country, and a clear need to mobilize support outside of regional strongholds to win presidential elections has led to campaigns that are rarely explicitly 'ethnic'. Consequently, Ghana has developed a form of competition that foregrounds local and national performance in delivering development – in terms of material projects or employment – in a way that productively

---

[68] This debate was again recalled in 2016. Unrecorded interview, academic, Cape Coast, 25 November 2016.

straddles the civic and patrimonial register. Politicians are expected to bring goods to their local constituents in line with the patrimonial register, but this is not generally presented as a redirection of resources away from other areas; rather it is – rhetorically at least – a contribution to national development. At the same time, regular transfers of power make it more difficult than in Kenya or Uganda to justify electoral malpractice as necessary to oust establishment elites. Repeated elections in Ghana have thus not weakened the patrimonial register, but they have discouraged the most exclusive forms of patrimonial politics by ensuring that the pursuit of patrimonial and civic virtue can be presented as compatible and even mutually reinforcing. To put this another way, one can be a good patrimonial leader in Ghana without necessarily raising fears of exclusion among non-co-ethnics.

In Kenya, by contrast, candidates and political parties are more closely associated with ethnic support bases and communities such as the Kikuyu, Luo and Kalenjin have at times voted as a near bloc (Throup and Hornsby 1998; Lynch 2011a). This reflects the weakness of political parties, the absence of effective political institutions that integrate individuals from different communities, and a divisive history of winner-takes-all politics that has led to pronounced socio-economic inequalities both between and within groups (Cheeseman, Kanyinga and Lynch 2020). The electoral dominance of ethnicity should not be overstated, however. There is much less bloc-voting by members of ethnic groups that do not stand presidential candidates, and in sub-national contests voters often need to choose between co-ethnics (Oloo 2005; MacArthur 2008; Long 2019). Even those engaged in ethnic mobilization typically also lay claim to civic virtue. In the 1990s Moi and his supporters insisted that KANU was the only national party, even as they stoked Kalenjin fears of a Kikuyu presidency. At the same time, the various rival opposition candidates claimed to be true nationalists, even as they complained of Kalenjin dominance (Throup and Hornsby 1998). At a more general level, and from the early 1990s to date, such claims to civic virtue have been expressed through a debate between opposition candidates, who cast themselves as promoting constitutionalism and democracy (Lockwood 2019a), and establishment candidates who emphasize stability and gradual progress (Lynch 2014). The decision of which side to join is informed by an array of factors – from individual trajectories and proclivities to the local popularity of particular presidential candidates – but the need to speak to the civic register stems, at least in part, from the fact that every presidential candidate understands that to win elections they must form a multi-ethnic coalition in order to appear credible to other communities. As noted earlier, while being a 'tribalist' may carry some currency locally, it is likely to be seen – even by some members of one's own community – as a disqualification for national office.

Throughout the postcolonial period, such claims to civic virtue have gone hand in hand with a rhetoric that revolves around accusations and counter-accusations about ethnic bias in state institutions. That has encouraged a focus on differences between the 'haves' and 'have nots' during political campaigns, which combined with the informalization of violence and a lack of accountability have led candidates on both sides of the political divide to make greater use of intimidation and violence than in Ghana (Mueller 2008; Lynch 2011b). In turn, the fear of ethnic bias offers a strong motivation to make – and heed – claims to patrimonial virtue (Bratton and Kimenyi 2008; Lynch 2011a, 2014). This ensures a much more tempestuous relationship between the patrimonial and civic registers than in Ghana, with politicians often enjoying strong support among those who have reason to believe that they may benefit from patrimonial reciprocity, but strong resistance from those who fear that they will be excluded.

Along with the historical personalization of power, the ability of leaders to mobilize ethnic groups in the absence of formal structures (Chapter 2) has discouraged the emergence of distinctive or enduring parties. Ambitious individuals seeking elected office gravitate to the party and alliance that is the most popular in their area at that point in time. As one FORD-Kenya leader explained, FORD-Kenya was dominant in his area 'so if [you] want to be a serious politician [you] need to be in FORD-Kenya'.[69] Failing to secure nomination for one party, aspirants readily look for another or run as independents.[70] This has rendered the party system in Kenya both highly unstable and less capable of checking the more exclusive and ethno-nationalist appeals of ambitious politicians. Being on the right party ticket is important, as there may be a 'party wave' that lifts all allied candidates, which is why primaries are vigorously contested (Oloo 2007; Wanyama 2010; Gadjanova 2019; Lockwood 2019b). But this matters less than in Ghana, and the parties of the presidential candidates have at times won a minority of seats in the National Assembly. Moreover, the ephemeral nature of all parties means that they neither channel nor constrain: ambitious politicians – and activists – can readily move from one party to another, for it is personal influence, not party service, that matters. Indeed, even in party strongholds it is often loyalty to a presidential candidate that matters most. As one parliamentary aspirant in Seme noted: 'Raila is an icon of the struggle ... people love him with a passion. It's Railamania ...

---

[69] Unrecorded interview, FORD-Kenya official, Bungoma, 17 July 2017.
[70] For example, unrecorded interview, MCA, Lodwar, 3 May 2017.

you cannot oppose him and succeed ... Even if you don't like him, you must pretend that you like him.'[71]

Partly as a result, new parties and alliances are regularly formed between elections, and even presidential aspirants can move from one party or alliance to another. Kenyatta shifted from KANU to TNA ahead of the 2013 election and then to the Jubilee Party ahead of the 2017 elections. More notably still, Odinga shifted from FORD-Kenya (1992) to NDP (1994), to LDP (2002) and NARC (2002) and, finally, to ODM (2007). Since then Odinga has remained in ODM but has headed different electoral alliances, from ODM's 'pentagon' in 2007, to Coalition for Reforms and Democracy (CORD) in 2013 and NASA in 2017. As a result, parties rely on multiple local networks and are intensely vulnerable to petty local factionalism and rivalry, since there are few rewards for loyalty. This has two somewhat paradoxical effects. On the one hand, the proliferation of parties and existence of some smaller parties that appeal to only one or two ethnic groups encourage a more exclusive form of patrimonial politics during campaigns. At the same time, the weakness of national political institutions and frequent accusations of election rigging and ethnic favouritism make it easier for politicians to justify contraventions of the civic register as an unfortunate, but necessary, means to protect 'their' community against the excesses of ethnic 'others'.[72]

On the other hand, party-swapping, and the complexity of Kenyan political alliances, means that political leaders regularly have to forgive past trespasses and bring their communities together in new alliances – as Uhuru Kenyatta and William Ruto did in 2013, when they brought the two communities that had experienced the worst post-election violence in 2007/2008 together into a new electoral vehicle (Lynch 2014). Along with the resonance of certain civic values for many Kenyans, this encourages leaders to emphasize the national good and their own commitment to political due process and the rule of law. Thus, while campaigns have a more exclusively patrimonial flavour, Kenyan politicians – especially those operating at a national level – cannot ignore the civic register.

In Uganda the story is different again, though here too politicians must make claims to both civic and patrimonial virtue. The political dominance of the NRM, and the absence of opposition parties with a different ethnic profile, has constrained the electoral salience of ethnicity. Meanwhile, the no-party system of 'individual merit' formalized patrimonialism in a way that undermined the significance of party labels, with voters invited to judge candidates on their local development record

---

[71] Interview KEN81a, parliamentary aspirant, Seme, 10 July 2017.
[72] For example, Interview KEN79a, former councillor, Seme, 14 July 2017; Interview KEN81a, parliamentary aspirant, Seme, 10 July 2017.

(Chapter 2). Taken together, these developments have resulted in a form of electoral patrimonialism that centres more on the abilities of aspirants and their personal loyalty to the president.

The dominance of the NRM derives in large part from the particularly strong benefits of incumbency that it enjoys – from considerable control over the economy and a high capacity for state violence to the relative weakness of associational life beyond parties and the inability of the opposition to form a united front (Beardsworth 2016). Yet the NRM itself is in some ways a shell, and so campaigning in Uganda is very different to Ghana: it is Museveni's influence and patronage that shape political possibilities for individuals, not the party. Museveni uses state resources and government policies (from employment programmes to compensation schemes) to reward supporters according to the patrimonial register (Titeca 2014; Vokes 2016). Yet at the same time, he draws upon memories of violence to justify the coercive suppression of the opposition as necessary to prevent a return to war and thus ensure national peace and development according to the civic register (Vokes and Wilkins 2016; Nkuubi 2017). In contrast, opposition parties denounce the authoritarianism and corruption of government as a form of patrimonial politics that undermines national interests, while simultaneously raising funds to give handouts and invest in local development projects – all the while making promises of more substantial rewards when they oust the NRM from power.

At the same time, the fact that both Museveni and his principal challenger for the past four elections hail from the western part of the country has curbed the salience of ethnicity, even as claims are made that Museveni has favoured the West and particularly his Bahima group. Indeed, with time, support for both the NRM and FDC has become more evenly spread across the country. This is most apparent in the long-standing opposition stronghold of Acholiland where the NRM managed to make significant inroads in 2011, which were then largely maintained in 2016 – when Museveni garnered 41 per cent and Besigye 42 per cent of the sub-regional popular vote – although it must be remembered that Ugandan elections are neither free nor fair. During these campaigns, the NRM gave out much money, claimed credit for (and promised further) development projects, insisted that they had brought relative peace to the region following years of conflict with the Lord's Resistance Army (LRA), and threatened economic marginalization and even a military takeover in the case of an opposition victory (Lynch 2016b). In contrast, the FDC argued 'that Museveni had overstayed ... that NRM was trying to use money and threats to impose weak leaders on the community ... and that people should stay firm and brave, and elect strong leaders that could defend people's interests' particularly as regards to land (Lynch 2016b).

The election was thus cast as a struggle over who was best placed to assist the area, rather than as a campaign in which particular parts of the country comprised ethnic 'zones' that belonged to a particular party.

The opposition's weakness – together with Museveni's decision not to campaign against independent candidates as long as they actively support his re-election (Wilkins 2018) – has meant that NRM-leaning independent candidates have won more parliamentary seats than opposition parties (Gibb 2016). In 2011, the NRM secured 164 open seats, as compared to 30 independents, 23 FDC and 20 from smaller parties; in 2016, the NRM took 199 open seats as compared to 44 independents, 29 FDC and 17 from other parties. Yet despite this, Uganda still features a campaign environment that foregrounds money and intimidation in ways that encourage opposition candidates to combine acts of localized assistance with a combative stand against the centre for the 'national' good. For their part, NRM (and NRM-leaning) candidates make offers of patronage that go hand in hand with those public goods that are valued according to the civic register – most notably, national development and stability. In this way, a less ethnicized form of patrimonial politics coexists with intimidation and the constant evocation of civic values.

6.6   Conclusion

Politicians in all three countries are widely regarded as elites, and electoral politics is understood as a route into that category. A widespread sense that many politicians are motivated by their own selfish interests – together with often intense competition – has encouraged campaigns in which candidates need to work hard to cultivate an image of being a 'good leader' who is caring and accessible and can promote and protect constituents' interests in a broad sense. Aspirants cultivate a reputation that they will be 'for' their constituents and/or the nation by playing on a sense of shared identity (be it ethnic, regional, national or ideological), but also through their track record and the campaign statements they make. While such efforts are often closely linked to the patrimonial register, they also need to speak to a civic register. Politicians are aided in this precarious balancing act by the productive ambiguity that surrounds the relationship between club and public goods, and thus between patrimonial preference and civic nationalism; by the adoption of different styles that can cut across the two registers; and by the use of a range of campaign activities that help politicians to tailor their messages for particular audiences.

The popular expectations and political incentives that candidates face vary significantly within and between countries. In states that feature more effective and inclusive parties and political organizations, less pronounced histories of winner-takes-all politics – and so less extensive socio-economic divisions – mean that aspirants are less likely to pursue exclusionary forms of patrimonialism and more likely to reference the civic register. In turn, this reduces the rhetorical stakes of electoral competition, leading to very different forms of moral economy. More specifically, the widespread perception that both the state and political parties are ethnically biased has encouraged more ethnically exclusive appeals in Kenya than in Ghana or Uganda. The nature of party organization also matters: the need to gain the support of nationally oriented parties offers strong incentives to limit certain kinds of ethno-nationalist appeals in Ghana, while weak parties ensure that parliamentary candidates in Kenya and Uganda need to rely more heavily on personalized networks of party mobilizers, which further skew the balance towards the patrimonial register.

The interconnection of socio-economic context and the structure of political institutions often exacerbates these tendencies. In Ghana, an experience of regular and peaceful transfers of power, and more inclusive development policies, has further dampened the more exclusive forms of patrimonial politics and ensured that local assistance is generally seen to be compatible with cross-national appeals to civic virtue. By contrast, in Kenya and Uganda a more problematic history of electoral malpractice has undermined public confidence that others will adhere to a civic register. Such scepticism further strengthens a more problematic form of patrimonial politics as voters who regard leaders as corrupt may nonetheless vote for them (Faller 2015 on Uganda), and those who eschew tribalism may nevertheless vote for co-ethnics due to a fear that others will be ethnically biased (Bratton and Kimenyi 2008 on Kenya). This then exacerbates the sense of unease around elections for those who worry that they might be excluded from resources and influence if their candidate loses at the polls, which encourages the use of extreme strategies to win power at any cost.

Candidates are also influenced by, and need to respond to, other actors. This includes those discussed in previous chapters, namely electoral administrators, observers and CSOs who tend to call on politicians to be virtuous civic leaders. It also includes a host of other actors that we have not been able to discuss in detail – from the judiciary and security forces to religious and traditional leaders, businessmen and campaign financiers, and gangs and militia. Their role is clearly more complex, messy and context dependent. Security forces, for example, have official mandates and rhetoric that emphasizes the civic register, but they can be ethnically biased (as was alleged during Kenya's post-election violence of 2007/2008) and/or become heavily involved in patrimonial logics (as in Uganda).

Finally, politicians make their own decisions – based on their own character, areas of competitive advantage and the opponents they face – about how to speak to the civic and patrimonial registers and what balance to strike. The decisions they make then help to shape the political landscape for those who follow. By instigating ethnic clashes and playing on historical tensions over the control of land, President Moi deliberately activated a range of inter-communal fault lines in a bid to retain power following the reintroduction of multiparty politics. This process directly contributed to the build-up of inter-ethnic distrust and instances of ethnicized political valence, both in the 1990s and again in 2007 (Branch and Cheeseman 2009). His counterparts in Ghana and Uganda at this time committed many democratic abuses but never sought to play divide-and-rule politics in quite this way.

However, while there is much scope for individual agency, successful politicians must also respond to popular expectations. One reason that Moi chose to play on historical grievances in Kenya was that he knew there would be considerable electoral benefits to deploying 'political tribalism' and calculated that these would be greater than the costs. By contrast, Ghanaian leaders well understand that such a strategy could easily backfire and would likely lose them support even within their 'own' communities. In other words, while the strategies adopted by politicians are not simply predetermined by popular expectations, voters – and their demands and decisions – help to co-produce electoral campaigns and outcomes. It is to these critical actors that the final chapter turns.

7   Navigating Multiple Moralities

Popular Expectations and Experiences of the Polls

Alan Kwadwo Kyeremanten is famous in Ghana, having been the country's ambassador to the United States and Minister of Trade, Industry and Private Sector Development. But most do not know him by this name. Instead, he is popularly known as Alan Cash. According to Kwadwo Kyeremanten himself, this nickname emerged during a political campaign in which he had stressed the importance of putting 'real cash' in the hands of the people. Others say that the name reflects his wealth and his willingness to hand out money in order to boost his own political career. In the mid-2000s, newspapers were full of articles reporting how Cash 'bagged a whooping 13billion [Cedis] from a fund-raising dinner dance he organised . . . to support his campaign activities'.[1] The wealth accumulated in this way was then used to fund a well-oiled patronage machine. For example, when he decided to run for leader of the New Patriotic Party (NPP) in 2007 to replace the outgoing John Kufour, Cash is said to have begun and ended his campaign by offering handouts:

[T]he Executives of each of the 230 Constituencies were promised amounts ranging between ¢350m to ¢500m, averaging ¢400m. Such is the amount being dished out to each of the 230 Constituency Executives . . . by Mr. 'Cash for the People', with a view to soliciting their votes.[2]

Both in name and in behaviour, then, Alan Cash epitomized key features of patrimonial leadership, making claims and promises rooted in reciprocity and the preferential treatment of supporters. When he sought to succeed John Kufuor as the NPP's leader and presidential candidate in 2007, his main rival was Nana Akufo-Addo, a technocrat known for his administrative capabilities. Given Akufo-Addo's disdain for popular politics – a well-placed NPP figure once told us that it was a struggle to persuade him to shake people's hands

---

[1] GhanaWeb, 'Alan "Cash" Bags 13 Billion', 9 October 2007, www.ghanaweb.com/Ghan aHomePage/NewsArchive/Alan-Cash-Bags-13-Billion-132061#.
[2] GhanaWeb, 'Buses for votes: Alan "Cash" sprays', 28 August 2007, www.ghanaweb.com /GhanaHomePage/NewsArchive/Buses-For-Votes-Alan-Cash-Sprays-129671.

and kiss babies on the campaign trail – patrimonial logic suggested that Cash would be successful.[3]

Yet when the votes had been counted it was not Kwadwo Kyeremanten who emerged victorious; Akufo-Addo won comfortably. Cash's defeat – not only in 2007 but also in subsequent party elections – demonstrates the importance of the moral economy of elections. Kwadwo Kyeremanten failed to realize his ambition of becoming the president of Ghana because he misunderstood the patrimonial register and underestimated the significance of civic ideals. Although he handed out gifts more freely than any other candidate, the way that he did it was not seen to be legitimate and so did not secure him reliable political support:

If there was any lesson in what is happening to Alan Cash, it is that loyalty is better than patronage. Alan Cash did not cultivate loyal and trusted supporters; he only used money to buy his way into their minds not their hearts.[4]

The story of Alan Cash is salutary, but far from unique. In a similar vein, Peter Lockwood (2019b) has shown how the high-spending incumbent governor of Kiambu County, William Kabogo, failed to win re-election in 2017 after his handouts were undermined by rumours that he had verbally abused women. People we spoke to in Kikuyu constituency stressed similar concerns and added that the rumours were generally regarded as plausible because the governor 'was very arrogant'.[5] Similarly, a candidate's efforts to secure the women's seat in Gulu were undermined by her association with a well-known military officer. As one interviewee explained:

[T]here were allegations that she was moving with one of the army officers who was actually distributing this money ... that particular officer had actually lost popularity in this sub-region and trust me if you are moving with someone who has no popularity that means you are associating with that person so even if you give me as much money as possible, I will take your money but I will not vote for you ... it worked against her.[6]

In a context where candidates clearly do have to be generous – and to be seen to be generous – the fate of these individuals raises a question: what is it that voters demand from candidates, and when do handouts serve to mobilize or undermine support? As we have already seen in Chapter 6, voters evaluate politicians in terms of a wide range of behaviours and

---

[3] Interview, NPP campaign worker, Accra, 22 June 2016.
[4] *The Herald*, 'Alan Cash crying now, he perhaps taught Nana Addo how to buy votes', 26 September 2014, http://theheraldghana.com/alan-cash-crying-now-he-perhaps-taught-nana-addo-how-to-buy-votes.
[5] Interview KEN24a, MCA aspirant, Kikuyu, 11 May 2017.
[6] Interview UGA80b, NGO worker, Gulu, 25 February 2016.

characteristics including their honesty, identity, gender, availability, ability to provide development, willingness to struggle for people's interests, and capacity to connect constituencies into networks of power and resources. This chapter shifts focus to consider how voters respond to evidence of electoral malpractice, and in particular what is commonly known as vote buying. We do not adopt this focus because African elections can simply be reduced to the exchange of money – the broad range of factors discussed in previous chapters demonstrates that this is clearly untrue – but because public debates over morality are particularly pronounced and insightful where money is concerned. Indeed, one of the main contributions of this chapter is to demonstrate that voters – including those living in poverty – are more circumspect about receiving electoral bribes than is commonly recognized (see, for example, Jensen and Justesen 2014).

We find that voters condemn a wide range of electoral manipulations including the use of violence and ballot-box stuffing. In so doing, they demonstrate strong support for civic values, most notably due process. The buying of votes is also widely condemned as improper, and the commoditization of elections is lamented. Those judgements also appear to be rooted in a civic register – and in many cases they are. Yet they also draw on a patrimonial register; the claims and denunciations made by voters, like those made by politicians, revolve around an uncertain distinction between virtuous generosity and immoral vote buying. The same individual may, for example, condemn one leader handing out money for seeking to bribe the electorate while, in the next breath, lauding a different candidate for the large amount of money that he has invested in the community. The distinction between these two judgements is not based on the amount given out, but rather on how it is morally interpreted. As Paul Nugent has argued, giving out money is only effective when banknotes can be 'converted into some kind of moral authority, which is weighed in the scales against other (non-material) claims to the exercise of leadership' (Nugent 2007: 255).

Significantly, individuals and communities evaluate material generosity not just in terms of the value of what is distributed but against the full range of evaluative criteria summarized earlier. In other words, whether a cash handout is seen to be virtuous depends in part on whether the person dispensing it is already seen to be a good leader according to the patrimonial register. As we have seen in Chapter 6, candidates are also expected to pay attention to the civic register and to demonstrate a willingness to invest in development more generally, especially at the national level. Consequently, leaders may be able to legitimate gift giving through the civic register if it can be construed as one component of a broader commitment to promoting the well-being of ordinary citizens. The risk, of course, is that excessive gift giving may undermine a leader's 'civic' credentials and so harm the chances of those who do not also have strong patrimonial connections.

When leaders who have cultivated moral authority through the patrimonial or civic register offer a gift, it is unlikely to be seen as a bribe at all, but rather as an act of beneficence. By contrast, leaders who have not earned such a reputation may be accused of trying to buy a community with 'dirty money'. This chapter seeks to explain when and why voters come to these different conclusions. Our research suggests that a candidate's commitment to the community, their reputation as someone who keeps their promises and their accessibility (Roelofs 2019) are particularly important in this regard. While those who manage to persuade voters of their authenticity will be rewarded for their gifts, leaders who fail this test may find that the distribution of money actually works against them – for example, because it is interpreted as signalling a corrupt relationship with national figures who have historically exploited the constituency or as a disrespectful attempt to simply buy support to the neglect of people's interests.

The different meanings that the handover of money can convey depending on the context highlight the limitations of many existing accounts of 'vote buying'. A rational choice approach, for example, might suggest that voters simply give their vote to the highest bidder in order to maximize their own utility (Blais 2000; Karahan et al. 2006). Yet rational choice analyses have famously struggled to explain why individuals bother to vote at all given the costs that they incur and the negligible likelihood that their vote will determine the outcome (Feddersen 2004). A second stream of research on vote buying has instead looked at who is most likely to be targeted for bribes and who is most likely to accept them, generally concluding that in both cases the answer is voters who live in poverty (Jensen and Justesen 2014). But while this finding provides valuable context, it does not tell us why some bribes are accepted and others not by members of the same economic group, nor whether those who receive bribes feel that they are under a moral obligation to vote a certain way. In recent years, Eric Kramon's work (2017) has encouraged a more sophisticated understanding of 'money for votes' by conceptualizing the distribution of gifts not as an economic contract between a leader and a potential supporter, but as a way in which leaders can convey viability and signal the kind of candidate that they really are. In seeing the handing out of gifts not as an exchange of money for votes, but as a way to provide information to voters about what kind of leader a candidate would be if elected, Kramon emphasizes the role that leaders play in the wider political economy of affection (Hydén 1980).

What Kramon's approach does not do, however, is to fully recognize that the political effectiveness of gift giving is shaped by its moral force, which we argue comes from a wider estimation of virtue. That estimation places the simplest form of gift giving – the handing out of cash at campaign events – in a context of longer-term behaviours and acts of generosity and advocacy that are not limited to rallies, or to the campaign period, or to assistance as development. As Schaffer has written of the Philippines, 'this moral calculus leads many voters to choose candidates whom they perceive to be caring, kind, and helpful; candidates who respect ... their fellow human beings, especially those who are poor' (2005: 15). Other virtues may also be important, and studies of African cases have emphasized the significance of being seen to be brave and courageous (Wanyande 2002; Oloo 2005) and, in some cases, of resisting co-optation and demonstrating independence from the president's patronage networks (Cheeseman 2008). In the latter case, which typically occurs after a community has felt marginalized for a significant period of time, leaders may even be able to make a virtue of their lack of resources, citing it as evidence of their political purity. It is therefore important to keep in mind that, while generosity is of great importance to perceptions of candidates in all three countries, exactly what is required to fulfil local expectations will vary because the expression of the patrimonial register is shaped by past practice and local moral debates.

In the analysis that follows, we draw on laboratory games, Afrobarometer surveys and the findings of three nationally representative surveys in addition to our interviews to demonstrate both the extent to which voters feel the resonance of key civic ideals and the capacity for elections to reinvigorate certain aspects of the patrimonial register – with significant implications for how we should understand the relationship between democracy, elections and the patrimonial register. Most notably, we show that, while repeated transfers of power may have strengthened popular and elite willingness to accept electoral outcomes in Ghana (Chapter 2), there is no evidence that this has reduced the significance of money in elections. Instead, the cost of elections to politicians has risen steadily during the multiparty period as the demands of voters have become increasingly taxing (Westminster Foundation for Democracy 2018). Teasing out how voters respond to this process – and whether politicians are wasting their money – is a challenging task and requires asking the right questions. Precisely because voters distinguish between straightforward vote buying, which is much more likely to be condemned, and reciprocal relationships with leaders who look after the community, which receives considerable support, existing survey questions that tend to focus on electoral handouts fail to fully capture popular sentiment. By asking about the transfer of money in different ways, we are able to demonstrate that, while popular attitudes towards 'vote buying' are broadly critical and similar across our case studies, suggesting relatively consistent support for the civic register, attitudes to candidates who hand out money in addition to performing a range of services for the community are much more positive and exhibit greater variation. This reveals both the power of the patrimonial register and the way that it is shaped by socio-economic context, historical precedence in terms of the distribution of development-shaped attitudes towards state–society relations, and institutional factors, most notably the strength of political parties.

Comparing across our cases, we find that voters are more likely to support patrimonial practices in Kenya, where parties are particularly weak, MPs have long been seen as the agents of local development and ethnic politics has come to have a particularly personalized flavour (Mueller 2008). Under these conditions, the prevalence of winner-takes-all dynamics undermines the provision of public goods (Miguel 2004), and hence public confidence that all communities will be treated equally. This is both because this kind of 'political tribalism' (Lonsdale 2004) increases the costs of investing in the civic register when others do not (Lynch 2011a), and because it empowers patrons to shut down dissent (Cheeseman 2015a). By contrast, while gifting has become a central feature of elections in Ghana, the presence of more effective political parties, along with the disruption of local political networks during the shifts from democratic to authoritarian rule in the 1970s and 1980s, means that it is less common and less accepted. Uganda falls in between the other two cases: a focus on the 'individual merit' of candidates has placed great pressure on candidates to fulfil the desires of their constituents, but the political dominance of the NRM and greater focus on state-led development programmes help to explain why some forms of gifting are less common than in Kenya.

Within each country, a number of socio-economic factors also prove to be significant in shaping popular attitudes. As Schaffer has argued, '[v]ote buying carries different meanings to different people, and these meanings can vary not only by class, but also by religion, ethnicity, levels of education, or the like' (2005: 22). In particular, voters who live in urban areas with relatively high degrees of service provision, are highly educated and are not poor, are more likely to express support for civic ideals and to be critical of gifting practices. One important implication of this finding is that attitudes to gifting are malleable and that urbanization and the expansion of education are likely to result in an evolution of the moral economy of elections.

7.1   A Short History of the Voter: Control, Consent and Competition

In all three countries, voting by secret ballot was initially a privilege offered to an elite who were deemed to have earned it – whether through education, the accumulation of wealth or evidence of loyalty to the government. In Ghana, the widespread use of indirect voting meant that a small minority of the population cast secret ballots in 1951; in Kenya, the franchise was severely restricted by property and 'loyalty' restrictions in 1957 (Branch 2006). But the franchise expanded with extraordinary speed; in the final late-colonial elections, all adults had the right to vote directly and secretly – at least in principle – in all three countries. Having begun as a badge of distinctive social status and respectability the vote became a mark of adulthood and respect that could be demanded by all – a sign of full political membership of a community. On the one hand, that community was national – the vote staked a claim to citizenship and the rights that entailed. On the other hand, the community might also be sub-national: voting could also be an assertion not simply of an ethnic, regional or local identity, but of claims to virtuous membership of that community (Horowitz 1985). So, of course, could abstaining from voting: the potential voters of Buganda and Volta who boycotted late-colonial elections (see Chapter 2) were making their own statement about what it was to be a virtuous Muganda or Ewe (Skinner 2015).

From the start, then, polls were seen as symbolically powerful events, doing political work that was not simply about the selection of national governments. That helps to explain why electoral participation was persistent after independence – even where, as in Kenya, there was no choice over the national government. Sporadic multiparty elections in Ghana (1969 and 1979) and Uganda (1980) saw significant turnout – especially in the Ugandan case. In those elections, local ideas of virtue and good leadership, and voters' sense of themselves and their politicians as members of moral communities, mattered greatly. In Ghana, for example, voters were concerned to choose MPs who would be good delegates to government (Dunn and Robertson 1973: 36–39). In Kenya, meanwhile, single-party rule allowed voters a degree of choice in selecting their local representatives (Barkan 1987), focussing minds and patronage networks away from national policy, which was now beyond reach, and towards the minutia of local politics (Cheeseman 2018b). When Barkan and John Okumu conducted a pioneering survey in Kenya in the 1970s (as discussed in Barkan 1976: 453), they found that the three things that constituents wanted their MPs to do above all else were to visit frequently (11 per cent), obtain projects and benefits (25 per cent) and tell the government what people in the constituency want (29 per cent).

There are a number of ways in which MPs could demonstrate this (Chapter 6), including raising questions in parliament and campaigning on key issues of local concern, but one of the most common was to make large donations to community development projects and to give personal gifts to voters as a kind of down payment on future returns from the individual's leadership. The cumulative effect of these trends was to strengthen and institutionalize the patrimonial relationships that ran through MPs and hence the legislature.

A similar situation prevailed during Uganda's 'no-party democracy' (Kasfir 1998) between 1986 and 2005, when political parties were officially banned, though Museveni's NRM was effectively a ruling party in all but name. Rather than voting on the basis of ideology or community, Museveni exhorted citizens to choose candidates on the basis of their 'individual merit' (Chapter 2), so polls became, in large part, a referendum on the development performance – or perceived potential – of the candidate (Furley 1999: 7; Furley and Katalikawe 1999: 21). In such circumstances, a common ethnic identity did not force individuals to support a predetermined candidate – but could become one way for voters to express demands for more responsive leadership. Through this mechanism, elections that were uncompetitive and stage-managed at the national level inspired considerable popular investment at the constituency level.

When and how electoral gift giving became a prominent part of electoral politics is contested. Accounts of the role of money in election campaigns are sometimes contradictory: there is an uneasy distinction between the distribution of cash on the campaign trail and a much wider set of gift-giving practices – fund raisings, donations, impromptu assistance with medical costs – that is not restricted to the election season, and people's memories of the past differ. In Kenya one interviewee claimed that gift giving began under Moi:

[F]rom '63 up to say '78 there was no money [in] politics . . . people were not using money . . . this money politics was introduced by Moi . . . so the problem now is that people who are going to government don't feel for the people they go there for their own gain.[7]

Another suggested a different chronology, claiming that things changed after the 1992 elections:

[7] Interview KEN53a, former activist, Seme, 20 June 2017.

I think in 1992, ... People were basically voting in parties. . . . these days you see things changing now people are resulting to how wealthy you are so if you can bribe the voters then they will most likely vote for you.[8]

Yet the 1992 elections themselves saw some very public distribution of cash at campaign events[9] and the documentary record suggests a much longer history to gift giving in Kenya than either of the above accounts. In the 1960s, Oginga Odinga's electoral politics were described as a combination of ethnic mobilization and 'a Tammany type operation of doling out small amounts of food and material assistance on the humblest level'.[10] A district administrator noted censoriously that in advance of the 1969 elections 'candidates went round giving donations and promising something'; diplomats' accounts of those elections also suggested considerable levels of gift giving.[11]

In Uganda, a civil society activist assured us that what he saw as the buying of votes is a recent phenomenon, a consequence of the return to multiparty politics:

Those who have money will buy votes, will buy the poor voters to vote for them and they buy them very cheaply. Sometimes if they are given a bar of soap, sometimes just a kilo of sugar, sometimes a kilo of salt and they will vote such a person.[12]

Yet in Uganda too, such practices are much older than this suggests. Even in pre-independence elections, candidates accused one another of gift giving.[13] Similarly, a campaigner for Museveni's UPM party in the 1980 elections first denied and then acknowledged gift giving:

[W]e could just buy a drink with your people talking, have lunch and after that you go. There was no giving money, this and that . . . [a] bit of money, some were giving, but not much money.[14]

In the 'no-party' constituent assembly elections of 1994, voters reportedly made clear that their expectations of candidates went beyond basic

---

[8] Interview KEN54a, voter, Kisumu, 21 June 2017.
[9] There were some striking press photographs at the time: see *Daily Nation*, 10 and 11 November and 19 December 1992.
[10] Coote, Nairobi to State, 29 June 1968, NARA RG 59 CFP files Box 2257 POL 13 KENYA 1/1/67.
[11] DO Kikuyu to DC Kiambu, 'Monthly report for the month of December 1969', 30 December 1969, KNA MA 12/29; McIlvaine, Nairobi to State, 13 December 1969, NARA RG59 CFP files Box 2257 POL 14 KENYA.
[12] Interview UGA79a, civil society activist, Gulu, 24 September 2015; see also Interview UGA38a, former MP, Kampala, 9 June 2015.
[13] *Uganda Argus*, 15 March 1961, '"No wild promises" by UPC – Arain', p. 5; Commissioner Special Branch to Kingston, Ministry of Defence and External Affairs, 2 February 1951, UKNA FCO 141/4926.
[14] Interview UGA69a, former civil servant, Fort Portal, 9 October 2015.

refreshments, declaring: '"Nothing for mere drinking water only!"' The campaign was 'a period in which "gifts", donations, drinks, food or more prosaically, "bribes" flowed abundantly among the people' (Gingyera-Pinycwa 1996: 25–26; see also Furley and Katalikawe 1999: 21). Another account of the same elections remarked on 'the extraordinary use of money to win over voters' and emphasized that '[i]t was not the choice of the candidates that money was spent. The voters themselves demanded it' (Mujaju 1996: 52–53).

Accounts of elections in Ghana report similar dynamics. A newspaper report on the 1954 campaign, for example, explained that 'wealth, family relationship, generosity, public and voluntarily [sic] duties performed by candidates are some of the factors influencing public opinion'.[15] Meanwhile in the 1979 elections, a candidate complained that 'it had become a fashion, especially on the part of the illiterate majority, to demand drinks and money whenever politicians approached them'.[16]

This is not to say that there has not been a real increase in the exchange of gifts and money around elections – the combination of greater political competition and enhanced access to campaign finance following financial liberalization and economic growth in the 1990s have increased the amounts spent on elections in a number of respects (Arriola 2013; Westminster Foundation for Democracy 2018). Yet it seems that these conflicting accounts of the past also reflect a technique of moral positioning – in other words that they reveal a chronic concern over the balance between virtuous generosity and the immoral purchase of votes, through which both politicians and voters seek to place themselves on the right side of history. In doing so, many leaders have taken up what on the face of it appears to be hypocritical positions. President Museveni, for example, is well known for denouncing vote buying but also gives generous donations on the campaign trail.[17]

Museveni is not alone. His main rival, Kizza Besigye, often appears as a recipient of donations, not a source of them, and denounces 'voter bribery', consciously playing up to the ideal that he is both a reform-minded opposition leader and a man of the people. Yet while this is feasible at the presidential level – where there is greater expectation that leaders will seek to promote the national good and greater acceptance that

[15] 'Candidates work 16 hours a day', *Daily Graphic*, 3 June 1954, p. 5.
[16] 'Don't influence electorate – UNC', *Daily Graphic*, 23 May 1979, p. 3.
[17] Excerpts from speech by Ugandan President Yoweri Museveni to launch his 1996 election manifesto, at the International Conference Centre, Kampala, 27 March 1996, FBIS, Kampala AFR-96-061; '"Chai" pleas surprise Museveni', *Daily Monitor*, 1 February 2006, p. 4; 'Museveni spends Shs 27bn on campaigns in two months', *Daily Monitor*, 22 January 2016.

candidates cannot be fully accessible to voters (Chapter 6) – at the parliamentary level FDC and NRM representatives alike face a popular expectation that they will give out gifts.[18] Indeed, while some opposition voters have been known to turn down handouts because they are seen to be immoral, others have done so because they were seen to be insufficiently generous.[19] As a former councillor noted in Seme: 'if people know you have and you don't [give], then the people say you're not a good leader'.[20] The situation is even more challenging for those closest to power, who are typically expected to be more generous on the basis that they have more to give. As Throup and Hornsby (1998) explain, the most dangerous political position for an MP to hold in Kenya in the 1980s was assistant minister, because those in this position were expected to enjoy access to power and patronage but actually lacked the influence to deliver roads, schools and other club goods.

The reintroduction of multiparty elections in Ghana and Kenya in the early 1990s and Uganda in 2006 occurred in the context of this history of gift giving. Far from taking place on virgin ground, the different political experience of each country shaped how voters interpreted their role and the elections in which they took part. In Kenya, the combination of the weakness of political parties and the socialization of voters into a localized form of politics meant that presidential elections tended to revolve around competition between ethnic Big Men, while legislative polls have continued to focus on the personal capacities of candidates to meet local concerns. Moreover, the creation of a Constituency Development Fund in 2002, which created a ring-fenced pot of money for committees chaired by MPs to invest in their constituencies (Ngacho and Das 2014), reinforced the idea that legislators were personally responsible for the delivery of development (Mitullah 2015). It is therefore unsurprising that a number of researchers have found that promises of future patronage and the giving of gifts are central to electoral competition at all levels of the political system. One reason for the popularity of devolution is that it has created more opportunities for patronage at the sub-national level and represented 'everyone's turn to eat' (D'Arcy and Cornell 2016: 246). In a similar vein, Eric Kramon estimates that Kenyans 'who were approached by a vote buyer were about 14 percentage points more likely to vote than those who were not' (2009: 1).

A focus on the role of individuals has also characterized Ugandan legislative elections, although the country's evolution into a dominant-party

[18] 'Dr Besigye "fires up" Mbale, reiterates defiance message' *Daily Monitor*, 8 January 2016, and 9 February 2016, 'Voter bribery only obstacle to my victory, says Besigye'.
[19] 'Youths turn down cash handout', *Daily Nation*, 15 November 2002.
[20] Interview KEN79a, former councillor, Seme, 14 July 2017.

state in which affiliation to the NRM is important to access both resources and office means that party labels have become increasingly significant (Carbone 2003) and go a long way towards overshadowing the role of ethnicity in national contests. Thus, Elizabeth Carlson (2015) finds that sharing the same ethnicity as a voter only boosts a candidate's hopes when they are also seen to have performed well. While Ugandans assume that members of their own community are more likely to look after their interests, 'coethnics only have an advantage when they are not shirkers' (2015: 358). This can be performed in a number of ways. FDC MPs, for example, may gain credibility by demonstrating that they are campaigning to make the country more democratic and inclusive. But a more common way of proving that you have been working hard is to distribute largesse, particularly in a context where the political elite assume that 'most voters tend to vote money not issues' (Bukuluki 2013: 35).[21]

By contrast, Ghana has historically seen less socialization into the 'development referenda' model, in part because both Kwame Nkrumah and J. J. Rawlings set the central state up as the focal point for both the design and implementation of development. Ghana introduced its own version of the Constituency Development Fund (Appiah-Agyekum et al. 2013) following the Kenyan model, but the proportion of development expenditure distributed in this way remains small. This very different history of political competition has been reinforced in recent years by the frequent transfer of power, which has constrained the evolution of a winner-takes-all dynamic. However, it is important not to exaggerate the difference between Ghana and our other cases. find that, while government budgeting does not demonstrate significant biases, actual expenditure in areas such as education was 'shaped by the incentives generated by Ghana's competitive clientelistic political settlement, which overrode rhetorical concerns with national unity and inclusive development' (2016: 44). These hidden biases notwithstanding, the fact that Ghanaian leaders pay such close attention to civic ideals such as national unity and inclusive development is indicative of an important political dynamic. As Gadjanova has argued, gift giving is often insufficient to ensure victory, and so 'parties are forced to pursue different linkage mechanisms to voters. One such mechanism involves defining and targeting broader constituencies through policy proposals' (2017: 593). This insight, and Ghana's distinctive political evolution, helps to explain why Lindberg finds that Ghanaian voters expect their MPs to supply private or club goods but actually take voting decisions based on

---

[21] Senior official in the Ministry of Finance, as quoted by Bukuluki.

their 'evaluations of the state of the national economy and of the government's policies' (2013: 945; see also Anebo 2001: 84–85).

Our research confirms that the moral economy of elections looks a little different in Ghana, as compared to Kenya and Uganda, but the difference is one of degree. MPs and activists in all three countries feel that voters expect – indeed, demand – a track record of material generosity from candidates both during and in between election campaigns. Moreover, in all three cases candidates seek to distinguish their response to these demands – which, as discussed in Chapter 6, are often presented as a virtuous demonstration of their willingness to listen to, and to help address, voters' particular needs and grievances, and thus of patrimonial virtue, but also as evidence of their commitment to the public good and thus of their civic virtue – from outright vote buying, which is seen to be illegitimate. In this way, the politicians that we engaged with typically attempted to interpret their own fulfilment of patrimonial responsibilities in a way that enabled them to also be seen to have upheld civic ideals. In Uganda, for example, an NRM activist presented the giving of money in some circumstances as a virtuous demonstration of a commitment to address local needs:

I see election as a community responsibility to make their choice freely but of course influenced by the statements you make, by the kind of contribution you give to them, because this is a poverty-stricken country. Somebody might bring a child to the hospital, some 40km away and the child dies at the hospital and you as a candidate, you give contribution to transport the dead body home. You become the darling of that family, the whole village.[22]

While in Ghana an incumbent MP presented gift giving – of multiple kinds – in similar terms:

[Y]ou must relate very well to them, and also, you must show concern for their needs. Even today, like this, all Junior High Schools within the district – um, I've bought shoes for them. I have 9,000 pairs of shoes that I'm sharing to all schools ... you know, it's a poor community .... People are in need, they come.[23]

Similarly, in Kenya, an incumbent politician explained:

[T]hey come to you asking for school fees, for this, for this, and you keep giving out even. Now I have spent three four thousand shillings this morning just giving it out, and you have been like that the whole day. My experience, and this is important, this little money that you give to people [will] have more impression than the projects.[24]

---

[22] Interview UGA77a, NRM activist, Gulu, 22 September 2015.
[23] Details withheld on the request of the interviewee.
[24] Details withheld on the request of the interviewee.

Empirically demonstrating the significance of these varied displays of generosity is complicated by the uncertain boundary between virtuous reciprocity and contributions to national development on the one hand, and improper vote buying on the other – and also by the fact that leaders are expected to engage in such activities both during and in between elections. In all three jurisdictions both handing out money and 'treating' – offering drinks and food to voters as an inducement to attend a rally – are against the official rules, and, while this is rarely enforced, candidates do not wish to broadcast such activities to domestic and international observers. Surveys on this topic are therefore challenging to interpret, as questionnaires often require respondents to assert a single morality, whereas – as we have suggested – most people live with an awareness of, and invest importance in, different registers of virtue. Yet careful analysis of surveys – particularly where questions are asked in more than one way – can reveal ambiguities and tensions over proper behaviour, as well as some clear patterns of difference.

To begin with, nationally representative Afrobarometer survey data provides clear evidence of the greater localization and personalization of politics in Kenya and to a lesser extent Uganda than in Ghana (Figure 7.1).[25] The vast majority of Kenyan respondents (85 per cent) and almost three-quarters of those in Uganda could name their MP. By comparison, only 66 per cent of Ghanaians could do likewise. Cross-national patterns of gift giving provide further evidence of differences. Citizens' evaluations of the extent of

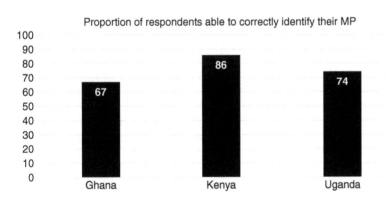

Figure 7.1 Levels of political knowledge (%)
Source: Authors' own survey data

[25] For full details of how the survey was carried out and for descriptive statistics see online appendix 2 at www.cambridge.org/moraleconomy.

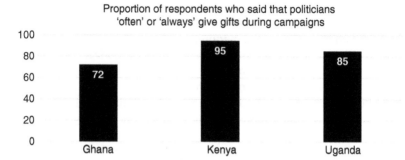

Figure 7.2 Extent of gift giving by candidates (%)[26]
Source: Afrobarometer (2017)

'vote buying' are not always reliable and, of course, may be inspired by hearsay as much as personal experience but are nonetheless indicative of how people think about the way that elections are conducted. According to Afrobarometer data, while almost all Kenyans (95 per cent) believe that politicians 'often' or 'always' give gifts in the course of an election campaign, this is considerably lower in Ghana, where almost 30 per cent of respondents said that gifting was not common (Figure 7.2). This result accords with our impressionistic sense from watching campaigns; cash handouts are considerably rarer in Ghana.

These findings are reinforced by our own survey data, which asks individuals about what they have *personally* seen, and so may be less susceptible to individuals reporting rumours (Figure 7.3). While the figures for locating development projects to benefit supporters are similar for all three countries, the purchasing of rival supporters' identity cards (so that they cannot vote for a rival) was twice as high in Kenya as Ghana, as was the proportion of people who said that they witnessed the handing out of money. For their part, significantly more Ugandans reported seeing money handed out than Ghanaians but report fewer instances of treating.

We also asked respondents whether or not they had been offered money themselves. In order to encourage individuals to answer honestly we did not ask them whether they had accepted a gift but simply whether they had been offered one. We would expect answers to this question to underestimate the actual frequency of such cash handouts, but the results indicate a similar pattern to that identified above: with 15 per cent of Kenyans and 14 per cent of Ugandans, but only 10 per cent of Ghanaians reporting that

[26] The full question was: 'How often (if ever) did a candidate or someone from a political party offer you something, like food or a gift, in return for your vote?'.

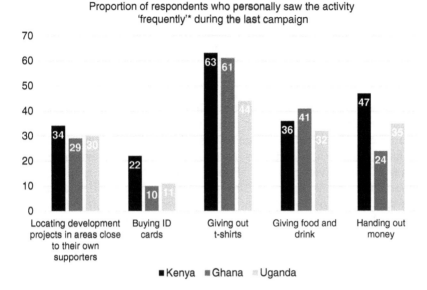

Figure 7.3 Personal experience of electoral manipulation
* The other options were 'once or twice' and 'never'.
Source: Authors' own survey data

they had been offered money to vote for a specific candidate. As we would expect from the different pressures placed on MPs in rural and urban areas (Chapter 6), more respondents reported having been offered money to vote for a candidate in rural constituencies (10 per cent compared to 6 per cent in Ghana, 17 per cent compared to 13 per cent in Uganda and 17 per cent compared to 16 per cent in Kenya), but it is worth noting that especially in the Kenyan case this difference was small.

It is also important not to exaggerate the significance of the cross-national variation in our sample. In all three countries, the majority of citizens believe that gifting is common, and in all three a minority of the population report having actually been offered money themselves. This caveat notwithstanding, the data suggests that the impact of institutional development and socialization on contemporary practice has been important. Popular expectations in Kenya and Uganda place MPs under even greater pressure to think and act locally, something that, as we shall see in 7.4, has a profound effect on the behaviour of political leaders.

7.2   The Meaning of Money

In order to better understand public attitudes towards the distribution of gifts, we asked a representative sample of the public in all three countries how they felt about a range of electoral practices. Questions took the form of: 'Can you tell me whether you think the action is not wrong at all, wrong but understandable, or wrong and should be punished: Stuffing the ballot box with fake votes/using hate speech/employing a gang to intimidate the supporters of rival candidates.' The results of the surveys, along with the conversations we have had with individuals in all three countries, evidence the allure of the civic register (Figure 7.4). The vast majority of respondents in all three countries believe that activities such as hate speech, the use of election gangs and ballot-box stuffing should be punished. Even when we look at whether an action is 'wrong but understandable' – breaking the rules might be seen to be understandable, for example, if the broader electoral context is seen to be manifestly unfair already – public attitudes are clear and

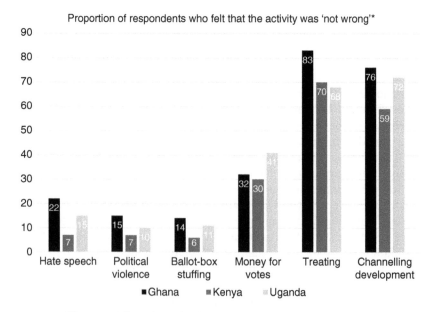

Figure 7.4 Popular attitudes towards electoral malpractice (%)
* Not wrong = 'not wrong at all' or 'wrong but understandable'. The other option was 'wrong and should be punished'.
Source: Authors' own survey data

consistent on these issues. Fully 86 per cent of Ghanaians believe that 'ballot-box stuffing' is always wrong, as do 89 per cent of Ugandans and 94 per cent of Kenyans. This demonstrates broad support for civic ideals such as due process.

The picture is a little different when it comes to 'handing out money for votes'. In this case, we still see clear majorities prepared to criticize the practice – 68 per cent in Ghana, 70 per cent in Kenya and 59 per cent in Uganda – but the extent of public disapprobation is markedly lower. These figures suggest that there is considerable support for the civic register, but also significant support for practices such as electoral bribery, even in their crudest form. This interpretation is supported by public attitudes towards 'giving food and drink to people that attend an event' and 'locating development projects in areas close to their supporters'. Strong majorities believe that treating voters or channelling development towards your own supporters is either 'not wrong' or 'wrong but understandable'. This of course is not necessarily evidence of support for the patrimonial register: voters may expect that parties will look after the interests of their supporters whether they cast their ballots along ethnic lines or on the basis of public policy. It is the broader context – the significance of identity politics, and the support for MPs who personally provide for their constituents – that suggests the patrimonial register is in play.

There are a number of reasons that we might expect the distribution of attitudes observed in Figure 7.4. Michael Bratton (2008) has pointed out that it makes sense that voters are most critical of acts such as political violence, because this may involve considerable harm being done to an individual who may not have intentionally or willingly been caught up in the situation. By contrast, practices such as treating and gifting, at least in the abstract, imply the consent of both the giver and the receiver. This is a good point, but we would express it in a slightly different way. Hate speech and political violence, for many of our respondents, transgress both patrimonial and civic norms and the same may be true of ballot-box stuffing if, for example, the preferred candidate of a community loses because a rival from the same group rigs the election in this way. By contrast, gifting, treating and channelling development to supporters contravene the civic register, but they are compatible with the patrimonial one. Moreover, the variation between the three 'willing giver, willing receiver' situations – gifting, treating and channelling development – suggests that our respondents are not only thinking about consent and the degree of impact, but also how legitimate each action is within a given moral worldview.

In any survey that asks sensitive questions there is a risk that answers reflect what respondents think survey enumerators want or expect to hear more than their true attitudes.[27] It is therefore possible that in some cases respondents told us what they thought we wanted to hear. But if this was the case, we would have expected closer adherence to the 'official rules' of the electoral game across the board – and voters are well aware that practices such as exchanging money for votes are not supposed to happen. Given this, it is particularly striking that these responses were given to a stranger. They are not therefore simply part of a hidden 'private' morality that stands in contrast to a 'public' disapproval of such practices – instead they were openly shared with a survey enumerator who, with their education and research background, might be expected to elicit 'socially desirable' answers. Instead, in the same setting and speaking to the same interviewer, citizens made distinctions between different forms of malpractice, and indeed between different sorts of giving, with the bribery of individuals seen to be much less acceptable than helping the community with development or offering refreshments at a rally.

The laboratory games that we played in all three countries provide further evidence of the strength of the civic register and the refusal of many citizens to accept electoral bribes.[28] In summary, the game involved two participants playing the role of politicians – 'Candidate A' and 'Candidate B' – competing for the support of a third participant who played the role of the 'voter'.[29] Candidate A – and only Candidate A – had the option of offering the voter a gift of money, which was specifically described as a bribe, in order to curry favour. Voters could then decide to cast their ballots – in the mocked-up ballot box provided – for Candidate A or Candidate B. For their part, Candidate B could not do anything to persuade the voter to support them and simply had to wait for the game to play out. The structure of the game meant that 'voters' would make the most money if they were given a gift but rejected Candidate A and

[27] This is especially troubling given that there is growing evidence that the presence of white researchers shapes how individuals respond to questions in contexts such as sub-Saharan Africa. In a study of player behaviour in laboratory games played in sixty villages in Sierra Leone, Cilliers et al. found that the mere presence of a white researcher made participants significantly more generous and concluded that the 'white-man mechanism' is rooted in the desire of participants 'to give more because they perceive this is what he wants them to do' (2015: 413).

[28] Voters were given no information about Candidates A and B other than whether Candidate A had paid a bribe. Payouts were between $0 and $10. The game was modified due to challenges experienced in Kenya, and so only the figures for Ghana and Uganda are reported here. For full details of how the lab games were carried out and for descriptive statistics see online appendix 3 at www.cambridge.org/moraleconomy.

[29] Around 360 people played each game. Participants were selected by positioning recruiters in areas of different socio-economic status in the location and approaching every fifth person who walked past with an invitation to attend. As only some of those who were approached attended, the sample is naturally skewed towards lower-income groups who were more willing to give up their spare time.

supported Candidate B instead. For their part, Candidate A would win the most money if they did not bribe but were voted for anyway – although this seemed unlikely, given that voters would go home with less money if they chose this option.

Faced with this situation, a majority of Candidate As – 58 per cent in Uganda and 63 per cent in Ghana – decided not to provide a cash incentive to voters. There are two possible explanations for this. First, participants playing this role may have been personally opposed to the idea of paying a bribe. Second, some Candidate As may have decided that voters would be unlikely to respond positively to a bribe and thus concluded that it was not worth paying one. In either case, the decision of the majority of Candidate As not to pay a bribe appears to demonstrate a recognition of the resonance of civic values or at the very least the limited resonance of patrimonial ones. However, the fact that a significant minority of Candidate As chose the other option and did offer a gift demonstrates that there was no consensus on this point. In total, around forty percent of candidate As appear to have concluded that the voter would definitely not support them without a bribe and that if one was offered they might be rewarded for their generosity.

The response of 'voters' suggests that in at least some cases they were right. A significant minority of those given a gift – 27 per cent in Uganda, 15 per cent in Ghana, 22 per cent overall – voted for the politician who gave it, even though they knew this would leave them worse off. This outcome suggests that, even in this artificially constructed situation, the giving of a gift created some sense of reciprocal obligation. More often, however, voters given a gift by Candidate A did not vote for them, suggesting that this bond has limited traction in this context. Perhaps the most interesting aspect of the game, though, was an unexpected result: 'voters' who did not receive a gift were more likely to vote for Candidate A than those who did: 10 per cent more in Uganda and 17 per cent more in Ghana.

Feedback received through a post-game survey and discussions with those who participated revealed that in many cases this was because voters decided to actively reward Candidate A for deciding not to pay a bribe – and were willing to leave with considerably less money in order to do this. Indeed, many of those that we talked to explicitly invoked an aspect of the civic register to explain their actions, saying that it was against the rules, unfair, or simply that they thought it was morally wrong. Even more strikingly, there were a number of instances in both countries in which participants refused to accept any money at all, either handing it back to research assistants or leaving the envelopes they had received on the table. In some cases, this was very public and so could perhaps be seen as a deliberate attempt at virtue signalling in a very particular context. But even if this was the case, the fact that these participants believed that rejecting money that came from a bribery game would enhance their reputation implies that support for certain civic values is widespread. Moreover, the fact that some people simply left their money on the table suggests that they were motivated by a genuine disapproval of transactional vote buying.

This raises the question of how the public in our three countries view transfers of money that are *not* simply transactional. In order to understand the way in which context shapes the morality of electoral gift giving, we used our surveys to ask about the behaviour of candidates in a very different way. As already discussed, we argue that voters interpret the morality of acts of gift giving in the context of a leader's behaviour and reputation. What is given and how it is given is important, because passing a small amount of cash to a mother to buy medicine for her children is clearly different to handing out bundles of notes to anyone who walks past on a street corner. But even the very same gifts made in the very same way can be interpreted differently based on the individual that makes them, their relationship to the individual and the community, and their perceived commitment to development more broadly. Those who have conformed to what it means to be a good leader within the patrimonial register are likely to be praised for their generosity – those who have not may be accused of 'vote buying'. To test this proposition, we included a question in the survey that explicitly locates the handing out of money around elections within the broader context of the kind of behaviour that is commonly demanded within the patrimonial register. Respondents were therefore asked how they felt about 'candidates campaigning for Parliament handing out gifts, money, paying fees and attending to other personal needs of their constituents'. This retains the idea of money being handed out for votes but places such activity in the context of a relationship in which the leader is attentive to the needs of the constituency. In order to make sure that we asked people to evaluate these actions in explicitly moral terms that evoke our two registers, we asked them to decide whether it was 'good, because it shows the leader is a good person', 'neutral' or 'bad, because vote buying is not good for the country'.[30] While the connection between the handing out of gifts and good leadership is a central feature of the patrimonial register, the notion that such practices are bad because they are not in the national interest epitomizes the civic register.

As expected, the responses we received varied significantly depending on the question that we asked. For the sake of clarity, from this point on

---

[30] For ease of graphic representation and analysis, the categories of 'good' and 'mostly good' have been merged, as have the categories of 'bad' and 'mostly bad'.

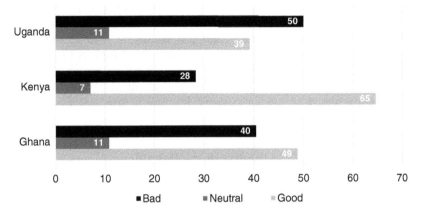

Respondents' evaluation of MP candidates 'handing out gifts, money, paying fees and attending to other personal needs of their constituents'*

Figure 7.5 Popular attitudes towards gift giving (%)
* 'Good' = 'good' and 'mostly good'. 'Bad' = 'bad' and 'mostly bad'.
Source: Authors' own survey data

we will refer to the question that only mentioned handing over money in return for votes as asking about 'vote buying' and the question that placed such activity in a wider context as asking about 'gift giving'. In all three countries, a large proportion of citizens answered that 'gift giving' was a good thing because it reflected good leadership (Figure 7.5), with a high of 65 per cent in Kenya. Significantly, a far higher proportion of respondents thought that this kind of gifting was 'good' as compared to those who were prepared to say that 'vote buying' was 'not wrong at all': 65 per cent as compared to 13 per cent in Kenya, 49 per cent against 9 per cent in Ghana and 39 per cent against 17 per cent in Uganda. The variation between our cases is also what we would have expected given the earlier discussion regarding the impact of political institutions and socialization, with much higher support for this kind of 'gift giving' in Kenya than in our other two cases, which sit relatively close together. While comparing between the two questions needs to be done with caution given the different answers available to respondents in each case, these variations support two of the main conclusions of this chapter. First, the perceived morality of financial transfers depends on the relationship between the individuals involved. Second, the legitimacy of patrimonial activities depends on the way in which individuals and communities have been socialized into assumptions about who should provide development and how that development should be delivered.

It is important to note, however, that not all voters were in favour of this kind of 'gift giving'. In Uganda, half of all voters believed that this was 'bad' – the most common response – and 40 per cent of Ghanaians agreed. Even in Kenya, 28 per cent of voters saw this as being morally wrong. The fact that 'gift giving' is seen to be more legitimate than 'vote buying' should therefore not blind us to the fact that even when we look at more contextual relationships there is strong evidence for the significance of civic ideals. Which voters align themselves with which register is a topic that we discuss in greater detail in 7.4.

7.3   Legitimacy Is in the Eye of the Beholder

We are not the first to point out that the giving of money may be subject to very different interpretations and that these matter. Schaffer and Schedler have argued that, when voters are offered private goods and services by politicians, they may see them as being a payment, a gift, a reparation or a sign (2005: 14–17). Each type of transaction has a very different meaning. While a payment is effectively a 'bribe' and 'the commodity citizens trade with are their votes', the other three do not always imply a 'quid pro quo' arrangement. Reparations are effectively payments for work or injustice already incurred and so do not have implications for future activity. Signs are just that – informational markers designed to reveal the personal qualities of the giver and so encourage positive evaluations, but stop short of compelling action. Gifts are unilateral transfers that may help to cement a relationship but do not necessarily incur a moral obligation on the receiver in the polling booth – the recipient may 'just grab the money, vote their conscience, and run' (Schaffer and Schedler 2005: 6). This, of course, might not be quite as clear cut as it sounds: in reality, the gift giver is likely to expect a degree of loyalty in the long term, even if each present is not tied to a specific obligation.

Translating our discussion in 7.2 into Schaffer and Schedler's language, voters in our three countries are much more likely to see 'gifts', 'signs' and 'reparations' as morally legitimate. As we were told in Uganda, many people know that gifting is against the law but do not condemn it:

The candidates of course use a lot of money. Yes, it is against the law but you find that it is like an acceptable wrong culture.[31]

---

[31] Interview UGA20a, NRM official and academic, Kampala, 20 September 2014.

The 'acceptable wrong culture' referred to in this quote is the patrimonial register of virtue by another name. Within this moral framework, gift giving is part of the legitimate activities of a good leader and is in turn legitimated by the other things – such as offering practical assistance – that a leader does. As one respondent in the Kenyan opposition stronghold of Kisumu thoughtfully explained, linking this broader point to the economic context in that constituency:

[T]he rate of poverty is very high, so for them maybe they are not looking at that act as bribery, but they are looking at it as an act that the person – the aspirant is trying to help them out in the situation that they are in.[32]

Handouts of money interpreted as 'payments', on the other hand, are more likely to be condemned as bribes, especially if they come from a candidate who has already aroused public suspicion. As one campaign activist put it in Kenya: 'If they like you, you are generous. If not, they tell you "you are buying us!"'[33]

These sentiments highlight a critical challenge for political leaders: if the money is given simply as a gift with no contractual element, voters may not feel obligated to deliver their vote in return. But if they explicitly frame the transfer as a purchase, voters may come to see their campaigns as being morally illegitimate. In turn, this may undermine their prospects – especially if voters believe that the ballot is secret, such that candidates cannot tell how they voted (Cheeseman and Klaas 2018). Using money in elections is therefore much more complicated than it might at first appear. This is especially the case given that candidates are not fully in control of the way that they are viewed. On the one hand, rival leaders may actively seek to 'decampaign' them by attacking their reputations (Chapter 6). On the other hand, questions about their past, and the source of their wealth, may prove difficult to shrug off.

As Nugent (2007) has pointed out in the Ghanaian context, when wealth is seen to be accumulated in the wrong way, acts of generosity may backfire and lead to accusations of illegitimacy. For example, during the Kenyan one-party state, candidates who were funded by the regime of Daniel arap Moi to defeat critical MPs sometimes lost elections even though they could easily outspend their rivals (Cheeseman 2008). The reason was that voters saw the money that they were able to distribute not as a sign of credibility, but as evidence that they had been 'bought' by Moi and would therefore be responsive to the president rather than to the constituency. This point holds more generally: when the wealth that

---

[32] Interview KEN22a, civil society activist, Kisumu, 19 March 2017.
[33] Interview KEN86a, activist, Kisumu.

a leader has accrued is seen to be illegitimately gained – and when a leader is seen to have sold out the community to promote their own interests (Chapter 6) – handouts may be taken as evidence not of their generosity, but of their tendency to 'eat on their own', as Kenyans would say, and thus of their failure to appropriately care for their kith and kin. When this happens, voters do not interpret the offer of money as a morally legitimate gift, but rather as an insulting attempt to buy their loyalty.

Political leaders therefore need to understand how wealth can be legitimized. As John Lonsdale has argued (1992b), conforming with community understandings of what constitutes good leadership is an important component of maintaining popular support; doing this successfully can 'cleanse' wealth and convert it into what Nugent (2007: 255) calls 'symbolic capital'. This means paying careful attention to what Lonsdale has called 'moral ethnicity' – local norms as to what constitutes good leadership and how Big Men should operate. Within Kikuyu moral ethnicity, for example, leaders are not expected to redistribute wealth for the sake of it – there is no conception of a deserving poor – but are instead expected to use their positions to benefit the community (Lonsdale 1992b). More broadly, politicians 'have to be careful about their public images because there is often a fine line between public adulation and disapprobation' (Nugent 2007: 255).

The need to fulfil local assumptions about leadership is particularly pressing given that most elections feature a number of candidates with a strong connection to the community. While giving bigger gifts in order to evidence one's wealth and virtue may be enough to generate a competitive edge for a candidate, leaders must keep in mind that voters who receive gifts from a number of candidates may use other criteria in order to choose between them. As one Ugandan explained:

[T]here are also situations where all candidates have the money so it doesn't become a factor. So, the voters start to look at your individual merit, yes, you all have money, what is your history in terms of community development? What is also your character? How do you relate to the people? Then you see people objectively selecting a candidate regardless of money.[34]

Under these circumstances, acts of generosity may be necessary but not sufficient to win. As a Kenyan activist put it, generosity 'is now an expectation, you must give us money in order for us to take you seriously'.[35] In this context, it is particularly important that a candidate is seen to be authentic – to belong. Elizabeth Carlson (2015), for example, shows that non co-ethnic candidates may struggle to gain recognition for their efforts, even if they otherwise conform to local expectations. Even co-ethnicity

---

[34] Interview UGA20a, NRM official and academic, Kampala, 20 September 2014.
[35] Interview KEN14a, civil society activist, Kisumu, 15 March 2017.

may not be enough to secure victory if other co-ethnics with a greater claim to the community's affections enter the race. One unsuccessful Ugandan candidate found this out to his cost when he left Kampala to campaign in his rural home only to face suspicion over his age, religion and – perhaps crucially – the fact he had no property in the constituency:

> I went for primaries. For consultation ... when I looked at the reports from my intelligence people, people were only ready to cheat me. They would praise you when you are around, then they would say, 'ah, this man has no house here!' The biggest supporter on the microphone [i.e. publicly] is the one saying, 'no no, we had better stay with this one [the rival candidate], [because] this man has no house here, he's a young man, he's a Muslim!'[36]

Gifting is therefore most effective when it is one of a number of different factors that confirm that a candidate both understands and is willing to live up to what it means to be a good leader within the patrimonial register. This is most likely to be the case when a leader with largesse also has a track record of delivering community development and/or of standing up for community interests, is regularly seen in the area and shares the identity of the majority of the electorate. The mutually reinforcing relationship between these different aspects of credibility was well summarized by a Ugandan NGO worker who, when asked to explain why the local MP was so popular, replied:

> Two things. One, he deliberately dedicates more time to the electorate. Not to the issues of the electorates to the national legislature, no, to the electorates. [He asks] what are the electorates struggling with? ... then he has the resources. He has real resources because he was part of the government structure.[37]

While these popular expectations can be manipulated by canny candidates (Chapter 6), they also place leaders under considerable pressure to conform. Popular demands have no doubt been shaped by the practice of politicians over many years, but they now set the limits for what is possible. When asked to explain the prevalence of money in politics, for example, a Ghanaian journalist initially said that he blamed MPs because 'the kind of things they tell the people [lead to popular expectations]'. Later, however, he reflected that to some extent this was impossible to avoid as 'if you tell the people the truth ... they will not vote for you'.[38] Numerous others agreed that the popular expectations place candidates under tremendous pressure to comply. As an unsuccessful Ugandan candidate who tried to avoid giving gifts explained:

[36] Interview UGA30a, civil society activist and former candidate, Kampala, 25 March 2015.
[37] Interview UGA23a, academic, Mukono, 23 March 2015.
[38] Interview GHA31a, journalist, Konongo, 29 August 2016.

They were seeing him [a rival] giving out money; they were seeing that I [who did not give out money] was a bad person ... how come this one is giving us and you are not?[39]

The same point was echoed in a number of interviews in Kenya. When personal generosity is interpreted as a 'sign' of virtue – and a measure of the likelihood that a candidate will keep their promises – deviating from the norm can be extremely costly. As one Kenyan respondent reflected, when asked whether gift giving was a necessity:

[I]f you don't give that money, they'll start abusing you and nicknaming you. They will brand you maybe you're mean, what, what – so many things![40]

In this way, the centrality of money in our three countries is co-produced by voters and politicians alike.

Adopting the lens of the moral economy of elections thus provides us with a number of valuable insights that existing accounts tend to overlook. It enables us to understand the way in which the giving of money can have very different meanings around elections, the reason that the candidate who spends the most does not always win, and why those who are often vying to represent poor constituencies broadcast their wealth rather than hiding it. But this is only half of the story. To return to Figures 7.3 and 7.5, there is far from universal agreement on the legitimacy of gifting and treating. Particularly where gifting is concerned, many people in our three countries stated that such activity was not only wrong but should be punished. This variation within our cases raises a number of important questions: what kinds of voters are most likely to view such practices as acceptable, why and what does this tell us about the compatibility of the civic and patrimonial registers of virtue?

7.4   Who Invests Most in the Patrimonial Register?

The existing literature has generated a number of fairly established predictions about where we should be most likely to see gifting and where it is most likely to meet with public acceptance. Schaffer (2005), for example, frames voter education efforts to eradicate 'vote-buying' in the Philippines as being predominantly conducted by an urban elite who target the urban and rural poor. The elite, being more educated and wealthier, are both more likely to have been sensitized into civic registers of virtue and less likely to need handouts. Other recent analyses typically

---

[39] Interview UGA18a, academic and former activist and candidate, Kampala, 24 September 2014.
[40] Interview KEN10a, activist, Seme, 14 March 2017.

fall into line with this framing. Within Kramon's understanding (2017), for example, handouts are most likely to take place in rural areas as this is where the future generosity of the MP is most significant to the lives of citizens. As Barkan (1995) has argued, because urbanites are more likely to live near, and to be able to benefit from, schools and hospitals, they are somewhat less dependent on the personal favour of their local representative. It is therefore those on the periphery who are the most dependent on their MPs for public services and so are particularly likely to focus on gifts as 'signs' of a candidate's future behaviour.

Cheeseman's (2015b) research on the impact of being 'middle class' in Kenya on support for key democratic principles reaches similar conclusions, although it emphasizes the significance of education over that of wealth. More specifically, Cheeseman finds that those who have completed university are significantly more likely to support civil liberties and to demand a high-quality democracy. Others have also found that education plays an important role in driving attitudes towards democracy. Looking at the case of Malawi, Geoffrey Evans and Pauline Rose conclude that, compared to those who receive no schooling, 'primary schooling promotes citizen endorsement of democracy and rejection of non-democratic alternatives even when it has taken place under authoritarian rule, without explicit civic education' (2007: 904). This leads to three fairly straightforward expectations, all of which are echoed in Bratton's (2008) research on vote buying in Nigeria: attitudes towards the acceptability of patrimonial electoral practices are likely to vary according to location, education and wealth/class.

The picture in our three countries is a little more complex than this suggests, however. We only find significant variations along these dimensions when it comes to public attitudes towards 'gift giving' – that is campaigns that use handouts, gifts and assistance. By contrast, there is very little variation when it comes to 'vote buying' – that is simply asking about the handing out of money in return for electoral support. We argue that this is strong evidence, first, of the consistent presence of the civic register across our cases (see Conclusion) and, second, that people draw on both civic and patrimonial registers in making distinctions between virtuous gift giving and improper vote buying. Where such practices are not set in the context of wider virtuous behaviours in the patrimonial register, individuals are more willing to reject them and – whether implicitly or explicitly – align that rejection with civic values, casting handouts as immoral vote buying. Consequently, while attitudes towards vote buying are fairly consistent across different sectors of society, things look very different when it comes to practices that are seen to be legitimate within the patrimonial register, even though they challenge civic virtue; in

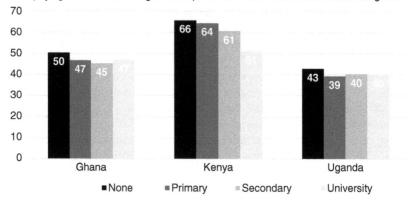

Proportion of respondents who said that MP candidates 'handing out gifts, money, paying fees and attending to other personal needs of their constituents' is 'good'*

Figure 7.6 Popular attitudes towards gift giving, by education
* 'Good' = 'good' and 'mostly good'. The other options were 'bad', 'mostly bad' and 'neutral'.
Source: Authors' own survey date

such cases, attitudes vary considerably. It is therefore only when it comes to gift giving that we see the kinds of variation in the holding of patrimonial values predicted by the literature.

This distinction is well demonstrated by the case of education. There is little evidence that higher levels of education are associated with disapprobation of vote buying. In Kenya, for example, it is actually those with no education at all that are most likely to say that gifting should be punished (72 per cent), and those who have only completed primary school are more likely to favour punishment (70 per cent) than those who have completed university (62 per cent). However, an education effect does appear when we shift our dependent variable to look at attitudes to politicians who campaign through handouts, gifts and assistance. As demonstrated in Figure 7.6, the proportion of respondents who felt that this kind of behaviour by political candidates was 'good' was highest among those with no education in all three countries. In Kenya, for example, there was a steady increase in opposition to this form of campaigning as one moves up the education scale, and the magnitude of this change – some 15 per cent – is large. This is strongly indicative of the way in which education can socialize individuals into aspects of the civic register.

The effect of education does not, however, appear to be uniform or linear. In both Ghana and Uganda there is very little difference between those who have finished primary, secondary school and university. The absence of a 'university' effect is surprising and may be due to the much smaller sample size in this category. This cannot explain the minimal differences we see in Ghana and Uganda when it comes to the impact of secondary schooling, though, because this is one of the largest categories. It is therefore important not to exaggerate the significance of education. What appears to matter most when it comes to attitudes towards patrimonial politics is the experience of schooling – more education appears to have only a limited effect once primary school has been completed – and overall the effect of education seems to be outweighed by other factors.[41]

It is considerably easier to measure the impact of education than that of wealth and income, which are notoriously difficult to capture due to the sensitivity of these topics and the incentives that respondents have to hide poverty (which may be embarrassing) and wealth (which may imply an individual should be paying more tax). This caveat notwithstanding, self-reported income demonstrates a similar relationship to patrimonialism as education, which is unsurprising given the correlation between the wealth and education in our cases. Again, this effect is only present when we focus on gifting and is not present when it comes to vote buying. To return to the Kenyan case, for example, when we move from those earning less than 3,000 KES (US$30) a month to those earning 28,000 KES (US$270), the proportion of people saying that vote buying should *not* be punished actually increases from 31 per cent to 36 per cent. When it comes to gift giving, however, there is a clear relationship between an individual's income and their attitude: only among those Kenyans who earn less than 3,000 KES each month is there an absolute majority who see gifting as 'good' (Figure 7.7). This makes intuitive sense for two reasons. First, those who earn more are less dependent on politicians' assistance and so can afford to take a more principled stance. Second, those who are in need are more likely to interpret a 'gift' as an informational cue that a politician is interested in the particular needs of a community, or willing to support development more generally, and thus to see such an action as virtuous. It is nonetheless important to note that the impact of income is much less clear-cut in Ghana and Uganda and that a significant proportion of poorer citizens in each country felt that gift giving was bad.[42]

---

[41] In a pooled multinomial logistic regression including country fixed effects, being better educated was not a statistically significant predictor of disapproving of MPs handing out gifts, money, paying fees and attending to other personal needs of their constituents in all three countries. See online appendix 2 at www.cambridge.org/moraleconomy.

[42] In the same logistic regression, being wealthier was a statistically significant predictor of an individual's acceptance of MPs handing out gifts. In individual country regressions, this held in Kenya and to a lesser extent Ghana and Uganda. See online appendix 2 at www.cambridge.org/moraleconomy.

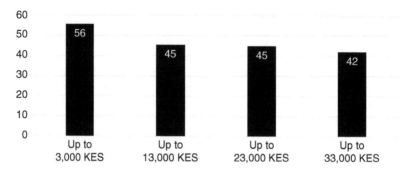

Proportion of respondents who said that MP candidates 'handing out gifts, money, paying fees and attending to other personal needs of their constituents' is 'good'*

Figure 7.7 Popular attitudes towards gift giving in Kenya, by monthly individual income
* 'Good' = 'good' and 'mostly good'. The other options were 'bad', 'mostly bad' and 'neutral'.
Source: Authors' own survey data

The situation is even more complex when it comes to geographical location. In line with wealth and education, there is no significant difference in attitudes between those living in areas demarcated as urban and rural by the national census frame where vote buying is concerned. As with the other variables discussed in this section, the expected pattern does start to emerge when we change our focus to look at broader processes of campaigning through handouts, gifts and assistance – but only to an extent. While those living in rural areas were more likely to say that gift giving was 'good' than their urban counterparts in Ghana and Uganda, the reverse was true in Kenya (Figure 7.8). This suggests that, as we noted in Chapter 6, we should be careful not to exaggerate the urban/rural divide.[43] It may also, however, reflect the fact that many areas that are now counted as 'urban' due to consistent population growth are located outside of major towns and so may be expected to have less distinctive attitudes to rural dwellers.

When we take a more fine-grained approach, moving beyond the urban/rural disctinction to look at how attitudes vary by region, and in particular in or close to the capital, a significant difference emerges. In

---

[43] In the same logistic regression, living in a rural area was not a statistically significant predictor of an individual's acceptance of MPs handing out gifts. In individual country regressions, it was in Kenya but not in our other two cases. See online appendix 2 at www .cambridge.org/moraleconomy.

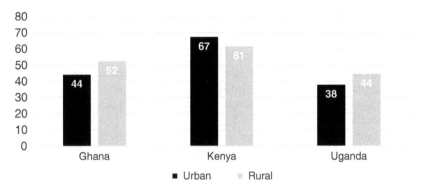

Figure 7.8 Popular attitudes towards gift giving, by location (%)
* 'Good' = 'good' and 'mostly good'. The other options were 'bad', 'mostly bad' and 'neutral'.
Source: Authors' own survey data

Ghana, for example, those living in Greater Accra were on average much less likely to say that gifting was 'good' (48 per cent) than those living in the comparatively remote Northern region (62 per cent). The same pattern holds in Kenya, where a smaller proportion of people in Nairobi (55 per cent) support gifting as compared to the former Coast (69 per cent) and North Eastern (72 per cent) provinces. It therefore seems likely that geographical location is significant, but that living in an area demarcated as 'urban' or 'rural' in terms of the national sampling frame is less relevant than the difference between residing in a developed urban city as compared to peripheral areas that are less likely to enjoy the same kinds of access to information and services.

With some important caveats, then, our data confirms the patterns predicted in the literature, but only when it comes to the broader understanding of 'gift giving', and even in this case the expected relations do not always materialize in all three countries. This finding has two important implications. First, it confirms the argument of this chapter that the transfer of money is much more likely to be rejected when it is perceived to represent a financial transaction and to be accepted when it occurs as part of a longer-term relationship in which a leader's efforts – both for the individual and for the community – have earned them a degree of moral authority. In so doing, our survey data also affirms the importance of understanding the moral economy of elections. As the example of Alan

Cash demonstrated at the start of this chapter, when voters believe that a candidate is using money as a substitute for moral character, rather than as a manifestation of their leadership qualities, they are unlikely to feel any obligation to provide political support – whether they accept a handout or otherwise.

Second, the (admittedly uneven) impact of education, wealth and location on support for patrimonial values suggests that future evolutions of the moral economy will be strongly shaped by current socio-economic trends, some of which seem likely to erode the resonance of the patrimonial register – at least in the very long run. At present, sub-Saharan Africa is witnessing rapid urbanization. It is estimated that the continent will be predominantly urban by 2040, although some countries such as Uganda that remain mostly rural may buck this trend. Levels of economic growth are not keeping pace with this process, but steady economic expansion, albeit punctuated with episodes of economic slowdown, has led to the gradual expansion of the middle class and a fall in poverty levels. The investment of governments in all three countries in free primary education has also changed the educational landscape, while the number of universities continues to steadily increase. Already, literacy levels have risen considerably since independence: between 1960 and 2018, they rose from 27 per cent to 76 per cent in Ghana and 20 per cent to 78 per cent in Kenya, while in Uganda – despite the disruptions of the 1970s – they rose from around 40 per cent in the late-colonial era to 72 per cent in 2015. While some have questioned the quality of the free education that is being provided and demonstrated that the growth of the middle class has been exaggerated (Cheeseman 2015b), it seems likely that the cumulative impact of these trends will transform society and, over time, reduce popular support for patrimonial political practices.

7.5   Political Identity and Popular Engagement

A final expectation that we had when designing this study was that we would see significant partisan variation in attitudes to certain aspects of patrimonial politics, with opposition supporters being more willing to condemn gifting and vote buying on the basis that such activities confer an advantage on the ruling party, given its greater access to state resources. This expectation is born out in Ghana and to a lesser extent in Uganda but not in Kenya, and in the former countries the effect is not significant (Figure 7.9).[44] Ahead of Ghana's 2016 elections, supporters of

---

[44] In the same logistic regression, being a supporter of an opposition party reduced acceptance of MPs handing out gifts, money, paying fees and attending to other personal needs

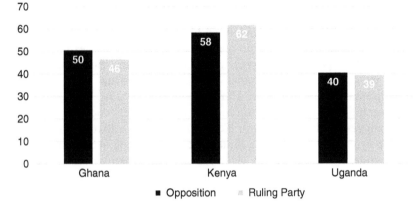

Figure 7.9 Popular attitudes towards gift giving, by partisan identity (%)
* 'Good' = 'good' and 'mostly good'. The other options were 'bad', 'mostly bad' and 'neutral'.
Source: Authors' own survey data

the ruling NDC were slightly more likely to say that 'gift giving' was 'good', at 50 per cent, as compared to their NPP counterparts at 46 per cent. In Uganda, 40 per cent of those who back the ruling NRM saw gifting as good, compared to 39 per cent who support an opposition party. By contrast, in Kenya, the opposition supporters behind NASA were slightly more likely to view gifting positively, at 61 per cent compared to 58 per cent for those who supported Jubilee.

These findings suggest that, while political positionality may shape attitudes towards gifting in some countries, this effect is considerably smaller than that of other variables. One possible explanation for why we do not find bigger political effects is that opposition supporters feel that they also benefit from patrimonial politics around elections. There are two very different logics that could ground such a perception. The first is that, while voters in all three countries have less opportunity to benefit from government resources when their party is out of power, they are not necessarily wholly excluded from patrimonial networks because they may

---

of their constituents. In individual country-level regressions, however, it is only significant in Ghana and Kenya. See online appendix 2 at www.cambridge.org/moraleconomy.

benefit – albeit in smaller ways – from the efforts of pro-government candidates to broaden their support base and from the activity of opposition leaders at various levels of the political system.

It is unclear to what extent opposition supporters benefit from the kinds of gifting that ruling party leaders and candidates might take part in. Jeremy Horowitz (2019) has demonstrated that, in countries with pronounced ethnic politics, leaders campaign in 'swing' and 'home' areas but rarely in opposition heartlands. However, reviewing Constituency Development Funds in Kenya, Harris and Posner (2019) find that they are geographically distributed more fairly than a purely clientelistic logic would suggest. It therefore seems likely that those who do not vote for the ruling party might benefit to a limited extent from the actions of ruling party candidates especially in closely contested constituencies. This is especially the case, of course, where candidates do not have clear reasons to think that certain types of citizen are unlikely to vote for them – for example because of their ethnicity – and so are incentivized to offer gifts and handouts across the board.

The potential for opposition supporters to benefit from the patrimonial behaviour of opposition leaders is easier to demonstrate. Especially in Ghana and Kenya, the main losing party or coalition in presidential elections has consistently been able to secure just under half of the seats in the legislature. As a result, many opposition supporters are represented by opposition MPs – and in the Kenyan case senators and governors – who strive to meet their patrimonial responsibilities in much the same way as their ruling party counterparts, investing in, and so helping to sustain, the patrimonial register. In this regard it is important to keep in mind that while Uganda has never seen a democratic transfer of power at the presidential level, and Kenya has only seen one opposition victory, legislative elections regularly see high levels of turnover. As a result, voters may feel not only that they can effectively make claims in the patrimonial register against their representatives, but also that they have the power to punish those who fail to meet their expectations. Indeed, it was under similar conditions – a lack of change in the national government and vibrant competition at the constituency level – that political competition in Kenya consolidated its highly personalized and localized dynamic in the 1970s and 1980s, creating the ideal conditions for the emergence of patrimonial ideals (Cheeseman 2008). Studies of local and legislative elections in opposition enclaves across our three cases provide support for this interpretation: leaders seeking to assert their authority in FDC, NASA and NPP heartlands have been shown to employ classic patrimonial strategies, alongside a range of other tactics (Ouma 2018; Waddilove 2019a).

The attitudes of opposition voters in Ghana, with its more open and democratic politics, may also be shaped by a rather different consideration, namely that opposition is not a permanent political status. The rotation of both political parties through power means that, although the NDC stood to gain most from financial transactions around elections during our fieldwork, the NPP had enjoyed this privilege between 2000 and 2008. In this context, opposition supporters can reasonably assume that their 'turn to eat' will come around again fairly soon and so have fewer reasons to fear that they will be excluded from access to state resources.

A second possible explanation for the limited impact of party identity is that opposition supporters feel a greater inclination to support civic values, but that they believe that the democratic system is so broken that there is little hope of reforming it – and so they may as well benefit while they can. As Julie Faller has argued in the case of Uganda, 'many voters do not object to, and may even prefer, corrupt politicians in a system where a single "honest" official is unlikely to reduce corruption overall' (2015: 428). It is difficult to empirically evaluate whether this logic plays a role in sustaining broader support for patrimonial values. It is certainly true that the electorate in Kenya and Uganda is highly sceptical of the potential for the political system to function as intended. Ahead of the 2016 Ugandan elections, an opinion poll revealed that a strong majority of people did not believe that elections could change the government, a point echoed by many commentators.[45] Anecdotal evidence from fieldwork in Kenya and Uganda also suggests that opposition leaders and supporters will often seek to justify transgressing the official rules on the basis that they have already been flouted – or will inevitably be flouted – by others and so it would be foolish to comply. Such justifications were far less common in Ghana, where the higher quality of elections makes this a less plausible line of defence. Thus, as we have argued throughout, evidence about the activity of rival political leaders, political experience and the way in which this experience conditions people's willingness to accept the credibility of key democratic institutions shapes how the moral economy plays out.

Whatever the reasons for slightly stronger support for gifting among opposition supporters in Ghana and Uganda, it is worth reflecting on

---

[45] Nic Cheeseman, Gabrielle Lynch and Justin Willis, 'In Uganda, many find it difficult to believe that Museveni could ever be defeated in an election', *Washington Post*, 3 November 2015, www.washingtonpost.com/news/monkey-cage/wp/2015/11/03/can-anyone-defeat-president-yoweri-museveni-in-uganda (3 January 2020); Magnus Taylor, 'Bit by bit, Uganda is laying the groundwork for future unrest', *International Crisis Group*, 13 December 2018, www.crisisgroup.org/africa/horn-africa/uganda/bit-bit-uganda-laying-groundwork-future-unrest (3 January 2020).

what this means for the relationship between the patrimonial register, elections and democracy. It is easy to assume that the prevalence of patrimonial practices and values has played a critical role in undermining democratic consolidation, and when it comes to support for irresponsible or ethnic chauvinist leaders this is clearly true (Chapter 6). But while patrimonial registers may facilitate abuse, they can also sustain popular support for the political process, not least by providing voters with a stronger relationship with, and connection to, political leaders and through them the wider political system. Relatively high levels of opposition support for the patrimonial register evidence our broader argument that one reason that so many people participate in elections that rarely generate national political change is that they are important arenas of both patrimonial and civic claims-making. In this sense, patrimonial politics may be productive by sustaining popular interest in political processes in countries such as Uganda, where the absence of genuinely competitive politics might otherwise be expected to generate widespread public disengagement – a point we develop further in the next chapter.

7.6   Conclusion

This chapter has explained how voters navigate the multiple moralities that characterize elections in Ghana, Kenya and Uganda. In deconstructing the idea that votes are simply 'brought' and 'sold', we have emphasized the fact that what is often described as vote buying occurs within a moral economy in which politicians are expected to be accessible and generous. Campaign handouts will not secure support for a candidate who is seen as otherwise inaccessible, unsympathetic or unwilling to speak for their people. The prevalence of gift giving is therefore not evidence that elections are amoral arenas, for the gifts themselves are subject to moral scrutiny.

In line with this point, we have argued that voters typically feel the pull of both registers of virtue and that the patrimonial register itself involves a form of accountability. We have also suggested that, when an individual that has received money from a candidate says that they wish for corruption-free elections and a free and fair process, they are not simply trying to hide their unsavoury actions from public scrutiny. Instead, they may genuinely value civic virtue and see this as a way to make demands. Yet they may also fear that relying on civic claims alone will render them vulnerable to exclusion from state resources, especially in a context in which others act 'patrimonially' (Chapter 6). Given this, even those who feel the pull of the civic register particularly strongly face powerful incentives to make patrimonial demands, especially when they suspect that others are doing so. As a result, political leaders may find themselves placed under pressure from below to deviate from the formal electoral rules.

We have also argued that the case of Ghana teaches us a valuable lesson: even when transfers of power have boosted acceptance of electoral outcomes, the civic register does not simply replace the patrimonial. Instead, there is considerable evidence that certain aspects of the patrimonial ideal of virtue are compatible with – and indeed may even be strengthened by – the institutionalization of certain formal rules. Numerous interviews and data collected by other researchers suggest that it has been the reintroduction and intensity of political competition that has forced candidates to spend ever-increasing amounts in a bid to impress their electorates (Chabal and Daloz 1999; Lindberg 2003). It should therefore not be a surprise that the cost of running for political office in Ghana is estimated to have increased by 59 per cent from 2012 to 2016 (Westminster Foundation for Democracy 2018: 5). One incumbent MP lamented his constituents' constant barrage of demands for private and club goods:

The educational issues, classroom blocks, you see these are the concerns of the electorates in the constituency and they see you as capable of doing all that. Mistakenly they think that you are a very rich person, aside that they come to you for money to settle their medical bills, money to pay rent, money to pay their children school fees. Yes. That's what they do on a regular basis. ... And if you don't respond positively to one, when he gets back home, 'this is the worst MP we have ever had!'[46]

Yet while Ghanaian MPs complained to us about the impossible demands that the cost of politics has placed upon them, these do seem less pronounced than in some other African states. The impact of political experience on how people think about the state and what they consider to be the right course of action in a given situation is demonstrated by the data from our surveys and interviews, which reveal significant variations between our countries. In particular, the weakness of political parties in Kenya, along with a national development strategy that has consistently identified MPs as the agents of local development, has sustained the prevalence and legitimacy of gifting. By contrast, in Ghana, where candidates cannot succeed without party support and the central government has often positioned itself as the provider of jobs and wealth, patrimonial politics operates within tighter limits.

These conclusions have significant implications for how we understand the impact of elections on political subjectivities and the broader

---

[46] Details withheld on the request of the interviewee.

democratic process. First, the persistence of patrimonial behaviours in one of Africa's most celebrated political systems demands that we recognize the ways in which formal democratic institutions may give a shot in the arm to what are often referred to as 'undemocratic' forms of behaviour. However, we have suggested that this should not necessarily be seen as a bad thing. While it is tempting to imagine that democratic consolidation occurs when civic registers eradicate their patrimonial counterparts, this is to forget the role that ethnic and personalistic ties can play in generating popular support for a political system. Indeed, it may be the case that in new democracies it is precisely the combination of strong civic registers coexisting with constrained patrimonial ideals that ensures that democratic political systems have stronger roots and are therefore more resilient to authoritarian reversal – a point that we return to in the Conclusion.

A final important lesson is that efforts to reduce practices such as vote buying that imagine that wily politicians are to blame, and that innocent voters just need to be better educated and informed to reject their overtures, are likely to fail. As discussed in Chapter 5, all too often civil society efforts at civic education assume that the problem of 'vote buying' is one of ignorance, selfishness or scepticism. Instead, the problem is rather different and much more intractable. Voters are not simply the passive recipients of gifts and favours; rather, patrimonial behaviours are co-produced in a way that locks citizens and candidates into a set of expected actions from which neither can easily extricate themselves.

Conclusion: The Electoral Fallacy Revisited

At the beginning of the 1990s, as the 'third wave' of democratization was reaching Africa, sceptics were asking whether the significance of elections was overstated; democracy, surely, requires multiple forms of institutional buttressing and popular engagement, not simply the secret ballot. As with so many broad movements within academic and popular thought, the idea that academics and policymakers mistake elections for democracy came to be known by a pithy shorthand: the electoral fallacy (Karl and Schmitter 1991). In response to successive waves of polls that failed to remove authoritarian leaders from power, a growing body of work emerged to explain how incumbents could use innovative rigging strategies to deliver elections without change (Abedanwi and Obadare 2011; Cheeseman and Klaas 2018). This critical re-evaluation of the role of elections in processes of political change was not confined to Africa; it drew on work in eastern Europe (Kalandadze and Orenstein 2009), Latin America (Burnell 2009) and Asia (Croissant et al. 2002; Stepan 2015) – and by political theorists (Møller 2007). At its most critical, the electoral fallacy has been invoked to suggest that we should neither use elections as a measure of democratic progress, nor allocate elections a special place within the literature on democratization. Some have gone as far as to suggest that elections in many countries are effectively meaningless, with the introduction of multi-partyism generating little evidence of 'any in-depth change in political culture' (Chabal and Daloz 1999: 35).

Our research confirms that there has long been a tendency to place unrealistic expectations on the electoral process. Yet we reject the argument that elections are unimportant political events or that they do not have a meaningful impact on those who participate in them and the broader political process. Electoral politics in Ghana, Kenya and Uganda are vibrant, exciting and important moments – even when they do not change the government – in large part because they are the sites of multiple moral projects that authorize individuals to make claims on those in power. In this sense, the great weakness of some critiques of elections that have emerged over the last twenty years – the fallacy of the fallacy, if you will – is that they have underestimated the impact of elections by misleadingly narrowing this down to the question of whether the polls result in a transfer of power.

Elections have multiple, sometimes contrary effects. The work that is done by adult suffrage and the secret ballot is not necessarily democratic in any straightforward sense. In the face of evident corruption, partiality and incompetence by government, elections can encourage people to believe that virtue may lie solely in shared ethnicity and personal ties, reducing politics to violent ethno-regional competition. By creating space for politicians and voters to make reciprocal claims to patrimonial virtue they may encourage people to think of themselves primarily not as national citizens, but as members of more local communities, demanding a very personal and local accountability. But the rhetoric of campaigns and elaborate technology of elections may also encourage voters to think and behave as national citizens. By helping to produce stateness – the appearance, more or less plausible, that the state is impartial – the processes of elections perpetuate existing forms of power at the same time as they highlight problems with, and impose constraints on, that power. Through this process, elections may encourage voters to see themselves as citizens with rights and those whose work makes the state to think of themselves – at least sometimes – as impartial, rule-bound functionaries. In this way, elections assert stateness and construct the imaginary of the disciplined citizen – even as they simultaneously fuel a range of personal, communal and clientelistic relationships that call this vision into question.

These multiple possibilities – sometimes contradictory, but sometimes compatible – are realized through an electoral moral economy whose outcomes are unpredictable and may confound the projects of power that they enable. Electoral officials speak the language of neutrality and discipline, advocating for peaceful and orderly polls (Chapter 3). Civil society organizations exhort their countrymen to honour their vote and to leave their parochial identities at the door when they enter the polling station (Chapter 5). International observers and the donors that fund them promote the importance of impartiality and due process and demand adherence to liberal democratic norms (Chapter 4). These moral projects, we have suggested, are rooted in a common civic register of virtue that locates what it means to do one's duty within a broader world view that emphasizes impartiality, meritocracy and citizenship. The fundamental animating principle of this register of virtue is that the ideal kind of state is one that is emancipated from social forces and is therefore free to operate in the interest of all citizens rather than one specific ethnic group or ruling clique. Across our three cases we have shown that this set of civic ideals is constantly rubbing up against, and often comes into direct competition with, another set of ideals, which we characterize as patrimonial.

In these three countries, when electoral officials deviate from the rules of the game in order to manipulate the outcome in favour of someone of their own family, ethnic group or region, they are often motivated by the notion that they owe their own community a greater responsibility than the wider nation or that they need to protect their community against the bias of others. Similarly, when political leaders present themselves as suitable people to represent their communities on the basis that they are best placed to promote and protect their particular interests against others (Chapter 6), they are drawing on a deeply rooted understanding of the reciprocal relationship between patrons and clients. Voters who respond by giving their support to such candidates, or who demand such preferential treatment and then ask that they deliver on their campaign promises, signal their own commitment to this relationship (Chapter 7). These kinds of claims, we have argued, are best understood as being located within a patrimonial register of virtue that reifies particularistic communal ties. These claims may and frequently do compete with one another, but collectively they sit in tension with the notion of civic-mindedness.

By drawing a contrast between these two registers of virtue we do not mean to imply that one is truly moral and the other not, or that the success of the democratic project requires the victory of the civic over the patrimonial. Instead, our argument is that both are inherently moral registers. Each is rooted in a conception of virtue that is based on particular understandings of community and what it is to be a good community member. Both registers, for example, imply a form of duty and a kind of social contract. Under the civic register, citizens owe their duty to the state, and the social contract is typically taken to refer to the willingness of individuals to fulfil their obligations – such as paying their taxes – in return for the provision of essential public services such as security. Here, the relevant community is the nation, and a sense of nationalism, along with an appeal to the national good, often underpins claims made within this register. A social contract also exists within the patrimonial register, but here the relevant community is sub-national and the social contract is often bounded to a particular ethnic, regional, religious or sectional group. Duty in this context is not something that one owes to the state, but rather to kith and kin, or other members of one's sub-national group. Both registers are therefore rooted in affective ties and their significance lies in the fact that as a result they carry moral weight.

We have argued that these registers are not necessarily easily compart-mentalized. Each of the main chapters that make up this volume has demonstrated the way in which the same individuals may make claims based on different registers or on both registers at the same time depend-ing on the context in which they are operating. It is true, of course, that certain institutions encourage people to see their role as being to strengthen democracy and take their force from specific moral projects within the civic register. Yet individuals often feel the pull of both civic and patrimonial ideals during the multiple processes that make up an election campaign. From a distance this complex array of claims may appear to cancel each other out, suggesting no change, but closer inspec-tion reveals significant differences in both group identities and under-standings of state–society relations.

These conclusions therefore do not suggest that elections are irrelevant, that international actors should disengage from them, or that academic and international attention should be focussed elsewhere. Rather, they suggest that we need to change the way we understand elections and engage with them. The electoral fallacy critique focusses on what elec-tions do not change: we argue that the moral work that goes on around the ballot is always changing things, though in unpredictable, and often unintended, ways.

At the same time, our analysis reinforces some of the warnings of the electoral fallacy literature regarding the limited capacity of elections, on their own, to institutionalize or promote democracy. The limited success of various international and domestic organizations to use elections as critical moments in which to instil particular democratic norms and values has demonstrated the complex challenges that such work faces and so provides evidence for the argument that there is no simple rela-tionship between holding elections and democratic consolidation. In particular, we have demonstrated the challenge that observers face in asserting their impartiality, the struggle of electoral officials to maintain their neutrality and the way in which many civil society groups become enmeshed in patrimonial politics. In all three cases, we find that contro-versies relating to the independence and motivations of these organiza-tions undermine their capacity to authorize norm change, weakening the power of claims made within the civic register.

In most of the elections that we review, there is no straightforward win for those seeking to push civic ideals, and implicit in our argument is the possibility that the civic register of virtue is unlikely to be wholly dominant in any situation, in Africa or elsewhere. Instead, a much more complex reality emerges in which multiple actors feel the pull of both registers of virtue. Successive transfers of power may increase confidence in elections – but it does not make the electorate believe absolutely in the impartiality of state institutions (Chapters 3 and 7). Despite this, the suspension of disbelief, as contingent and partial as it may be, makes the work of observers, officials and civil society groups considerably easier and encourages public support for a wider democratic project that fore-grounds civic virtue. In this sense, our findings provide support for one of the key assumptions of the electoral fallacy literature, namely the import-ance of transfers of power to the fostering of a wide range of democratic norms and values.

It is important to note, however, that even when power has changed hands on numerous occasions, as in Ghana, we do not see the straightfor-ward replacement of patrimonial beliefs and behaviours with civic ones. Alternance encourages participation in electoral processes and acceptance of outcomes and thus reduces the stakes of political competition. But it can also provide a shot in the arm for patrimonial claims-making between leaders and their supporters. This is because the uncertainty of electoral outcomes encourages a wider set of individuals to believe that it is possible that their representatives will secure access to state resources. As a result, the contingent acceptance of institutions can go hand in hand with height-ened competition and the intensification of the distribution of largesse and development projects in return for political support, especially in areas that have previously been locked out of power. This suggests two important lessons. First, that the relationship between the patrimonial and civic is not zero sum – rather, the strengthening of civic ideals in one area may strengthen patrimonial ideals in another. Second, patrimonial claims-making is not necessarily the death knell of democracy. While it is true that patrimonial behaviour can undermine the credibility of key institutions and foster corruption, claims-making in this register typically encourages individuals to participate in the political process through activities such as rally attendance and voting. On its own this does not make for democrats of course, but it does, over time, help to build popular expectations that leaders will be selected through elections. And this, in turn, helps to ensure that electoral politics – as imperfect as it often is – becomes part and parcel of the fabric of political life. In such contexts, removing patrimonial logics could simply result in popular disengagement from political processes.

By way of conclusion, this chapter first considers how generalizable our argument is likely to be. Following this, we end with a discussion of the implications of our findings for those working within and beyond the academy. In particular, we call for a stronger academic and policy focus on the impact that elections have on voters' relationships to one another and to the state; a keener awareness of the limitations of election observa-tion and civic education as they are currently constituted; and, a greater appreciation of the potential for patrimonial values to generate engagement with, and to an extent strengthen support for, democratic processes.

C.1   The Reach of the Moral Economy of Elections

How broadly does the understanding of the moral economy of elections presented here apply? Our findings are based on three Anglophone African cases that are not representative of the whole continent. It is perfectly plausible that a similar investigation would come to different conclusions if it focussed on Francophone or Lusophone states, with their particular colonial legacy or countries with a longer experience with democracy – such as Senegal – or a shorter one, such as South Sudan. Even greater differences are likely if we move to states with very different histories and institutional frameworks. But this is not to say that we would expect to find elections taking place outside of a moral economy. Election campaigns, with their focus on candidates and the responsibilities of office holders and voters, are intimately bound up with contested ideas of virtue and what constitutes good leadership. In other words, a moral economy operates around all elections in all countries, just as it does around wider public debates about the conduct of those in office and national policy priorities.

Instead, the question is how the moral economy manifests itself: what registers of virtue are prominent, how they are expressed and what balance exists between them. Our identification of the patrimonial and civic register evolved out of years of engaging in and listening to conversations about politics in East and West Africa, and we are deeply aware of the historical roots of these processes, though our sense is that the most significant of those roots lies in colonial and postcolonial soil. Different historical experiences are likely to bring to the fore different moral economies.

The very nature of elections, with their focus on 'one person, one vote' and the disciplinary power of the polling station, means that we would expect the civic register to be present wherever meaningful contests are held. By contrast, we have shown that the particular form that the patrimonial register takes, and its relative significance, is not set in stone but instead varies across our three cases and over time as a result of socio-economic factors, the structure of political institutions, historical experiences and the decisions taken by political leaders at key moments. Moving beyond our three cases further variation is likely, both in terms of the number and nature of registers that animate the moral economy of elections and their relative import.

Aspects of the patrimonial register are likely to be found in almost all political systems, in terms of the expectations placed on individuals on the basis of kin and community and the added responsibilities that leaders may be put under due to their identity. Although it is rarely discussed in these terms, pronounced racial voting patterns in the United States (Greenwald et al. 2009), the presence of regional parties in Italy and the United Kingdom (Bull and Gilbert 2001; Bohrer and Krutz 2005), the existence of separatist movements in Spain (Muro 2005), and so on, all suggest the existence of patrimonial considerations. How the patrimonial register plays out in these cases is likely to be very different, however, for a number of reasons. To return to the four factors identified earlier, in some established democracies greater trust in the politcal system, the existence of institutions that bridge communal divides and processes of economic development that have ensured citizens' basic needs have combined to reduce the propensity towards winner-takes-all politics and the importance of personal patronage. Along with the more effective enforcement of rules against electoral bribery and treating, this appears to have rendered the patrimonial register weaker than in our three cases (for a longer discussion of vote buying see Mares and Young 2016) and means that there is less of an emphasis on individual leaders personally delivering resources to constituents.

In addition to variation in the form and weight of the patrimonial register, it seems likely that additional registers will hold sway in different countries due to varying processes of state formation and socio-economic development, the most obvious candidates being class solidarity (Evans 2000), and religious belief systems with distinctive attitudes to state–society relations, such as Salafism (Anjum 2016). Indeed, there is some evidence that these registers are also at play in some other African states, with Salafist beliefs challenging the civic register in parts of the Sahel (Elischer 2019), and a history of trade union activity supporting a range of class-based and populist appeals in Southern Africa (Cheeseman and Larmer 2015).

Other factors beyond the scope of this study are also likely to play a role in shaping the moral economy of elections. As noted in the Introduction, the intensity of patrimonial claims-making is also likely to be influenced by the structure of the electoral system. Our three cases operate first-past-the-post electoral systems that place a considerable emphasis on constituency-level political processes. While the presidential election remains the most important contest, and the focus of the most pronounced winner-takes-all dynamics, many of the relationships that we have described are between individuals and their MPs – or councillors, senators, governors and so on. As Dan Paget (2019a) has argued in the case of Tanzania, the need to contest constituency-based elections is an important driver of party and candidate activity and may lead to the holding of more campaign events – such as rallies – at which patrimonial claims are made. It is therefore plausible that the kind of patrimonial claims-making described in Chapter 6 operates in a very different way in countries that employ systems of proportional representation in which voters are elected from a party list, such as Namibia and South Africa (Barkan 1995), or are highly authoritarian, such as Rwanda (Reyntjens 2011) – and may feature very different dynamics where both factors come into play (Stroh 2010).

The quality of democracy is also likely to shape the intensity of claims-making. While we purposefully chose our cases to vary in terms of both historical experience and respect for political rights and civil liberties, none of them falls into the 'closed' authoritarian category in which political change is least likely (Roessler and Howard 2010). Even in the heavily controlled Ugandan political system, opposition parties have won up to 40 per cent of the official vote in national elections, making politics generally competitive in a way that it is not in, say, Cameroon. This no doubt infuses the moral economy of elections with an energy that would be much less apparent if every candidate at all levels was repeatedly returned unopposed.

Thus, while we argue that the moral economy of elections is at play everywhere, the content of that moral economy needs to be empirically deduced rather than assumed. It is beyond the scope of this book to investigate additional registers and the different kinds of moral claims-making that occur as part of the moral economy of elections in different parts of the world. Undertaking such a project is complicated by the lack of relevant data on these issues and the dearth of literature that has sought to understand elections from this perspective. Our thinking about the moral economy of elections evolved through 300 interviews, three nationally representative surveys, thousands of pages of archival work and a series of laboratory games. The same set of complementary data does not exist for any other country. Our hope is that this book may inspire others to take up this challenge of collecting the necessary evidence to document the moral economy of elections in other parts of the world and, in so doing, reveal how common, or rare, the particular manifestation is that we have identified.

What is possible in the space available is to demonstrate that the two registers we have identified, and the tension between them, can be discerned in the secondary literature on some other countries that share similar political and economic contexts. It therefore seems likely that our focus on the interaction between the civic and patrimonial register is relevant beyond our three cases. For example, research conducted on other countries in Africa by scholars using the Afrobarometer survey data find evidence of similar public attitudes and tensions to those that we discuss in Chapter 7. People's judgements on electoral virtue do not fit simply with either patrimonial or civic registers but suggest a tension between the two. For example, Michael Bratton's (2008) analysis of an Afrobarometer survey conducted ahead of Nigeria's 2007 election found that 79 per cent of respondents said that political violence was 'never justified' (Bratton 2008: 3). By contrast, only 58 per cent agreed with the proposition that efforts by politicians to 'purchase support at the polls' were 'wrong and punishable'. This differentiation between violence and ballot-box stuffing, which are widely condemned, and handing out money for votes, which is much more likely to be accepted, matches the pattern we describe in Chapter 7. The Afrobarometer survey did not include a question that placed gifting in a wider context of community service, as ours did, and so it is not possible to compare public attitudes on this more contextual understanding of financial exchanges. However, Bratton does find that popular attitudes were more tolerant of voters taking money – with only 49 per cent saying this was 'wrong and punishable' – than of politicians giving it. This implies that Nigerians also recognize that what matters is not so much receiving money, which can be legitimate in the context of an ongoing relationship with an authentic community leader, but whether or not an individual actually changes their vote on the basis of taking a 'bribe'.

This interpretation is supported by the fact that, when asked to imagine how they would respond to a handout from a hypothetical candidate, only 8 per cent of Nigerians said that they would accept the money and vote for the candidate. Far more respondents (42 per cent) said they would accept but vote for another candidate. This is further evidence that efforts to sway the electorate using money are only likely to be successful if the candidate already enjoys moral authority. Just as importantly – given our argument, following Kramon (2017) and others, that handouts are so prevalent because they help to signal virtue rather than simply buy votes – 41 per cent said that they would not refuse the money. Even more strikingly, only 24 per cent said that they thought other voters would refuse money if it was offered. This is significant, because we know that, when it comes to sensitive questions about activities that break official rules, individuals often mask their own behaviour and opinions, and so answers about how they think others behave may actually serve as a more reliable guide. Clearly, Nigerian voters think in moral terms about elections – what behaviours are right, what it means to be a good leader and a good citizen. As in Kenya, Ghana and Uganda, this may not stop them accepting handouts from politicians, but it does mean that their votes cannot be simply 'bought' (Bratton 2008: 13). Indeed, when viewed as 'immoral', money may have a detrimental impact on a candidate's chances. In this vein, Kristen Kao, Ellen Lust and Lise Rakner have found that handouts have a negative effect on the likelihood that poor Malawians will support a candidate. They argue that this is because the 'poor see the handouts as an attempt to buy their support in the short-term in order to exploit them in the future, while wealthier citizens see handouts as a token of appreciation for their time' (2020: 31).

There are multiple tensions in play here. Voters think in terms of civic virtue, as well as patrimonial virtue, and patrimonialism cannot simply be reduced to material clientelism. Daniel Young's study of Afrobarometer data on Kenya and Zambia provides further evidence for both points, concluding that, while the offering of gifts is widespread, it 'does not determine voting behaviour, at least in terms of support for an MP's re-election bid' (2009: iv). More important is whether an MP meets local expectations in terms of listening to and being present for the community (2009: 8). In this sense, electoral clientelism is constrained by the moral economy in two ways; voters may seek to uphold the civic register and reject vote buying, or they may feel that the exchange of money did not confer an obligation on them because it failed to imply good leadership within the patrimonial register.

Scholarship on Francophone Africa also suggests the significance of the tensions we have described. The seminal work of Richard Banégas on Benin, which has much influenced our argument, argues that multiparty elections from the 1990s have provided a focus for novel forms of material distribution and exchange, shifting political dynamics and enabling a new kind of political accountability:

[C]lientelist redistribution may appear as civic virtue, a manifestation of accountability, and so constitutes as such a paradoxical means of learning, and experimenting with, the rules of pluralism. (Banégas 1998: 87; our translation)

Revisiting the theme in 2014, as President Yayi Boni displayed increasingly authoritarian behaviours, Banégas suggested both that the consequent popular commitment to elections was strong enough to endure such efforts and that electoral experience had disciplined voters into an 'economy of patience', which channelled political action into the moment of the ballot (Banégas 2014a: 115). The results of the 2016 election – when Yayi Boni's chosen successor lost the presidential election – vindicated this judgement. At the same time, however, Banégas offered a reminder of the inherent limitations of the 'highly corrupt model of "collusive transactions"' (Banégas 2014b: 458) that enabled this accountability: picking up on Bayart's use of Gramsci (and echoing Abrahamsen 1997), he has characterized the politics that emerged in the 1990s as a 'passive revolution', managed from above, that ultimately maintained an existing social order (Banégas 2014a: 100, 116). In Benin it seems, as in Ghana, repeated elections and frequent transfers of power have become the norm. But this has not led to a reduction in the intensity of patrimonial claims placed on political candidates, and the cost of parliamentary campaigning gives a clear advantage to wealthy candidates (Koter 2017). If anything, the intensity of competition and possibility of change re-energized a patrimonial register that had been held in check under the one-party state.

Cameroon has also seen a re-energization of patrimonial politics alongside the elaboration of bureaucratic electoral forms, but here without any consequent alternations of power, and perhaps with diminishing returns in terms of popular participation. Forced into a return to multi-partyism in 1992, President Paul Biya has established a reputation as an electoral authoritarian rivalling that of Museveni, winning multiparty elections repeatedly amidst multiple allegations of fraud and establishing a 'seigneurial' state that rewards loyalty – and punishes support for the opposition – through the skewed allocation of state resources (Sindjoun 1997: 109; Takougang 2003). Elections in Cameroon may be dismissed as no more than a shared fantasy, persisting only because of their utility to powerful national and international actors (Pommerolle 2016), but they are not irrelevant. On the contrary, multi-partyism has 'channelled' political change (Menthong 1998: 41) and ensured substantial continuity in terms of who actually holds power. Antoine Socpa (2000) argued that this has entailed widespread electoral 'gift giving', in which the distribution of material largesse has become the essential counterpart to a politics of promise. He presents this as a politics of commands ('drink, eat, and vote for our party') and counter-commands ('take it, eat and drink, because this is your money! But don't vote for them!') (Socpa 2000: 92).

As Socpa's depiction implies, there is an element of moral argument here – and also an element of popular demand, directed at candidates for the ruling party in particular: 'You speak well – but can we eat your words?' (Socpa 2000: 98). Socpa, however, sees this as 'anti-democratic' and not as a form of accountability. He suggests that it has driven an increasingly ethno-regional politics and the notorious weakness of Cameroon's opposition parties, since aspiring politicians need money to campaign and so are readily vulnerable to being bought off: '[p]oliticians ruin the state, and ruin themselves' (Socpa 2000: 104). Biya's regime may sustain itself partly by displays of patrimonial virtue, but it relies also on fear and intimidation (Pommerolle 2008). While some of the population reportedly view him as a legitimate ruler (Letsa 2017: 675), participation in the 2016 elections was very low.

As the case of Cameroon demonstrates, the moral economy of elections works in very different ways in different places. Frederick Schaffer's (2005) account of the Philippines, for example, has a number of similarities to our own but also reveals important variations. He too document the way in which voters seek out candidates that they perceive to be caring and helpful (see Chapter 7) and finds that anti-vote-buying campaigns in the Philippines, Thailand and Taiwan typically have little impact (2005: 5–6; see Chapter 4). However, where we document the centrality of a form of communality in Ghana, Kenya and Uganda that often revolves around ethnic or regional identities, Schaffer pays more attention to class, noting that it is 'a key category for this analysis' and that 'class distinctions are important and real to most Filipinos' (2005: 9–10). Socio-economic status is of course also relevant in our cases, and like Schaffer we witnessed the patronizing disdain that the wealthy sometimes have for the poor, who are often seen to accept bribes out of ignorance (2005: 11). But class distinctions are not as clearly drawn and do not dominate the moral economy of elections in our three countries to the extent that it makes sense to speak of a 'politics of dignity' (2005: 11) as Schaffer does. Moreover, we find that individuals from all social backgrounds invest in the patrimonial register, if not always in equal measure (Chapter 7). Schaffer's account of the Philippines therefore provides further evidence of the value of thinking with the moral economy, but also of the need to understand how it operates on a case-by-case basis.

This short discussion reveals that the detail of our findings cannot simply be generalized across Africa or beyond it. But it also suggests that understanding elections in terms of claims-making by politicians and voters who live across different notions of virtue may help us to understand the vigour, unpredictability and sheer political productiveness of the electoral form across markedly different contexts.

C.2   The Broader Implications of the Moral Economy of Elections

Approaching elections in terms of a moral economy – in which the making of claims to virtue shapes people's ideas of political possibilities and proper behaviour – suggests that we need to pay greater attention to the complexity of political subjectivities. A rich and persuasive set of articles and books considers the importance of ethnicity for vote choice (Posner 2007; Bratton and Kimenyi 2008), whether or not elections meet international standards (Kelley 2009), and what the relationship is between political competition and conflict (Basedau et al. 2007; Branch and Cheeseman 2009). Insightful studies have demonstrated the capacity of elections to generate a spike in ethnic identification (Eifert, Miguel and Posner 2010) or the way that transfers of power shape popular support for democracy (Bratton 2004). Yet the assumption is often that voters – and politicians and officials – inhabit a singular moral world, accepting a particular set of behaviours as right. The moral economy approach suggests that people live between and across registers of virtue – that there are many ways to be good.

For instance, our analysis provides further evidence for the idea that in Ghana repeated transfers of power have helped to make electoral participation and the acceptance of electoral outcomes seem virtuous: it is widely accepted that it is good to vote and right to respect the results. But this 'democratization by elections' (Lindberg 2006) has its limits, even in this more successful case: most notably, it is associated with persistent patrimonial politics. Ethnicity, localism, personal ties and of a set of loyalties that rest on a sense of sub-national community are still powerful. In Kenya and Uganda, where elections have been more problematic but nonetheless sit comfortably above the threshold identified by van Ham and Lindberg (2018) as necessary for them to have democratizing effects, the story is more complicated still. Contested and controversial elections appear to do relatively little to encourage broader confidence in, or commitment to, the rules of the democratic game. They may, however, sustain mass political engagement in important ways, and the continued enthusiasm of popular participation challenges the idea that all good things go together. A lively electoral politics can be sustained by a tension between civic and patrimonial behaviours: people can understand themselves as citizens, but also as Baganda, Asante or Luo; they can feel a strong moral obligations to family and neighbours as well as to the nation within the political arena.

Our findings also have significant implications beyond the academy. Chapters 3 to 5 demonstrated that there is an inherent limitation to the capacity of election observers, officials and civil society organizations to encourage greater adherence to civic registers of virtue. In addition to the obvious logistical challenge of communicating effectively with millions of citizens, these organizations face a deeper challenge: despite their claims to neutrality, they are often viewed as being deeply enmeshed in partisan or patrimonial politics by voters. This is not just because observers or civil society groups have made mistakes in the past or demonstrated bias in this or that election. If this were the problem, it would be relatively easy to remedy through a process of lesson learning and a greater commitment to operating consistently. Instead the issue is more profound: civil society leaders and officials are known to have patrimonial ties because they operate in contexts in which it would be almost unfeasible for them not to. Extricating themselves from these ties and expectations would require an unprecedented level of social alienation – and even then, it might not be possible to persuade voters that they had done so or that voters should follow suit.

International observers who are not members of ethnic groups and do not have relatives or kin engaged in political activities face a different problem. The issue in this case is not the challenge of demonstrating neutrality when one is socially embedded, but rather the election observers' dilemma. Operating conservatively and not condemning the vast majority of elections enable observers to continue to operate in countries in which they might otherwise be excluded and hence to play a role in promoting iterative reform. It also, however, undermines their credibility in the eyes of opposition supporters. Yet moving in the other direction, applying higher standards and rejecting a greater number of outcomes risks further undermining popular confidence in democratic institutions by confirming their fragility. It also has the potential to further weaken confidence in observation itself, because every election that observers condemn demonstrates that their presence is not sufficient to deter rigging. Observers are therefore stuck between a rock and a hard place: whichever option they take, they may undermine the foundations of their own authority. Moreover, the one thing that changes this situation – a transfer of power that encourages greater acceptance of electoral outcomes more generally – is beyond observers' control.

This does not mean that international donors, observers, officials and civil society groups should give up on their work. But it does suggest the need for a much more realistic appraisal of what can be achieved through these methods. At a more granular level, we have argued that some of the ways that voter education programmes are designed should be rethought. The basic assumption that voters are innocent figures led astray by manipulative leaders is a gross oversimplification and leads to the unhelpful conclusion that educating citizens about the rules will change their behaviour. Instead, we need to better appreciate the ways in which patrimonial registers, and the kinds of electoral manipulation that they encourage, are co-produced. It will also be counter-productive to simply tell voters that accepting money from candidates is morally wrong. In the vast majority of cases, they are already aware that this is true within the civic register, but also understand that it is not only acceptable but legitimate and, in many cases, required within the patrimonial register. Civic education drives are therefore more likely to be successful if they work on the basis of a combination of patrimonial and civic claims – for example, voters may be much more responsive to a message that they may take money from candidates but should always vote for the individual that they think will do the best job than an argument that suggests they should never take money at all.

Some would argue that the ultimate aim of international and domestic electoral support programmes should be to eradicate patrimonialism, rather than to authorize it: elections are, after all, 'national exercises'. This is an understandable position, but our research has also counselled against the idea that undermining patrimonial claims would be a straightforward victory for democracy. This might inspire confidence in the impartiality and efficiency of institutions seen as key to democracy – the electoral management body, the courts, the civil service as a whole. But as Almond and Verba (1963) recognised over fifty years ago, it would likely also weaken the affective ties that bind many voters to political systems, while also reducing people's sense of the moral accountability of their politicians and engender political apathy. Patrimonial ideals may exist in tension with civic ones, but it is also true that the affective power of claims to reciprocity, communality and preference is an important source of popular engagement with formal political processes. If democracy is understood as responsible, accountable government that serves the aspirations and needs of its people – that is, by what it does, rather than through reference to a specific model – then the evidence from Ghana, Kenya and Uganda suggests that it might best be pursued not by simply eradicating patrimonialism, but rather by channelling it in ways that build on its affective power while constraining its more divisive and corrupting potential.

Appendix 1: Research Methods

The research supporting this book mainly involved archive work, interviews and nationally representative surveys. This appendix provides a brief description of how this research was conducted. For more details, in particular on the surveys and lab games, please go to www.cambridge.org/moraleconomy.

A1.1 Archives

There are significant limits to the archival record, for the preservation and accessibility of government records have been uneven: broadly, the national archival record is better for Kenya than for Uganda or Ghana, but in all cases it is very sparse indeed for the period after the mid-1970s. That record is supplemented, however, by local archive collections in Uganda, which offer a fascinating window on to the bureaucratic world that local election officials sought to make. It is also complemented to some extent by diplomatic archives in the United Kingdom and United States, which offer occasional insights into high politics up to the 1970s, and more effectively by other sources: national newspapers including online records and national archives, and in some cases party newspapers (though we found only sporadic examples of these); and the records of radio and television broadcasts available through monitoring services, which are rich for some periods. Locally recruited research assistants helped us to go through major national newspapers in all three countries around the time of elections from independence to the time of writing. 'Grey' literature – the publications of international observers, non-governmental organizations and of electoral management bodies – offered a further substantial source of material on more recent events, very different in their nature to the early archival records, but nonetheless deeply revealing of the assumptions and habits of mind of those involved in elections.

A1.2   Interviews and Field Notes

Informal observations and discussions were recorded in field diaries; these remain confidential, since they often record opinions that were offered in confidence. The formal interviews followed no single-set script; mostly, they combined personal histories with discussions of attitudes and were intended to explore the links between electoral experience and political subjectivity. Interviewees included candidates, activists, party officials, election workers and individuals active in civil society organizations. The overwhelming majority of interviews were conducted in English, and at least one of the authors was present at every interview, as the main interviewer, unless otherwise indicated in the footnote. In this – as in other aspects of the work – we were very aware of our positionality as researchers, in terms of the assumptions that both we and those with whom we talked brought to our conversations. As white researchers from Europe, we were very likely to be understood as advocates of a particular idea of electoral virtue; as academics we embodied ideas about the advantages of education. We could not dispel such assumptions; nowhere could we claim that we were anything other than outsiders, evidently part of an international gaze that expects and encourages certain kinds of behaviour and deplores others. Our only remedy for that problem was our attentiveness to multiple sources, historical and contemporary.

Most interviews were recorded and transcribed; interviewees were provided with an information sheet explaining the project and were asked to give formal consent to interview and to the audio recording and public deposit of interview material. In a number of cases – especially in Kenya and Uganda – interviewees declined recording and/or public deposit. As researchers, we felt concerned that in some cases consent had been given even though it appeared that material was sensitive. References to interview material in this book have therefore been anonymized according to a simple code: KEN1 being the first interviewee in Kenya; KEN1a being the first interview with that person; in a small number of cases we have withheld details entirely from references. In cases where consent was given and where we were confident that the material did not expose the interviewee or others to risk, we have deposited transcripts in the ESRC data archive, identified by the code explained earlier.

A1.3   Surveys

Three nationally representative surveys were conducted, one in each country. While some questions were borrowed from the Afrobarometer in order to enable comparability with existing data sets, most were written originally for this project. In general, the same questions were asked in each country, although due to the specific history of the three states some questions about past experience and events were tailored to the individual case. The surveys were implemented in conjunction with a local public opinion company that could provide a team of enumerators with the necessary language skills and local knowledge so that each respondent could be interviewed in the language of their choice. In each case, the research team visited the relevant country to conduct focus groups on key questions in order to ensure that the appropriate language was used in order to inspire the correct meaning. Surveys were translated into the main languages in each country, and the quality of translations was checked by the research team through back translation using independent individuals who had not been involved in the initial translation exercise.

The training of survey enumerators was supervised by Cheeseman, who has past experience of conducting surveys in Nigeria. Interviews were conducted in households, with the respondent and household selected randomly in order to give all members of the population an equal and known chance of participating. Each survey included two components: first, a nationally representative sample of at least 1,200 people; second, an oversample of at least 250 people in each of the three constituencies selected for fieldwork. This was designed to enable us to both talk about the national picture and to gain an insight into public opinion in our main interview sites.

In each case, the survey sample was stratified using the national census sampling frame in order to ensure a representative distribution on key variables such as rural/urban and region/ethnicity. Starting points were selected at random, with one supervisor managing four enumerators and ensuring that they followed the walk and randomization protocol. The researchers remained on the ground to oversee the start of the survey in each country in order to identify and correct any mistakes or confusion that had not been corrected during training. Particular attention was paid to the importance of not overlooking poorer households by only considering formal houses and large roads when walking from the selected starting point. In contrast with some surveys such as the Afrobarometer, enumerators were not asked to alternate respondents male/female in order to ensure gender parity. This is because there may not be gender parity in some urban and rural settings, and we made the decision to reflect each locality as accurately as possible.

Survey responses were entered directly into a tablet to minimize transcription errors and enable geo-coding. The data was checked carefully for errors and patterns that might suggest enumerator error or that questions had not been understood as intended. Where national averages are provided, this is based on the nationally representative sample. All survey data will be made available to other researchers at the end of the project, via the ESRC data archive and Professor Cheeseman's website, www.democracyinafrica.org.

Bibliography

Aapengnuo, Clement Mweyang (2010) 'Misinterpreting ethnic conflicts in Africa', *Africa Center for Strategic Studies*, Security Brief no. 4, https://africacen ter.org/publication/misinterpreting-ethnic-conflicts-in-africa.

Abdulai, Abdul-Gafaru and Gordon Crawford (2010) 'Consolidating democracy in Ghana: Progress and prospects?', *Democratization*, 17, no. 1: 26–67.

Abdulai, Abdul-Gafaru and Sam Hickey (2016) 'The politics of development under competitive clientelism: insights from Ghana's education sector', *African Affairs*, 115, no. 458: 44–72.

Abrahamsen, Rita (1997) 'The victory of popular forces or passive revolution? A neo-Gramscian perspective on democratisation', *The Journal of Modern African Studies*, 35, no. 1: 129–152.

Abrahamsen, Rita (2000) *Disciplining Democracy: Development Discourse and Good Governance in Africa*. London: Zed Books.

Abrahamsen, Rita and Gerald Bareebe (2016) 'Briefing: Uganda's 2016 elections: not even faking it any more', *African Affairs*, 115, no. 461: 751–765.

Abrams, Philip (1988) 'Notes on the difficulty of studying the state (1977)', *Journal of Historical Sociology*, 1, no. 1: 58–89.

Adebanwi, Wale and Ebenezer Obadare (2011) 'The abrogation of the electorate: an emergent African phenomenon', *Democratization*, 18, no.2: 311–335.

Adedeji, Adebayo (1994) 'An alternative for Africa', *Journal of Democracy*, 5, no.4: 119–132.

Adejumobi, Said (2000) 'Elections in Africa: a fading shadow of democracy?' *International Political Science Review*, 21, no. 1: 59–73.

Afram, Alexander and Kafui Tsekpo (2017) 'Missing numbers in Ghana's election 2016: low turnout or a bloated register?', *Pambazuka News*, www.pambazuka.org/author/alexander-afram-and-kafui-tsekpo.

Agnew, John and J. Nicholas Entrikin (eds.) (2004) *The Marshall Plan Today: Model and Metaphor*. Abingdon: Routledge.

Agyeman-Duah, Baffour (1987) 'Ghana, 1982–6: the politics of the PNDC', *The Journal of Modern African Studies*, 25, no. 4: 613–642.

Ake, Claude (1991) 'Rethinking African democracy', *Journal of Democracy*, 2, no. 1: 32–44.

Ake, Claude (1993) 'The unique case of African democracy', *International Affairs*, 69, no.2: 239–244.

Alava, Henni and Jimmy Spire Ssentongo (2016) 'Religious (de)politicisation in Uganda's 2016 elections', *Journal of Eastern African Studies*, 10, no.4: 677–692.

Allen, Chris (1997) 'Who needs civil society?' *Review of African Political Economy*, 24, no. 73: 329–337.

Allen, Tim (1991) 'Understanding Alice: Uganda's holy spirit movement in context', *Africa: Journal of the International African Institute*, 61, no. 3: 370–399.

Allen, Tim and Koen Vlassenroot (2010) *The Lord's Resistance Army: Myth and Reality*. London: Zed Books.

Allman, Jean (1990) 'The youngmen and the porcupine: Class, nationalism and Asante's struggle for self-determination, 1954–57', *The Journal of African History*, 31, no.2: 263–279.

Almond, Gabriel and Sidney Verba (1963) *The Civic Culture: Political Attitudes and Democracy in Five Nations*. Princeton, NJ: Princeton University Press.

Anderson, David M. (2003) 'Briefing: Kenya's elections 2002: The dawning of a new era?' *African Affairs*, 102, no. 407: 331–342.

Anderson, David M. (2005) '"Yours in struggle for Majimbo". Nationalism and the party politics of decolonization in Kenya, 1955–64', *Journal of Contemporary History*, 40, no.3: 547–564.

Anebo, Felix K. G. (2001) 'The Ghana 2000 elections: voter choice and electoral decisions', *African Journal of Political Science/Revue Africaine de Science Politique*, 6, no. 1: 69–88.

Anglin, Douglas (1998) 'International election monitoring: the African experience', *African Affairs*, 97, no. 389: 471–495.

Anjum, Ovamir (2016) 'Salafis and democracy: doctrine and context', *The Muslim World*, 106, no. 3: 448–473.

Anyang' Nyong'o, Peter (1983) 'Struggles for political power and class contradictions in Kenya', *Contemporary Marxism*, no. 7: 154–168. www.jstor.org/stable/i29765739.

Anyang' Nyong'o, Peter (1988) 'Political instability and the prospects for democracy in Africa', *Africa Development/Afrique et Développement*, 13, no. 1: 71–86.

Appiah-Agyekum, N. N., N. Y. Boachie Danquah and E. K. Sakyi (2013) 'Local government finance in Ghana: disbursement and utilisation of the MPs share of the District Assemblies Common Fund', *Commonwealth Journal of Local Governance*, 12, May: 90–109.

Apter, David (1955) *The Gold Coast in Transition*. Princeton, NJ: Princeton University Press.

Apter, David (1968) 'Ghana'. In James Coleman and Carl Rosberg (eds.), *Political Parties and National Integration in Tropical Africa*. Berkeley and Los Angeles: University of California Press: 259–315.

Apter, David (2013) *The Political Kingdom in Uganda. A Study in Bureaucratic Nationalism*. London: Routledge (first edition 1961).

Arhin, Kwame (1983) 'Rank and class among the Asante and Fante in the nineteenth century', *Africa*, 53, no. 1: 2–22.

Arnold, Thomas Clay (2001) 'Rethinking moral economy', *American Political Science Review*, 95, no. 1: 85–95.

Arriola, Leonardo R. (2013) *Multi-ethnic Coalitions in Africa: Business Financing of Opposition Election Campaigns*. Cambridge: Cambridge University Press.

Arthur, Peter (2010) 'Democratic consolidation in Ghana: The role and contribution of the media, civil society and state institutions', *Commonwealth and Comparative Politics*, 48, no. 2: 203–226.

Asunka, Joseph, Sarah Brierley, Miriam Golden, Eric Kramon and George Ofosu (2017) 'Electoral fraud or violence: the effect of observers on party manipulation strategies', *British Journal of Political Science*, 49, no. 1: 129–151.

Atieno Odhiambo, E. S. (1987) 'Democracy and the ideology of order in Kenya'. In Michael G. Schatzberg (ed.), *The Political Economy of Kenya*. Westport, CT: Praeger: 177–201.

Atieno Odhiambo, E. S. (2004) 'Hegemonic enterprises and instrumentalities of survival: Ethnicity and democracy in Africa'. In Bruce J. Berman, Dickson Eyoh and Will Kymlicka (eds.), *Ethnicity and Democracy in Africa*. Oxford: James Currey: 167–182.

Attwood, William (1967) *The Reds and the Blacks: A Personal Adventure*. New York: Harper & Row.

Aubyn, Festus. K. (2012) 'Election observation and democratic consolidation in Africa: the Ghanaian experience'. In Kwesi Aning and Kwaku Danso (eds.), *Managing Election-related Violence for Democratic Stability in Ghana*. Accra: Friedrich Ebert Stiftung: 240–275.

Aubynn, Anthony Kwesi (2002) 'Behind the transparent ballot box: The significance of the 1990s elections in Ghana'. In Michael Cowen and Liisa Laakso (eds.), *Multi-party Elections in Africa*. Oxford: James Currey: 75–103.

Austen, Ralph (1993) 'The moral economy of witchcraft, an essay in comparative history'. In Jean Comaroff and John L. Comaroff (eds.), *Modernity and its Malcontents: Ritual and Power in Postcolonial Africa*. Chicago: University of Chicago Press: 89–110.

Austin, Dennis (1970) *Politics in Ghana, 1946–60*. Oxford: Oxford University Press (first edition 1964).

Austin, Dennis (1976) 'The Convention People's Party in 1958'. In Dennis Austin (ed.), *Ghana Observed. Essays on the Politics of a West African Republic*. Manchester: Manchester University Press: 34–48.

Austin, Dennis and Robin Luckham (eds.) (1975) *Politicians and Soldiers in Ghana 1966–72*. London: Frank Cass.

Ayee, Joseph R. A. (2008) 'The evolution of the New Patriotic Party in Ghana', *South African Journal of International Affairs*, 15, no. 2: 185–214.

Ayee, Joseph R. A. (2011) 'Manifestos and elections in Ghana's Fourth Republic', *South African Journal of International Affairs*, 15, no.2: 185–214.

Ayee, Joseph R. A. (2017) 'Ghana's elections of 7 December 2016: a postmortem', *South African Journal of International Affairs*, 24, no.3: 311–330.

Ayelazuno, Jasper (2009) 'The politicisation of the Mirigu-Kandiga conflict in Ghana's 2008 elections: questioning the electoral peace paradigm', *Conflict Trends*, no. 2: 45–50.

Ayittey, George (2006) *Indigenous African Institutions*. Leiden: Brill.

Baamara, Layla, Camille Floderer and Marine Poirier (2016) 'Introduction: Conjuguer la campagne au pluriel'. In Layla Baamara, Camille Floderer and Marine Poirier (eds.), *Faire campagne, ici et ailleurs. Mobilisations électorales et pratiques politiques ordinaire*. Paris: Karthala: 7–24.

BakamaNume, Bakama (1997) 'An electoral geography of Uganda: From the gun to the ballot, a "politics of success" or legitimation?', *East African Geographical Review*, 19, no. 1: 44–56.

Baku, Kofi (1991) 'Kobina Sekyi of Ghana: An annotated bibliography of his writings', *The International Journal of African Historical Studies*, 24, no. 2: 369–381.

Banégas, Richard (1998) 'Marchandisation du vote, citoyenneté et consolidation democratique au Benin', *Politique Africaine*, 69: 75–88.

Banégas, Richard (2007) 'Commodification of the vote and political subjectivity in Africa: Reflections based on the case of Benin'. In Romain Bertrand, Jean-Louis Briquet and Peter Pels (eds.), *Cultures of Voting: The Hidden History of the Secret Ballot*. London: Hurst: 180–196.

Banégas, Richard (2014a) 'L'autoritarisme à pas de caméléon? Les derives de la revolution passive démocratique au Bénin', *Afrique Contemporaine*, 249: 99–118.

Banégas, Richard (2014b) 'Benin: Challenges for democracy', *African Affairs*, 113, no.452: 449–459.

Banerjee, Mukulika (2014) *Why India Votes?* New Delhi/London: Routledge.

Bang, Henrik (2005) 'Among everyday makers and expert citizens'. In Janet Newman (ed.), *Remaking Governance: People, Politics and the Public Sphere*. Bristol: Policy Press: 159–178.

Barkan, Joel D. (1976) 'Comment: Further reassessment of "conventional wisdom": Political knowledge and voting behavior in rural Kenya', *American Political Science Review*, 70, no. 2: 452–455.

Barkan, Joel D. (1979a) 'Bringing home the pork: Legislative behavior, rural development and political change in East Africa'. In J. Smith and L. D. Musolf (eds.), *Legislatures in Development: Dynamics of Change in New and Old States*. Durham, NC: Duke University Press: 265–288.

Barkan, Joel D. (1979b) 'Legislators, elections, and political linkage'. In Joel D. Barkan and John Okumu (eds.), *Politics and Public Policy in Kenya and Tanzania*. New York: Praeger: 64–92.

Barkan, Joel D. (1987) 'The electoral process and peasant-state relations in Kenya'. In Fred Hayward (ed.), *Elections in Independent Africa*. Boulder, CO: Westview: 213–237.

Barkan, Joel D. (1993) 'Kenya: Lessons from a flawed election', *Journal of Democracy*, 4, no. 3: 85–99.

Barkan, Joel D. (1995) 'Elections in agrarian societies', *Journal of Democracy*, 6, no. 4: 106–116.

Barkan, Joel D. (2008) 'Legislatures on the rise?' *Journal of Democracy*, 19, no. 2: 124–137.

Barkan, Joel D. (2013) 'Kenya's 2013 elections: Technology is not democracy', *Journal of Democracy*, 24, no.3: 156–165.

Barkan, Joel D. and Njuguna Ng'ethe (1998) 'Kenya tries again', *Journal of Democracy*, 9, no.2: 32–42.

Barkan, Joel D. and John J. Okumu (1978) '"Semi-competitive" elections, clientelism, and political recruitment in a no-party state: the Kenyan experience'. In

Guy Hermet, Richard Rose and Alain Rouquié (eds.), *Elections without Choice.* London: Palgrave Macmillan: 88–107.

Basedau, Matthias, Gero Erdmann and Andreas Mehler (2007) *Votes, Money and Violence: Political Parties and Elections in Sub-Saharan Africa.* Johannesburg: Nordiska Afrikainstitutet and Kwazulu-Natal Press.

Bauer, G. (2019) 'Ghana: Stalled patterns of women's parliamentary representation'. In Susan Franceschet, Mona Lena Krook and Netina Tan (eds.), *The Palgrave Handbook of Women's Political Rights.* London: Palgrave Macmillan: 607–625.

Bawa, Sylvia and Francis Sanyare (2013) 'Women's participation and representation in politics: perspectives from Ghana', *International Journal of Public Administration*, 36, no. 4: 282–291.

Bayart, Jean-François (1978) 'Clientelism, elections and systems of inequality and domination in Cameroun: A reconsideration of the notion of social and political control'. In Guy Hermet, Richard Rose and Alain Rouquié (eds.), *Elections without Choice.* London: Palgrave Macmillan: 66–87.

Bayart, Jean-François, F. Constantin, C. Coulon and D. Martin (1978) 'Par le canal du scrutin. Comment dépouiller les élections Africaines?'. In Dmitri Lavroff (ed.), *Aux Urnes l'Afrique! Élections et pouvoirs en Afrique noire.* Paris: Pedone: 1–24.

Bayart, Jean-François (1986) 'Civil society in Africa'. In Patrick Chabal (ed.), *Reflections on the Limits of Power.* Cambridge: Cambridge University Press: 109–125.

Bayart, Jean-François and Stephen Ellis (2000) 'Africa in the world: a history of extraversion', *African Affairs*, 99, no. 395: 217–267.

Beardsworth, Nicole (2016) 'Challenging dominance: the opposition, the coalition and the 2016 election in Uganda', *Journal of Eastern African Studies*, 10, no. 4: 749–768.

Beardsworth, Nicole, Nic Cheeseman and Simukai Tinhu (2019) 'Zimbabwe: the coup that never was, and the election that could have been', *African Affairs*, 118, no. 472: 580–596.

Beek, Jan (2016) *Producing Stateness: Police Work in Ghana.* Leiden: Brill.

Beller, Emily and Michael Hout (2006) 'Welfare states and social mobility. How educational and social policy may affect cross-national differences in the association between occupational origins and destinations', *Research in Social Stratification and Mobility*, 24, no. 4: 353–365.

Bennett, George (1953) 'The gold coast general election of 1954', *Parliamentary Affairs*, 7, no. 4: 430–439.

Bere, R.M. (1955) 'Land and chieftainship among the Acholi', *Uganda Journal*, 19, no. 1: 49–56.

Berg-Schlosser, Dirk (1982) 'Modes and meaning of political participation in Kenya', *Comparative Politics*, 14, no. 4: 397–415.

Berman, Bruce J. (1998) 'Ethnicity, patronage and the African state: the politics of uncivil nationalism', *African Affairs*, 97, no. 388: 305–341.

Berman, Bruce J., Jill Cottrell and Yash Ghai (2009) 'Patrons, clients, and constitutions: ethnic politics and political reform in Kenya', *Canadian Journal of African Studies/La Revue canadienne des études africaines*, 43, no. 3: 462–506.

Berman, Bruce J. and Stephen J. Larin (2016) 'Introduction: the moral economies of ethnic and nationalist claims'. In Bruce J. Berman, André Laliberté and Stephen J. Larin (eds.), *The Moral Economies of Ethnic and Nationalist Claims*. Vancouver: UBC Press: 3–22.

Berry, Sara (1998) 'Unsettled accounts: stool debts, chieftaincy disputes and the question of Asante constitutionalism', *The Journal of African History*, 39, no. 1: 39–62.

Bertrand, Romain, Jean-Louis Briquet and Peter Pels (2007) 'Introduction: towards a historical ethnography of voting'. In Romain Bertrand, Jean-Louis Briquet and Peter Pels (eds.), *Cultures of Voting. The Hidden History of the Secret Ballot*. London: Hurst: 1–15.

Bienen, Henry (1974) *Kenya: the Politics of Participation and Control*. Princeton, NJ: Princeton University Press.

Bierschenk, Thomas and Jean-Pierre Oliver de Sardan (2014) 'Studying the dynamics of African bureaucrats. An introduction to states at work'. In Thomas Bierschenk and Jean-Pierre Oliver de Sardan (eds.), *States at Work. Dynamics of African Bureaucracies*. Leiden: Brill: 3–32.

Bing, John (1974) 'Tribe and elections in Uganda', PhD thesis, Washington University.

Björkdahl, Annika (2002) 'Norms in international relations: some conceptual and methodological reflections', *Cambridge Review of International Affairs*, 15, no. 1: 9–23.

Blais, André (2000) *To Vote or not to Vote?: The Merits and Limits of Rational Choice Theory*. Pittsburgh: University of Pittsburgh Press.

Bland, Gary (2015) 'Measuring the quality of Kenya's March 2013 election', *Election Law Journal*, 14, no. 2: 136–147.

Boafo-Arthur, Kwame (1998) 'The international community and Ghana's transition to democracy'. In Kwame Ninsin (ed.), *Ghana: Transition to Democracy*, Nairobi: African Books Collective: 167–186.

Bob-Milliar, George (2012a) 'Party factions and power blocs in Ghana: a case study of power politics in the National Democratic Congress', *The Journal of Modern African Studies*, 50, no. 4: 573–601.

Bob-Milliar, George (2012b) 'Political party activism in Ghana: factors influencing the decision of the politically active to join a political party', *Democratization*, 19, no. 4: 668–689.

Bob-Milliar, George (2014) 'Party youth activists and low-intensity electoral violence in Ghana: a qualitative study of party foot soldiers' activism', *African Studies Quarterly*, 15, no. 1: 125–153.

Bob-Milliar, George M. and Jeffrey W. Paller (2018) 'Democratic ruptures and electoral outcomes in Africa: Ghana's 2016 election', *Africa Spectrum*, 53, no. 1: 5–35.

Bodewes, Christine (2010) 'Civil society and the consolidation of democracy in Kenya: an analysis of a Catholic parish's efforts in Kibera slum', *The Journal of Modern African Studies*, 48, no. 4: 547–571.

Bodewes, Christine (2014) *Civil Society in Africa: The Role of a Catholic Parish in a Kenyan slum*. Newcastle upon Tyne: Cambridge Scholars Publishing.

Bohrer, Robert E. and Glen S. Krutz (2005) 'The devolved party systems of the United Kingdom: sub-national variations from the national model', *Party Politics*, 11, no. 6: 654–673.

Bompani, Barbara (2016) '"For god and for my country": Pentecostal-charismatic churches and the framing of a new political discourse in Uganda'. In Adriaan Van Klinken and Ezra Chitando (eds.), *Public Religion and the Politics of Homosexuality in Africa*. Abingdon: Routledge: 19–34.

Boone, Catherine (1994) 'State and ruling classes in postcolonial Africa: the enduring contradictions of power'. In Joel Migdal, Atul Kohli and Vivienne Shue (eds.), *State Power and Social Forces: Domination and Transformation in the Third World*. Cambridge: Cambridge University Press: 108–140.

Boone, Catherine (2011) 'Politically allocated land rights and the geography of electoral violence: the case of Kenya in the 1990s', *Comparative Political Studies*, 44, no. 10: 1311–1342.

Booth, William James (1994) 'On the idea of the moral economy', *American Political Science Review*, 88, no. 3: 653–667.

Botchway, Thomas Prehi (2018) 'Civil society and the consolidation of democracy in Ghana's Fourth Republic', *Cogent Social Sciences*, 4, no. 1: 1–17.

Bouka, Yolande, Marie E. Berry and Marilyn Muthoni Kamuru (2019) 'Women's political inclusion in Kenya's devolved political system', *Journal of Eastern African Studies*, 13, no. 2: 313–333.

Branch, Daniel (2006) 'Loyalists, Mau Mau and elections in Kenya: the first triumph of the system, 1957–58', *Africa Today*, 53, no. 2: 27–50.

Branch, Daniel and Nic Cheeseman (2006) 'The politics of control in Kenya: understanding the bureaucratic-executive state, 1952–78', *Review of African Political Economy*, 33, no. 107: 11–31.

Branch, Daniel and Nic Cheeseman (2009) 'Democratization, sequencing, and state failure in Africa: lessons from Kenya', *African Affairs*, 108, no. 430: 1–26.

Brass, J. (2016) *Allies or Adversaries: NGOs and the State in Africa*. Cambridge: Cambridge University Press.

Brass, Jennifer, Wesley Longhofer, Rachel S. Robinson and Allison Schnable (2018) 'NGOs and international development: a review of thirty-five years of scholarship', *World Development*, 112: 136–149.

Bratton, Michael (2004) 'The "alternation effect" in Africa', *Journal of Democracy*, 15, no. 4: 147–158.

Bratton, Michael (2008) 'Vote buying and violence in Nigerian election campaigns', Afrobarometer Working Paper 99, Michigan: Afrobarometer, http://afrobarometer.org/sites/default/files/publications/Working%20papers/afropaperno99.pdf.

Bratton, Michael (2013a) 'Voting and democratic citizenship in Africa: where next?'. In Michael Bratton (ed.), *Voting and Democratic Citizenship in Africa*. Boulder, CO: Lynne Rienner: 277–287.

Bratton, Michael (2013b) 'Where do elections lead in Africa?'. In Michael Bratton (ed.), *Voting and Democratic Citizenship in Africa*. Boulder, CO: Lynne Rienner: 17–38.

Bratton, Michael and Philip Alderfer (1999) 'The effects of civic education on political culture: evidence from Zambia', *World Development*, 27, no. 5: 807–824.

Bratton, Michael and Mwangi S. Kimenyi (2008) 'Voting in Kenya: putting ethnicity in perspective', *Journal of Eastern African Studies*, 2, no. 2: 272–289.

Bratton, Michael and Gina Lambright (2001) 'Uganda's referendum 2000: the silent boycott?', *African Affairs*, 100, no. 400: 429–452.

Bratton, Michael and Carolyn Logan (2015) 'The viability of political opposition in Africa: popular views', Afrobarometer Policy Paper 26, https://afrobarom eter.org/sites/default/files/publications/Policy%20papers/ab_r6_policypa perno26.pdf.

Bratton, Michael, Robert Mattes and Emmanuel Gyimah-Boadi (2005) *Public Opinion, Democracy, and Market Reform in Africa*. Cambridge: Cambridge University Press.

Bratton, Michael and Nicholas Van de Walle (1997) *Democratic Experiments in Africa: Regime Transitions in Comparative Perspective*. Cambridge: Cambridge University Press.

Briggs, Ryan C. (2012) 'Electrifying the base? Aid and incumbent advantage in Ghana', *The Journal of Modern African Studies*, 50, no. 4: 603–624.

Brinkman, Inge (2019) 'Social diary and news production: authorship and read-ership in social media during Kenya's 2007 elections', *Journal of Eastern African Studies*, 13, no. 1: 72–89.

Brisset-Foucault, Florence (2013) 'Buganda royalism and political competition in Uganda's 2011 elections', *Journal of Eastern African Studies*, 7, no. 3: 509–529.

Brosché, Johan, Hanne Fjelde and Kristine Höglund (2019) 'Electoral violence and the legacy of authoritarian rule in Kenya and Zambia', *Journal of Peace Research*, 57, no. 1: 111–125.

Brown, Stephen (2001) 'Authoritarian leaders and multiparty elections in Africa: how foreign donors help to keep Kenya's Daniel arap Moi in power', *Third World Quarterly*, 22, no. 5: 725–739.

Brunk, Gregory (1980) 'The impact of rational participation models on voting attitudes', *Public Choice*, 35, no. 5: 549–564.

Bukuluki, Paul (2013) '"When I steal, it is for the benefit of me and you": is collectivism engendering corruption in Uganda?', *International Letters of Social and Humanistic Sciences*, no. 5: 27–44.

Bull, Anna Cento and Mark Gilbert (2001) *The Lega Nord and the Northern Question in Italian Politics*. New York: Palgrave.

Burbidge, Dominic (2014) '"Can someone get me outta this middle class zone?!" Pressures on middle class Kikuyu in Kenya's 2013 election', *The Journal of Modern African Studies*, 52, no. 2: 205–225.

Burnell, Peter (2009) 'New challenges to democratization'. In Peter Burnell and Richard Youngs (eds.), *New Challenges to Democratization*. Abingdon: Routledge: 13–34.

Bwengye, Francis (1985) *The Agony of Uganda*. London: Regency Press.

Byrd, Robert O. (1963) 'Characteristics of candidates for election in a country approaching independence: the case of Uganda', *Midwest Journal of Political Science*, 7, no. 1: 1–27.

Callaway, Barbara (1970) 'Local politics in Ho and Aba', *Canadian Journal of African Studies/La Revue canadienne des études africaines*, 4, no. 1: 121–144.

Carbone, Giovanni (2003) 'Political parties in a "no-party democracy". Hegemony and opposition under "movement democracy" in Uganda', *Party Politics*, 9, no. 4: 485–501.

Card, Emily and Barbara Callaway (1970) 'Ghanaian politics: the elections and after', *Africa Report*, 15, no. 3: 10–15.

Carlson, Elizabeth (2015) 'Ethnic voting and accountability in Africa: a choice experiment in Uganda', *World Politics*, 67, no. 2: 353–385.

Carothers, Thomas (1997) 'The observers observed', *Journal of Democracy*, 8, no. 3: 17–31.

Carothers, Thomas (2002) 'The end of the transition paradigm', *Journal of Democracy* 13, no. 1: 5–21.

Carter Centre (2016) *25 Years of Election Observation at The Carter Center: A Retrospective*. Atlanta, GA: Carter Center.

Carter Center (2017) *Kenya 2017 General and Presidential Elections*. Atlanta, GA: Carter Center.

Carter Center (2018) *Youth and women's consultations on political participation in Kenya: Findings and recommendations*. www.cartercenter.org/resources/pdfs/ne ws/peace_publications/democracy/kenya-youth-and-women-political-partici pation-report.pdf.

CCEDU [Citizen's Coalition for Electoral Democracy in Uganda] (2015) *Towards the 2016 General Elections: A Voter Mobilization Guide*. Kampala: CCEDU.

Centre for Governance and Development (2005) *You and your MP, Bunge Series June 2005*. Nairobi: Centre for Governance and Development.

CEON-U [Citizens Election Observers Network – Uganda] (2016) 'Uganda General Elections 2016: Revisiting The Democracy Construct', Kampala, CEON-U: www.ccedu.org.ug/index.php/publications/publications/reports/23 -ceon-report/file.

Chabal, Patrick and Jean-Pascal Daloz (1999) *Africa Works: Disorder as Political Instrument*. London: James Currey and IAI.

Chacha, Babere K. (2010) 'Pastors or bastards? The dynamics of religion and politics in the 2007 general elections in Kenya', In Karuti Kanyinga and Duncan Okello (eds.), *Tensions and Reversals in Democratic Transitions: The Kenya 2007 General Elections*. Nairobi: Society for International Development: 101–139.

Chambers, Simone and Jeffrey Kopstein (2001) 'Bad civil society', *Political Theory*, 29, no. 6: 837–865.

Chazan, Naomi (1987) 'The anomalies of continuity: perspectives on Ghanaian elections since independence'. In Fred Hayward (ed.), *Elections in Independent Africa*. Boulder, CO: Westview: 61–86.

Chazan, Naomi (1992) 'Ethnicity and politics in Ghana', *Political Science Quarterly*, 97, no. 3: 461–485.

Chazan, Naomi (1993) 'Between liberalism and statism: African political culture and democracy'. In Larry Diamond (ed.), *Political Culture and Democracy in Developing Countries*. Boulder, CO: Lynne Rienner: 67–106.

Chazan, Naomi and Victor T. Le Vine (1979) 'Politics in a "non-political" system: the March 30, 1978 referendum in Ghana', *African Studies Review*, 22, no. 1: 177–207.

Cheeseman, Nic (2008) 'The Kenyan elections of 2007: an introduction', *Journal of Eastern African Studies*, 2, no. 2: 166–184.

Cheeseman, Nic (2015a) *Democracy in Africa: Successes, Failures, and the Struggle for Political Reform*. Cambridge: Cambridge University Press.

Cheeseman, Nic (2015b) '"No bourgeoisie, no democracy"? The political attitudes of the Kenyan middle class', *Journal of International Development*, 27, no. 5: 647–664.

Cheeseman, Nic (2016) 'Patrons, parties, political linkage, and the birth of competitive authoritarianism in Africa', *African Studies Review*, 59, no. 3: 181–200.

Cheeseman, Nic (ed.) (2018a) *Institutions and Democracy in Africa. How the Rules of the Game Shape Political Developments*. Cambridge: Cambridge University Press.

Cheeseman, Nic (2018b) 'Introduction: understanding African politics: bringing the state back in'. In Nic Cheeseman (ed.), *Institutions and Democracy in Africa*. Cambridge: Cambridge University Press, 1–38.

Cheeseman, Nic, Jonathan Fisher, Jamie Hitchin and Idayat Hassan (2020) 'Social media disruption: Nigeria's WhatsApp politics', *Journal of Democracy*, 31, no. 3: 145–159.

Cheeseman, Nic, Karuti Kanyinga and Gabrielle Lynch (2020) 'The political economy of Kenya: community, clientelism, and class'. In Nic Cheeseman, Karuti Kanyinga and Gabrielle Lynch (eds.), *Oxford Handbook of Kenyan Politics*. Oxford: Oxford University Press: 1–25.

Cheeseman, Nic, Karuti Kanyinga, Gabrielle Lynch, Mutuma Ruteere and Justin Willis (2019) 'Kenya's 2017 elections: winner-takes-all politics as usual?', *Journal of Eastern African Studies*, 13, no. 2: 215–234.

Cheeseman, Nic and Brian Klaas (2018) *How to Rig an Election*. New Haven: Yale University Press.

Cheeseman, Nic and Miles Larmer (2015) 'Ethnopopulism in Africa: opposition mobilization in diverse and unequal societies', *Democratization*, 22, no. 1: 22–50.

Cheeseman, Nic, Gabrielle Lynch and Justin Willis (2014) 'Democracy and its discontents: understanding Kenya's 2013 elections', *Journal of Eastern African Studies*, 8, no. 1: 2–24.

Cheeseman, Nic, Gabrielle Lynch and Justin Willis (2016) 'The man who overstayed', *Foreign Policy*, https://foreignpolicy.com/2016/02/16/the-man-who-overstayed-uganda-museveni.

Cheeseman, Nic, Gabrielle Lynch and Justin Willis (2017a) 'Ghana: The ebbing power of incumbency', *Journal of Democracy*, 28, no. 2: 92–104.

Cheeseman, Nic, Gabrielle Lynch and Justin Willis (2017b) 'Were the Kenyan elections conducted successfully? What worked and what didn't', *Foreign*

Affairs, www.foreignaffairs.com/articles/africa/2017-08-15/were-kenyan-elections-conducted-successfully.

Cheeseman, Nic and Sishuwa Sishuwa (2020) 'Democracy', *African Studies Review*, in press.

Chege, Michael (1981) 'A tale of two slums: electoral politics in Mathare and Dagoretti', *Review of African Political Economy*, 8, no. 20: 74–88.

Chege, Michael (2008) 'Kenya: back from the brink?', *Journal of Democracy*, 19, no. 4: 125–139.

Chege, Michael (2020) 'The political economy of foreign aid to Kenya (1963-2015)'. In Nic Cheeseman, Karuti Kanyinga and Gabrielle Lynch (eds.), *The Oxford Handbook of Kenyan Politics*. Oxford: Oxford University Press.

Cilliers, Jacobus, Oeindrila Dube and Bilal Siddiqi (2015) 'The white-man effect: how foreigner presence affects behaviour in experiments', *Journal of Economic Behaviour & Organization*, 118: 397–414.

Chua, Amy (2003) *World on Fire: How Exporting Free Market Democracy Breeds Ethnic Hatred and Global Instability*. London: Heinemann.

CJPC [Catholic Justice and Peace Commission] (2016) *Peaceful and Prosperous Kenya... My Responsibility. Lenten Campaign 2016*. Nairobi: CJPC.

CJPC [Catholic Justice and Peace Commission] (2017) *Peaceful and Credible Elections: Leaders of Integrity. Lenten campaign 2017*. Nairobi: CJPC.

Cloward, Karisa (2019) 'Strange bedfellows: the personalisation of NGO-Government relations', unpublished working paper.

Cloward, Karisa and Keith Weghorst (2019) 'Career sequences and legislative candidacy in Kenya: the rise of the NGO aspirant', unpublished working paper.

Cohen, Andrew (1957) 'Uganda's progress and problems', *African Affairs*, 56, no. 223: 111–122.

Coleman, James S. (1960) 'The politics of sub-Saharan Africa'. In Gabriel Almond and James S. Coleman (eds.), *The Politics of the Developing Areas*. Princeton, NJ: Princeton University Press: 247–368.

Coles, Kimberley (2004) 'The construction of democracy through technique', *Cultural Anthropology*, 19, no. 4: 551–580.

Collier, Paul (2009) *Wars, Guns and Votes. Democracy in Dangerous Places*. New York: HarperCollins.

Collord, Michaela (2016) 'From the electoral battleground to the parliamentary arena: understanding intra-elite bargaining in Uganda's national resistance movement', *Journal of Eastern African Studies*, 10, no. 4: 639–659.

Comaroff, John and Jean Comaroff (1999) 'Introduction'. In John Comaroff and Jean Comaroff (eds.), *Civil Society and the Political Imagination in Africa: Critical Perspectives*. Chicago:University of Chicago Press: 1–43.

Commonwealth Secretariat (2011) *Uganda Presidential and Parliamentary Elections. Report of the Commonwealth Observer Group*. At https://thecommon wealth.org/sites/default/files/news-items/documents/Uganda-COG-Final-Rep ort.pdf.

Commonwealth Secretariat (2012) *Ghana Presidential and Parliamentary Elections. 7 December 2012. Report of the Commonwealth Observer Group*. At http://thecom monwealth.org/sites/default/files/inline/GhanaElections-FinalReport2012.pdf.

Conroy-Krutz, Jeffrey and Carolyn Logan (2012) 'Museveni and the 2011 Ugandan election: did the money matter?', *The Journal of Modern African Studies*, 50, no. 4: 625–655.

Cook, Nicolas (2018) 'Ghana: current issues and U.S. relations in brief', Washington: Congressional Research Service, 18 July 2018, https://fas.org/sg p/crs/row/R45260.pdf.

Cooper, Frederick (2012) 'Decolonization and citizenship. Africa between empires and a world of nations'. In Els Bogaerts and Remco Raben (eds.), *Beyond Empire and Nation: Decolonizing Societies in Africa and Asia, 1930s to 1970s*. Leiden: KITLV: 40–67.

Cornell, Agnes and Michelle D'Arcy (2014) '*Plus ça change?* County-level politics in Kenya after devolution', *Journal of Eastern African Studies*, 8, no. 1: 173–191.

Cortell, Andrew P. and James W. Davis Jr (2000) 'Understanding the domestic impact of international norms: a research agenda', *International Studies Review*, 2, no. 1: 65–87.

Cottrell, Jill and Yash Ghai (2007) 'Constitution making and democratization in Kenya (2000–2005)', *Democratization*, 14, no. 1: 1–25.

Cowen, Michael and Karuti Kanyinga (2002) 'The 1997 elections in Kenya. The politics of communality and locality'. In Michael Cowen and Liisa Laakso (eds.), *Multi-party Elections in Africa*. Oxford:James Currey: 128–171.

Crabbe, Justice V. C. R. A. C. (2013) *Democratic Governance in Ghana: How Political Polarization May be Abated*. Accra: CDD-Ghana.

CRECO [Constitution and Reform Education Consortium] (2019) *Digital Audit of the Democracy, Rights and Governance Civil Society Sector in Kenya: An Analysis of the Digital Civic Space*. Nairobi: CRECO.

Crick, Bernard (2002) 'Education for citizenship: the citizenship order', *Parliamentary Affairs*, 55, no. 3: 488–504.

Croissant, Aurel, Gabriele Bruns and Marei John (2002) 'Electoral politics in Southeast and East Asia: a comparative perspective'. In Aurel Croissant and Marei John (eds.), *Electoral Politics in Southeast and East Asia*. Singapore: Friedrich Ebert Stiftung: 321–368.

D'Arcy, Michelle and Agnes Cornell (2016) 'Devolution and corruption in Kenya: everyone's turn to eat?', *African Affairs*, 115, no. 459: 246–273.

Daddieh, Cyril K. and George M. Bob-Milliar (2012) 'In search of 'honorable' membership: parliamentary primaries and candidate selection in Ghana', *Journal of Asian and African Studies*, 47, no. 2: 204–220.

Dagne, Ted and Zarina Harding (2001) 'Uganda: recent elections and current conditions', CRS Report for Congress, www.everycrsreport.com/files/200107 19_RS20969_ccd7743e6b0a8e866a25ce93ea8471d1daf427df.pdf.

Deacon, Gregory (2015) 'Driving the devil out: Kenya's born-again election', *Journal of Religion in Africa*, 45, no. 2: 200–220.

Deacon, Gregory and Gabrielle Lynch (2013) 'Allowing Satan in? Moving toward a political economy of neo-Pentecostalism in Kenya', *Journal of Religion in Africa*, 43, no. 2: 108–130.

Debrah, Emmanuel (2011) 'Measuring governance institutions' success in Ghana: the case of the electoral commission, 1993–2008', *African Studies*, 70, no. 1: 25–45.

Decalo, Samuel (1992) 'The process, prospects and constraints of democratization in Africa', *African Affairs*, 91, no. 362: 7–35.

de Torrenté, Nicolas (2013) 'Understanding the 2011 Ugandan elections: the contribution of public opinion surveys', *Journal of Eastern African Studies*, 7, no. 3: 530–548.

Diamond, Larry (1994) 'Toward democratic consolidation', *Journal of Democracy*, 5, no. 3: 4–17.

Diamond, Larry and Marc F. Plattner (eds.) (1999) *Democratization in Africa*. Baltimore and London: Johns Hopkins Press.

Dicklitch, Susan (1998) *The Elusive Promise of NGOs in Africa: Lessons from Uganda*. Basingstoke: Macmillan.

Dicklitch, Susan (2001) 'NGOs and democratization in transitional societies: lessons from Uganda', *International Politics*, 38: 27–46.

Dodsworth, Susan and Nic Cheeseman (2018) 'Ten challenges in democracy support – and how to overcome them', *Global Policy*, 9, no. 3: 301–312.

Dodsworth, Susan and Nic Cheeseman (2019) 'Defending Democracy: when parliaments protect political space', unpublished paper presented at Uppsala University.

Doom, Ruddy and Koen Vlassenroot (1999) 'Kony's message: a new koine? The Lord's Resistance Army in northern Uganda', *African Affairs*, 98, no. 390: 5–36.

Dorman, Sara Rich (2019) 'Citizenship'. In Gabrielle Lynch and Peter VonDoepp (eds.), *Routledge Handbook of Democratization in Africa*. Abingdon: Routledge: 460–472.

Dulani, Boniface (2019) 'The struggle for presidential term limits'. In Gabrielle Lynch and Peter VonDoepp (eds.), *Routledge Handbook of Democratization in Africa*. Abingdon: Routledge: 104–116.

Dunn, John and A.F. Robertson (1973) *Dependence and Opportunity. Political Change in Ahafo*. Cambridge: Cambridge University Press.

Dunn, John (1980) 'From democracy to representation: an interpretation of a Ghanaian election'. In John Dunn (ed.), *Political Obligation in its Historical Context: Essays in Political Theory*. Cambridge: Cambridge University Press: 112–156.

Dunning, Thad and Lauren Harrison (2010) 'Cross-cutting cleavages and ethnic voting: an experimental study of cousinage in Mali', *American Political Science Review*, 104, no.1: 21–39.

Ekeh, Peter (1975) 'Colonialism and the two publics in Africa: a theoretical statement', *Comparative Studies in Society and History*, 17, no.1: 91–112.

Eifert, Benn, Edward Miguel and Daniel N. Posner (2010) 'Political competition and ethnic identification in Africa', *American Journal of Political Science*, 54, no.2: 494–510.

Elder, Claire, Susan Stigant and Jonas Claes (2014) *Elections and Violent Conflict in Kenya: Making Prevention Stick*. Washington, DC: United States Institute of Peace.

Electoral Commission of Ghana (2010) *Ghana Elections 2008*. Accra: Friedrich Ebert Stiftung.

Electoral Commission of Kenya (nd, but circa 2006) *Election Handbook*. Nairobi: ECK.

Elischer, Sebastian (2013) *Political Parties in Africa: Ethnicity and Party Formation.* Cambridge: Cambridge University Press.

Elischer, Sebastian (2019) 'Governing the faithful: state management of Salafi activism in the Francophone Sahel', *Comparative Politics*, 51, no.2: 199–218.

Elklit, Jørgen (1999) 'Electoral institutional change and democratization: you can lead a horse to water, but you can't make it drink', *Democratization*, 6, no.4: 28–51.

Elklit, Jørgen and Andrew Reynolds (2005) 'A framework for the systematic study of election quality', *Democratization*, 12, no.2: 147–162.

Elklit, Jørgen and Palle Svensson (1997) 'What makes elections free and fair?', *Journal of Democracy*, 8, no.3: 32–46.

Engholm, Geoffrey (1963) 'The Westminster model in Uganda', *International Journal*, 18, no.4: 468–487.

Erdmann, Gero and Ulf Engel (2007) 'Neopatrimonialism reconsidered: critical review and elaboration of an elusive concept', *Journal of Commonwealth and Comparative Politics*, 45, no.1: 95–119.

Erdmann, Gero, Matthias Basedau, and Andreas Mehler (2007) 'Introduction: research on electoral systems, parties and party systems in Africa'. In Matthias Basedau, Gero Erdmann and Andreas Mehler (eds.), Votes, Money and Violence: Political Parties and Elections in Sub-Saharan Africa. Uppsala: Nordiska Afrikainstitutet: 7–20.

Erlich, Aaron and Nicholas Kerr (2016) '"The local mwananchi has lost trust": design, transition and legitimacy in Kenyan election management', *The Journal of Modern African Studies*, 54, no.4: 671–702.

European Union (2011) *Uganda. Final Report. General Elections March 2011.* Brussels: European Union.

European Union (2016) *Uganda. Final Report. Presidential, Parliamentary and Local Government Elections 18 February 2016.* Brussels: European Union.

European Union (2017) *Final Report. Republic of Kenya, General Elections 2017.* Brussels: European Union.

European Union External Action Service (2016) *Handbook for EU Election Observation*, 3rd Edition 2016, Brussels: European Union.

Evans, Alice (2018) 'Cities as catalysts of gendered social change? reflections from Zambia. *Annals of the American Association of Geographers*, 108, no.4, 1096–1114.

Evans, Alice (2019) 'How cities erode gender inequality: a new theory and evidence from Cambodia', *Gender & Society*, 33, no.6: 961–984.

Evans, Geoffrey and Pauline Rose (2007) 'Support for democracy in Malawi: does schooling matter?', *World Development*, 35, no.5: 904–919.

Evans, Geoffrey (2000) 'The continued significance of class voting', *Annual Review of Political Science*, 3, no. 1: 401–417.

Evans, Tessa Devereaux and Nicolas van de Walle (2019) 'The impact of foreign aid'. In Gabrielle Lynch and Peter VonDoepp (eds.), *Routledge Handbook of Democratization in Africa*. Abingdon: Routledge: 63–77.

Eyoh, Dickson (1998) 'African perspectives on democracy and the dilemmas of postcolonial intellectuals', *Africa Today*, 45, nos. 3 and 4: 281–306.

Faller, Julie K. (2015) 'The system matters: corruption and vote choice in Uganda', *Commonwealth and Comparative Politics*, 53, no.4: 428–456.

Fassin, Didier (2005) 'Compassion and repression: the moral economy of immigration policies in France', *Cultural Anthropology*, 20, no.3: 362–387.

Fatton, R. (1995) 'Africa in the age of democratization: the civic limitations of civil society', *African Studies Review*, 38, no.2: 67–99.

Feddersen, Timothy J. (2004) 'Rational choice theory and the paradox of not voting', *Journal of Economic Perspectives*, 18, no.1: 99–112.

Ferree, Karen E., Clark C. Gibson, and James D. Long (2014) 'Voting behavior and electoral irregularities in Kenya's 2013 election', *Journal of Eastern African Studies*, 8, no.1: 153–172.

Ferree, Karen, Danielle F. Jung, Robert A. Dowd and Clark C. Gibson (2020 'Election ink and turnout in a partial democracy', *British Journal of Political Science*, 50, no. 3: 1175–1191.

Ferree, Karen E. and James D. Long (2016) 'Gifts, threats, and perceptions of ballot secrecy in African elections', *African Affairs*, 115, no. 461: 621–645.

Finkel, S. E., C. A. Sabatini and G. B. Bevis (2000) 'Civic education, civil society and political mistrust in a developing democracy: the case of the Dominican Republic', *World Development*, 28, no. 11: 1851–1874.

Finkel, Steven E. and Amy Erica Smith (2011) 'Civic education, political discussion, and the social transmission of democratic knowledge and values in a new democracy: Kenya 2002', *American Journal of Political Science*, 55, no.2: 417–435.

Finnström, Sverker (2008) *Living with Bad Surroundings: War, History, and Everyday Moments in Northern Uganda*. Durham, NC: Duke University Press.

Fisher, Jonathan (2013a) '"Image management" and African agency: Ugandan regional diplomacy and donor relations under Museveni'. In William Brown and Sophie Harman (eds.), *African Agency in International Politics*. Abingdon: Routledge: 111–127.

Fisher, Jonathan (2013b) 'The limits–and limiters–of external influence: donors, the Ugandan electoral commission and the 2011 elections', *Journal of Eastern African Studies*, 7, no.3: 471–491.

Fisher, Jonathan (2014) 'When it pays to be a "fragile state": Uganda's use and abuse of a dubious concept', *Third World Quarterly*, 35, no.2: 316–332.

Foeken, Dick and Ton Dietz (2000) 'Of ethnicity, manipulation and observation: the 1992 and 1997 elections in Kenya', in Foeken, Dick, Ton Dietz, Jon Abbink and Gerti Hesseling (eds), Election Observation and Democratization in Africa. Geneva: Springer: 122–149.

Foeken, Dick, Ton Dietz, Jon Abbink and Gerti Hesseling (2000) *Election Observation and Democratization in Africa*. Geneva: Springer.

Freeden, Michael (1996) *Ideologies and Political Theory: a Conceptual Approach*. Oxford: Oxford University Press.

Fridy, Kevin S. (2007) 'The elephant, umbrella and quarrelling cocks: disaggregating partisanship in Ghana's Fourth Republic', *African Affairs*, 106, no.423: 281–305.

Fridy, Kevin S. and Victor Brobbey (2009) 'Win the match and vote for me: the politicisation of Ghana's Accra Hearts of Oak and Kumasi Asante Kotoko football clubs', *The Journal of Modern African Studies*, 47, no.1: 19–39.

Fourie, Elsje (2014) 'Model students: policy emulation, modernization, and Kenya's Vision 2030', *African Affairs*, 113, no.453: 540–562.

Furley, Oliver (1999) *Democratisation in Uganda*. Leamington Spa: Research Institute for the Study of Conflict and Terrorism.

Furley, Oliver and James Katalikawe (1999) *No-Party Democracy: Uganda's Elections to the Constituent Assembly, 1994*. Kampala: Centre for Basic Research.

Gadjanova, Elena (2017) 'Electoral clientelism as status affirmation in Africa: evidence from Ghana', *Journal of Modern African Studies*, 55, no.4: 593–621.

Gadjanova, Elena (2019) 'Treacherous coattails: gubernatorial endorsements and the presidential race in Kenya's 2017 election', *Journal of Eastern African Studies*, 13, no.2: 272–293.

Gadjanova, Elena, Gabrielle Lynch, Jason Reifler and Ghadafi Saibu (2019) Social media, cyber battalions, and political mobilisation in Ghana, www .elenagadjanova.com/uploads/2/1/3/8/21385412/social_media_cyber_batta lions_and_political_mobilisation_in_ghana_report_final.pdf.

Galaty, John (2005) 'Double-voiced violence in Kenya'. In Vigdis Broch-Due (ed.), *Violence and Belonging: The Quest for Identity in Post-Colonial Africa*. London: Routledge: 173–194.

Geschiere, Peter (1997) *The Modernity of Witchcraft: Politics and the Occult in Postcolonial Africa*. Charlottesville: University of Virginia Press.

Galston, William A. (2001) 'Political knowledge, political engagement and civic education', *Annual Review of Political Science*, 4: 217–234.

Garber, Larry, and Glenn Cowan (1993) 'The virtues of parallel vote tabulations', *Journal of Democracy*, 4, no.2: 95–107.

Garigue, Philip (1954) 'Changing political leadership in West Africa' *Africa*, 24, no.3: 220–232.

Garrigou, Alain (1992) *Le vote et la vertu. Comment les Français sont devenus électeurs*. Paris: Presses de Sciences Po.

Gathaka, Jephthah K. (2012) *You and Your Vote: Elections, Voters and Leadership. A Voter's Manual*. Nairobi: The Ecumenical Centre for Justice and Peace.

Gay, Lauriane (2014) 'A "hot cake": the land issue in the Buganda kingdom during Uganda's 2011 elections', in Sandrine Perrot, Sabiti Makara, Jérôme Lafargue and Marie-Aude Fouéré (eds.), Elections in a Hybrid Regime: Revisiting the 2011 Uganda Polls. Kampala: Fountain Publishers: 248–265.

Gazibo, Mamoudou (2019) 'Electoral administration'. In Gabrielle Lynch and Peter VonDoepp (eds.), *Routledge Handbook of Democratization in Africa*. Abingdon: Routledge: 174–188.

Geisler, Gisela (1993) 'Fair? What has fairness got to do with it? Vagaries of election observations and democratic standard', *The Journal of Modern African Studies*, 31, no.4: 613–637.

Genovese, Elizabeth Fox (1973) 'The many faces of moral economy: a contribution to a debate', *Past & Present*, 58: 161–168.

Gertzel, Cherry (1970) *The Politics of Independent Kenya*. Evanston, IL: Northwestern University Press.

Gertzel, Cherry (1974) *Party and Locality in Northern Uganda, 1945–62*. London: University of London.

Ghana, Republic of (1967) *Parts I and II of the Report of the Commission of Enquiry into Electoral and Local Government Reform*. Accra: Government Printer.

Gibb, Ryan (2016) 'The elections in Uganda, February 2016', *Africa Spectrum*, 51, no.2: 93–101.

Gibson, Clarke and James Long (2009) 'The presidential and parliamentary election in Kenya, December 2007', *Electoral Studies*, 28, no.3: 497–502.

Gingyera-Pinycwa, A. G. G. (1996) 'Constituent Assembly elections in Jonam Constituency, Nebbi District'. In Makara, et al., *Politics, Constitutionalism and Electioneering in Uganda*: 19–45.

Gloppen, S, C. Atoo, E. Kasimbazi, A. Kibandama, J. Kiiza, S. Makara, G. Okiror, L. Rakner, S. Rwengabo, L. Svåsand, R. Tabaro and A. Tostensen (2006) *Uganda's 2006 Presidential and Parliamentary Elections*. Bergen: Chr Michelsen Institute.

Golaz, Valérie, and Claire Médard (2014) 'Election results and public contestation of the vote: an overview of the Uganda 2011 general elections'. In Sandrine Perrot, Sabiti Makara, Jérôme Lafargue and Marie-Aude Fouéré (eds.), Elections in a Hybrid Regime: Revisiting the 2011 Uganda Polls. Kampala: Fountain Publishers: 54–109.

Goldschmidt, Jenny (1980) 'Ghana between the second and third republican era: recent constitutional developments and their relation to traditional laws and institutions', *The Journal of Legal Pluralism and Unofficial Law*, 12, no.18: 43–61.

Gray, Robert (1963) 'Political parties in new African nations: an anthropological view', *Comparative Studies in Society and History*, 5, no.4: 449–461.

Green, Elliott (2010) 'Patronage, district creation, and reform in Uganda', *Studies in Comparative International Development*, 45, no.1: 83–103.

Greenberg, Ari and Robert Mattes (2013) 'Does the quality of elections affect the consolidation of democracy?'. In Michael Bratton (ed.), *Voting and Democratic Citizenship in Africa*. Boulder, CO: Lynne Rienner: 239–252.

Greenwald, Anthony G., Colin Tucker Smith, N. Sriram, Yoav Bar-Anan and Brian A. Nosek (2009) 'Implicit race attitudes predicted vote in the 2008 US presidential election', *Analyses of Social Issues and Public Policy*, 9, no.1: 241–253.

Grignon, François, Marcel Rutten and Alamin Mazrui (2001a) 'Observing and analysing the 1997 general elections: an introduction'. In Marcel Rutten, Alamin Mazrui and Francois Grignon (with Francois as written earlier on in the reference) (eds.), *Out for the Count. The 1997 General Elections and Prospects for Democracy in Kenya*. Kampala: Fountain Publishers: 1–27.

Grignon, François, Alamin Mazrui and Marcel Rutten (2001b) 'Conclusion'. In Marcel Rutten, Alamin Mazrui and Francois Grignon (with Francois as written earlier on in the reference) (eds.), *Out for the Count. The 1997 General Elections and Prospects for Democracy in Kenya*. Kampala: Fountain Publishers: 594–603.

Gyampo, Ransford Edward van, Emmanuel Graham and Eric Yobo (2017) 'Ghana's 2016 general election: accounting of the monumental defeat of the National Democratic Congress (NDC)', *Journal of African Elections*, 16, no. 1: 24–45.

Gyampo, Ransford Edward Van (2019) 'Generational dynamics and youth politics'. In Gabrielle Lynch and Peter VonDoepp (eds.), *Routledge Handbook of Democratization in Africa*. Abingdon: Routledge: 329–342.

Gyekye-Jandoh, Maame Adwoa A. (2016) 'Civic election observation and general elections in Ghana and the Fourth Republic: enhancing government legitimacy and the democratization process'. In I Kwame A. Ninsin (ed.), *Ghana's Electoral Politics*, Dakar: CODESRIA: 115–135.

Gyimah-Boadi, Emmanuel (1994) 'Ghana's uncertain political opening', *Journal of Democracy*, 5, no.2: 75–86.

Gyimah-Boadi, Emmanuel (1996) 'Civil society in Africa', *Journal of Democracy*, 7, no.2: 118–131.

Gyimah-Boadi, Emmanuel (2001) 'A peaceful turnover in Ghana', *Journal of Democracy*, 12, no. 2:103–117.

Gyimah-Boadi, Emmanuel (2009) 'Another step forward for Ghana', *Journal of Democracy*, 20, no. 2: 138–152

Gyimah-Boadi, Emmanuel (2015) 'Africa's waning democratic commitment', *Journal of Democracy*, 26, no.1: 101–113.

Gyimah-Boadi, Emmanuel and Marton T. Markovits (2008) 'Civil society and governance'. In Baffour Agyeman-Duah (ed.), *Ghana: Governance in the Fourth Republic*. Tema, Ghana: Digibooks Ghana Ltd.

Gyimah-Boadi, Emmanuel, Mike Oquaye and F. K. Drah (2000) *Civil Society Organizations and Ghanaian Democratization*. Accra, Ghana: Center for Democracy & Development.

Gyimah-Boadi, Emmanuel and H. Kwasi Prempeh (2012) 'Oil, politics and Ghana's democracy', *Journal of Democracy*, 23, no. 3: 94–108.

Ham, C. van and Lindberg, S. (2018) 'Elections: the power of elections in multiparty Africa'. In Nic Cheeseman (ed.), *Institutions and Democracy in Africa*. Cambridge: Cambridge University Press: 213–237.

Harding, Robin (2015) 'Attribution and accountability: voting for roads in Ghana', *World Politics*, 67, no. 4: 656–689.

Harrington, John and Ambreena Manji (2015) 'Restoring Leviathan? The Kenyan supreme court, constitutional transformation and the presidential election of 2013', *Journal of Eastern African Studies*, 9, no.2: 175–192.

Harris, J. Andrew, and Daniel N. Posner (2019) '(Under what conditions) Do politicians reward their supporters? Evidence from Kenya's constituencies development fund', *American Political Science Review*, 113, no.1: 123–139.

Haste, Helen, and Amy Hogan (2006) 'Beyond conventional civic participation, beyond the moral-political divide: young people and contemporary debates about citizenship', *Journal of Moral Education*, 35, no.4: 473–493.

Hauser, Ellen (1999) 'Ugandan relations with Western donors in the 1990s: what impact on democratisation?', *The Journal of Modern African Studies*, 37, no.4: 621–641.

Hayward, Fred (1987) 'Introduction'. In Fred Hayward (ed.), *Elections in Independent Africa*. Boulder, CO: Westview: 1–23.

Hearn, Julie (1998) 'The "NGO-isation" of Kenyan society: USAID and the restructuring of health care', *Review of African Political Economy*, 75: 89–100.

Hearn, Julie (2007) 'African NGOs: the new compradors?', *Development and Change*, 38, no.6: 1095–1110.

Hermet, Guy, Richard Rose and Alain Rouquié (eds.) (1978) *Elections Without Choice*. London: Macmillan.

Hermet, Guy (1978) 'State-controlled elections: a framework'. In Guy Hermet, Richard Rose and Alain Rouquié (eds.), *Elections Without Choice*. London: Macmillan: 1–18.

Holmquist, Frank and Michael Ford (1995) 'Stalling political change: Moi's yay in Kenya', *Current History*, 94, no.591: 177–181.

Hornsby, Charles (1989) 'The social structure of the national assembly in Kenya, 1963–83', *The Journal of Modern African Studies*, 27, no.2: 275–296.

Hornsby, Charles (2011) *Kenya: A History Since Independence*. London: I B Tauris.

Horowitz, Donald L. (1993) 'Democracy in divided societies', *Journal of Democracy*, 4, no.4: 18–38.

Horowitz, Donald L. (1985) *Ethnic Groups in Conflict*. California: University of California Press.

Horowitz, Jeremy (2019) 'Ethnicity and the swing vote in Africa's emerging democracies: evidence from Kenya', *British Journal of Political Science*, 49, no. 3: 901–921.

Hughes, Lotte (2016) 'Rights, wrongs, and reciprocity: Change and continuity among Kenyan Maasai'. In Bruce J. Berman, André Laliberté and Stephen Larin (eds.), *The Moral Economies of Ethnic and Nationalist Claims*. Vancouver: UBC Press: 70–100.

Huntington, Samuel (1965) 'Political development and political decay', *World Politics*, 17, no. 3: 386–430.

Huntington, Samuel (1991 and 2009) 'How countries democratize', *Political Science Quarterly*, 124, no.1: 31–69.

Hyde, Susan D. (2007) 'The observer effect in international politics: evidence from a natural experiment', *World Politics*, 60, no.1: 37–63.

Hyde, Susan D. and Nikolay Marinov (2014) 'Information and self-enforcing democracy: the role of international election observation', *International Organization*, 68, no.2: 329–359.

Hyden, Goran and Colin Leys (1972) 'Elections and politics in single-party systems: the case of Kenya and Tanzania', *British Journal of Political Science*, 2, no.4: 389–420.

Hyden, Goran (1980) *Beyond Ujamaa in Tanzania: Underdevelopment and an uncaptured peasantry*, California: University of California Pres.

Hyden, Goran (2006) *African Politics in Comparative Perspective*. Cambridge: Cambridge University Press.

Ibingira, G. S. K. (1973) *The Forging of an African Nation: The Political and Constitutional Evolution of Uganda from Colonial Rule to Independence, 1894–1962*. New York: The Viking Press.

Ibrahim, Jibrin (1986) 'The political debate and the struggle for democracy in Nigeria', *Review of African Political Economy* 13, no.37: 38–48.

Ichino, Nahomi and Matthias Schündeln (2012) 'Deterring or displacing electoral irregularities? Spillover effects of observers in a randomized field experiment in Ghana', *The Journal of Politics*, 74, no.1: 292–307.

IEA [Institute of Economic Affairs] (2014) *The Story of the Institute of Economic Affairs: 25 Years of Shaping the Future*. IEA: Accra.

Ignatieff, Michael (2017) *The Ordinary Virtues: Moral Order in a Divided World*. Cambridge: Harvard University Press.

Ihonvbere, Julius (1996) 'Where is the third wave? A critical evaluation of Africa's non-transition to democracy', *Africa Today*, 43, no.4: 5–28.

Independent Review Commission [IREC] (2008) *Report of the Independent Review Commission on the General Elections Held in Kenya on 27th December 2007.* Nairobi, Government Printer.

Ingham, Kenneth (1974) *The Kingdom of Toro in Uganda.* London: Methuen.

Interim National Election Commission (1992) *A Guide to the Candidate.* Accra: Republic of Ghana.

Ishiyama, John (2012) 'Explaining ethnic bloc voting in Africa', *Democratization*, 19, no.4: 761–788.

Ismail, Zenobia (2018) 'The Alternation Fallacy: Turnover Without Transformation in Zambia (1991–2015)'. PhD University of Cambridge.

Izama, Angelo and Michael Wilkerson (2011) 'Uganda: Museveni's triumph and weakness', *Journal of Democracy*, 22, no.3: 64–78.

Jeffries, Richard (1980) 'The Ghanaian elections of 1979', *African Affairs*, 79, no.316: 397–414.

Jeffries, Richard (1989) 'Ghana: the political economy of personal rule'. In Donal Cruise O'Brien, John Dunn and Richard Rathbone (eds.), *Contemporary West African States.* Cambridge: Cambridge University Press: 75–99.

Jeffries, Richard (1998) 'The Ghanaian elections of 1996: towards the consolidation of democracy?', *African Affairs*, 97, no.387: 189–208.

Jeffries, Richard and Clare Thomas (1993) 'The Ghanaian elections of 1992', *African Affairs*, 92, no.368: 331–366.

Jenkins, Sarah (2012) 'Ethnicity, violence, and the immigrant-guest metaphor in Kenya', *African Affairs*, 111, no. 445: 576–596.

Jensen, Peter Sandholt and Justesen, Morgens K. (2014) 'Poverty and vote buying: survey-based evidence from Africa', *Electoral Studies*, 33: 220–232.

Jesuit Hakimani Centre (2017) *Election Agenda 2017 and Beyond: Election Issuefication.* Nairobi: Jesuit Hakimani Centre.

Jinadu, L. Adele (1997) 'Matters arising: African elections and the problem of electoral administration', *African Journal of Political Science/Revue Africaine de Science Politique*, 2, no.1: 1–11.

Jockers, Heinz, Dirk Kohnert and Paul Nugent (2010) 'The successful Ghana election of 2008: a convenient myth?', *The Journal of Modern African Studies*, 48, no. 1: 95–115.

de Kadt, Daniel and Evan S. Lieberman (2020 'Nuanced accountability: voter responses to service delivery in Southern Africa', *British Journal of Political Science*, 50, no. 1: 185–215.

Kagwanja, Peter and Roger Southall (2009) 'Introduction: Kenya–A democracy in retreat?', *Journal of Contemporary African Studies*, 27, no.3: 259–277.

Kalandadze, Katya and Mitchell A. Orenstein (2009) 'Electoral protests and democratization beyond the color revolutions', *Comparative Political Studies*, 42, no.11: 1403–1425.

Kamungi, Prisca (2009) 'The politics of displacement in multiparty Kenya', *Journal of Contemporary African Studies*, 27, no.3: 345–364.

Kanyinga, Karuti (1994) 'Ethnicity, patronage and class in a local arena: 'high' and 'low' politics in Kiambu, Kenya, 1982–92'. In Peter Gibbon (ed.), *The*

New Local Level Politics in East Africa. Uppsala: Nordiska Afrikainstitutet, 66–86.

Kanyinga, Karuti (1998) 'Contestation over political space: The state and the demobilisation of opposition politics in Kenya'. In Adebayo Olukoshi (ed.), *The Politics of Opposition in Contemporary Africa*. Uppsala: Nordiska Afrikainstitutet: 39–90.

Kanyinga, Karuti (2009) 'The legacy of the white highlands: land rights, ethnicity and the post-2007 election violence in Kenya', *Journal of Contemporary African Studies*, 27, no.3: 325–344.

Kanyinga, Karuti, James Long and David Ndii (2010) 'Was it rigged? A forensic analysis of vote returns in Kenya's 2007 elections'. In Karuti Kanyinga and Duncan Okello (eds.), *Tensions and Reversals in Democratic Transitions: The Kenya 2007 General Elections*. Nairobi: Society for International Development and Institute for Development Studies, University of Nairobi: 373–415.

Kanyinga, Karuti and Collins Odote (2019) 'Judicialisation of politics and Kenya's 2017 elections', *Journal of Eastern African Studies*, 13, no. 2: 235–252.

Kanyinga, Karuti, Duncan Okello and Akoko Akech (2010) 'Contradictions of transition to democracy in fragmented societies: the Kenya 2007 general elections in perspective'. In Karuti Kanyinga and Duncan Okello (eds.), *Tensions and Reversals in Democratic Transitions: The Kenya 2007 General Elections*. Nairobi: Society for International Development and Institute for Development Studies, University of Nairobi: 1–28.

Kao, Kristen, Ellen Lust and Lise Rakner (2020) 'Poverty and clientelism: Do the poor embrace handouts?', Unpublished Working Paper.

Karahan, Gökhan R., Laura Razzolini and William F. Shughart (2006) 'No pretense to honesty: county government corruption in Mississippi', *Economics of Governance*, 7, no.3 : 211–227.

Kariuki, Joseph (2005) 'Choosing the president: electoral campaigns in northern central Kenya'. In Hervé Maupeu, Musambayi Katumanga and Winnie Mitullah (eds.), *The Moi Succession: The 2002 Elections in Kenya*. Nairobi: Transafrica Press.

Karl, Terry Lynn and Philippe Schmitter (1991) 'What democracy is . . . and is not', *Journal of Democracy*, 2, no.3: 75–88.

Karlström, Mikael (1996) 'Imagining democracy: political culture and democratisation in Buganda', *Africa*, 66, no.4: 485–505.

Karlström, Mikael (1999) 'Civil society and its presuppositions: lessons from Uganda'. In John Comaroff and Jean Comaroff (eds.), *Civil Society and the Political Imagination in Africa: Critical Perspectives*. Chicago: University of Chicago Press: 104–123.

Karugire, Samuel R. (1988) *The Roots of Instability in Uganda*. Kampala: New Vision Press.

Karume, Shumbana and Eleonora Mura (2012) 'Reflections on African Union electoral assistance and observation'. In Raul Cordenillo and Andrew Ellis (eds.), *The Integrity of Elections: The Role of Regional Organizations*. Stockholm: International IDEA: 21–37.

Kasfir, Nelson (1991) 'The Uganda elections of 1989: power, populism and democratisation'. In Holger Hansen and Michael Twaddle (eds.), *Changing Uganda*. London: James Currey: 247–278.

Kasfir, Nelson (1998) '"No-party democracy" in Uganda', *Journal of Democracy*, 9, no.2: 49–63.

Kasfir, Nelson (2000) '"Movement" democracy, legitimacy and power in Uganda'. In Justus Mugaju and Joseph Oloka-Onyango (eds.), *No-party Democracy in Uganda: Myths and Realities*. Kampala: Fountain Press: 60–78.

Kassimir, Ronald (1995) 'Catholics and political identity in Toro'. In Holger Hansen and Michael Twaddle (eds.), *Religion and Politics in East Africa*. London: James Currey: 120–140.

Katusiimeh, Mesharch W. (2004) 'Civil society organisations and democratic consolidation in Uganda', *African Journal of International Affairs*, 7, nos.1 & 2: 99–116.

Kavulla, Travis R. (2008) 'Our enemies are God's enemies': the religion and politics of Bishop Margaret Wanjiru, MP', *Journal of Eastern African Studies*, 2, no.2: 254–263.

KCCB [Kenya Conference of Catholic Bishops] (2017) *Civic, Voter and Peace Education Handbook*. Nairobi: Kenya.

Keating, Michael (2011) 'Can democratization undermine democracy? Economic and political reform in Uganda', *Democratization*, 18, no.2: 415–442.

Kelly, Bob and R. B. Bening (2013) 'The Ghanaian elections of 2012', *Review of African Political Economy*, 40, no.137: 475–484.

Kelley, Judith (2008) 'Assessing the complex evolution of norms: the rise of international election monitoring', *International Organization*, 62, no.2: 221–255.

Kelley, Judith (2009) 'The more the merrier? The effects of having multiple international election monitoring organizations', *Perspectives on Politics*, 7, no.1: 59–64.

Kelley, Judith (2012) *Monitoring Democracy: When International Election Observation Works, and Why It Often Fails*. Princeton, NJ: Princeton University Press.

Kenya, Republic of (1969) *Guide to the General Election*. Nairobi: Government Printer.

Kenya, Republic of (2008) *Report of the Independent Review Commission on the General Elections Held in Kenya on 27 December 2007*. Nairobi: Government Printers.

Khadiagala, Gilbert M. (2008) 'The failure of leaders and institutions: reflections on the 2007 election malaise in Kenya', *African Renaissance*, 5, no.1: 53–60.

Kimambo, Isaria, Goran Hyden, S. Maghimbi and Kazuhiko Sugimura (eds.) (2008) *Contemporary Perspectives on African Moral Economy*. Dar es Salaam: University of Dar es Salaam.

Klaas, Brian (2015) 'Bullets over ballots: how electoral exclusion increases the risk of coups d'état and civil wars', DPhil Thesis, Oxford: University of Oxford, https://ora.ox.ac.uk/objects/uuid:2492d39d-522f-494e-9549-28b3f6fc7db3.

Klopp, Jacqueline (2001) '"Ethnic clashes" and winning elections: the case of Kenya's electoral despotism', *Canadian Journal of African Studies*, 35, no.3: 473–517.

KNCHR [Kenya National Commission of Human Rights] (2007) *Public Accountability Statement: Statement of Successes and Challenges, 2006–2007.* Nairobi: KNCHR.

Knighton, Ben (2010) 'Going for *cai* at Gatundu: reversion to a Gikuyu ethnic past or building a Kenyan national future?' In Dan Branch, Nic Cheeseman and Leigh Gardner (eds.), *Our Turn to Eat: Politics in Kenya since 1950.* Berlin: Lit Verlag: 107–128.

Kobo, Ousman (2010) '"We are citizens too": the politics of citizenship in independent Ghana', *The Journal of Modern African Studies*, 48, no.1: 67–94.

Korir, Rt. Rev Cornelius arap (2017) 'Preface'. In KCCB [Kenya Conference of Catholic Bishops], *Civic, Voter and Peace Education Handbook.* Nairobi: Kenya: 6–7.

Koter, Dominika (2017) 'Costly electoral campaigns and the changing composition and quality of parliament: evidence from Benin', *African Affairs*, 116, no.465: 573–596.

Kramon, Eric (2009) 'Vote buying and Turnout in Kenya's 2002 elections', Los Angeles: University of California. www.sscnet.ucla.edu/polisci/wgape/papers/17_Kramon.pdf.

Kramon, Eric (2017) *Money for Votes. The Causes and Consequences of Electoral Clientelism in Africa.* Cambridge: Cambridge University Press.

Kyle, Keith (1999) *The Politics of the Independence of Kenya.* Hampshire: Palgrave.

Langer, Arnim, Abdul Raufu Mustapha and Frances Stewart (2009) 'Diversity and discord: ethnicity, horizontal inequalities and conflict in Ghana and Nigeria', *Journal of International Development*, 21, no.4: 477–482.

Large, Daniel (2008) 'Beyond "dragon in the bush": the study of China–Africa relations', *African Affairs*, 107, no. 426: 45–61.

Lavroff, Dmitri (ed.) (1978) *Aux Urnes l'Afrique! Élections et pouvoirs en Afrique noire.* Paris: Pedone.

Lawrance, Benjamin (2005) 'Bankoe v. Dome: traditions and petitions in the Ho-Asogli amalgamation, British Mandated Togoland, 1919–39', *The Journal of African History*, 46, no. 2: 243–267.

Lawson, J. S. (1951) 'Operation "elections." An account of the steps taken to prepare the people of the gold coast for the exercise of the franchise', *Parliamentary Affairs*, 4, no.3: 332–340.

LeBas, Adrienne (2010) 'Ethnicity and the willingness to sanction violent politicians: evidence from Ghana', Afrobarometer Working Paper No. 125. https://afrobarometer.org/publications/wp125-ethnicity-and-willingness-sanction-violent-politicians-evidence-kenya.

LeBas, Adrienne (2013) *From Protest to Parties: Party-building and Democratization in Africa.* Oxford: Oxford University Press.

Le Vine, Robert A. (1962) 'Wealth and power in Gusiiland'. In Paul Bohannen and George Dalton (eds.), *Markets in Africa.* Evanston, IL: Northwestern University Press: 520–536.

Le Vine, Victor (1987) 'Autopsy on a regime: Ghana's civilian interregnum, 1969–72', *The Journal of Modern African Studies*, 25, no.1: 169–178.

Lentz, Carola (2014) '"I take an oath to the state, not the government": career trajectories and professional ethics of Ghanaian public servants'. In Thomas Bierschenk and Olivier de Sardan (eds.), *States at Work: Dynamics of African Bureaucracies*. Leiden: Brill: 175–204.

Letsa, Natalie Wenzell (2017) '"The people's choice": popular (il)legitimacy in autocratic Cameroon', *The Journal of Modern African Studies*, 55, no.4: 647–679.

Levitsky, Steven and Lucan Way (2002) 'The rise of competitive authoritarianism', *Journal of Democracy*, 13, no. 2: 51–65.

Levitsky, Steven and Lucan Way (2006) 'Linkage versus leverage. Rethinking the international dimension of regime change', *Comparative Politics*, 38, no. 4: 379–400.

Levitsky, Steven and Lucan Way (2010) *Competitive Authoritarianism: Hybrid Regimes After the Cold War*. Cambridge: Cambridge University Press.

Leys, Colin (1967) *Politicians and Policies. An Essay on Politics in Acholi, Uganda, 1962–65*. Nairobi: East African Publishing House.

Lindberg, Staffan I. (2003) 'It's our time to "chop"': Do elections in Africa feed neo-patrimonialism rather than counter-act it?', *Democratization*, 10, no.2: 121–140.

Lindberg, Staffan I. (2006) *Democracy and Elections in Africa*. Baltimore, MD: Johns Hopkins University Press.

Lindberg, Staffan I. (2010) 'What accountability pressures do MPs in Africa face and how do they respond? Evidence from Ghana', *The Journal of Modern African Studies*, 48, no.1: 117–142.

Lindberg, Staffan I. (2013) 'Have the cake and eat it: the rational voter in Africa', *Party Politics*, 19, no.6: 945–961.

Lindberg, Staffan I. and Minion Morrison (2005) 'Exploring voter alignments in Africa: core and swing voters in Ghana', *The Journal of Modern African Studies*, 43, no.4: 565–586.

Lindberg, Staffan I. and Minion Morrison (2008) 'Are African voters really ethnic or clientelistic? Survey evidence from Ghana', *Political Science Quarterly*, 123, no.1: 95–122.

Lindemann, Stefan (2011) 'Just another change of guard? Broad-based politics and civil war in Museveni's Uganda', *African Affairs*, 110, no.440: 387–416.

Lockwood, Peter (2019a) 'Before there is power, there is the country': civic nationalism and political mobilisation amongst Kenya's opposition coalitions, 2013–2018', *Journal of Modern African Studies*, 57, no. 4: 541–561.

Lockwood, Peter (2019b) 'The buffalo and the squirrel: moral authority and the limits of patronage in Kiambu County's 2017 gubernatorial race', *Journal of Eastern African Studies*, 13, no.2: 353–370.

Long, James D. (2008) 'Electoral fraud and the erosion of democratic gains in Kenya'. Working Group in African Political Economy (WGAPE) meeting, April 2008, online at https://pdfs.semanticscholar.org/58b1/a04d99 a402792895365cf95d39808fbd65c3.pdf.

Long, James D. (2019) 'Voting behaviour'. In Gabrielle Lynch and Peter VoDoepp (eds.), *Routledge Handbook of Democratization in Africa*. Abingdon: Routledge: 191–204.

Lonsdale, John (1986) 'Political accountability in African history'. In Patrick Chabal (ed.), *Political Domination in Africa. Reflections on the Limits of Power*. Cambridge: Cambridge University Press: 126–157.

Lonsdale, John (1992a) 'The moral economy of Mau Mau. Wealth, poverty and civic virtue in Kikuyu political thought', in Bruce J. Berman and John Lonsdale (eds.), *Unhappy Valley. Conflict in Kenya and Africa*. London: James Currey: 315–504.

Lonsdale, John (1992b) 'The political culture of Kenya', online at http://rossy.ruc.dk/ojs/index.php/ocpa/article/view/3906/2080.

Lonsdale, John (1994) 'Moral ethnicity and political tribalism'. In Preben Kaarsholm and Jan Huttin (eds.), *Inventions and Boundaries: Historical and Anthropological Approaches to the Study of Ethnicity and Nationalism*. Roskilde, Denmark: Institute for Development Studies, Roskilde University: 131–150.

Lonsdale, John (2004) 'Moral and political argument in Kenya'. In Bruce Berman, Dickson Eyoh and Will Kymlicka (eds.), *Ethnicity and Democracy in Africa*. Oxford: James Currey: 73–95.

Low, Donald Anthony (1962) *Political Parties in Uganda, 1949–62*. London: University of London.

Low, Donald Anthony (1964) 'The advent of populism in Buganda', *Comparative Studies in Society and History*, 6, no.4: 424–444.

Lugano, Geoffrey (2020) 'Civil society and the state'. In Nic Cheeseman, Karuti Kanyinga and Gabrielle Lynch (eds.), *Oxford Handbook of Kenyan Politics*. Oxford: Oxford University Press: 310–324.

Lumumba-Kasongo, Tukumbi (2005) 'The problematics of liberal democracy and democratic process: lessons for deconstructing and building African democracies'. In Tukumbi Lumumba-Kasongo (ed.), *Liberal Democracy and Its Critics in Africa: Political Dysfunction and the Struggle for Social Progress*. Dakar: CODESRIA: 1–25.

Lynch, Gabrielle and Gordon Crawford (2011) 'Democratization in Africa 1990–2010: an assessment', *Democratization*, 18, no.2: 275–310.

Lynch, Gabrielle. (2011a) *I Say to You. Ethnic Politics and the Kalenjin in Kenya*. Chicago: University of Chicago.

Lynch, Gabrielle (2011b) 'The wars of who belongs where: the unstable politics of autochthony on Kenya's Mt Elgon', *Ethnopolitics*, 10, nos.3–4: 391–410.

Lynch, Gabrielle (2014) 'Electing the 'alliance of the accused': the success of the Jubilee Alliance in Kenya's Rift Valley', *Journal of Eastern African Studies*, 8, no.1: 93–114.

Lynch, Gabrielle (2016a) '*Majimboism* and Kenya's moral economy of ethnic territoriality'. In Bruce Berman, André Laliberté and Stephen Larin (eds.), *Moral Economies and Ethnic and Nationalist Claims*. Vancouver: UBC Press: 49–69.

Lynch, Gabrielle (2016b) 'Uganda 2016: The struggle to win Acholi minds', *Review of African Political Economy blog*, http://roape.net/2016/03/03/uganda-2016-the-struggle-to-win-acholi-minds.

Lynch, Gabrielle, Nic Cheeseman and Justin Willis (2019) 'From peace campaigns to peaceocracy: elections, order and authority in Africa', *African Affairs*, 118, no. 473: 603–627.

Macarthur, Julie (2008) 'How the west was won: regional politics and prophetic promises in the 2007 Kenya elections', *Journal of Eastern African Studies*, 2, no.2: 227–241.

Mackenzie, W. J. M. (1954) 'Representation in plural societies', *Political Studies*, 2, no.1: 54–69.

Mackenzie, W. J. M. (1957) 'The export of electoral systems', *Political Studies*, 5, no.3: 240–257.

Mackenzie, W. J. M. (1960) 'Some conclusions'. In W. J. M. Mackenzie and K. Robinson (eds.), *Five Elections in Africa: a Group of Electoral Studies*. Oxford: Clarendon Press: 462–488.

Madanda, Aramanzan (2017) 'Inclusion and exclusion: the case of gender equality in the 2016 elections'. In Joseph Oloka-Onyango and Josephine Ahikire (eds.), *Controlling Consent: Uganda's 2016 Elections*. Trenton, New Jersey: Africa World Press: 173–192.

Mafeje, Archie (1971) 'The ideology of tribalism', *The Journal of Modern African Studies*, 9, no.2: 253–261.

Makara, Sabiti, Geoffrey Tukahebwa and Foster Byarugaba (eds.) (1996) *Politics, Constitutionalism and Electioneering in Uganda. A Study of the 1994 Constituent Assembly Elections*. Kampala: Makerere University Press.

Makara, Sabiti, Lise Rakner and Lars Svåsand (2009) 'Turnaround: the national resistance movement and the reintroduction of a multiparty system in Uganda', *International Political Science Review / Revue internationale de science politique*, 30, no.2: 185–204.

Makara, Sabiti (2010) 'Deepening democracy through multipartyism: the bumpy road to Uganda's 2011 elections', *Africa Spectrum*, 45, no. 2: 81–94.

Manji, Ambreena (2020) *Land, Constitutionalism and the Struggle for Justice in Kenya*. Woodbridge: Boydell & Brewer.

Mann, Michael (2005) *The Dark Side of Democracy. Explaining Ethnic Cleansing*. Cambridge: Cambridge University Press.

Mansfield, Edward D. and Jack L. Snyder (2007) 'The "sequencing fallacy"', *Journal of Democracy*, 18, no.3: 5–10.

Mapuva, Jephias (2013) 'Elections and electoral processes in Africa: a gimmick or a curse?', *African Journal of History and Culture*, 5, no. 5: 87–95.

March, James and John. P. Olsen (2011) 'The logic of appropriateness'. In Robert Goodin (ed.), *The Oxford Handbook of Political Science*. Oxford: Oxford University Press: 478–498.

Mares, Isabela and Lauren Young (2016) 'Buying, expropriating, and stealing votes', *Annual Review of Political Science*, 19: 267–288.

Mattes, Robert (2002) 'South Africa: democracy without the people', *Journal of Democracy*, 13, no.1: 22–28.

Mattes, Robert and Shaheen Mozaffar (2016) 'Legislatures and democratic development in Africa', *African Studies Review*, 59, no.3: 201–215.

McFaul, Michael (2004) 'Democracy promotion as a world value', *The Washington Quarterly*, 28, no.1: 147–163.

Médard, Claire and Valérie Golaz (2013) 'Creating dependency: land and gift-giving practices in Uganda', *Journal of Eastern African Studies*, 7, no. 3: 549–568.

Meinert, Lotte and Anne Mette Kjær (2016) '"Land belongs to the people of Uganda": politicians' use of land issues in the 2016 election campaigns', *Journal of Eastern African Studies*, 10, no.4: 769–788.

Menthong, Hélène-Laure (1998) 'Vote et communautarisme au Cameroun: "un vote de cœur, de sang et de raison"', *Politique Africaine*, 69: 40–52.

Mercer, Claire (2002) 'NGOs, civil society and democratization: a critical review of the literature', *Progress in Development Studies*, 2, no.1: 5–22.

Mercer, Claire (2003) 'Performing partnership: civil society and the illusions of good governance in Tanzania', *Political Geography*, 22, no. 7: 741–763.

Merloe, Patrick (2015) 'Election monitoring vs. disinformation', *Journal of Democracy*, 26, no.3: 79–93.

Mesfin, Berouk (2008) *Democracy, Elections and Political Parties: A Conceptual Overview with Special Emphasis on Africa*. Pretoria: Institute for Security Studies Papers, no. 166. https://media.africaportal.org/documents/PAPER166.pdf.

Meyer, Birgit (2008) 'Powerful pictures: popular Christian aesthetics in southern Ghana', *Journal of the American Academy of Religion*, 76, no.1: 82–110.

Migdal, Joel (2001) 'The state in society approach. A new definition of the state and transcending the narrowly constructed world of rigor'. In Joel Migdal (ed.), *State in Society: Studying How State and Society Transform and Constitute One Another*. Cambridge: Cambridge University Press: 3–38.

Miguel, Edward (2004) 'Tribe or nation? Nation building and public goods in Kenya versus Tanzania', *World Politics*, 56, no.3: 327–362.

Mitchell, Timothy (1991) 'The limits of the state: beyond statist approaches and their critics', *American Political Science Review*, 85, no.1: 77–96.

Mitullah, W. V. (2015) 'Constituency development fund: issues and challenges of management'. In Orieko P. Chitere and Roberta Mutiso (eds.), *Working with Rural Communities. Participatory Action Research in Kenya*. Nairobi: University of Nairobi Press: 263–273.

Mitullah, Winnie (2020) 'Gender mainstreaming and the campaign for equality'. In Nic Cheeseman, Karuti Kanyinga and Gabrielle Lynch (eds.), *Oxford Handbook of Kenyan Politics*. Oxford: Oxford University Press: 163–177.

Mkandawire, Thandika (1999) 'Crisis management and the making of choiceless democracies'. In Richard Joseph (ed.), *State, Conflict and Democracy in Africa*. Boulder: Lynne Rienner: 119–136.

Moehler, Devra C. (2013) 'Critical citizens and submissive subjects: election losers and winners in Africa'. In Michael Bratton (ed.), *Voting and Democratic Citizenship in Africa*. Boulder, CO: Lynne Rienner: 219–237.

Moehler, Devra C. and Staffan I. Lindberg (2009) 'Narrowing the legitimacy gap: turnovers as a cause of democratic consolidation', *The Journal of Politics*, 71, no.4: 1448–1466.

Møller, Jørgen (2007) 'The gap between electoral and liberal democracy revisited. Some conceptual and empirical clarifications', *Acta Politica*, 42, no. 4: 380–400.

Monga, Célestin (1995) 'Civil society and democratisation in Francophone Africa', *The Journal of Modern African Studies*, 33, no.3: 359–379.

Monga, Célestin (1997) 'Eight problems with African politics', *Journal of Democracy*, 8, no.3: 156–170.

Morgenthau, Ruth S. (1964) *Political Parties in French-Speaking West Africa*. Oxford: Clarendon Press.

Morrison, Minion (2004) 'Political parties in Ghana through four republics: a path to democratic consolidation', *Comparative Politics*, 36, no.4: 421–442.

Moskowitz, Kara (2019) *Seeing Like a Citizen. Decolonization, Development and the Making of Kenya, 1945–1980*. Athens, Ohio: Ohio University Press.

Mozaffar, Shaheen (2002) 'Patterns of electoral governance in Africa's emerging democracies', *International Political Science Review*, 23, no.1: 85–101.

Mozaffar, Shaheen and Andreas Schedler (2002) 'The comparative study of electoral governance: introduction', *International Political Science Review*, 23, no.1: 5–27.

Mueller, Susanne D. (1984) 'Government and opposition in Kenya, 1966–69', *The Journal of Modern African Studies*, 22, no.3: 399–427.

Mueller, Susanne D. (2008) 'The political economy of Kenya's crisis', *Journal of Eastern African Studies*, 2, no.2: 185–210.

Mueller, Susanne D. (2011) 'Dying to win: elections, political violence, and institutional decay in Kenya, *Journal of Contemporary African Studies*, 29, no.1: 99–117.

Mugisha, Anne (2004) 'Museveni's machinations', *Journal of Democracy*, 15, no.2: 140–144.

Muhula, Raymond (2020) 'The limits of multipartyism (1992–2005)'. In Nic Cheeseman, Karuti Kanyinga and Gabrielle Lynch (eds.), *Oxford Handbook of Kenyan Politics*. Oxford: Oxford University Press: 69–81.

Muhumuza, William (1997) 'Money and power in Uganda's 1996 elections', *African Journal of Political Science*, 2, no.1: 168–179.

Muhumuza, William (2009) 'From fundamental change to no change: the NRM and democratization in Uganda', *Democracy*, 76, no.6: 21–42.

Mujaju, Akiiki (1996) 'Constituent assembly elections in Fort Portal municipality, Kabarole District' in S. E. Makara, G. B. Tukahebwa and F. Byarugaba (eds), *Politics, Constitutionalism and Electioneering in Uganda: A Study of the 1994 Constituent Assembly Elections*. Kampala: Makerere University Press: 47–63.

Murunga, Godwin and Shadrack Nasong'o (2006) 'Bent on self-destruction: the Kibaki regime in Kenya', *Journal of Contemporary African Studies*, 24, no. 1: 1–28.

Murison, Jude (2013) 'Judicial politics: election petitions and electoral fraud in Uganda', *Journal of Eastern African Studies*, 7, no.3: 492–508.

Muro, Diego (2005) 'Nationalism and nostalgia: the case of radical Basque nationalism', *Nations and Nationalism*, 11, no.4: 571–589.

Mushemeza, Elijah D. (2001) 'Issues of violence in the democratisation process in Uganda', *Africa Development*, 26, no.1/2: 55–72.

Mutahi, Patrick (2005) 'Political violence in the elections'. In Herve Maupeu, Musambayi Katumanga and Winnie Mitullah (eds.), The Moi Succession: The 2002 Elections in Kenya.. Nairobi: Transafrica Press: 69–96.

Mutahi, Patrick and Mutuma Ruteere (2019) 'Violence, security and the policing of Kenya's 2017 elections', *Journal of Eastern African Studies*, 13, no.2: 253–271.

Mwenda, Andrew (2007) 'Personalizing power in Uganda', *Journal of Democracy*, 18, no. 3: 23–37.

Nasong'o, Shadrack W. and Gordon R. Murunga (2007) 'Prospects for democracy in Kenya'. In Godwin R. Murunga and Shadrack W. Nasong'o (eds.), *Kenya. The Struggle for Democracy*. Dakar: CODESRIA: 3–18.

Nathan, Noah L. (2016) 'Local ethnic geography, expectations of favouritism, and voting in urban Ghana', *Comparative Political Studies*, 49, no.14: 1896–1929.

Ndegwa, Stephen N. (1996) *Two Faces of Civil Society: NGOs and Politics in Africa*. Boulder, Colorado: Kumarian Press.

Nevitte, Neil and Santiago A. Canton (1997) 'The role of domestic observers', *Journal of Democracy*, 8, no. 3: 47–61.

Ngacho, Christopher and Debadyuti Das (2014) 'A performance evaluation framework of development projects: an empirical study of Constituency Development Fund (CDF) construction projects in Kenya', *International Journal of Project Management*, 32, no.3: 492–507.

Ninsin, Kwame (1993) 'The electoral system, elections and democracy in Ghana'. In Kwame Ninsin and F. K. Drah (eds.), *Political Parties and Democracy in Ghana's Fourth Republic*. Accra: Department of Political Sciences, Legon: 175–191.

Ninsin, Kwame (1998a) 'Civic associations and the transition to democracy'. In Kwame Ninsin (ed.) *Ghana: Transition to Democracy*. Dakar: CODESRIA: 49–81.

Ninsin, Kwame (1998b) 'Postscript: elections, democracy and elite consensus'. In Kwame Ninsin (ed.), *Ghana: Transition to Democracy*. Dakar: CODESRIA: 211–229.

Ninsin, Kwame (2006) 'The contradictions and ironies of elections in Africa', *Africa Development*, 31, no.3: 1–10.

Njogu, Kimani (2005) 'Ahadi ni deni'. In Herve Maupeu, Musambayi Katumanga and Winnie Mitullah (eds.), The Moi Succession: *The 2002 Elections in Kenya.*. Nairobi: Transafrica Press: 401–432.

Nketiah, Eric Sakyi (2005) 'A History of Women in Politics in Ghana', MPhil Dissertation, University of Cape Coast, https://erl.ucc.edu.gh/jspui/handle/12 3456789/1815.

Nkrumah, Kwame (1961) *I Speak of Freedom: A Statement of African Ideology*. London: Heinemann.

Nkuubi, James (2017) 'Of "yellow" police, a cadre army and the liberation war psychosis: the question of electoral security'. In Joseph Oloka-Onyango and Josephine Ahikire (eds.), *Controlling Consent: Uganda's 2016 Elections*. Trenton, NJ: Africa World Press: 401–430.

Norris, Pippa (2015) *Why Elections Fail*. Cambridge: Cambridge University Press.

Nugent, Paul (1995) *Big Men, Small Boys and Politics in Ghana: Power, Ideology and the Burden of History, 1982–1994*. London: Pinter Publishers Ltd.

Nugent, Paul (1996) 'An abandoned project? The nuances of chieftaincy, development and history in Ghana's Volta Region', *The Journal of Legal Pluralism and Unofficial Law*, 28, nos. 37–38: 203–225.

Nugent, Paul (1999) 'Living in the past: rural, urban and ethnic themes in the 1992 and 1996 elections in Ghana', *The Journal of Modern African Studies*, 37, no.2: 287–319.

Nugent, Paul (2001a) 'Ethnicity as an explanatory factor in the Ghana 2000 elections', *African Issues*, 29, no. 1/2: 2–7.

Nugent, Paul (2001b) 'Winners, losers and also rans: money, moral authority and voting patterns in the Ghana 2000 elections', *African Affairs*, 100, no. 400: 405–428.

Nugent, Paul (2007) 'Banknotes and symbolic capital'. In Matthias, Basedau, Gero Erdmann and Andreas Mehler (eds.), *Votes, Money and Violence: Political Parties and Elections in Sub-Saharan Africa*. Uppsala: Nordiska Afrikainstitutet: 252–275.

Nyabola, Nanjala (2018) *Digital Democracy, Analogue Politics: How the Internet Era is Transforming Politics in Kenya*. London: Zed Books Ltd.

Nyairo, Joyce (2015) 'The circus comes to town: performance, religion and exchange in political party campaigns'. In Kimani Njogu and Peter W. Wekesa (eds.), *Kenya's 2013 Election: Stakes, Practices and Outcomes*. Nairobi: Twaweza Communications Ltd: 124–143.

Nyangira, Nicholas (1987) 'Ethnicity, class, and politics in Kenya'. In Michael Schatzberg (ed.), *The Political Economy of Kenya*. New York, NY: Praeger: 15–31.

Nye, Joseph S. (1990) 'Soft power', *Foreign Policy*, 80: 153–171.

Nzongola-Ntalaja, Georges (2004) 'Citizenship, political violence and democratization in Africa', *Global Governance*, 10, no.4: 403–409.

Nzongola-Ntalaja, Georges (2006) 'Democratic transition in Africa', *The Constitution*, 6, no.1: 1–19.

Obi, Cyril (2011) 'Taking back our democracy? The trials and travails of Nigerian elections since 1999', *Democratization*, 18, no.2: 366–387.

Ocitti, Jim (2000) *Political Evolution and Democratic Practice in Uganda, 1952–1996*. Edwin Mellen: Lewiston and Lampeter.

Ocobock, Paul (2017) *An Uncertain Age: The Politics of Manhood in Kenya*. Athens: Ohio University Press.

Odeh, Lemuel (2016) 'African Union Election Observation Mission: opportunities and challenges', unpublished paper: University of Ilorin, Ilorin, www .academia.edu/23189415/AFRICAN_UNION_ELECTION_OBSERVER_ MISSION_OPPORTUNITIES_AND_CHALLENGES.

Odukoya, Adelaja (2007) 'Democracy, elections, election monitoring and peace-building in West Africa', *African Journal of International Affairs*, 10, nos.1 & 2: 147–160.

Okoth-Ogendo, H. W. (1972) 'The politics of constitutional change in Kenya since independence, 1963–69', *African Affairs*, 71, no.282: 9–34.

Oloka-Onyango, Joseph and Josephine Ahikire (2017) 'How do you control consent?'. Joseph Oloka-Onyango and Josephine Ahikire (eds), Controlling *Consent: Uganda's 2016 Elections*. Trenton, NJ and London: Africa World Press: 1–16.

Oloka-Onyango, Joseph and J. J. Barya (1997) 'Civil society and the political economy of foreign aid in Uganda', *Democratization*, 4, no.2: 113–138.

Oloo, Adams (2005) 'The Raila Factor in Luoland'. In Herve Maupeu, Musambayi Katumanga and Winnie Mitullah (eds.), The Moi Succession: The 2002 Elections in Kenya. Nairobi: Transafrica Press: 159–196.

Oloo, Adams (2007) 'The contemporary opposition in Kenya: between internal traits and state manipulation', In Godwin R. Murunga and Shadrack W. Nasong'o (eds.), Kenya: the Struggle for Democracy. London: Zed Books: 90–123.

Olukoshi, Adebayo (1998) 'The democracy debate in Africa – an outline'. In Steve Kayizzi-Mugerwa, Adebayo Olukoshi and Lennet Wohlgemuth (eds.), Towards a New Partnership with Africa: Challenges and Opportunities. Uppsala: Nordiska Afrikainstitutet: 15–41.

Omach, Paul (2014) 'Peace, security and elections in northern Uganda'. In Sandrine Perrot, Sabiti Makara, Jérôme Lafargue and Marie-Aude Fouéré (eds), Elections in a Hybrid Regime: Revisiting the 2011 Ugandan Polls: 348–371.

Omanga, Duncan (2019) 'WhatsApp as "digital publics": the Nakuru Analysts and the evolution of participation in county governance in Kenya', Journal of Eastern African Studies, 13, no.1, 175–191.

Omobowale, Ayokunle O. (2008) 'Clientelism and social structure: an analysis of patronage in Yoruba social thought', Africa Spectrum, 43, no.2: 203–224.

Omotola, J. Shola (2013) 'The Electoral Commission of Ghana and the conduct of the 2012 elections', Journal of African Elections, 12, no.2: 34–55.

Opalo, Ken Ochieng' (2019) 'The politics of legislative development'. In Gabrielle Lynch and Peter VonDoepp (eds.), Routledge Handbook of Democratization in Africa. Abingdon: Routledge.

Oquaye, Mike (1995) 'The Ghanaian elections of 1992 – a dissenting view', African Affairs, 94, no.375: 259–275.

Orvis, Stephen (2003) 'Kenyan civil society: bridging the urban-rural divide?', The Journal of Modern African Studies, 41, no.2: 247–268.

Osaghae, Eghosa E. (1995) 'Amoral politics and democratic instability in Africa: a theoretical exploration', Nordic Journal of African Studies, 4, no. 1: 62–78.

Osaghae, Eghosa E. (1999) 'Democratization in sub-Saharan Africa: faltering prospects, new hopes', Journal of Contemporary African Studies, 17, no.1: 5–28.

Osaghae, Eghosa E. (2004) 'Making democracy work in Africa: from the institutional to the substantive', Journal of African Elections, 3, no. 1: 1–12.

Osborn, Michelle (2008) 'Fuelling the flames: rumour and politics in Kibera', Journal of Eastern African Studies, 2, no.2: 315–327.

Osei, Anja (2012) Party-voter Inkage in Africa: Ghana and Senegal in Comparative Perspective. Konstanz: Springer VS.

Osei, Anja (2016) 'Formal party organisation and informal relations in African parties: evidence from Ghana', The Journal of Modern African Studies, 54, no.1: 37–66.

Ost, David (2004) 'Politics as the mobilization of anger: emotions in movements and in power', European Journal of Social Theory, 7, no.2: 229–244.

Otayek, René (1998) 'Les elections en Afrique sont-elles un objet scientifique pertinent?', Politique Africaine, 69: 3–11.

Oucho, John O. (2002) Undercurrents of Ethnic Conflict in Kenya. Leiden, Netherlands: Brill.

Oucho, John O. (2010) 'Undercurrents of post-election violence in Kenya: issues in the long-term agenda'. In Karuti Kanyinga and Duncan Okello (eds.), *Tensions and Reversals in Democratic Transitions: The Kenya 2007 General Elections*. Nairobi: Society for International Development: 491–532.

Ouma, Seth (2018) 'Democracy, development and dynasty politics: Kenya's Luo Nyanza as a laboratory, 1992–2017', MSc dissertation, University of Oxford.

Ovadia, Jesse S. (2011) 'Stepping back from the brink: a review of the 2008 Ghanaian election from the capital of the northern region', *Canadian Journal of African Studies*, 45, no.2: 310–340.

Owusu, Maxwell (1971) 'Culture and democracy in West Africa: some persistent problems', *Africa Today*, 18, no.1: 68–76.

Owusu, Maxwell (1975) 'Politics in Swedru'. In Dennis Austin and Robin Luckham (eds), Politicians and Soldiers in Ghana 1966–1972. London: Frank Cass: 233–263.

Owusu, Maxwell (1979) 'Politics without parties: reflections on the Union Government proposals in Ghana', *African Studies Review*, 22, no. 1: 89–108.

Owusu, Maxwell (1992) 'Democracy and Africa – a view from the village', *The Journal of Modern African Studies*, 30, no.3: 369–396.

Oyugi, Walter O. (1987) 'Bureaucracy and democracy in Africa'. In Walter O. Oyugi and Afrifa Gitonga (eds.), *Democratization: Theory and Practice in Africa*. Nairobi: East African Educational Publishers: 99–110.

Pachai, Bridglal (1965) 'An outline of the history of municipal government at Cape Coast', *Transactions of the Historical Society of Ghana*, 8: 130–160.

Paget, Dan (2019a) 'The authoritarian origins of well-organized opposition parties: the rise of Chadema in Tanzania', *African Affairs*, 118, no.473: 692–711.

Paget, Dan (2019b) 'The rally-intensive campaign: a distinct form of electioneering in sub-Saharan Africa', *The International Journal of Press/Politics*, 24, no.4: 444–464.

Pastor, Robert (1999) 'The role of electoral administration in democratic transitions: implications for policy and research', *Democratization*, 6, no.4: 1–27.

Peiffer, Caryn and Pierre Englebert (2012) 'Extraversion, vulnerability to donors, and political liberalization in Africa', *African Affairs*, 111, no.444: 355–378.

Pels, Peter (2007) 'Imagining elections: modernity, mediation and the secret ballot in late colonial Tanganyika'. In Romain Bertrand, Peter Pels and Jean-Louis Briquet (eds), Cultures of Voting: The Hidden History of the Secret Ballot. London: Hurst: 100–113.

Perrot, Sandrine, Sabiti Makara, Jérôme Lafargue and Marie-Aude Fouéré (eds.) (2014) *Elections in a Hybrid Regime: Revisiting the 2011 Uganda Polls*. Kampala: Fountain Publishers.

Perrot, Sandrine, Jérôme Lafargue and Sabiti Makara (2014) 'Introduction: looking back at the 2011 multiparty elections in Uganda'. In Perrot, Sandrine, Sabiti Makara, Jérôme Lafargue and Marie-Aude Fouéré, (eds.), *Elections in a Hybrid Regime: Revisiting the 2011 Ugandan Polls*. Kampala: Fountain Publishers: 1–34.

Perrot, Sandrine (2016) 'Partisan defections in contemporary Uganda: the micro-dynamics of hegemonic party-building', *Journal of Eastern African Studies*, 10, no.4: 713–728.

Peters, Ralph-Michael (2001) 'Civil society and the election year 1997 in Kenya'. In Marcel Rutten, Alamin Mazrui and François Grignon (eds.), *Out for the Count: The 1997 General Elections and Prospects for Democracy in Kenya*. Kampala: Fountain Publishers: 29–49.

Peterson, Derek and Edgar C. Taylor (2013) 'Rethinking the state in Idi Amin's Uganda: the politics of exhortation', *Journal of Eastern African Studies*, 7, no.1: 58–82.

Peterson, Derek (2020) 'Colonial rule and the rise of African politics (1930–1964)'. In Nic Cheeseman, Karuti Kanyinga and Gabrielle Lynch (eds.), *Oxford Handbook of Kenyan Politics*. Oxford: Oxford University Press: 29–42.

Piccolino, Giulia (2016) 'Infrastructural state capacity for democratization? Voter registration and identification in Côte d'Ivoire and Ghana compared', *Democratization*, 23, no.3: 498–519.

Pinkston, Amanda Leigh (2016) 'Insider democracy: private sector weakness and the closed political class in democratic Africa', PhD dissertation, Harvard University, https://dash.harvard.edu/handle/1/33840666.

Pitcher, Anne, May H. Moran and Michael Johnston (2009) 'Rethinking patrimonialism and neopatrimonialism in Africa', *African Studies Review*, 51, no.1: 125–156.

Pommerolle, Marie-Emmanuelle (2008) 'La démobilisation collective au Cameroun: entre régime postautoritaire et militantisme extraverti', *Critique Internationale*, 3: 73–94.

Pommerolle, Marie-Emmanuelle (2016) 'Donors and the making of "credible" elections in Cameroon'. In Tobias Hagmann and Filip Reyntjens (eds.), *Aid and Authoritarianism in Africa: Development without Democracy*. London: Zed Books: 119–138.

Porter, Theodore (2006) 'Speaking precision to power: the modern political role of social science', *Social Research*, 73, no.4: 1273–1294.

Posner, Daniel N. (2004) 'The political salience of cultural difference: why Chewas and Tumbukas are allies in Zambia and adversaries in Malawi', *American Political Science Review*, 98, no. 4: 529–545.

Posner, Daniel N. (2007) 'Regime change and ethnic cleavages in Africa', *Comparative Political Studies*, 40, no. 11: 1302–1327.

Posner, Daniel N. and Daniel J. Young (2007) 'The institutionalization of political power in Africa', *Journal of Democracy*, 18, no.3: 126–140.

Prempeh, H. Kwasi (2008) 'Presidents untamed', *Journal of Democracy*, 19, no.2: 109–123.

Prasad, Monica, Andrew J. Perrin, Kieran Bezila, Steve G. Hoffman, Kate Kindleberger, Kim Manturuk, Ashleigh Smith Powers and Andrew R. Payton. 'The undeserving rich: "moral values" and the white working class', *Sociological Forum*, 24, no. 2: 225–253.

Price, Robert (1974) 'Politics and culture in contemporary Ghana: the Big-man Small-boy syndrome', *Journal of African Studies*, 1, no.2: 173–204.

Provizer, Norman (1977) 'The national electoral process and state building: proposals for new methods of election in Uganda', *Comparative Politics*, 9, no.3: 305–326.

Putnam, Robert D. (1994) *Making Democracy Work: Civic Traditions in Modern Italy*. Princeton, NJ: Princeton University Press.

Pykett, Jessica (2007) 'Making citizens governable? The crick report as governmental technology', *Journal of Education Policy*, 22, no.3: 301–319.

Pykett, Jessica, Michael Saward and Anja Schaefer (2010) 'Framing the good citizen', *British Journal of Politics and International Relations*, 12: 523–538.

Quantin, Patrick (1998) 'Pour une analyse comparative des elections africaines', *Politique Africaine*, 69: 12–28.

Rajak, Dinah (2010) '"HIV/AIDS is our problem": the moral economy of treatment in a transnational mining company', *Journal of the Royal Anthropological Institute, NS*, 16: 551–571.

Rathbone, Richard (1973) 'Businessmen in politics: party struggle in Ghana, 1949–57', *Journal of Development Studies*, 9, no.3: 391–401.

Rathbone, Richard (1978) 'Ghana'. In John Dunn (ed.), *West African States: Failure and Promise*. Cambridge: Cambridge University Press: 22–35.

Rathbone, Richard (ed.) (1992) *British Documents on the End of Empire: Ghana*. London: HMSO. vol. II, pp. 251–255.

Reid, Richard (2017) *A History of Modern Uganda*. Cambridge: Cambridge University Press.

Resnick, Danielle (2017) 'Democracy, decentralization, and district proliferation: the case of Ghana', *Political Geography*, 59: 47–60.

Reyes-Foster, Beatriz M. (2014) 'Creating order in the bureaucratic register: an analysis of suicide crime scene investigations in Southern Mexico', *Critical Discourse Studies*, 11, no.4: 377–396.

Reynolds, Andrew (1999) 'Women in the legislatures and executives of the world: knocking at the highest glass ceiling', *World Politics*, 51, no.4: 547–572.

Reyntjens, Filip (2011) 'Behind the façade of Rwanda's elections', *Georgetown Journal of International Affairs*, 12, no. 2: 64–69.

Robert-Nicoud, Nathalie Raunet (2019) 'Elections and borderlands in Ghana', *African Affairs*, 184, no.473: 672–691.

Robbins, Paul and Julie T. Sharp (2003) 'Producing and consuming chemicals: the moral economy of the American lawn', *Economic Geography*, 79, no.4: 425–451.

Robinson, William (2013) 'Promoting polyarchy: 20 years later', *International Relations*, 27, no.2: 228–234.

Roelofs, Portia (2019) 'Beyond programmatic versus patrimonial politics: contested conceptions of legitimate distribution in Nigeria', *The Journal of Modern African Studies*, 57, no.3: 415–436.

Roessler, Philip G. and Marc M. Howard (2009) 'Post-cold war political regimes: when do elections matter?'. In Staffan I. Lindberg (ed.), *Democratization by Elections: A New Mode of Transition*. Baltimore, MD: Johns Hopkins University Press: 101–127.

Rogan, Tim (2017) *The Moral Economists. R. H. Tawney, Karl Polanyi, E. P. Thompson, and the Critique of Capitalism*. Princeton: Princeton University Press.

Rokkan, Stein (1961) 'Mass suffrage, secret voting and political participation', *European Journal of Sociology*, 2, no.1: 132–152.

Rose, Nikolas (1991) 'Governing by numbers: figuring out democracy', *Accounting, Organizations and Society*, 16, no.7: 673–692.

Russell, A. C. (1951) 'The gold coast general elections, 1951', *Journal of African Administration*, 3, no. 1: 65–77.

Rutten, Marcel, Alamin Mazrui and François Grignon (2001) *Out for the Count. The 1997 General Elections and the Prospects for Democracy in Kenya*. Kampala: Fountain Publishers.

Rutten, Marcel (2000) 'The Kenyan general elections of 1997: implementing a new model for international election observation in Africa'. In Foeken, Dick, Ton Dietz, Jon Abbink and Gerti Hesseling (eds.), *Election Observation and Democratization in Africa*. London: Palgrave Macmillan: 295–320.

Rutten, Marcel (2001) 'The Kenya 1997 general elections in Maasailand: of "sons" and "puppets" and how KANU defeated itself'. In Marcel Rutten, Alamin Mazrui and François Grignon (eds.), *Out for the Count: The 1997 General Elections and Prospects for Democracy in Kenya*. Kampala: Fountain Publishers: 405–439.

Sabar, Galia (2002) *Church, State, and Society in Kenya: From Mediation to Opposition, 1963–1993*. London: Frank Cass.

Sabar-Friedman, Galia (1997) 'Church and state in Kenya, 1986–1992: the churches' involvement in the "game of change"', *African Affairs*, 96, no.382: 25–52.

Sandbrook, Richard and Jay Oelbaum (1997) 'Reforming dysfunctional institutions through democratisation? Reflections on Ghana', *The Journal of Modern African Studies*, 35, no.4: 603–646.

Sanger, Clyde and John Nottingham (1964) 'The Kenya general election of 1963', *The Journal of Modern African Studies*, 2, no.1: 1–40.

de Sardan, J. P. Olivier (1999) 'A moral economy of corruption in Africa?' *The Journal of Modern African Studies*, 37, no.1: 25–52.

Saward, Michael (2006) 'The representative claim', *Contemporary Political Theory*, 5, no.3: 297–318.

Sayer, Andrew (2007) 'Moral economy as critique', *New Political Economy*, 12, no.2: 261–270.

Schaffer, Frederic C. (1998) *Democracy in Translation. Understanding Politics in an Unfamiliar Culture*. Ithaca and London: Cornell University Press.

Schaffer, Frederic C. (2002) 'Might cleaning up elections keep people away from the polls? Historical and comparative perspectives', *International Political Science Review*, 23, no. 1: 69–84.

Schaffer, Frederic C. (2005) '"Clean elections and the great unwashed." Vote buying and voter education in the Philippines', Paper no. 21, School of Social Science, Princeton NJ. http://citeseerx.ist.psu.edu/viewdoc/download?doi=10.1.1.520.359&rep=rep1&type=pdf.

Schaffer, Frederic C. (ed.) (2007a) *Elections for Sale: The Causes and Consequences of Vote Buying*. Boulder: Lynne Rienner.

Schaffer, Frederic C. (2007b) 'How effective is voter education?'. In Schaffer (ed.), Elections for Sale: The Causes and Consequences of Vote Buying. Boulder: Lynne Rienner: 161–179.

Schaffer, Frederic C. (2008) *The Hidden Costs of Clean Election Reform*. Ithaca and London: Cornell.

Schaffer, Frederic C. and Andreas Schedler (2005) 'What is vote-buying? The limits of the market model', Conference paper delivered at Stanford University. https://polsci.umass.edu/file/904/download?token=wqyQOKoP.

Schaffer, Frederic C. and Andreas Schedler (2007) 'What is vote-buying?'. In Frederic C. Schaffer (ed.), *Elections for Sale. The Causes and Consequences of Vote-Buying*. Boulder, CO: Lynne Rienner: 17–30.

Schatzberg, Michael G. (1993) 'Power, legitimacy and "democratisation" in Africa', *Africa*, 63, no. 4: 445–461.

Schedler, Andreas (2002) 'The menu of manipulation', *Journal of Democracy*, 13, no. 2: 36–50.

Schmitz, Afra (2018) '"Once they all pick their guns you can have your way": campaigning and talking about violence in northern Ghana'. In M. Soderberg Kovacs and Jesper Bjarnesen (eds.), *Violence in African Elections: Between Democracy and Big Man Politics*. Uppsala: Nordiska Afrikainstitutet: 233–249.

Schroven, Anita 'The people, the power and the public service: political identification during Guinea's general strikes in 2007', *Development and Change*, 41, no. 4: 659–677.

Schuessler, Alexander (2000) 'Expressive voting', *Rationality and Society*, 12, no.1: 87–119.

Scott, James C. (1977) *The Moral Economy of the Peasant: Rebellion and Subsistence in Southeast Asia*. New Haven: Yale University Press.

Sekindi, Fred (2017) 'Presidential election disputes in Uganda. A critical analysis of the Supreme Court decisions', *Journal of African Elections*, 16, no. 1: 154–179.

Shaloff, Stanley (1974) 'The Cape Coast *asafo* company riot of 1932', *The International Journal of African Historical Studies*, 7, no.4: 591–607.

Shils, Edward (1960) 'Political development in the new states, Part I', *Comparative Studies in Society and History*, 2, no.3: 265–292.

Signé, Landry (2019) 'Executive power and horizontal accountability'. In Gabrielle Lynch and Peter VonDoepp (eds.), *Routledge Handbook of Democratization in Africa*. Abingdon: Routledge.

Siméant, Johanna (2010) '"Économie morale" et protestation – detours Africains', *Genèses*, 81: 118–136.

Simpser, Alberto and Daniela Donno (2012) 'Can international election monitoring harm governance?', *The Journal of Politics*, 74, no.2: 501–513.

Sindjoun, Luc. (1997) 'Élections et politique au Cameroun: concurrence déloyale, coalitions de stabilité hégémonique et politique d'affection', *African Journal of Political Science/Revue Africaine de Science Politique*, 2, no.1: 89–121.

Sives, Amanda (2001) 'A review of commonwealth election observation', *Commonwealth and Comparative Politics*, 39, no.3: 132–149.

Sjöberg, Fredrik (2011) *Competitive Elections in Authoritarian States: Weak States, Strong Elites and Fractional Societies in Central Asia and Beyond*. Uppsala: Uppsala Universitet.

Sjögren, Anders (2018) 'Wielding the stick again: the rise and fall of state violence during presidential elections in Uganda'. In Mimmi Soderberg Kovacs and

Jesper Bjarnesen (eds.), *Violence in African Elections: Between Democracy and Big Man Politics*. Uppsala: Nordiska Afrikainstitute: 47–66.

Skinner, Kate (2007) 'Reading, writing and rallies: the politics of "freedom" in southern British Togoland, 1953–56', *The Journal of African History*, 48: 123–147.

Skinner, Kate (2015) *The Fruits of Freedom in British Togoland: Literacy, Politics and Nationalism, 1914–2014*. Cambridge: Cambridge University Press.

Skitka, Linda J. and Christopher W. Bauman (2008) 'Moral conviction and political engagement', *Political Psychology*, 29, no.1: 29–54.

Smith, Daniel (2002) 'Consolidating democracy? The structural underpinnings of Ghana's 2000 elections', *The Journal of Modern African Studies*, 40, no.4: 621–650.

Smith, Rogers M. (2001) 'Citizenship and the politics of people-building', *Citizenship Studies*, 5, no.1, 73–96.

Socpa, Antoine (2000) 'Les dons dans le jeu électoral au Cameroun', *Cahiers d'études africaines*, 40, no.157: 91–108.

Steel, Robert Walter (1948) 'The population of Ashanti: a geographical analysis', *The Geographical Journal*, 112, no. 1/3: 64–77.

Steeves, Jeffrey S. (1999) 'The political evolution of Kenya: the 1997 elections and succession politics' *Journal of Commonwealth & Comparative Politics*, 37, no.1: 71–94.

Steinhart, Edward (1973) 'Royal clientage and the beginnings of colonial modernization in Toro, 1891–1900', *International Journal of African Historical Studies*, 6, no.2: 262–285.

Stepan, Alfred (2015) 'India, Sri Lanka, and the majoritarian danger', *Journal of Democracy*, 26, no.1: 128–140.

Stewart, Francis (ed.) (2008) *Horizontal Inequalities and Conflict: Understanding Group Violence in Multiethnic Societies*. Basingstoke: Palgrave.

Stockwell, John and Donald Perley (1978) *In Search of Enemies: a CIA story*. New York: Norton.

Stoeltje, Beverly J. (2010) 'Custom and politics in Ghanaian popular culture'. In Toyin Falola and Fallou Ngom (eds.), *Facts, Fiction, and African Creative Imaginations*. New York: Routledge: 60–74.

Stroh, Alexander (2010) 'Electoral rules of the authoritarian game: undemocratic effects of proportional representation in Rwanda', *Journal of Eastern African Studies*, 4, no.1: 1–19.

Takougang, Joseph (2003) 'The 2002 legislative election in Cameroon: a retrospective on Cameroon's stalled democracy movement', *The Journal of Modern African Studies*, 41, no.3: 421–435.

Takyi, Baffour K., Chris Opoku-Agyeman and Agnes Kutin-Mensah (2010) 'Religion and the public sphere: religious involvement and voting patterns in Ghana's 2004 elections', *Africa Today*, 56, no.4: 62–86.

Tankard, Margaret L and Elizabeth Levy Paluck (2016) 'Norm perception as vehicle for social change', *Social Issues and Policy Review*, 10, no.1: 181–211.

Tapscott, Rebecca (2016) 'Where the wild things are not: crime preventers and the 2016 Ugandan elections', *Journal of Eastern African Studies*, 10, no.4, 693–712.

Technical Working Group (2018) *Points Taken: A CSO Proposal for Setting the Electoral Reform Agenda in Kenya. The Report of the National Election Observer Symposium.* Nairobi: ELOG.

Tettey, Wisdom J. (2019) 'Digital media, networked spaces, and politics'. In Gabrielle Lynch and Peter VonDoepp (eds.), *Routledge Handbook of Democratization in Africa.* Abingdon: Routledge: 378–391.

Thompson, Edward P. (1971) 'The moral economy of the English crowd in the eighteenth century', *Past & Present*, 50: 76–136.

Throup, David (1993) 'Elections and political legitimacy in Kenya', *Africa*, 63, no.3: 371–396.

Throup, David (1995) 'Render unto Caesar the things that are Caesar's: the politics of church-state conflict in Kenya 1978–1990'. In Holger Bernt Hansen and Michael Twaddle (eds.), *Religion and Politics in East Africa.* London: James Currey: 143–176.

Throup, David and Charles Hornsby (1998) *Multi-Party Politics in Kenya.* Oxford and Nairobi: James Currey and EAEP.

Titeca, Kristof (2014) 'The commercialisation of Uganda's 2011 election in the urban informal economy: money, boda-bodas and market vendors'. In Perrot, Sandrine, Sabiti Makara, Jérôme Lafargue and Marie-Aude Fouéré (eds), Elections in a Hybrid Regime: Revisiting the 2011 Ugandan Polls. Kampala: Fountain Publishers: 178–207.

Trawick, Paul (2001) 'The moral economy of water: equity and antiquity in the Andean commons', *American Anthropologist*, 103, no. 2: 361–379.

Tripp, Aili Mari (2001) 'The politics of autonomy and co-optation in Africa: the case of the Uganda Women's Movement', *The Journal of Modern African Studies*, 39, no.1: 101–128.

Tripp, Aili Mari (2004) 'The changing face of authoritarianism in Africa: the case of Uganda', *Africa Today*, 50, no.3: 3–26.

Tripp, Aili Mari (2010) *Museveni's Uganda: Paradoxes of Power in a Hybrid Regime.* Boulder, CO: Lynne Rienner.

Tripp, Charles (2006) *Islam and the Moral Economy: The Challenge of Capitalism.* Cambridge: Cambridge University Press.

Tsikata, Dzodzi, Maame Gyejye-Jandoh and Martin Hushie (2013) *Political Economy Analysis of Civil Society in Ghana.* Accra: STAR-Ghana.

Twumasi, Yaw (1975) 'The 1969 election'. In Dennis Austin and Robin Luckham (eds.), Politicians and Soldiers in Ghana 1966–72. London: Frank Cass: 140–163.

UHRC [Uganda Human Rights Commission] (2016) *Protection and Promotion of Human Rights in Electoral Processes for the 2016 General Elections.* Kampala: UHRC.

van Stapele, Naomi (2020) 'Youth and masculinity'. In Nic Cheeseman, Karuti Kanyinga and Gabrielle Lynch (eds.), *Oxford Handbook of Kenyan Politics.* Oxford: Oxford University Press: 178–90.

Verdon, Michel (1980) 'Re-defining pre-colonial Ewe polities: the case of Abutia', *Africa*, 50, no. 3: 280–292.

Vernon, James (1993) *Politics and the People. A Study in English Political Culture, c. 1815–1867.* Cambridge: Cambridge University Press.

VonDoepp, Peter (2019) 'Civil society'. In Gabrielle Lynch and Peter VonDoepp (eds.), *Routledge Handbook of Democratization in Africa*. Abingdon: Routledge: 364–377.

Vokes, Richard (2016) 'Primaries, patronage, and political personalities in South-western Uganda', *Journal of Eastern African Studies*, 10, no. 4: 660–676.

Vokes, Richard and Sam Wilkins (2016) 'Party, patronage and coercion in the NRM's 2016 re-election in Uganda: imposed or embedded?', *Journal of Eastern African Studies*, 10, no. 4: 581–600.

Waddilove, Hannah (2019a) 'Support or subvert? Assessing devolution's effect on central power during Kenya's 2017 presidential rerun', *Journal of Eastern African Studies*, 13, no.2, 334–352.

Waddilove, Hannah (2019b) 'The power and politics of devolution in Kenya, 2012–17', PhD dissertation, University of Warwick.

Walker, Andrew (2008) 'The rural constitution and the everyday politics of elections in Northern Thailand', *Journal of Contemporary Asia*, 38, no.1: 84–105.

Wanyama, Fredrick O. (2010) 'Voting without institutionalized political parties: primaries, manifestos and the 2007 general elections in Kenya'. In Karuti Kanyinga and Duncan Okello (eds.), *Tensions and Reversals in Democratic Transitions: The Kenya 2007 General Elections*. Nairobi: Society for International Development: 61–100.

Wanyande, Peter (2002) 'The power of knowledge: the impact of voter education and electoral behaviour in a Kenyan constituency'. In Ludeki Chweya (ed.), *Electoral Politics in Kenya*. Nairobi: ClariPress: 47–69.

Ward, Kevin (1995) 'The Church of Uganda amidst conflict. The interplay between Church and politics in Uganda since 1962'. In Holger Hansen and Michael Twaddle (eds.), *Religion and Politics in East Africa*. London: James Currey: 72–103.

Welbourn, Francis (1965) *Religion and Politics in Uganda, 1952–62*. Nairobi: East African Publishing House.

Westad, Odd Arne (2005) *The Global Cold War: Third World Interventions and the Making of Our Times*. Cambridge: Cambridge University Press.

Westminster Foundation for Democracy and CDD Ghana (2018) '*The Cost of Politics in Ghana*'. London: Westminster Foundation for Democracy, www.wfd.org/wp-content/uploads/2018/04/Cost_Of_Politics_Ghana.pdf.

Whitfield, Lindsay (2009) '"Change for a better Ghana": party competition, institutionalization and alternation in Ghana's 2008 elections', *African Affairs*, 108, no.433: 621–641.

Widner, Jennifer (1992) *The Rise of a Party-State in Kenya. From Harambee! to Nyayo!*, Berkeley and Los Angeles, CA: University of California Press.

Wilkins, Sam (2016) 'Who pays for pakalast? The NRM's peripheral patronage in rural Uganda', *Journal of Eastern African Studies*, 10, no.4: 619–638.

Wilkins, Sam (2018) 'The dominant party system in Uganda: subnational competition and authoritarian survival in the 2016 elections', PhD Dissertation, University of Oxford.

Willetts, Peter (1975) 'The politics of Uganda as a one-party state, 1969–70', *African Affairs*, 74, no.296: 278–299.

Willis, Justin (2008) 'What has he got up his sleeve? Advertising the Kenyan presidential candidates in 2007', *Journal of Eastern African Studies*, 2, no.2: 264–271.

Willis, Justin (2009) 'The King of the Mijikenda, and other stories about the kaya: Heritage, politics and histories in multi-party Kenya'. In Derek Peterson and Giacomo Macola (eds.), *Recasting the Past: History Writing and Political Work in Modern Africa*. Athens, OH: Ohio University Press: 233–250.

Willis, Justin (2015) '"Peace and order are in the interest of every citizen": elections, violence and state legitimacy in Kenya, 1957–74', *International Journal of African Historical Studies*, 48, no.1: 99–116.

Willis, Justin, Gabrielle Lynch and Nic Cheeseman (2016) 'La machine électorale: culture matérielle des bureaux de vote au Ghana, au Kenya et en Ouganda', *Politique Africaine*, 144: 27–50.

Willis, Justin, Gabrielle Lynch and Nic Cheeseman (2017) '"A valid electoral exercise"? Uganda's 1980 elections and the observers' dilemma', *Comparative Studies in Society and History*, 59, no. 1: 211–238.

Willis, Justin, Gabrielle Lynch and Nic Cheeseman (2018) 'Voting, nationhood and citizenship at the end of empire in Africa', *The Historical Journal*, 61, no.4: 1113–1135.

Wiseman, John (1995) 'Introduction: the movement towards democracy'. In John Wiseman (ed.), *Democracy and Political Change in Sub-Saharan Africa*. London and New York: Routledge: 1–10.

Wolf, Thomas P. (2020) 'The science, suspicion and sustainability of political polling'. In Nic Cheeseman, Karuti Kanyinga and Gabrielle Lynch (eds.), *The Oxford Handbook of Kenyan Politics*. Oxford: Oxford University Press: 325–341.

Wolff, Jonathan (1994) 'Democratic voting and the mixed-motivation problem', *Analysis*, 54, no.4: 193–196.

Young, Daniel (2009) 'Is clientelism at work in African elections? A study of voting behaviour in Kenya and Zambia', Michigan: Afrobarometer Working Paper No. 106, www.files.ethz.ch/isn/98869/AfropaperNo106.pdf.

Young, Tom (1993) 'Introduction: elections and electoral politics in Africa', *Africa*, 63, no. 3: 299–312.

Zolberg, Aristide R. (1966) *Creating Political Order. The Party-States of West Africa*. Chicago: Rand McNally and Co.

Zolberg, Aristide R. (1968) 'The structure of political conflict in the new states of tropical Africa', *American Political Science Review*, 62, no.1: 70–87.

Index